The Romantic I

This comprehensive survey of British   )f
six poets whose names are most closely associated with the Romantic era –
Wordsworth, Coleridge, Blake, Keats, Byron, and Shelley – as well as works
by other significant but less widely studied poets such as Leigh Hunt,
Charlotte Smith, Felicia Hemans, and Letitia Elizabeth Landon. Along with
its exceptional coverage, the volume is alert to relevant contexts, and opens
up ways of understanding Romantic poetry.

The Romantic Poetry Handbook encompasses the entire breadth of the
Romantic Movement, from Anna Laetitia Barbauld to Thomas Lovell
Beddoes and John Clare. In its central section 'Readings' it explores tensions,
change, and continuity within the Romantic Movement, and examines a
wide range of individual poems and poets through sensitive, attentive, and
accessible analyses. In addition, the authors provide a full introduction, a
detailed historical and cultural timeline, biographies of the poets whose
works are featured, and a helpful guide to further reading.

The Romantic Poetry Handbook is an ideal text for undergraduate and
postgraduate students of British Romantic poetry. It will also appeal to
those with a general interest in poetry and Romantic literature.

Michael O'Neill, is Professor of English at Durham University, UK. He has
published widely on many aspects of Romantic literature, especially the
work of Percy Bysshe Shelley, Victorian poetry, and an array of British, Irish,
and American twentieth- and twenty-first-century poets. His most recent
book is, as editor, *John Keats in Context* (2017). He has also published three
volumes of poetry.

Madeleine Callaghan, is Lecturer in Romantic Literature at the University
of Sheffield, UK. She is co-editor of *Twentieth Century British and Irish
Poetry: Hardy to Mahon* (2011), Assistant Editor of *The Oxford Handbook
of Percy Bysshe Shelley* (2012), and author of *Shelley's Living Artistry:
Letters, Poems, Plays* (2017).

Wiley Blackwell Literature Handbooks

This new series offers the student thorough and lively introductions to literary periods, movements, and, in some instances, authors and genres, from Anglo-Saxon to the Postmodern. Each volume is written by a leading specialist to be invitingly accessible and informative. Chapters are devoted to the coverage of cultural context, the provision of brief but detailed biographical essays on the authors concerned, critical coverage of key works, and surveys of themes and topics, together with bibliographies of selected further reading. Students new to a period of study or to a period genre will discover all they need to know to orientate and ground themselves in their studies, in volumes that are as stimulating to read as they are convenient to use.

Published

The Science Fiction Handbook
M. Keith Booker and Anne-Marie Thomas

The Seventeenth-Century Literature Handbook
Marshall Grossman

The Twentieth-Century American Fiction Handbook
Christopher MacGowan

The British and Irish Short Story Handbook
David Malcolm

The Crime Fiction Handbook
Peter Messent

The Literary Theory Handbook, second edition
Gregory Castle

The Anglo-Saxon Literature Handbook
Mark C. Amodio

The American Short Story Handbook
James Nagel

The Romantic Poetry Handbook
Michael O'Neill and Madeleine Callaghan

The Romantic Poetry Handbook

Michael O'Neill
and
Madeleine Callaghan

WILEY Blackwell

This edition first published 2018
© 2018 John Wiley & Sons Ltd

The right of Michael O'Neill and Madeleine Callaghan to be identified as the authors of this work has been asserted in accordance with law.

Registered Office(s)
John Wiley & Sons, Inc., 111 River Street, Hoboken, NJ 07030, USA
John Wiley & Sons Ltd, The Atrium, Southern Gate, Chichester, West Sussex, PO19 8SQ, UK

Editorial Office
9600 Garsington Road, Oxford, OX4 2DQ, UK

For details of our global editorial offices, customer services, and more information about Wiley products visit us at www.wiley.com.

Wiley also publishes its books in a variety of electronic formats and by print-on-demand. Some content that appears in standard print versions of this book may not be available in other formats.

Limit of Liability/Disclaimer of Warranty
While the publisher and authors have used their best efforts in preparing this work, they make no representations or warranties with respect to the accuracy or completeness of the contents of this work and specifically disclaim all warranties, including without limitation any implied warranties of merchantability or fitness for a particular purpose. No warranty may be created or extended by sales representatives, written sales materials or promotional statements for this work. The fact that an organization, website, or product is referred to in this work as a citation and/or potential source of further information does not mean that the publisher and authors endorse the information or services the organization, website, or product may provide or recommendations it may make. This work is sold with the understanding that the publisher is not engaged in rendering professional services. The advice and strategies contained herein may not be suitable for your situation. You should consult with a specialist where appropriate. Further, readers should be aware that websites listed in this work may have changed or disappeared between when this work was written and when it is read. Neither the publisher nor authors shall be liable for any loss of profit or any other commercial damages, including but not limited to special, incidental, consequential, or other damages.

Library of Congress Cataloging-in-Publication Data

Names: O'Neill, Michael, 1953– author. | Callaghan, Madeleine, author.
Title: The Romantic poetry handbook / by Michael O'Neill and Madeleine Callaghan.
Description: 1 | Hoboken : Wiley-Blackwell, 2018. | Series: Wiley Backwell literature handbooks | Includes bibliographical references and index.
Identifiers: LCCN 2017031756 (print) | LCCN 2017037559 (ebook) | ISBN 9781118308691 (pdf) | ISBN 9781118308714 (epub) | ISBN 9781118308738 (hardback) | ISBN 9781118308721 (paper)
Subjects: LCSH: English poetry–19th century–History and criticism–Handbooks, manuals, etc. | English poetry–18th century–History and criticism–Handbooks, manuals, etc. | Romanticism–Great Britain–Handbooks, manuals, etc. | BISAC: LITERARY CRITICISM / European / English, Irish, Scottish, Welsh.
Classification: LCC PR590 (ebook) | LCC PR590 .O64 2018 (print) | DDC 821/.709145–dc23
LC record available at https://lccn.loc.gov/2017031756

Cover Image: Joseph Mallord William Turner 1775–1851
A detail from 'Venice: Looking across the Lagoon at Sunset: 1840' / Tate Images
Cover Design: Wiley

Set in 10/13pt Sabon by SPi Global, Pondicherry, India
Printed and bound in Malaysia by Vivar Printing Sdn Bhd

10 9 8 7 6 5 4 3 2 1

Contents

Acknowledgements   viii

Part 1   Introduction   1

**Part 2   Timeline of the Late Eighteenth Century
            and Romantic Period**   21

Part 3   Biographies   47
Anna Laetitia Barbauld (1743–1825)   49
Thomas Lovell Beddoes (1803–1849)   51
William Blake (1757–1827)   54
Robert Burns (1759–1796)   57
Lord George Gordon Byron (1788–1824)   59
John Clare (1793–1864)   61
Samuel Taylor Coleridge (1772–1834)   63
Felicia Hemans (1793–1835)   66
(James Henry) Leigh Hunt (1784–1859)   69
John Keats (1795–1821)   72
Letitia Elizabeth Landon (1802–1838)   74
Thomas Moore (1779–1852)   77
Mary Robinson (1758–1800)   80
Percy Bysshe Shelley (1792–1822)   82
Charlotte Smith (1749–1806)   85
Robert Southey (1774–1843)   87
William Wordsworth (1770–1850)   90
Ann Yearsley (1753–1806)   93

Part 4   Readings   95

First-Generation Romantic Poets   95
Anna Laetitia Barbauld, 'Epistle to William Wilberforce,
    Esq., on the Rejection of the Bill for Abolishing the Slave Trade';
    'The Rights of Woman'; *Eighteen Hundred and Eleven, A Poem*   97
Charlotte Smith, *Elegiac Sonnets*   101
Charlotte Smith, *Beachy Head*   107
Ann Yearsley, 'Poem on the Inhumanity of the Slave-trade';
    'Bristol Elegy'   110
William Blake, *Songs of Innocence and of Experience*   115
William Blake, *The Marriage of Heaven and Hell*;
    The Book of Urizen; 'The Mental Traveller'   124
Mary Robinson, *Sappho and Phaon*   132
Robert Burns, Lyrics   137
William Wordsworth and S. T. Coleridge, *Lyrical Ballads*   144
William Wordsworth, 'Resolution and Independence';
    'Ode: Intimations of Immortality'; 'Elegiac Stanzas, Suggested
    by a Picture of Peele Castle in a Storm, Painted by Sir George
    Beaumont'; 'Surprized by Joy'   152
William Wordsworth, *The Prelude*   163
William Wordsworth, *The Excursion*   174
Samuel Taylor Coleridge, Conversation Poems: 'The Eolian Harp',
    'This Lime-Tree Bower My Prison', 'Frost at Midnight',
    and 'Dejection: An Ode'   179
Samuel Taylor Coleridge, *The Rime of the Ancient Mariner*;
    Kubla Khan; 'The Pains of Sleep'; *Christabel*   187
Robert Southey, *Thalaba the Destroyer* and *The Curse of Kehama*   196

Second-Generation Romantic Poets   203
Thomas Moore, *Irish Melodies*   205
Leigh Hunt, *The Story of Rimini*   211
Lord Byron, *Lara*; 'When We Two Parted';
    'Stanzas to Augusta'; *Manfred*   215
Lord Byron, *Childe Harold's Pilgrimage*   223
Lord Byron, *Don Juan*, Cantos 1–4   232
Percy Bysshe Shelley, *Queen Mab*; *Alastor*;
    Laon and Cythna [*The Revolt of Islam*]   242
Percy Bysshe Shelley, 'Hymn to Intellectual Beauty';
    'Mont Blanc'; 'Ozymandias'; 'Ode to the West Wind';
    the late poems to Jane Williams   251

Percy Bysshe Shelley, *Prometheus Unbound*; *Adonais*;
    The Triumph of Life   260
John Keats, *Endymion*; 'Sleep and Poetry'; The Sonnets   268
John Keats, *Hyperion* and *The Fall of Hyperion*   277
John Keats, The 1820 Volume   284

Third-Generation Romantic Poets   295
John Clare: Lyrics   297
Felicia Hemans, *Records of Woman: With Other Poems*   304
Letitia Elizabeth Landon, 'Love's Last Lesson'; 'Lines of Life';
    'Lines Written under a Picture of a Girl Burning a Love-Letter';
    'Sappho's Song'; 'A Child Screening a Dove from a Hawk.
    By Stewardson'   311
Thomas Lovell Beddoes, *Death's Jest-Book* and Lyrics   318

Part 5   Further Reading   325
General Critical Reading   327
Anna Laetitia Barbauld (1743–1825)   328
Thomas Lovell Beddoes (1803–1849)   328
William Blake (1757–1827)   329
Robert Burns (1759–1796)   329
Lord George Gordon Byron (1788–1824)   329
John Clare (1793–1864)   330
Samuel Taylor Coleridge (1772–1834)   330
Felicia Hemans (1793–1835)   331
(James Henry) Leigh Hunt (1784–1859)   331
John Keats (1795–1821)   331
Letitia Elizabeth Landon (1802–1838)   331
Thomas Moore (1779–1852)   332
Mary Robinson (1758–1800)   332
Percy Bysshe Shelley (1792–1822)   332
Charlotte Smith (1749–1806)   333
Robert Southey (1774–1843)   333
William Wordsworth (1770–1850)   333
Ann Yearsley (1753–1806)   334

Index   **335**

Acknowledgements

The authors would like to thank all those at Wiley Blackwell who have made this book possible. The book is a joint venture, with each author taking primary responsibility for different sections. Michael O'Neill has taken primary responsibility for the volume's overall design, and has written the introduction and the sections on Beddoes, Blake, Burns, Clare, Hunt, Moore, Robinson, Southey, and Wordsworth (with the exception of the section on *Lyrical Ballads*). He has also written the sections on Byron's *Childe Harold's Pilgrimage* and *Don Juan*, Coleridge's conversation poems, the final section on Keats (his 1820 volume), and the section on Shelley's *Queen Mab*, *Alastor*, and *Laon and Cythna*. Madeleine Callaghan has drawn up the timeline, written the biographies, taken principal responsibility for preparing the further reading, and written the remaining sections on Byron, Coleridge, Keats and Shelley, and the sections on Barbauld, Hemans, Landon, *Lyrical Ballads*, Smith, and Yearsley. The authors are grateful to the Universities of Durham and Sheffield for help of various kinds, and would like particularly to acknowledge the intellectual stimulus and collegiality provided by Anna Barton, Adam Piette, Stephen Regan, Mark Sandy, Sarah Wootton, and Angela Wright. They are also grateful to the readers of their original proposal and of the final manuscript for many valuable suggestions. As will be evident from the text, notes, and further reading, they are indebted to the work of many critics and scholars who have shaped their understanding of the poetry of the period. Michael O'Neill is especially grateful to Duncan Wu for showing him advance proofs of the latter's brilliantly thought-provoking *30 Great Myths about the Romantics* (Malden, MA: Wiley Blackwell, 2015). For assistance with the index, the authors are grateful to Sharon Tai.

Part 1 **Introduction**

Part I Introduction

The Romantic Poetry Handbook seeks to enhance an understanding and appreciation of British Romantic poetry. Its intended audience is readers at all levels of familiarity with the work that it addresses. It takes its cue from Coleridge's comment in *Biographia Literaria* that 'A poem is that species of composition, which is opposed to works of science, by proposing for its *immediate* object pleasure, not truth'.[1] Coleridge does not finally outlaw 'truth', but he reminds us that poetry involves play, aesthetic delight, miracles of rare devices, 'pleasure'. The word catches the professional literary critic off guard, with its seeming suggestion of something amoral, frivolous, irresponsible. Yet Coleridge invites reflection on the process and upshot of reading poems rather than, say, scientific papers. Certainly, the boldness of his investment in 'pleasure' – even when that pleasure takes the form of responding to the representation of difficult, painful or sorrowful experience – is one we take to be a clarion-call for critical practice at a time when the word 'pleasure' is almost transgressively non-utilitarian. Put simply, then, the book's '*immediate* object' is to convey the two authors' enjoyment of Romantic poetry.

Jerome J. McGann argues that 'The Romantic – prototypically Coleridgean – concept of poetic pleasure is a philosophic category of human Being', claiming that 'Though a subjective experience' such pleasure 'is metaphysically transcendent'. There is a link in Coleridge between the aesthetic and the metaphysical, but it is not our purpose to enlist Romantic poetry in support of the 'transcendent Form of Being' that McGann half-stigmatizes.[2] Our purpose is simpler, to read the poetry as poetry and not another thing. As McGann's work shows, the idea of 'Romantic poetry' is the subject of

The Romantic Poetry Handbook, First Edition. Michael O'Neill and Madeleine Callaghan.
© 2018 John Wiley & Sons Ltd. Published 2018 by John Wiley & Sons Ltd.

critical critique in recent decades. Much work has questioned assumptions underpinning the category of 'Romantic poetry'. The current volume responds to the stimulating provocation supplied by much of this work, often associated with critics writing from a new historicist perspective, but it owes its existence to a belief in the arresting achievement of poets writing in the last two decades of the eighteenth century and, principally, the first three of the nineteenth century, though beyond 1830 as well. Readings of a range of poems provide a concerted attempt to explore, illuminate, and define the nature of that achievement. At the outset, we would highlight, among the many pointers towards what makes Romantic poets original and significant, Wordsworth's assertion in his Note to 'The Thorn' that 'the Reader cannot be too often reminded that Poetry is passion: it is the history or science of feelings'.[3]

Definitions

The idea of the 'Romantic' is entangled with seemingly endless problems of definition. When did British Romanticism begin? What, if any, are its essential characteristics? Is it merely a retrospective construction that bears witness to our need for an order to be imposed upon the flux and chaos of literary history? We acknowledge, in Stuart Curran's words, that it is 'possible that we are holding up a mirror to ourselves and calling the reflection Romanticism'.[4] But we also note the contemporary awareness which Shelley proclaims in *A Defence of Poetry* of living through 'a memorable age in intellectual [and poetic] achievements'.[5] We concede that not every poet in the period betrays characteristics that can be termed 'Romantic' and that it is easy to overlook figures who don't neatly fit or who challenge subsequent categorizations: the belated admission of Byron, the poet who felt that he and his contemporaries were 'upon the wrong revolutionary poetical system', into the canon of the major Romantics proves the point.[6] We allow for possibly problematic overlaps and gaps between 'Romantic poetry' and 'Romantic-period poetry', and we have responded enthusiastically to the expansion of the canon undertaken in work on Romantic poetry in recent decades.

Accounts of the 'Romantic' that overlook the claims on our attention of writers who fail to fit a schematic critical version can be unnecessarily exclusive, and our readings indicate a wish to break away from fixation on the work of a few major writers. We by no means abandon the idea of literary or aesthetic merit, but we allow it to be explored and tested in the way that it is explored and tested by poets of the period. Our understanding of Romantic poetry has benefited from the work of those many critics and scholars who have made it possible and necessary to enlarge the number of poets writing in the period on whom critical attention can and should be brought. We acknowledge that challenges to a particular model of Romantic poetry mean that René Wellek's pithy formulation of Romanticism (first published in 1949) as 'imagination for the view of poetry, nature for the view of the world, and symbol and myth for poetic style' is under assault.[7]

And yet those ideas named by Wellek still hold a central role in thinking about Romantic poetry. Romantic poetry prizes the imagination, praises nature, deploys symbol, and reformulates myth. The prizing of the imagination found in the poetry and poetics of the period may not be to everyone's taste; it doesn't mean that it isn't present. In addition, Romantic poetry often contains a powerful capacity for self-critique. Coleridge's *Kubla Khan* imagines a recreation of vision, but it does so in a spirit of conditionality. Wordsworth sees nature as a ministering force that 'never did betray / The heart that loved her' (123–4), yet earlier in the same poem, 'Lines Written a Few Miles above Tintern Abbey', he worries whether trust in the gifts of insight and memory bequeathed by natural scenes 'Be but a vain belief' (50). Poets may reach for the image that embodies symbolic resolution of tensions. Yet often symbolic resolutions in Romantic poetry invite and seem aware of deconstructive energies; they participate in the dialogic instinct present in philosophers as diverse as Plato and Hume, whose influence on Romantic poetry lies more in their drive to present their thought through dramatic means than in their supposedly paraphrasable positions. In its dealings with analytical thought, Romantic poetry shapes procedures that put into the foreground the value of imaginative thinking and experiencing as ongoing actions of consciousness. One can speak of *Adonais* as showing the influence on Shelley of Platonic conceptions and imagery, yet to describe it as a poem written by a Platonist, someone who adopts fully a supposedly Platonic world-view, ignores its self-shaped existence as a drama of feeling and thought. Comparable energies are operative in the reworking of myth in Romantic poetry. The Romantics remake traditional myth, as in Keats's *Endymion*, in ways that serve less to consolidate the truth of a new story than to remind us that all human stories can be endlessly reinterpreted. And yet this two-sidedness does not mean that imagination, nature, symbol, and myth are not crucially important in the work of Romantic poetry.

Certainly doubleness and doubt haunt and energize Romantic poetry,[8] and the imps that bedevil literary history mockingly disrupt any attempt to fix a point of origin: 1784, with Smith's *Elegiac Sonnets*? 1786, with Burns's *Poems, Chiefly in the Scottish Dialect*? 1789, with Blake's *Songs of Innocence*? 1798, with Wordsworth and Coleridge's *Lyrical Ballads*?[9] But the fact that there are multiple claimants for a point of origin does not invalidate the sense that something new has come into being. Our solution is to accommodate all four writers as occupying the field of the Romantic, to see Smith and Burns as participating in a process of adumbration of, approach to, and involvement in the Romantic, while Blake and Wordsworth are claimed – to the degree that comparative word-length involves an implicit claim about significance – as figures at the heart of a process that then runs its generational course through to the later asylum poems of John Clare. Chronological messiness and complications are no reason to invalidate the emergence of a force and energy into literary history that we may justifiably call 'Romantic'. We recognize the force of Seamus Perry's point that, unless we think about the various functions that the word 'Romantic' has been made to perform, we risk 'covert prescriptiveness', but like him we see the word as serving an 'organising' function, allowing us to adopt 'a way of learning about' the particulars of Romantic poetry.[10]

Thought, Feeling, History

To return to our earlier quotation from Wordsworth, Romantic poetry gives prominence to 'passion': feeling at its most intense. But it is also often 'the history or science of feelings', less a licensed outpouring than a troubled exploration. T. S. Eliot contended that in and around the Romantic period poets 'thought and felt by fits, unbalanced'.[11] Yet if there is much fascination in poetry of the period with the 'unbalanced', there is a preoccupation, too, with reconciliation, harmony, often difficult to attain, but striven for with impassioned intelligence. These are not static conditions, but glimpsed outcomes of what might, oxymoronically, be termed a permanent process: Coleridge describes the 'poet, in *ideal* perfection' as one who 'brings the whole soul of man into activity'[12] – and the word that asks to be singled out there is 'activity', activity involving the 'whole soul', including its endless potential for division. Romantic poetry matters because it recognizes the facts of division and disunity and longs to repair rents in the fabric of experience. These recognitions and longings enmesh with its high valuation of what we are told by both heart and head, by 'feelings' which, as Wordsworth writes in the Preface to *Lyrical Ballads* (1800), 'are modified by our thoughts, which are indeed the representatives of all our past feelings' (p. 60).

Our working assumption is that Romantic poems warrant attention and praise for their high intelligence and intense dramatizations rather than wary criticism because of their supposed recourse to aesthetic mystifications. Robert Browning, a major heir of the Romantics, offers in 'Childe Roland to the Dark Tower Came', a nightmarish, possibly ironized version of his predecessors' commitment to quest, a quest that, as Harold Bloom has argued, is often internalized.[13] But he also reminds us at his poem's close of a central virtue of Romantic questers, whether conveyed through the motif of intrepid pursuit in, say, Shelley's *Alastor* or through the verve of Byron's refusal to disengage from the human comedy in the English cantos of *Don Juan*. That virtue is courage, courage displayed when, almost mocking his refusal to despair, Browning's speaker asserts, 'And yet / Dauntless the slug-horn to my lips I set, / And blew' (202–4).[14] Such 'dauntlessness', pointed up by the tenacious rhyme that places 'set' against 'yet' (each six-line stanza has only two rhymes), is a feature typical of our poets. Their poems concede doubt as they hope for certainty, yet they press on, as in so many of Shelley's poems; they deal with what is unique to the poet and what has wider significance, as in Wordsworth's 'Ode: Intimations of Immortality'; they constantly brave extremes of passionate feeling, as in Hemans's *Records of Woman*.

The poetry we discuss was written in a period of turbulent change politically, historically, and culturally, and in a detailed time-chart we plot the major events of the period, alongside dates associated with the poets and poems of the period. The period is an age of revolution in politics. The War of American Independence represents a struggle that would result in a constitution and a polity that prefigure modern ideas of equality and democracy. It may have had flaws, as commentators such as Alan Ryan have brought out, but it served as a lodestar of hope to those fired by the desire of liberty. Above all, it generated confidence in a people's political agency, as the ardent revolutionist Tom Paine saw and articulated. Specifically, the new American constitution encouraged the view, ascribed by Ryan to Thomas Jefferson, chief among the Founding Fathers, 'that it was the inalienable right of every generation to imagine its own future and rebuild its institutions as it chose'.[15] The French Revolution and the libertarian opinions of Rousseau and others that, in part, led to it was, for the critic and essayist William Hazlitt, one of the prime movers of Wordsworth's 1790s poetry, as M. H. Abrams notes, quoting Hazlitt's comment on Wordsworth: 'His Muse … is a levelling one.'[16]

The Revolution created exhilaration but also dismay. It may have been heavenly bliss for the young Wordsworth to have been alive at such a time (*The Prelude*, 1805, X.692–3). Yet for Edmund Burke, staunch supporter of the American cause, the French Revolution presented itself, from the outset and well before fraternity turned into fratricide, as a terrifying rationalist assault on the links and bonds, the feelings that held society and culture together, and enabled the establishment and maintenance of an unwritten but deeply important 'partnership not only between those who are living, but between those who are living, those who are dead, and those who are to be born'.[17] Burke's wary pessimism is a powerful presence in the period, even when it is contested. Byron illustrates ambivalences found in writers of his generation. The Revolution resulted in the overthrow of 'old opinions', in a phrase from *Childe Harold's Pilgrimage*, canto 3 (771). At the same time, he offers a tempered and ironic view of the Revolution as a force that 'overthrew' 'good with ill' (774) and allowed for the return, after the resulting war with Napoleon and the re-establishment at the Congress of Vienna of former political structures, of 'Dungeons and thrones' (777).[18]

The Revolution appears in the work of all the Romantics as an event of fundamental significance, as we bring out in our comments, say, on Wordsworth's *The Prelude* or Shelley's *Prometheus Unbound*. War is a central historical experience in the period, as is noticed by Simon Bainbridge in accounting for the great popularity of Walter Scott's verse romances such as *The Lady of the Lake* and *Marmion*, works responsible for a 'transforming of war', couched in 'the conventions of romance'.[19] That process of transforming conflict varies from poet to poet, but 'Visions of Conflict', to quote Bainbridge's well-chosen subtitle, run through Romantic poetry, sometimes confronting grim realities with near-journalistic aplomb, as in *Childe Harold's Pilgrimage*, sometimes recasting them with mythologizing, epic ambition, as in Keats's *Hyperion* poems. The period is often one of upheaval and crisis in British domestic affairs, as many poems reveal, and we touch, as appropriate, on relevant contexts in our commentary. It is also a time in which poets write with a strong awareness of history as the sum total of cultural and human experience. Multiple perspectives arise: there is the sense, as Isaiah Berlin paraphrases Vico, that 'man is not distinguishable from the actual process of his development'[20] and there is, too, a sense of history's prefigurings and patternings, of its millennial or cyclical or Utopian trajectories.[21]

Biography, Groupings, and Genres

The volume never loses sight of the fact that poems are written by talented individuals. To that end, and to aid in understanding of their writings, we offer brief biographies of the eighteen poets we have selected – Barbauld, Smith, Yearsley, Blake, Robinson, Burns, Wordsworth, Coleridge, Southey, Moore, Hunt, Byron, Shelley, Clare, Hemans, Keats, Landon, and Beddoes. For convenience, we organize these biographies in alphabetical order, though in our 'Readings' section, to point up the inter-generational nature of Romantic poetry, its layerings of inheritance and bequest, we group poets into three main areas or observable generations (we are aware of chronological overlap and complication here, but would argue that the essential usefulness of the organizing device holds).[22] In 'Readings', the main part of the book, as noted above, individual accounts of poems and poets are supplied to bring out the diversity and range of Romantic poetic achievement. And in a section on further reading, as in our notes, we offer suggestions for more detailed exploration and study.

The book seeks in its 'Readings' to bring out Romantic poetry's capacity to move, affect, provoke, re-examine, imagine, and re-imagine. We focus on a great range of kinds of poems: epic, lyric, including odes, sonnets, and songs, conversation poems in blank verse, narratives, romances, satires, and meditations in many metres and styles – Spenserian stanzas, couplets, *ottava rima*, *terza rima*. The same form may serve different purposes, as the use of the iambic pentameter couplet reveals: Anna Barbauld pens her controversial state of the nation poem, *Eighteen Hundred and Eleven*, in stingingly incisive couplets; Leigh Hunt deploys couplets for more sympathetically inward accounts of psychological process in *The Story of Rimini*, even if that poem has its own transgressive impulses; Keats is politically liberal and imaginatively adventurous in his handling of the form in *Endymion*, whilst being more poised, ironic, and detached in his management of the couplet in the later work, *Lamia*. But the three poets use the same form in different ways: Barbauld uses closed heroic couplets deriving from the practice of Pope, possibly, as Daniel P. Watkins suggests, to mirror ironically the 'restrictions' that 'British society' has enjoined on the abolition of slavery.[23] Hunt enjambs freely, varies the position of his caesural pauses, moving them on many occasions to a position after the seventh syllable rather than the standard Augustan practice of placing them after the fourth or sixth syllables, and uses feminine rhymes: all in the cause of a libertarian assault on the assumptions propelling the closed heroic couplet. Keats, after following Hunt's more liberal practice in earlier poems such as *Endymion*, strives in *Lamia* for a mode that consciously looks back to Dryden, with its reduction of run-on lines, its uses of the occasional alexandrine and triplet, its lexical and prosodic strength married to narrative focus.[24]

For his part, George Crabbe reminds us, as do Hunt, Keats, and Byron (the example we supply in our 'Readings' is *Lara*), of the couplet's durability as a medium for narrative, offering both distillation and flow. Crabbe is able in a poem such as *Peter Grimes* to employ the couplet for a mode of seemingly uneventful if quietly harrowing literary delineation, finally taking us into the guilt-ridden mind of Peter, who has enslaved, tormented, and murdered 'parish-boys' (62). Crabbe uses the couplet for forms of trenchant understatement, as when he describes the indifference of others to Peter's beating of a boy: 'some, on hearing cries, / Said calmly, "Grimes is at his exercise"' (77–8). Contemporaries felt that Crabbe wrote in a different manner from the innovative style associated with Wordsworth and Coleridge that laid emphasis on the imagination. Hazlitt saw Crabbe as intent only on making 'an exact image of any thing on the earth', and Wordsworth felt that '19 out of 20 of Crabbe's pictures are mere matters of fact with which the Muses have just about as much to do as they have with a collection of medical reports, or of law cases'.[25] But Crabbe's understatements connect with as much as they differ from Wordsworth's indirections, and he shares with other Romantic-period writers an ability to depict and understand the workings of human evil. The poem slides, stage by stage, into Peter's dawning acquaintance with the horror of his actions, hinted at in the apparently factual description of the local seascape, 'The bounding marsh-bank and the blighted tree' (174). Related to Peter's state of mind, this scene of stagnation takes one into a permanent circle of hell, which one enters fully in Peter's death-bed confession, when first-person narration replaces the previous detachment as we hear of Peter's being haunted by the ghosts of the dead boys:

> But there they were, hard by me in the tide,
> The three unbodied forms – and 'Come', still 'come!' they cried. (326–7)

Those 'unbodied forms' take on an unbudgeable if spectral reality in that final lengthened alexandrine (an extra iambic foot).[26]

Crabbe is one of many poets who illustrate the rich diversity of poets in the period, and while he is not included in our 'Readings', we urge readers to embrace this diversity. In reading across our sections on the poets, readers are encouraged both to recognize shared techniques and concerns, and to explore the individual nature of our chosen poets' talents and experimentations.

Nowhere is this experimentation more evident than in the Romantics' fascination with hybrid genres: poems such as Shelley's *Prometheus Unbound*, subtitled a 'lyrical drama', a wording probably indebted to Wordsworth and Coleridge's *Lyrical Ballads*, one of the foundational texts for British Romanticism in its hospitality to plain speech and imaginative effects, and in its grasp of the fact that poetry is less a question of decorative figuration than of passion demanding unique expression. That the cumulative line of Wordsworth's narrative 'Michael', first included in the 1800 version of the volume, should be the simple yet complexly affecting, 'And never lifted up a single stone' (475), speak eloquently about Romanticism's new emphasis on a showing forth of 'the essential passions of the heart' (59), in Wordsworth's phrase from the Preface to *Lyrical Ballads*. Crucially, this showing forth results in a poetry that, in *Lyrical Ballads*, interweaves narrative and lyric; lyric, with its concern for feeling and the arrangements of metre and rhythm, often has commerce with the story-telling dynamic central to narrative, yet the story told by Wordsworthian narrative in particular is often one that centres less on what happens than what a protagonist and, in turn, a reader feel about what has happened – in the case of 'Michael', what the old shepherd feels about his life now that it is clear that his son, Luke, sent to London to make his way and help pay off an outstanding debt, has gone to the bad, been driven overseas, never to return to help his father complete the sheepfold, symbol of the covenant between father and son.

It is possible that the reader will discern in the poem echoes of the test set Abraham by God when he is told to sacrifice his son Isaac, a sacrifice that is stopped even as Abraham is ready to strike. Michael, too, might be thought to sacrifice his son on the altar of economic necessity.[27] If so, he pays the price, so the poem hints, as it associates him with another patriarch, the tragic figure of Lear, for whom his daughter Cordelia will 'never' come again. These literary and biblical associations arise quietly, and in an unforced way. They correspond not to a Romantic desire to exhibit literary knowledge, but to Wordsworth's understanding that his tale bears witness to a suffering intensity and depth of implication that rivals even as it calls up memories of ancestral texts. In *Prometheus Unbound*, Shelley displays an even more ambitious originality, one that depends on our awareness of how he is vying with and outdoing precursor texts, in this case, the *Prometheus Bound* and its lost sequel by Aeschylus. Whereas Pope and Dryden offer satirical mock-epic as their best, admiring response to the formidable achievement of Homer, Virgil, and Milton, Shelley, drawing on but revising Aeschylus, Dante, and Milton, among others, writes a work that imagines a creative revival of hope, imagination, and love, a mode of responding to political defeat with Utopian fortitude. Shelley writes that 'Didactic poetry is my abhorrence' (*Major Works*, p. 232); he makes his appeal to the reader's imagination.

Romantic Poetry and the Reader

The reader comes of age in Romantic poetry, continually appealed to as completer and maker of meaning, as the focus of the poetry's imaginative designs. 'All deities reside in the human breast', Blake asserts in plate 11 of *The Marriage of Heaven and Hell*, his magnificent retort to orthodox theology,[28] and one heard again in many Romantic relocations of deity or its replacements, Shelley's 'Hymn to Intellectual Beauty', for example. But he might well have written, his own remarkable *Songs of Innocence and of Experience* in mind, that 'All meanings reside within the reader's head – and heart'. Over and over, Romantic poetry transfers the burden of meaning-making to the reader and tests the process of doing so, whether through tactics of incompletion and fragmentation that invite the rounding out of a broken arc, or through concluding questions as in Shelley's 'Ode to the West Wind' or Keats's 'Ode to a Nightingale', or through moments of aporia, enigma, or uncertainty, as at the close of Wordsworth's 'Simon Lee', or, indeed, through Prefaces that purport to explain all, but only generate further questions, as in Coleridge's 1816 version of *Kubla Khan*.

If dramatic monologue will become the Victorian mode par excellence, its roots are visible in many Romantic predecessors, even as the Romantics place their emphasis less on limited partiality of viewpoint than on unignorable subjectivity: Felicia Hemans's *Records of Woman* comes to mind, with its invitations to empathize with a range of female speakers, such as Arabella Stuart or Properzia Rossi. So, too, as suggested above, do Blake's *Songs*. Intent on 'Shewing the Two Contrary States of the Human Soul', as the title page of the joint *Songs* has it, the poems seek to 'show' the state of soul of their speakers.[29] This state may be the concern for others and acceptance of his fate displayed by the speaker in 'The Chimney Sweeper' in *Innocence*. The poem is certainly conscious of the misery inflicted on young children through the practice of sending them up chimneys to clean them from soot, but its mode is less that of head-on critique than of an entrance into the speaker's way of thinking. This way of thinking carries a loaded reproach to the poem's readers; it also conveys the value of the speaker's innocence, itself contrasted with that of Tom Dacre's more naïve, yet more visionary (or possibly fantasizing) approach. The poem comes to a potentially disturbing close in its last line, 'So if all do their duty they need not fear harm' (24), a typical Blakean riddle coiling itself inside the line. Does it indicate the speaker's indoctrinated response to being told about 'duty', non-adherence to which can lead to 'harm'? This seems likely, and avoids us having to suppose the late intervention of an ironized or unironized authorial surrogate. If so, it makes us aware of how vital perspective and angles of approach are to Blake's work, if we are to hear the precise inflections of words such as 'duty'.

In poems from *Experience*, Blake reminds us of the role played by what in 'London' he calls 'The mind-forg'd manacles' (8): manacles forged, that is, by and for the mind. It is this mind-manacling that is central to many Romantic poets' vision of oppression. At the same time they sense the possibility of a mental unchaining, which will have liberating effects. They do not deny the influence of contexts and material pressures, but they centre their investigations of the human condition on what it is to possess a mind, heart, and soul. From Burns's lament over 'Man's inhumanity to Man' in 'Men Were Made to Mourn' to Landon's vision of escape from socially intimidating and corrupting pressures in 'Lines of Life', the Romantic poetic vision appeals directly and forcefully not only to what we know, or can be persuaded to imagine, but also to an unconquerable impulse in human beings for a better way.

To put it so might seem uncritically to subscribe to what Jerome J. McGann stigmatized as the 'Romantic ideology', by which he means 'an uncritical absorption in Romanticism's own self-representations'.[30] Yet even if a neutral or hostile tone towards such 'self-representations' is sometimes nowadays preferred, to adapt a line from Donald Davie's 'Remembering the 'Thirties',[31] it is worth asserting that Romantic poetry demands that we bring our full humanity and capacity for thought and feeling to bear on its creations. The luxury of detached uninvolvement is rarely available in their work. Even in *Lamia*, where Keats subjects to appraisal both 'cold philosophy' (2.230) and warm imaginings,[32] the subsequent poetic contest offers the difficult pleasure of continuous if differently directed sympathy and recoil. Nor for that matter is it often the case that the Romantics allow us easily to adopt a single position. One reason why the ode makes so spectacular a generic return in the period is because, with its architecture of turn and counter-turn, the form is a plastic medium for the revelation of complicated feelings: loss and asserted recovery in Wordsworth's 'Ode: Intimations of Immortality', for instance, or depression accompanied by an imaginative rallying that belies the poem's stated loss of the 'shaping spirit of Imagination' (86) in Coleridge's 'Dejection: An Ode'.

The result is nothing less than an astonishing transformation of resources made available by eighteenth-century poets such as Thomson, Cowper, Gray, and Collins. We attend in the volume to those resources, evident in the use to which the influence exerted by Cowper's *The Task* on Coleridge's 'Frost at Midnight' is put. There, Cowperesque self-awareness undergoes a characteristic Romantic transformation. Coleridge discovers that the self opens up new depths as it alights, through processes of imaginative association, on mysteries of growth, development, hope, and a vision of connectedness. As Coleridge lays open to view the very pulse of conscious being, 'the interspersed vacancies / And momentary pauses of the thought' (51–2), he draws attention to the capacity of Romantic poets to move, in their depiction of the self, from the classical 'I think', in Christian la Cassagnère's terms, to revelation of 'an "I" watching a stream of thought or of imagery in the making and in the welling from a self below the self'.[33] In revaluations of eighteenth-century ideas of the sublime, the self's discovery of its capacity for what Wordsworth will call 'unknown modes of being' (*The Prelude*, 1805, I.420) is revelatory, even apocalyptic.

Self, World, and Metapoetry

Romantic absorption in the self's creative power quickly turns to the risky, exhilarating business of world-discovering and even world-making. Wordsworth's *The Prelude* replaces Milton's Christian story of Adam and

Eve's fall from paradise and subsequent hope of redemption by 'one greater man' (I.4) with the account of his imagination's fall from early communion with nature and subsequent recovery.[34] The 'Mind of Man' is Wordsworth's 'haunt, and the main region of my Song' (40), as he wrote in a Prospectus at the head of *The Excursion* (1814) intended to outline the nature of an overall project, the ambitious long poem *The Recluse*, which he never completed.[35] And it is so (without gender implications) in the work of many of the major Romantic poets because it is in and through the mind that life is lived, that the ideas and ideals shaped therein are projected onto and help shape 'the very world', to quote Wordsworth again, 'which is the world / Of all of us, the place on which, in the end, / We find our happiness, or not at all' (*The Prelude*, 1805, X.725–7).

Wordsworth helps us understand Romantic poetry through his comments on what he sought to do in his poetry. Metapoetic commentary is frequent in the period: the awareness of living 'A being more intense' (*Childe Harold's Pilgrimage* 3.6.47) in the act of creation is dramatized by Byron in *Childe Harold's Pilgrimage* and taken to brilliantly comic extremes in his *Don Juan*. It is evident in Keats's turn on his use of the word 'forlorn' (71) at the start of the final stanza of 'Ode to a Nightingale', in Shelley's assertion that, were he capable of a more peaceful state, he 'would ne'er have striven // As thus with thee in prayer in my sore need' (51–2) in 'Ode to the West Wind', in Letitia Landon's question, 'Why write I this?' in 'Lines of Life',[36] and in the orchestrated enquiries into and provisional answers to the question 'what is the value of poetry?' which haunt Romantic poetry. It is a sign of the poetic art's significance in the period that such self-consciousness abounds; at the same time it speaks of and to an anxiety, sometimes latent, sometimes overt, about the way in which poetry is its own guarantor in a period dominated, for the Shelley of *A Defence of Poetry*, by an 'excess of the selfish and calculating principle' (p. 696).

'Readings'

The book's 'Readings' are central to its attempt to respond to and recreate the experience of reading Romantic poetry. As noted above, they begin with accounts of first-generation poets, including poets who might on a different if parallel account be thought of as precursors to Romantic poets, Barbauld, Burns, Robinson, Smith, and Yearsley. All five poets reinvigorate forms, especially the sonnet, song, and lyric, and bring eighteenth-century concerns with sensibility and sympathy into new regions of feeling and thought. Their work heralds and runs alongside the productions of poets traditionally regarded as composing the first generation of Romantic poetry proper, Blake, Coleridge,

Southey, and Wordsworth, poets who explore the possibilities and dangers of the unleashed imagination as they respond, above all else, to the challenge and stimulus of a revolutionary age. It is our sense that the very liminality of poets one is tempted to call precursors should lead us to be wary of imposing artificial fences, and we have thus included Barbauld, Burns, Robinson, Smith, and Yearsley in our grouping of first-generation Romantic poets.

Claims could, of course, be made for other writers to be included such as Helen Maria Williams or John Thelwall. In 'The Bastille, A Vision', from her novel *Julia*, Williams writes with keen interest in feeling as she captures the glad surprise at the coming of freedom – 'I lose the sense of care! / I feel the vital air – / I see, I *see* the light of day!' (50–2) – that is forever haunting Romantic 'Visions of bliss' (53).[37] Thelwall's poetry and ideas about poetics and prosody are at last beginning to receive the attention they deserve.[38] It is, indeed, impossible to deny critical perceptiveness to a figure who could roundly describe passages of Coleridge's *Religious Musings* (to its author) as 'the very acme of abstruse, metaphysical, mystical rant', or poetic sensibility and skill to a poet who, in Coleridge's own conversation mode, speaks to Coleridge of 'Thy Sara and my Susan, and, perchance, / Alfoxden's musing tenant, and the maid / Of ardent eye who with fraternal love / Sweetens his solitude' ('Lines Written at Bridgwater ...', 123–6).[39] At once formal and conversational, Thelwall gives us an imperishable vignette of Wordsworth and Dorothy Wordsworth in these lines from 1797. We can only plead restrictions of time and space as an explanation for exclusions; the book seeks to be wide-ranging but it does not essay comprehensiveness.

We then look at the revisionary and independent work of the next generation of poets, Byron, Hunt, Keats, Moore, and Shelley and beyond them the poets of a discernibly later grouping, poets whose major work is written in the 1820s and 1830s, even later in the case of Clare: Beddoes, Clare, Hemans (whose career covers several decades, though we focus on her later 1820s work), and Landon – all poets in whom a sophisticated sense of working within and against a tradition, a tradition carving itself into being in the writings of the first two generations of Romantic poets, can be felt as a creatively enabling presence. Here boundaries productively criss-cross: words like 'Romantic' and 'Victorian' have the solidity of monolithic nation-states, but something of the tendency, too, of nations to forego wholly discrete identities. Tennyson's early volumes, for example, show a deep responsiveness to the poetry of Keats and Shelley. His close friend Arthur Hallam classed Tennyson with Keats and Shelley as 'Poets of Sensation' and contended that 'There is a strange earnestness in his worship of beauty which throws a charm over his impassioned song', comments that link him with the Shelley of 'Hymn to Intellectual Beauty' or the Keats of the odes.[40]

Echoes of the older poets abound in Tennyson's work, yet in his attraction to distilled portraits of weariness and despair, as in 'Mariana', there is a concentration on landscape as the correlative of mood, which declines the more overt if highly dynamic and often intricate poetry of process typical of the Romantics. Tennyson absorbs himself in a brooding attention to externals, which is less Keats's self-forgetfulness in the presence of being than a constant pressure, almost nightmarish in intensity, to fetch out images that hurt and connect, in Auden's phrase ('The Novelist'). Harold Bloom suggests with typical acuteness that the poem 'remains the finest example in the language of an embowered consciousness representing itself as being too happy in its happiness to want anything more',[41] and the allusion there to the opening of Keats's 'Ode to a Nightingale' serves to define the difference between Keats and Tennyson. We read Tennyson less as a latter-day Romantic poet, though he illustrates with unusual complexity the enduring vitality of Romantic legacies, than as a poet who shapes a consciously post-Romantic body of work. Even though Beddoes, Clare, Hemans, and Landon wrote poems that appeared after Tennyson's youthful volumes, they participate in Romantic currents of thought and feeling with a different, more participative sympathy, and it is on their work that we focus.

But we are conscious of poetry's refusal to obey 'keep out' signs erected by custodians of chronological or periodic order, and we offer all our responses as prompts for further thought about the nature of Romantic poetry as well as about the achievement of many Romantic poems. Our 'Readings' sometimes focus on an individual poem or volume, sometimes on groupings of poems, usually by genre, sometimes by theme. We point up the ability of Romantic poets to write major long poems, such as Wordsworth's *The Excursion* and Southey's *Thalaba* and *The Curse of Kehama*. We also include accounts of individual collections: Wordsworth and Coleridge's *Lyrical Ballads*, Moore's *Irish Melodies*, Keats's 1820 volume, Hemans's *Records of Woman*. In addition, we draw explicit attention to the generic experimentation which is a notable feature of the poetic output of writers such as Byron and Shelley. We choose, for example, to devote one section on Byron to his eastern tale *Lara* (the most psychologically compelling of the tales), along with two lyrics and his dramatic poem *Manfred*. Honouring Byron's variegated creativity, the section also finds a thematic continuity in the poet's concern with performing the self. Elsewhere, as in our second section on Blake, we track the developing trajectory of a poet's career. Our general hope and intention throughout our 'Readings' is that the varying nature of the focal lens we supply will encourage appropriate flexibility of approach and response. Always to the fore is the verbal thisness, the imaginative life, of our chosen poems.

Notes

1   *Coleridge's Poetry and Prose*, ed. Nicholas Halmi, Paul Magnuson, and Raimonda Modiano (New York: Norton, 2004), p. 493. Unless indicated otherwise, this edition is used for all of Coleridge's writings.

2   Jerome J. McGann, 'The Anachronism of George Crabbe', *ELH* 48 (1981): 555–72 (at 564).

3   Qtd, as is all of Wordsworth's writing, unless indicated otherwise, from *William Wordsworth*, ed. Stephen Gill, 21st-Century Oxford Authors (Oxford: Oxford University Press, 2010), p. 728.

4   Stuart Curran, 'Romantic Poetry: Why and Wherefore?', in *The Cambridge Companion to British Romanticism*, ed. Stuart Curran, 2nd edn (Cambridge: Cambridge University Press, 2010), p. 210.

5   *Percy Bysshe Shelley: The Major Works*, ed. Zachary Leader and Michael O'Neill (Oxford: Oxford University Press, 2003), p. 700. Shelley is quoted from this edition, unless stated otherwise.

6   *Byron's Letters and Journals*, ed. Leslie Marchand, 12 vols (London: Murray, 1973–82), 5.265 (hereafter *BLJ*).

7   'The Concept of Romanticism in Literary History', in *Concepts of Criticism* (New Haven, CT: Yale University Press, 1963), pp. 128–98 (at p. 161).

8   See Michael O'Neill, 'Introduction: Romantic Doubleness', in *Romantic Poetry: An Annotated Anthology*, ed. Michael O'Neill and Charles Mahoney (Malden, MA: Wiley Blackwell, 2008), pp. xxi–xxix.

9   For a salutary caution against making too bold claims for supposed points of origin, see Duncan Wu's demolition of the 'myth' (his word) of the idea that 'Wordsworth's Preface to *Lyrical Ballads* Was a Manifesto for the Romantic Revolution', to quote his chapter title, in *30 Great Myths about the Romantics* (Malden, MA: Wiley Blackwell, 2015), pp. 82–9 (at p. 82).

10 Seamus Perry, 'Romanticism: The Brief History of a Concept', in *A Companion to Romanticism*, ed. Duncan Wu (Oxford: Blackwell, 1998), pp. 4, 9.

11 T. S. Eliot, 'The Metaphysical Poets', in *The Complete Prose of T. S. Eliot*, vol. 2, *The Perfect Critic*, ed. Anthony Cuda and Ronald Schuchard (Baltimore: Johns Hopkins University Press, 2014), p. 381.

12 *Coleridge's Poetry and Prose*, p. 495.

13 Harold Bloom, 'The Internalization of Quest-Romance' (1970), in *Romanticism: Critical Concepts in Literary and Cultural Studies*, ed. Michael O'Neill and Mark Sandy, 4 vols (London: Routledge, 2006), 1.102–21.

14 *Robert Browning*, Oxford Authors, ed. Adam Roberts, intro. Daniel Karlin (Oxford: Oxford University Press, 1997).

15 Alan Ryan, *On Politics: A History of Political Thought from Herodotus to the Present* (London: Penguin, 2012), p. 611.

16 Hazlitt in *The Spirit of the Age* (1825), qtd from M. H. Abrams, 'English Romanticism: The Spirit of the Age' (1963), in *Romanticism*, ed. O'Neill and Sandy, 1.74.

17 See Edmund Burke, *Reflections on the Revolution in France* (1790; London: Dodsley, 1791), p. 144.

18 Qtd from *Lord Byron: The Major Works*, ed. Jerome J. McGann (Oxford: Oxford University Press, 2008).

19 Simon Bainbridge, *British Poetry and the Revolutionary and Napoleonic Wars: Visions of Conflict* (Oxford: Oxford University Press, 2003), p. 2.

20 Isaiah Berlin, *Vico and Herder: Two Studies in the History of Ideas* (London: Chatto & Windus, 1976), p. 65.

21 For essays that explore Romantic writers' conceptions and depictions of history, see *Rethinking British Romantic History, 1770–1845*, ed. Porscha Fermanis and John Regan (Oxford: Oxford University Press, 2014).

22 For the idea of a 'third generation', and for emphasis on the 'generational' nature of Romantic poetry, see Donald H. Reiman, 'Keats and the Third Generation', in *The Persistence of Poetry: Bicentennial Essays on Keats*, ed. Robert M. Ryan and Ronald A. Sharp (Amherst: University of Massachusetts Press, 1998), pp. 109–19 (at p. 109).

23 Daniel P. Watkins, *Anna Laetitia Barbauld and Eighteenth-Century Visionary Poetics* (Baltimore: Johns Hopkins University Press, 2012), p. 186.

24 See Walter Jackson Bate, *The Stylistic Development of Keats* (1945; London: Routledge, 2016), p. 151. For a brief, valuable reminder of Dryden's presence in the period (he is a writer edited by Walter Scott, among other things), see *John Dryden*, poems sel. Charles Tomlinson (London: Faber, 2004), p. xiv.

25 Qtd, as is the text of *Peter Grimes*, from *Romanticism: An Anthology*, ed. Duncan Wu, 3rd edn (Malden, MA: Blackwell, 2006), p. 142.

26 For fine discussion of Crabbe's descriptive effects and handling of the couplet, see Fiona Stafford, '"Of Sea or River": Crabbe's Best Description', *Romanticism* 20 (2014): 162–73.

27 See *Lyrical Ballads*, ed. Michael Mason (London: Longman, 1992), p. 341.

28 Qtd, as is all of Blake's writings unless indicated otherwise, from *Blake: Complete Writings*, ed. Geoffrey Keynes (Oxford: Oxford University Press, 1966). For more on Romanticism and religion, see Robert M. Ryan, *The Romantic Reformation: Religious Politics in English Literature, 1789–1824* (Cambridge: Cambridge University Press, 1997).

29 *Blake: Complete Writings*, p. 210.

30 Jerome J. McGann, *The Romantic Ideology: A Critical Investigation* (Chicago: University of Chicago Press, 1983), p. 1.

31 Qtd from *New Lines*, ed. Robert Conquest (London: Macmillan, 1956).

32 John Keats, 'Sleep and Poetry', in *John Keats: The Complete Poems*, ed. John Barnard, 3rd edn (Harmondsworth: Penguin, 1988). All poetry by John Keats will be quoted from this edition, unless specified otherwise.

33 'The Self', in *A Handbook to English Romanticism*, ed. Jean Raimond and J. R. Watson (Basingstoke: Macmillan, 1992), p. 239.

34 *John Milton: The Complete Poems*, ed. with preface and notes by John Leonard (London: Penguin, 1998).

35 See Kenneth R. Johnston, *Wordsworth and 'The Recluse'* (New Haven, CT: Yale University Press, 1984).

36 Qtd from Letitia Elizabeth Landon, *Selected Writings* (Peterborough, Ont.: Broadview, 1997).

37 Qtd from *Romanticism*, ed. Wu.

38 See, among others, *John Thelwall: Selected Poetry and Poetics*, ed. Judith Thompson (New York: Palgrave Macmillan, 2015) and Richard Gravil, '"Mr Thelwall's Ear"; or, Hearing *The Excursion*', in *Grasmere 2011: Selected*

Papers from the Wordsworth Summer Conference, ed. Richard Gravil (Humanities Ebooks, 2011), pp. 171–202.

39 Qtd from *Romanticism*, ed. Wu.

40 Qtd from Tennyson, *Poems of 1842*, ed. Christopher Ricks (London: Methuen, 1968), p. 365.

41 *Poetry and Repression: Revisionism from Blake to Stevens* (New Haven, CT: Yale University Press, 1976), p. 152.

Part 2 Timeline of the Late Eighteenth Century and Romantic Period

In assembling this timeline, the authors are indebted to the work of other scholars, notably Duncan Wu, in his 'A Romantic Timeline 1770–1851', in *Romanticism: An Anthology*, 4th edn (Malden, MA: Wiley Blackwell, 2012), pp. li–lxxxix.

Date	Current event	Literary or artistic landmark
1743		20 June: Anna Laetitia Barbauld (*née* Aikin) is born
		20 May: Toussaint Louverture, Haitian revolutionary is born
1744	15 March: France declares war on Great Britain	
1745	19 August: Jacobite rising of 1745 begins at Glenfinnan in Scotland	
	4 December: Jacobite rising: The Scottish Jacobite army reaches Derby, England, causing panic in London; two days later it begins retreat	
	18 December: Jacobite rising: A Jacobite victory at the Clifton Moor Skirmish	
	23 December: Jacobite rising: A Jacobite victory at the Battle of Inverurie	
1749		4 May: Charlotte Smith (*née* Turner) is born

The Romantic Poetry Handbook, First Edition. Michael O'Neill and Madeleine Callaghan.
© 2018 John Wiley & Sons Ltd. Published 2018 by John Wiley & Sons Ltd.

Date	Current event	Literary or artistic landmark
1751	31 March: Frederick, Prince of Wales dies and is succeeded by his son, the future George III of the United Kingdom	
1752	June: Benjamin Franklin proves that lightning is electricity	
1753	7 July: Royal assent to the Jewish Naturalization Act (British Parliament extends citizenship to Jews)	15 July: Ann Yearsley (*née* Cromartie) is baptized
1754	25 March: The Clandestine Marriages Act of 1753 comes into force in England and Wales, placing marriage in that jurisdiction on a statutory basis for the first time	
1755		15 April: *A Dictionary of the English Language* is published by Samuel Johnson
1756	15 May: Britain declares war on France, officially starting the Seven Years War (involving many world powers, but the principal opponents were France and Great Britain)	
1757	23 June: Battle of Plassey: 3,000 troops serving with the British East India Company defeat Nawab of Bengal's army and allies	28 November: William Blake is born
1758		27 November: Mary Robinson (*née* Darby) is born
1759	1 May: Josiah Wedgwood founds the Wedgwood pottery company in England	25 January: Robert Burns is born
1762	9 July: Catherine II becomes empress of Russia	
1763	10 February: Seven Years War ends	
1765	22 March: The Parliament of Great Britain passes the Stamp Act, imposing the first direct tax levied from Great Britain on the American colonies	
	24 March: Great Britain passes the Quartering Act, requiring the American colonies to house British troops	

Date	Current event	Literary or artistic landmark
1766	18 March: American Revolution: The British Parliament repeals the unpopular Stamp Act. The Declaratory Act claims the right to tax colonies	
1768	The first voyage (of three) of James Cook begins; the Royal Navy and Royal Society expedition to the South Pacific Ocean aboard HMS *Endeavour* takes place from 1768 to 1771	
1770	7 May: Marie Antoinette marries Louis Auguste (later King Louis XVI of France)	7 April: William Wordsworth is born
1771		25 December: Dorothy Wordsworth is born
1772	Second voyage of James Cook begins (1772–5)	21 October: Samuel Taylor Coleridge is born
1773	December 16: Boston Tea Party, where a group of American colonists trespass onto ships owned by the East India Company and dump their cargo of tea into Boston Harbour in order to protest against British tax policies	
1774	Intolerable (or Coercive) Acts: British Parliament pass four acts ending self-governance of Massachusetts following the Boston Tea Party	12 August: Robert Southey is born 29 September: Johann Wolfgang von Goethe's novel, *The Sorrows of Young Werther*, is published
1775	American Revolution begins James Watt builds a successful prototype of a steam engine	
1776	James Cook's third and final voyage begins	
1778		10 April: William Hazlitt is born
1779	14 February: Captain James Cook dies on the Sandwich Islands 21 June: Spain declares war on England, coming out on the side of the United States in the Revolutionary War	28 May: Thomas Moore is born

Date	Current event	Literary or artistic landmark
1780	June: Gordon Riots (anti-Catholic) in London	25 September: Charles Maturin is born
1781		Immanuel Kant publishes the *Critique of Pure Reason*
1783	3 September: Treaty of Paris: A treaty between the United States and Great Britain is signed in Paris, ending the American Revolutionary War; and treaties are signed between Britain, France, and Spain at Versailles ending hostilities with the Franco-Spanish Alliance. The treaty formally recognised America's status as a free nation 19 December: William Pitt becomes Prime Minister (serving 1783–1801 and 1804–6)	
1784		June: Charlotte Smith's *Elegiac Sonnets* are published 19 October: Leigh Hunt is born 13 December: Samuel Johnson dies
1785		June: Ann Yearsley publishes *Poems, on Several Occasions* August: William Cowper publishes *The Task* 15 August: Thomas de Quincey is born 18 October: Thomas Love Peacock is born
1786		26 January: Benjamin Robert Haydon is born 7 June: William Beckford's *Vathek* is published, unauthorized 31 July: Robert Burns publishes *Poems, Chiefly in the Scottish Dialect*
1787	22 May: Society for Effecting the Abolition of the Slave Trade is founded by Thomas Clarkson and Granville Sharp, with support from John Wesley, Josiah Wedgwood, and others 17 September: American constitution drafted and signed	

Date	Current event	Literary or artistic landmark
1788	7 June: Grenoble, France: Day of the Tiles (agitation against the government) George III's mental health breaks down	22 January: George Gordon Noel Byron is born
1789	4 February: George Washington is elected the first President of the United States 14 July: Storming of the Bastille (French Revolution)	William Blake publishes *Songs of Innocence* and *The Book of Thel*
1790	8 January: George Washington delivers the inaugural State of the Union address 11 February: Two Quaker delegates petition the United States Congress for the abolition of slavery 17 April: Benjamin Franklin dies 14 July: Louis XVI swears oath of loyalty to the new French constitution (establishing constitutional monarchy) October: Slaves revolt in Haiti (the Ogé Rebellion)	November: Edmund Burke publishes *Reflections on the Revolution in France*; Mary Wollstonecraft anonymously publishes *A Vindication of the Rights of Men*
1791	French royal family are ordered to remain in Paris, try to flee France, but are prevented July–August: Slave riots in San Domingo, Haiti October: Wolfe Tone founds the United Irishmen to fight for Irish nationalism	Anna Laetitia Barbauld publishes 'An Epistle to William Wilberforce' Thomas Paine publishes *The Rights of Man* (Part 1) Robert Burns publishes *Tam O'Shanter* Ann Radcliffe publishes *The Romance of the Forest* 5 December: Wolfgang Amadeus Mozart dies
1792	20 April: France declares war on Austria and Prussia (beginning French Revolutionary Wars) 21 May: Thomas Paine is charged with sedition 10 August: Mob storms royal palace and Louis XVI of France and family are arrested and taken into custody	Mary Wollstonecraft publishes *A Vindication of the Rights of Woman* Thomas Paine publishes *The Rights of Man* (Part 2) 4 August: Percy Bysshe Shelley is born

Date	Current event	Literary or artistic landmark
	Thomas Paine escapes to France	
	21 September: France declares itself a republic	
	December: Trial of Thomas Paine for seditious libel	
1793	21 January: Louis XVI is guillotined	14 February: William Godwin publishes *Political Justice*
	1 February: France declares war on 1st Coalition of Austria, Prussia, Britain, Holland, and Spain	13 July: John Clare is born
	16 October: Marie Antoinette is executed	25 September: Felicia Hemans (*née* Browne) is born
	28 December: Thomas Paine is arrested in France	
1794	4 February: France abolishes slavery in its territories (before reintroducing it in 1802)	10 May: Ann Radcliffe publishes *The Mysteries of Udolpho*
	7 May: Suspension of Habeas Corpus Act (enacted on 16 May)	12 May: William Godwin publishes *Caleb Williams*
	12 May: Radicals (including John Thelwall on 13 May) arrested	
	28 July: Robespierre is executed; end of the Terror	
	6 November: Paine released from prison	
	November–December: All arrested radicals are found not guilty	
1795	18 January: Batavian Revolution in Amsterdam. William V, Prince of Orange, flees the country	31 [or 29] October: John Keats is born
	8 April: The Prince of Wales marries Caroline	December: Robert Southey publishes *Joan of Arc*
1796	9 March: Marriage of Napoleon Bonaparte and Joséphine de Beauharnais	Matthew Lewis publishes *The Monk*
	April: Napoleon begins Italian campaign	16 April: Samuel Taylor Coleridge publishes his first volume, *Poems*
	23 June: Peace of Bologna ends Napoleon's first successful invasion of the Papal States	21 July: Robert Burns dies
	17 November: Catherine the Great dies	December: Ann Yearsley publishes *The Rural Lyre*

Date	Current event	Literary or artistic landmark
1797	4 March: John Adams becomes second President of the United States 16 April–15 May: Royal Navy mutinies	30 August: Mary Godwin (later Mary Shelley) born 10 September: Mary Wollstonecraft dies December: Ann Radcliffe publishes *The Italian*
1798	Napoleon captures Switzerland, Rome, and Naples 23 May: Uprising of the United Irishmen 1 July: Napoleon invades Egypt 1 August: Battle of the Nile. Great Britain defeats the French forces	Thomas Malthus publishes *Essay on Population* William Wordsworth and Samuel Taylor Coleridge publish *Lyrical Ballads* anonymously
1799	9 November: Napoleon becomes First Consul 14 December: George Washington dies	
1800		January: Maria Edgeworth publishes *Castle Rackrent* anonymously 25 April: William Cowper dies 20 November: Mary Robinson publishes *Lyrical Tales* 26 December: Mary Robinson dies
1801	28 January: The governor of Spanish San Domingo surrenders his territory to Toussaint Louverture. Louverture forms a central assembly to write a constitution that abolishes slavery on the island and begins social reform 16 February: Pitt the Younger resigns as Prime Minister and is succeeded by Henry Addington 23 March: Tsar Paul I of Russia is assassinated. He is succeeded by his son, Alexander I June: General Enclosure Act 15 July: Napoleon signs a Concordat with Pope Pius VII	*Lyrical Ballads* (1800) published under William Wordsworth's name

Date	Current event	Literary or artistic landmark
1802	27 March: The Treaty of Amiens between France and Great Britain ends the war (until May 1803) August: Napoleon becomes Life Consul of France	24 February: Walter Scott publishes *Minstrelsy of the Scottish Border* 18 April: Erasmus Darwin dies 14 August: Letitia Elizabeth Landon is born
1803	7 April: Toussaint Louverture dies in prison 18 May: Great Britain declares war on France July: Robert Emmet leads a failed uprising in Ireland 20 September: Robert Emmet is executed	30 June: Thomas Lovell Beddoes is born 15 August: Warrant issued for the arrest of William Blake for sedition
1804	21 February: First voyage of the steam locomotive (by Richard Trevithick) 10 May: William Pitt's second term begins 18 May: Napoleon proclaimed emperor 2 December: Napoleon's coronation ceremony	11–12 January: Blake tried for sedition and acquitted 12 February: Immanuel Kant dies 4 July: Nathaniel Hawthorne is born
1805	4 March: Thomas Jefferson begins second term as President 26 May: Napoleon crowned King of Italy 21 October: Battle of Trafalgar (Lord Nelson is mortally wounded) 2 December: Napoleon defeats Russian and Austrian armies at Austerlitz	9 May: Friedrich Schiller dies. 19 July: William Hazlitt publishes *An Essay on the Principles of Human Action*
1806	23 January: William Pitt dies 6 August: Holy Roman Empire is dissolved 14 October: Napoleon defeats Prussian forces at Jena 21 November: Berlin Decree: Napoleon declares the blockade of Great Britain	6 March: Elizabeth Barrett Browning is born 20 May: John Stuart Mill is born

Date	Current event	Literary or artistic landmark
1807	25 March: Abolition of the Slave Trade Act receives royal assent, thereby abolishing the slave trade in the British Empire, but it did not abolish slavery itself	January: Charles and Mary Lamb publish *Tales from Shakespeare* February: Charlotte Smith's *Beachy Head* is posthumously published 8 May: William Wordsworth publishes *Poems, in Two Volumes*
1808	January: Act Prohibiting Importation of Slaves comes into effect in the United States (passed 2 March 1807) 2 May: Peninsular War begins (lasting until 1814) where Napoleon's empire and the allied powers of Spain, Britain, and Portugal fought for control of the Iberian Peninsula	Thomas Moore publishes *Irish Melodies* (with many editions published between 1808 and 1834) 3 January: Leigh and John Hunt found *The Examiner* 22 February: Walter Scott publishes *Marmion* May: Felicia Dorothea Browne (later Hemans) publishes her first book of poetry 1 June: Coleridge publishes *The Friend* 20 September: Covent Garden theatre burns down December: Goethe publishes *Faust, Part One*; Hannah More publishes *Coelebs in Search of a Wife*
1809	February: *Quarterly Review* is founded 12 February: Abraham Lincoln is born 4 March: James Madison becomes 4th US President 13 March: Byron enters the House of Lords May: Napoleon takes Vienna 17 May: Papal States annexed to France 10 June: Pope Pius VII excommunicates Napoleon July: Napoleon arrests and imprisons Pope Pius VII	19 January: Edgar Allan Poe is born 12 February: Charles Darwin is born March: Byron publishes *English Bards and Scotch Reviewers* 31 May: Joseph Haydn dies 8 June: Thomas Paine dies 2 July: Byron and John Cam Hobhouse begin their Grand Tour 6 August: Alfred Tennyson born 18 September: Covent Garden theatre reopens

Date	Current event	Literary or artistic landmark
1810	9 April: Sir Francis Burdett imprisoned for libel 15 June: William Cobbett found guilty of treasonous libel	1 March: Frédéric Chopin is born 24 March: Mary Tighe dies 8 May: Walter Scott publishes *The Lady of the Lake*
1811	5 February: Prince of Wales made head of state following the recognition of the king as insane March: Luddite riots	18 July: William Makepeace Thackeray is born 22 October: Franz Liszt is born 29 August: Shelley elopes with Harriet Westbrook 30 October: Jane Austen publishes *Sense and Sensibility*
1812	11 May: Spencer Perceval (Prime Minister) assassinated 18 June: America declares war on Great Britain 22 June: Napoleon declares war on Russia 9 July: William Cobbett released from prison September: Napoleon's forces enter Moscow 19 October: Napoleon's forces retreat from Moscow	January: Anna Laetitia Barbauld publishes *Eighteen Hundred and Eleven* 7 February: Charles Dickens is born 10 March: Byron publishes cantos 1 and 2 of *Childe Harold's Pilgrimage* 22 March: Leigh Hunt's article on the Prince Regent is published in *The Examiner* 7 May: Robert Browning is born
1813	17 March: Prussia declares war on France 12 August: Austria declares war on France 27 August: Napoleon's final victory at Dresden 19 October: Napoleon defeated at Leipzig 9 November: Metternich (the Austrian Empire) offers a peace settlement to Napoleon	23 January: Coleridge's *Remorse* opens at Drury Lane theatre to plaudits 28 January: Jane Austen publishes *Pride and Prejudice* 3 February: Leigh Hunt sentenced to two years for libel 5 May: Søren Kierkegaard is born 18 May: Wordsworth becomes the Distributor of Stamps for Westmorland 22 May: Richard Wagner is born June: Percy Bysshe Shelley privately publishes *Queen Mab* 11 August: Henry James Pye (poet laureate) dies October: Madame de Staël publishes *De l'Allemagne* 4 November: Robert Southey becomes poet laureate

Date	Current event	Literary or artistic landmark
1814	31 March: Allies enter Paris 10 April: Napoleon defeated and exiled to Elba 11 April: Napoleon abdicates as French emperor 24 August: British troops occupy Washington, DC November: John Walter (proprietor of *The Times*) introduces the steam press 24 December: American–British hostilities cease with Treaty of Ghent	1 February: Byron publishes *The Corsair* March: Frances Burney publishes *The Wanderer* 9 May: Jane Austen publishes *Mansfield Park* 7 July: Walter Scott anonymously publishes *Waverley* 28 July: Percy Bysshe Shelley elopes with Mary Godwin to the continent, bringing Jane (Claire Clairmont) along with them 17 August: William Wordsworth publishes *The Excursion* 13 September: Shelley, Mary, and Jane return from the continent
1815	8 January: Battle of New Orleans won by Americans over British forces 3 February: Leigh Hunt released from jail 1 March: Napoleon escapes from Elba 20 March: Napoleon enters Paris after escaping from Elba, beginning his 'Hundred Days' rule 5–12 April: Mount Tambora (in the Dutch East Indies) erupts 18 June: Napoleon defeated at Waterloo and exiled to St Helena 22 June: Napoleon abdicates, naming Napoleon II as his successor 8 July: Louis XVIII returns to Paris to claim the French throne 9 November: Sir Humphry Davy announces his invention of the Davy lamp 20 November: Napoleonic Wars end (Treaty of Paris)	2 January: Byron marries Annabella Milbanke 24 February: Walter Scott publishes *Guy Mannering* 27 April: William Wordsworth publishes his collected *Poems* May: William Wordsworth publishes *The White Doe of Rylstone* 12 May: Byron appointed to sub-committee of management at Drury Lane theatre 1 June: John Gillray dies 1 October: John Keats enrols as a medical student at Guy's Hospital December: Jane Austen publishes *Emma*; Thomas Love Peacock publishes *Headlong Hall*

Date	Current event	Literary or artistic landmark
1816	9 July: Argentina declares independence from Spain November: Spa Fields riots in London	10 February: Percy Bysshe Shelley publishes *Alastor; or, The Spirit of Solitude* February: Leigh Hunt publishes *Rimini* 21 April: Charlotte Brontë is born 25 April: Byron leaves England for the continent 2 May: Percy Bysshe Shelley, Mary Godwin, and Claire Clairmont (was Jane) leave England for Geneva 4 May: Walter Scott publishes *The Antiquary* 5 May: John Keats publishes his first poem, 'To Solitude' 25 May: Byron and Shelley meet for the first time in Sécheron, near Geneva; Samuel Taylor Coleridge publishes *Kubla Khan* and 'The Pains of Sleep' 17 June: Mary Godwin begins writing *Frankenstein* 7 July: Richard Brinsley Sheridan dies 8 September: Shelley, Mary Godwin, and Claire Clairmont return to England 9 November: Harriet Shelley (Westbrook) commits suicide 18 November: Byron publishes *Childe Harold's Pilgrimage* III 30 December: Shelley marries Mary Godwin
1817	4 March: James Monroe becomes 5th President of the United States; habeas corpus is suspended in Great Britain June: Uprisings in provinces of Great Britain 18 June: William Hone tried for publishing blasphemous material 6 November: Princess Charlotte dies in childbirth	19 January: Percy Bysshe Shelley publishes 'Hymn to Intellectual Beauty' in *The Examiner* 13 February: Robert Southey's *Wat Tyler* (composed in 1794) published in an unauthorized version 14 February: William Hazlitt and Leigh Hunt publish *The Round Table* 1 March: John Keats publishes *Poems*

Date	Current event	Literary or artistic landmark
	20 December: William Hone is acquitted	April: *Blackwood's Edinburgh Magazine* is founded
		3 July: Byron publishes *Manfred*
		9 July: William Hazlitt publishes *Characters of Shakespeare's Plays*
		11 July: Samuel Taylor Coleridge publishes *Biographia Literaria* and *Sibylline Leaves*
		12 July: Henry David Thoreau is born
		14 July: Madame de Staël dies
		18 July: Jane Austen dies
		December: Jane Austen's *Northanger Abbey* and *Persuasion* are posthumously published
1818	28 January: Habeas corpus restored	1 January: Mary Shelley publishes *Frankenstein* anonymously
	12 February: Chile proclaims its independence from Spain	11 January: Percy Bysshe Shelley publishes 'Ozymandias' in *The Examiner*
	17 November: Queen Charlotte dies	12 January: Shelley publishes *The Revolt of Islam*
		31 January: Walter Scott publishes *Rob Roy*
		28 February: Byron publishes *Beppo*
		22 April–19 May: John Keats publishes *Endymion*
		28 April: Byron publishes *Childe Harold's Pilgrimage* IV
		29 April: William Hazlitt publishes *A View of the English Stage*
		5 May: Karl Marx is born
		18 May: Charles Lamb publishes *Works* (in two volumes)
		30 July: Emily Brontë is born
		November: Thomas Love Peacock publishes *Nightmare Abbey*

Date	Current event	Literary or artistic landmark
1819	24 May: Princess Victoria is born	8 February: John Ruskin is born
	16 August: Peterloo Massacre of protesters by cavalry at St Peter's Fields, Manchester	1 April: John Polidori publishes *The Vampyre* under Byron's name
	12 October: Richard Carlile tried for blasphemy, blasphemous libel, and sedition	15 April: John Hamilton Reynolds publishes *Peter Bell. A Lyrical Ballad*
	21 November: Carlile is sentenced to six years in prison	22 April: William Wordsworth publishes *Peter Bell*
	December: Simón Bolívar becomes first President of the Republic of Gran Colombia (which includes present-day Venezuela, Colombia, Panama, and Ecuador)	31 May: Walt Whitman is born
		15 July: Byron publishes cantos 1 and 2 of *Don Juan* anonymously
		1 August: Herman Melville is born
		14 August: William Hazlitt publishes *Political Essays*
1820	January: A constitutionalist military insurrection at Cádiz leads to a revolution	1 January: *London Magazine* starts publishing
	29 January: George III dies and George IV ascends the throne	16 January: Leigh Hunt starts publishing *The Indicator*; John Clare publishes *Poems Descriptive of Rural Life and Scenery*
	23 February: Cato Street Conspiracy (to kill the Cabinet) in Great Britain	17 January: Anne Brontë is born
	9 March: King Ferdinand VII of Spain accepts the new constitution, beginning the Trienio Liberal	28 January: Robert Southey publishes *Poetical Works* in 14 volumes
	17 August: Trial of Queen Caroline for infidelity begins	June: Thomas Love Peacock publishes 'The Four Ages of Poetry'
	3 December: James Monroe re-elected US President	1 July: John Keats publishes *Lamia, Isabella, The Eve of St. Agnes, and Other Poems*
		6 July: William Wordsworth publishes *The River Duddon*
		14 August: Percy Bysshe Shelley publishes *Prometheus Unbound…, with Other Poems*
		17 September: Keats leaves England for Rome
1821	March: Beginning of the Greek War of Independence	23 February: John Keats dies
	5 May: Napoleon dies in exile in St Helena	6 April: William Hazlitt publishes the first volume of *Table Talk*
	24 June: Venezuela becomes independent from Spain	July: Percy Bysshe Shelley publishes *Adonais*

Date	Current event	Literary or artistic landmark
	19 July: George IV is crowned King of the United Kingdom of Great Britain and Ireland	September: John Clare publishes *The Village Minstrel*
	15 September: Guatemala, El Salvador, Honduras, Nicaragua, and Costa Rica gain independence from Spain by the Act of Independence of Central America	1 October: Thomas de Quincey publishes *Confessions of an English Opium-Eater* (part I) in *London Magazine* (part II is published in November)
	28 November: Panama declares independence from Spain	11 November: Fyodor Dostoyevsky is born
	1 December: The Dominican Republic declares independence from Spain	12 December: Gustave Flaubert is born
		19 December: Byron publishes *Sardanapalus, The Two Foscari,* and *Cain: A Mystery*
1822	3 July: Charles Babbage publishes a proposal for a 'difference engine' (a prototype of the modern computer)	February: William Hazlitt publishes 'The Fight' in *New Monthly Magazine*
	12 August: Viscount Castlereagh (UK foreign secretary) commits suicide	15 June: Hazlitt publishes *Table Talk,* volume II
	7 September: Brazil declares its independence from Portugal	8 July: Percy Bysshe Shelley dies
		16 August: Shelley is cremated
	27 December: Louis Pasteur is born	14 October: The first edition of *The Liberal* is published (a project devised by Hunt, Shelley, and Byron)
		December: Charles Lamb publishes *Elia*
		24 December: Matthew Arnold is born
1823	5 October: Thomas Wakley founds *The Lancet* in London	February: Mary Shelley publishes *Valperga*
	2 December: Monroe Doctrine introduced in the United States	23 April: William Hazlitt publishes 'My First Acquaintance with Poets' in *The Liberal*
		9 May: Hazlitt publishes *Liber Amoris*
		June: Felicia Hemans publishes *The Siege of Valencia*
		25 August: Mary Shelley returns to England with her son, Percy Florence Shelley
		12 December: Hemans's *The Vespers of Palermo* performed at Covent Garden theatre

Date	Current event	Literary or artistic landmark
1824	16 June: Royal Society for the Prevention of Cruelty to Animals founded in Great Britain	4 January: Byron lands at Missolonghi, Greece, to fight in the Greek War of Independence
		March: Samuel Taylor Coleridge elected a royal associate of the Royal Society of Literature
		19 April: Byron dies
		7 May: Ludwig van Beethoven's *Symphony No. 9 in D minor* first performed
		June: Mary Shelley publishes her edition of Shelley's *Posthumous Poems*
		June: James Hogg anonymously publishes *Private Memoirs and Confessions of a Justified Sinner*
		July: Letitia Elizabeth Landon's *The Improvisatrice, and other Poems* published
		September: Sir Timothy Shelley suppresses publication of Shelley's posthumous poetry
		30 October: Charles Maturin dies
1825	4 March: John Quincy Adams begins term as US President	11 January: William Hazlitt anonymously publishes *The Spirit of the Age*
	27 September: The world's first modern railway, the Stockton and Darlington Railway, opens in England	9 March: Anna Laetitia Barbauld dies
		16 April: Henry Fuseli dies
		May: Felicia Hemans publishes *The Forest Sanctuary and Other Poems*
		June: Barbauld's niece, Lucy Aikin, publishes Barbauld's works anonymously
		7 November: Charlotte Dacre dies
1826	1 April: Samuel Morey patents an internal combustion engine	23 January: Mary Shelley publishes *The Last Man*
	4 July: John Adams and Thomas Jefferson die	March: William Blake publishes *Job*
		28 April: William Hazlitt anonymously publishes *The Plain Speaker*

Date	Current event	Literary or artistic landmark
1827	10 April: George Canning succeeds Lord Liverpool as British Prime Minister 8 August: George Canning dies	26 March: Ludwig van Beethoven dies April: John Clare publishes *The Shepherd's Calendar, with Village Stories and Other Poems* 12 August: William Blake dies 15 December: Helen Maria Williams dies
1828	22 January: Duke of Wellington becomes Prime Minister	January: Volumes I and II of William Hazlitt's *Life of Napoleon Buonaparte* are published 16 April: Francisco Goya dies May: Felicia Hemans publishes *Records of Woman* 12 May: Dante Gabriel Rossetti is born 19 November: Franz Schubert dies
1829	4 March: Andrew Jackson becomes US President April: Catholic Emancipation Act 19 June: Metropolitan Police Service in London established by Sir Robert Peel (begin patrolling on 29 September)	December: Samuel Taylor Coleridge publishes *On the Constitution of Church and State*
1830	3 February: The London Protocol establishes the full independence of Greece from the Ottoman Empire 26 June: King George IV dies and is succeeded by his brother, William IV June–July: France invades Algeria 27–9 July: The July Revolution begins in France 4 October: Belgium's provisional government declare independence 22 November: Earl Grey succeeds the Duke of Wellington as Prime Minister of the United Kingdom	Felicia Hemans's *Songs of the Affections, with Other Poems* is published May: Volumes III and IV of William Hazlitt's *Life of Napoleon Buonaparte* are published June: Effingham Wilson publishes Alfred Tennyson's *Poems, Chiefly Lyrical* 18 September: William Hazlitt dies 5 December: Christina Rossetti is born 10 December: Emily Dickinson is born

Date	Current event	Literary or artistic landmark
1831	May–June: Merthyr Rising: Coal miners and others riot in Merthyr Tydfil, Wales for improved working conditions 8 September: The coronation of King William IV of the United Kingdom 27 December: Charles Darwin embarks on his historic voyage aboard HMS *Beagle* 27 December: The Christmas Rebellion begins in Jamaica	16 March: *The Hunchback of Notre-Dame* is published by Victor Hugo 11 November: Nat Turner, American slave rebel, dies 14 November: Georg Hegel dies
1832	4 January: The Christmas Rebellion ends in Jamaica 28 February: Charles Darwin and the crew of HMS *Beagle* arrive at South America for the first time May: Greece is recognized as a sovereign nation 7 June: The Reform Act becomes law in the United Kingdom 3 December: Andrew Jackson is re-elected US President	Edward Moxon publishes *The Poetical Works of Leigh Hunt* Percy Bysshe Shelley, *The Mask of Anarchy*, is posthumously published, with a preface by Leigh Hunt Leigh Hunt, *The Poetical Works of Leigh Hunt*, is published by subscription 27 January: Lewis Carroll (Charles Dodgson) is born 22 March: Johann Wolfgang von Goethe dies 6 June: Jeremy Bentham dies 22 July: Napoleon II of France dies 21 September: Sir Walter Scott dies December: *Faust* Part 2 is posthumously published
1833	29 July: William Wilberforce dies 1 August: British Parliament passes the Slavery Abolition Act 1833, abolishing slavery in British colonies (with exceptions) 29 August: British Parliament enacts the Factory Acts, limiting child labour December: American Anti-Slavery Society founded	Hartley Coleridge publishes his *Poems* Robert Browning anonymously publishes *Pauline, a Fragment of a Confession* Elizabeth Barrett anonymously publishes a translation of Aeschylus' *Prometheus Bound* 15 May: Edmund Kean dies 7 September: Hannah More dies

Date	Current event	Literary or artistic landmark
1834	1 August: Slaves officially freed by Slavery Abolition Act 1833 14 August: British Parliament passes the Poor Law Amendment Act 16 October: Fire destroys Palace of Westminster (Houses of Parliament)	Samuel Taylor Coleridge, *Poetical Works*, is published Felicia Hemans publishes *National Lyrics, and Songs for Music* and *Scenes and Hymns of Life* 17 February: John Thelwall dies 24 March: William Morris is born 25 July: Samuel Taylor Coleridge dies 27 December: Charles Lamb dies 29 December: Thomas Malthus dies
1835	7 January: HMS *Beagle* anchors off the Chonos Archipelago on her second voyage 18 April: Lord Melbourne succeeds Sir Robert Peel as British Prime Minister	Robert Browning's *Paracelsus* is published Thomas Moore, *The Fudges in England*, published William Wordsworth, *Yarrow Revisited, and Other Poems*, published March: Mary Shelley publishes *Lodore* July: John Clare, *The Rural Muse*, published 16 May: Felicia Hemans dies 21 November: James Hogg dies
1836	23 February–6 March: The Battle of the Alamo 2 October: Charles Darwin returns to England aboard HMS *Beagle* 7 December: Martin Van Buren wins United States presidential election	March: First monthly part of Charles Dickens's *The Pickwick Papers* is published 7 April: William Godwin dies
1837	20 June: King William IV dies 20 June: Queen Victoria accedes to the throne of the United Kingdom	10 February: Alexander Pushkin dies 5 April: Algernon Charles Swinburne is born
1838	28 June: Coronation of Queen Victoria 13 May: The People's Charter, demanding universal suffrage, is presented to British Parliament (to be rejected)	Elizabeth Barrett publishes *The Seraphim, and Other Poems* William Wordsworth's *The Sonnets of William Wordsworth* is published 15 October: Letitia Elizabeth Landon dies

Date	Current event	Literary or artistic landmark
1839	First Opium Wars begin between Britain and China	January to May: *The Poetical Works of Percy Bysshe Shelley* (in four volumes), edited by Mary Shelley, is published by Edward Moxon
		19 January: Paul Cézanne is born
		February: De Quincey publishes the first of his 'Lake Reminiscences' in *Tait's Edinburgh Magazine*
		4 August: Walter Pater is born
1840	10 February: Queen Victoria of the United Kingdom marries her cousin Prince Albert of Saxe-Coburg and Gotha	Matthew Arnold publishes *Alaric at Rome*
		Robert Browning publishes *Sordello*
		William Wordsworth publishes *The Poetical Works of William Wordsworth* in six volumes
	30 September: The frigate *Belle-Poule* arrives in Cherbourg, bringing back the remains of Napoleon from Saint Helena to France	*The Poetical Works of Thomas Moore*, in 10 volumes, published starting in 1840 and ending in 1841
		6 January: Frances Burney dies
	4 November: William Henry Harrison elected President of the United States	2 June: Thomas Hardy is born
		5 October: John Addington Symonds is born
1841	26 January: Britain occupies Hong Kong	Robert Browning publishes *Pippa Passes*
	4 April: William Henry Harrison dies; he is succeeded by Vice President John Tyler (sworn in 6 April)	25 February: Pierre-Auguste Renoir is born
		9 November: Edward VII of the United Kingdom is born
	21 May: New Zealand becomes a British colony	
1842		Alfred Tennyson, *Poems*, is published
		Robert Browning publishes *Dramatic Lyrics*
		William Wordsworth, *Poems, Chiefly of Early and Late Years*, is published
		Leigh Hunt publishes *The Palfrey*
		11 January: William James is born
		18 March: Stéphane Mallarmé is born
		23 March: Stendhal dies

Date	Current event	Literary or artistic landmark
1843	7 April: The Indian Slavery Act, 1843 abolishes slavery within the territories of the East India Company	21 March: Robert Southey dies 4 April: William Wordsworth becomes poet laureate 15 April: Henry James is born 7 June: Friedrich Hölderlin dies 16 October: Søren Kierkegaard's *Fear and Trembling* is published
1844	27 February: The Dominican Republic becomes independent from Haiti April: The Fleet Prison for debtors in London is closed 28 August: Friedrich Engels and Karl Marx meet for the first time 4 December: James K. Polk elected President of the United States	Elizabeth Barrett publishes *Poems* Leigh Hunt publishes *Imagination and Fancy* 30 March: Paul Verlaine is born 28 July: Gerard Manley Hopkins is born 15 October: Friedrich Nietzsche is born 23 October: Robert Bridges is born
1845	Friedrich Engels publishes *The Condition of the Working Class in England* in Leipzig 26 July to 10 August: Isambard Kingdom Brunel's steamship *Great Britain* makes its first transatlantic crossing from Liverpool to New York 9 September: Potato blight breaks out in Ireland, heralding the beginning of the Great Famine	Robert Browning publishes *Dramatic Romances and Lyrics* Edgar Allan Poe publishes *The Raven and Other Poems* 10 January: Robert Browning sends Elizabeth Barrett the note that begins their courtship May: Frederick Douglass's *Narrative of the Life of Frederick Douglass, an American Slave* is published by the Boston Anti-Slavery Society
1846	Cholera epidemic in England 14 February: James K. Polk annexes the Republic of Texas to the United States 13 May: America declares war and officially begins the Mexican–American War 15 May: Corn Laws are repealed in the United Kingdom 10 June: The California Republic declares independence from Mexico 23 September: Discovery of the planet Neptune	Edward Lear publishes *A Book of Nonsense* 7 January: John Hookham Frere dies May: The Brontë sisters publish *Poems by Currer, Ellis, and Acton Bell* 22 June: Benjamin Robert Haydon commits suicide 12 September: Elizabeth Barrett and Robert Browning get married

Date	Current event	Literary or artistic landmark
1847	11 February: Thomas Edison is born	Christina Rossetti publishes *Verses by Christina G. Rossetti*
		Percy Bysshe Shelley, *The Works of Percy Bysshe Shelley*, edited by Mary Shelley, is posthumously published
		The Princess, by Alfred Tennyson, is published
		Ralph Waldo Emerson publishes *Poems*
		20 May: Mary Lamb dies
		19 October: Charlotte Brontë publishes *Jane Eyre* (as Currer Bell)
		14 December: Emily Brontë and Anne Brontë publish *Wuthering Heights* and *Agnes Grey* in a three-volume set (as Ellis Bell and Acton Bell)
1848	February: The French Second Republic is proclaimed	Pre-Raphaelite Brotherhood is founded by Dante Gabriel Rossetti, William Holman Hunt, and John Everett Millais
	2 February: Mexican–American War officially ends	
	21 February: Karl Marx and Friedrich Engels publish *The Communist Manifesto*	*Life, Letters, and Literary Remains of John Keats* is published in two volumes, edited by Richard Monckton Milnes
	15 March: The Hungarian Revolution of 1848 begins	7 June: Paul Gauguin is born
	10 April: Chartist 'Monster Rally' held in London	24 September: Branwell Brontë dies
	23 June to 26 June: The June Days Uprising in France	October: Elizabeth Gaskell's first novel, *Mary Barton: A Tale of Manchester Life*, is anonymously published
	7 November: Zachary Taylor elected President of the United States	19 December: Emily Brontë dies
	10 December: Prince Louis-Napoleon Bonaparte is elected first President of the French Second Republic	
1849	8 February: The new Roman Republic is proclaimed	Matthew Arnold publishes *The Strayed Reveller, and Other Poems* (published under 'A')
	13 August: Hungarian Revolution fails	Robert Browning publishes *Poems*
		A. H. Clough (with Thomas Burbidge) publishes *Ambarvalia*
		6 January: Hartley Coleridge dies

Date	Current event	Literary or artistic landmark
		6 January: Hartley Coleridge dies
		26 January: Thomas Lovell Beddoes dies
		22 May: Maria Edgeworth dies
		28 May: Anne Brontë dies
		7 October: Edgar Allan Poe dies
		1 November: Wordsworth's *Poetical Works* (six volumes) begins publishing
		De Quincey publishes 'The English Mail-Coach' (anonymously) in *Blackwood's* (October and December issues)
1850	18 March: American Express founded by Henry Wells and William Fargo	Thomas Lovell Beddoes's *Death's Jest-Book, or, The Fool's Tragedy* is posthumously published (with a memoir by T. F. Kelsall)
	9 July: President Zachary Taylor dies (Vice President Millard Fillmore becomes US President)	26 January: Francis Jeffrey dies
		8 February: Kate Chopin is born
	9 September: California becomes 31st state of the United States	16 March: Nathaniel Hawthorne's *The Scarlet Letter* is published
		7 April: William Lisle Bowles dies
		23 April: William Wordsworth dies
		May: Alfred Tennyson anonymously publishes *In Memoriam A.H.H.*
		July: William Wordsworth's *The Prelude; or, Growth of a Poet's Mind: An Autobiographical Poem*, on which he has worked since 1798, is posthumously published
		18 August: Honoré de Balzac dies
		November: A new edition of Elizabeth Barrett Browning's *Poems*, including *Sonnets from the Portuguese*, is published
		19 November: Alfred Tennyson becomes poet laureate

Part 3 **Biographies**

Anna Laetitia Barbauld (1743–1825)

Anna Laetitia Barbauld, *née* Aikin, was born into a middle-class Dissenting family. Her father, a schoolmaster, taught her Latin and Greek from a young age. In 1758 he took up a teaching post at Warrington Academy, Lancashire and the family moved with him. Legal and social discrimination saw Dissenters barred from leading universities, and Warrington Academy became their intellectual hub and sanctuary, allowing Barbauld to make the acquaintance of figures such as Joseph Priestley (1733–1804) and William Enfield (1741–97). Though prevented from officially enrolling as a student at the school, she was precocious in her learning and poetic ability, and began writing poetry on diverse topics from the mid-1760s. In 1774, she married a graduate from Warrington Academy, Reverend Rochemont Barbauld, and settled in Palgrave, Suffolk, where they opened a successful school for boys. In 1777, they adopted her brother John Aikin's second son, Charles Rochemont Aikin. Barbauld taught prose composition, and her work with children inspired her to write her *Hymns in Prose for Children* (1781) and the subsequent four-volume work, *Lessons for Children* (1787–8). *Hymns in Prose for Children* was particularly successful, running through many editions. It is among the books that inspired William Blake's *Songs of Innocence* (1789).[1] These publications cemented her reputation as synonymous with children's education.

In 1785 the Barbaulds resigned from teaching at their school and travelled on the continent. On their return, in 1787 they settled in Hampstead, and Barbauld focused on her writing career while her husband continued to teach pupils. She began to compose various works of social and political criticism, particularly essays on the legal discrimination against Dissenters and the moral responsibilities of governments. Such political concerns are clearly visible in her poetry, particularly in 'Epistle to William Wilberforce, Esq., on

The Romantic Poetry Handbook, First Edition. Michael O'Neill and Madeleine Callaghan.
© 2018 John Wiley & Sons Ltd. Published 2018 by John Wiley & Sons Ltd.

the Rejection of the Bill for Abolishing the Slave Trade' (1791), where Barbauld's detached voice offers a balanced though scornful denunciation of British attitudes to slavery. Barbauld also began to write literary criticism; she provided prefaces to editions of Mark Akenside (1794), William Collins (1797), and Addison and Steele (1804). After the couple moved to Stoke Newington in 1802, Barbauld's domestic life became increasingly troubled owing to her husband's apparent mental illness. In 1808, they separated because of her fears of physical violence. Barbauld's husband committed suicide in the same year. After widespread and sometimes brutal condemnation of her poem *Eighteen Hundred and Eleven*, Barbauld ceased publishing poetry. Her poetry and selected prose were published by her niece, Lucy Aikin, in 1825, the year Barbauld died. Despite her success as an author, Barbauld is often considered to be less concerned with female emancipation than some of her peers, as Caroline Franklin argues: 'Dissenters Anna Barbauld and Helen Maria Williams were politically radical, yet accepted conventional gender distinctions.'[2] However, her sex did not prevent her from addressing vital political questions in *Eighteen Hundred and Eleven*; her jeremiad may have finished her career but it also affirmed her prophetic gift.

Notes

1 Mary Waters, 'Anna Barbauld', *The Literary Encyclopedia*, first published 23 March 2002; last revised 30 November [http://www.litencyc.com/php/speople.php?rec=true&UID=249, accessed 16 April 2015].
2 Caroline Franklin, 'Enlightenment Feminism and the Bluestocking Legacy', in *The Cambridge Companion to Women's Writing in the Romantic Period*, ed. Devoney Looser (Cambridge: Cambridge University Press, 2015), pp. 115–28 (at p. 121).

Source

William McCarthy, 'Barbauld, Anna Letitia (1743–1825)', *Oxford Dictionary of National Biography*, Oxford University Press, 2004; online edn, January 2008 [http://www.oxforddnb.com/view/article/1324, accessed 6 June 2015]; Anna Letitia Barbauld (1743–1825): doi:10.1093/ref:odnb/1324; Mary Waters, 'Anna Barbauld', *The Literary Encyclopedia*, first published 23 March 2002; last revised 30 November [http://www.litencyc.com/php/speople.php?rec=true& UID=249, accessed 16 April 2015].

Biography

Betsy Rodgers, *Georgian Chronicle: Mrs. Barbauld and Her Family* (London: Methuen, 1958).

Thomas Lovell Beddoes (1803–1849)

Born in 1803 in Clifton, Bristol, Beddoes was the second of four children born to Anna (*née* Edgeworth, sister of the novelist Maria Edgeworth) and Dr Thomas Beddoes, an acclaimed physician and author. After the death of his father in 1808, Beddoes and his family relocated to Great Malvern, Worcestershire in 1811 and then to Bath in 1814. Excelling at Charterhouse School (enrolling in 1817), Beddoes then went up to Pembroke College, Oxford in 1820.

Beddoes's first publication was a short poem in heroic couplets, 'The Comet', which appeared in the *Morning Post*, 5 July 1819; its prophetic and controlled voice recalls Byron's 'Darkness'. On beginning his degree at Oxford, he entered into a period of intense creativity. He published *The Improvisatore, in Three Fyttes, with other Poems* in March 1821, despite coming to regret the collection, and in November 1822, Rivington published *The Brides' Tragedy*. Earning the notice of Bryan Waller Procter (Barry Cornwall, a respected contemporary poet) and George Darley, this drama showed Beddoes earning his spurs as a playwright in the Jacobean tradition, and between 1823 and 1825 he wrote various dramatic fragments, including *The Second Brother, Torrismond, Love's Arrow Poisoned*, and *The Last Man*. These early publications reveal his ability to write a blank verse deeply inspired by the Elizabethan and Jacobean periods, yet speaking with his own often macabre, haunting, and sardonic voice. An additional major source of inspiration was Percy Bysshe Shelley, especially but by no means only as the author of the drama *The Cenci*, and in 1824 he stood guarantor with Procter, Kelsall (later Beddoes's literary executor), and Nicholas Waller for the publication of Shelley's *Posthumous Poems*.

The Romantic Poetry Handbook, First Edition. Michael O'Neill and Madeleine Callaghan.
© 2018 John Wiley & Sons Ltd. Published 2018 by John Wiley & Sons Ltd.

After his mother's death in Florence in 1824 (he did not arrive at her deathbed in time), Beddoes returned to Oxford to complete his studies, but he soon left England to move to Germany to study medicine. Enrolled in the medical school in Göttingen, Beddoes was both an excellent academic asset to the university and a liability owing to his misconduct (financial as well as personal). Having written a large part of *Death's Jest-Book, or, The Fool's Tragedy* by 1829, Beddoes was devastated by the negative reactions of Procter, Kelsall, and J. G. H. Bourne, which intensified his descent into drinking and debauchery. Ironically, this is now the work by Beddoes that attracts the most critical praise, but the censure of his friends led him to never publish it, despite reworking it frequently in the 1830s and 1840s. After being asked to leave the university in Göttingen, Beddoes began to study again in Würzburg, receiving his degree in September 1831. His involvement in radical politics, however, saw him banished from Bavaria in 1832 and he moved to Switzerland, until finally he was expelled from Zürich in 1840 and returned to Germany. Though his interests had moved from the poetic to the political, Beddoes kept writing satiric and lyric poetry and revising *Death's Jest-Book*. He met Konrad Degen, a baker for whom he apparently developed romantic feelings, and when he returned to England for a visit in 1846–7, Beddoes's dissipation disturbed his family and friends. When he returned to Frankfurt, he contracted blood poisoning from a diseased cadaver. After falling out with Degen, he returned to Basel in despair. He committed suicide and was found on 26 January 1849; his friends and family hushed up the tragic circumstances of his death. One of the most significant third-generation Romantic poets, as Michael Bradshaw writes, 'Beddoes's career was impelled by early acclaim which he avidly watched unfold in the pages of *Blackwood's* and *The London Magazine*, but which he could never replicate with his mature writing'.[1] However, critics have brought and continue to bring Beddoes's significant achievements into the larger Romantic arena.

Note

1 Michael Bradshaw, 'Third-Generation Romantic Poetry: Beddoes, Clare, Darley, Hemans, Landon', in *The Cambridge History of English Poetry*, ed. Michael O'Neill (Cambridge: Cambridge University Press, 2010), pp. 542–60 (at p. 544).

Source

Alan Halsey, 'Beddoes, Thomas Lovell (1803–1849)', *Oxford Dictionary of National Biography*, Oxford University Press, 2004; online edn, May 2007 [http://www.oxforddnb.com/view/article/1920, accessed 9 September 2015]; Thomas Lovell Beddoes (1803–1849): doi:10.1093/ref:odnb/1920; Shelley S. Rees, 'Thomas Lovell Beddoes', *The Literary Encyclopedia*, first published 13 February 2006 [http://www.litencyc.com/php/speople.php?rec=true&UID=324, accessed 09 September 2015].

Biography

James R. Thompson, *Thomas Lovell Beddoes*, Twayne English Author Series (Boston: Twayne, 1985).

William Blake (1757–1827)

William Blake, poet, artist, and engraver, was born in Soho, London, on 28 November 1757 into a family of London shopkeepers and artisans. From childhood onwards, Blake had visionary experiences, and his father, while being circumspect about the content of his son's visions, encouraged his artistic leanings. At the age of ten, Blake went to drawing school and was apprenticed at fourteen to James Basire, a printmaker who was also engraver to the Royal Society and the Society of Antiquaries. Blake presumably lived with his master for seven years. In 1779 he was admitted to the Royal Academy as a student, and after passing a three-month probationary period, he was entitled to attend exhibitions and lectures for six years. Blake's long-held interest in poetry began to grow, and his range of reading, from Milton's poetry to theology, combined with his interest in revolutionary changes to society, began to influence his writing and art. *Poetical Sketches* (1783), Blake's first poetry collection, is not always reprinted in its entirety in selections of his poetry, but its original engagements with conventional themes and styles anticipate his later work.

Blake married Catherine Boucher in August 1782. Catherine may have been illiterate, entering an X in place of a signature on the register. After a few early quarrels, notably with Blake's brother Robert, when Blake made his wife apologize to his brother, their marriage was happy, with Catherine steadfastly supporting her husband throughout his career. He exhibited his art several times at the Royal Academy and began to attend the New Jerusalem church, which based its teachings on the thought of Emanuel Swedenborg. A commission from John and Josiah Boydell to create his largest copy engraving, *Beggar's Opera*, after a painting by William Hogarth, helped the Blakes move to the well-appointed 13 Hercules Buildings, Lambeth

The Romantic Poetry Handbook, First Edition. Michael O'Neill and Madeleine Callaghan.
© 2018 John Wiley & Sons Ltd. Published 2018 by John Wiley & Sons Ltd.

where they enjoyed a period of prosperity. Always a prolific worker, Blake engraved and wrote *The Book of Thel* (1789) and the *Songs of Innocence* (1789), but commercial success was stymied, in part, owing to Blake's practice of engraving each individual copy. He was also at work on a number of commissions, including Erasmus Darwin's *The Botanic Garden* (1791) and Mary Wollstonecraft's *Original Stories from Real Life* (1791). Blake rejected Swedenborg's teachings and published *The Marriage of Heaven and Hell* (1790), which reverses traditional doctrine in favour of a sensual, Satanic voice. *Visions of the Daughters of Albion* (1793) reinforces Blake's radical and apocalyptic world-view, along with *America a Prophecy* (1793) and *Europe* (1794), which blend real places and people with Blake's imaginative scheme. In 1794 *Songs of Innocence and of Experience* was published. Blake was commissioned in 1795 to engrave plates for Edward Young's *Night Thoughts*, but the project failed to be a commercial success. He began to work on *Vala, or, The Four Zoas*, but it was never completed. His friendship with William Hayley led Hayley to invite Blake to work for him, and in 1800 Blake moved with his wife to Felpham, Sussex. After an initial period of content, tension grew between Hayley and Blake, and the Blakes intended to move back to London. However, in 1803, while the couple were still in Felpham, a soldier, John Scolfield, entered Blake's garden, and the subsequent quarrel between Blake and Scolfield led to the soldier accusing Blake of sedition. Though Blake was later acquitted of all charges, it was a stressful period. Blake remained productive, beginning *Milton* (engraved 1809) and *Jerusalem* (completed 1820), and writing 'Auguries of Innocence' and 'The Mental Traveller' (1804). Despite the showing of two of his watercolours in the 1808 Royal Academy exhibition, Blake felt neglected, and in 1809 he held the only exhibition of his work, which met with critical disregard and mockery of his mental state: no sales are recorded, and the Blakes lived in some poverty. However, Blake became a friend of John Linnell, an artist, who offered him various commissions, and their friendship lasted until Linnell's death. Blake found himself surrounded by young followers introduced to him by Linnell, and his creativity continued up to his death on 12 August 1827. Blake's radical apocalyptic poetry and engravings reveal the importance of his maxim, 'One Power alone makes a Poet – Imagination, The Divine Vision'.[1]

Note

1 William Blake, 'Marginalia: On William Wordsworth, *Poems: Including Lyrical Ballads*, Volume I (1815)', in *Blake's Poetry and Designs: Illuminated Works, Other Writings, Criticism*, sel. and ed. Mary Lynn Johnson and John E. Grant, 2nd edn (New York: Norton, 2008), p. 446.

Source

Robert N. Essick, 'Blake, William (1757–1827)', *Oxford Dictionary of National Biography*, Oxford University Press, 2004; online edn, October 2005 [http://www.oxforddnb.com/view/article/2585, accessed 14 September 2015]; William Blake (1757–1827): doi:10.1093/ref:odnb/2585; David Punter, 'William Blake', *The Literary Encyclopedia*, first published 07 July 2001 [http://www.litencyc.com/php/speople.php?rec=true&UID=5182, accessed 14 September 2015]; Duncan Wu, 'William Blake (1757–1827)', in *Romanticism: An Anthology*, ed. Duncan Wu, 4th edn (Oxford: Wiley Blackwell, 2012), pp. 174–80.

Biographies

Peter Ackroyd, *Blake* (London: Sinclair-Stevenson, 1995).
Kathleen Raine, *William Blake* (Oxford: Oxford University Press, 1970).

Robert Burns (1759–1796)

Burns, whose inventiveness spanned energetic, humorous poetry in Scottish dialect and also meditative lyric, united such disparate thinkers as Byron, Wordsworth, Coleridge, and Hazlitt in praise for his poetic ability. He was one of the key influences on later Romantic poets. Born in Alloway, Ayrshire on 25 January 1759, Burns was the eldest of seven children. His father, William Burnes, was a tenant farmer whose refusal of Calvinism's strictures had a profound influence on his son; his father insisted on Burns receiving an education alongside the vernacular tradition of the locale. Burns began writing songs in 1774 to woo a local girl, and his education repaid him as he came to marry the rhythms of local speech with the poetic eloquence of his literary models. He also founded the Tarbolton Bachelors' Club, an early rural Scottish debating society, and became a freemason in 1781. But his father's early death in 1784 meant that Burns was responsible for his siblings and mother thereafter. He took over farming, yet this did not prevent him from producing a prodigious output of poetry. On 22 May 1785, Elizabeth Paton, a servant, gave birth to his daughter, Elizabeth, but the pair never married. Dallying with several young women, Burns also impregnated Jean Armour and continued his various flirtations with other women, despite the fury of Jean Armour's father. Planning to flee to Jamaica, Burns was also busy arranging the publication of *Poems, Chiefly in the Scottish Dialect*, which came out in 1786, when Burns discovered he was the father of twins. Six hundred and twelve copies of his collection were published, and all were sold within a month, to major critical fanfare.

A second, expanded edition of 3,000 copies, the Edinburgh volume of his poems, was a great success. The Scottish and English luminaries of the day welcomed Burns, despite his continued indiscretions with women, and Burns

The Romantic Poetry Handbook, First Edition. Michael O'Neill and Madeleine Callaghan.
© 2018 John Wiley & Sons Ltd. Published 2018 by John Wiley & Sons Ltd.

was invited to meet such figures as philosopher and historian Professor Adam Ferguson, the playwright John Home, sixteen-year-old Walter Scott, among others. By 1787, Burns undertook a series of tours in Scotland and northern England, and he reacquainted himself with Jean Armour, despite his resolution never to marry her. She became pregnant again, but Burns continued in his resolve. His tours had reinvigorated his fascination with Scottish dialect and folklore, and this fascination would translate into poetry that reflected his interest. On returning to Edinburgh, he agreed to contribute to, and even became the editor of, a large, six-volume anthology with music collected by engraver James Johnson (the first volume appeared in May 1787 and the last in 1803). Apparently married to Jean Armour by 1788, Burns then trained as an excise officer. By early 1794, the depression that had sporadically afflicted him returned. Burns took to excessive drinking and suffered painfully with rheumatism. He died in Dumfries on 21 July 1796. After his death, several volumes of previously private work were published, including *The Jolly Beggars* (1799), *The merry muses of Caledonia: a collection of favourite Scots songs, ancient and modern, selected for use of the Crochallan Fencibles* (*c.*1800; a collection of bawdy verses), and *Letters Addressed to Clarinda* (1802).

Source

Robert Crawford, 'Burns, Robert (1759–1796)', *Oxford Dictionary of National Biography*, Oxford University Press, 2004; online edn, May 2011 [http://www. oxforddnb.com/view/article/4093, accessed 7 September 2015]; Robert Burns (1759–1796): doi:10.1093/ref:odnb/4093; Duncan Wu, 'Robert Burns (1759–1796)', in *Romanticism: An Anthology*, ed. Duncan Wu, 4th edn (Oxford: Wiley Blackwell, 2012), pp. 265–7.

Biographies

Robert Crawford, *The Bard: Robert Burns, A Biography* (Princeton: Princeton University Press, 2009).

James A. Mackay, *Burns: A Biography of Robert Burns* (Edinburgh: Mainstream, 1992).

Lord George Gordon Byron (1788–1824)

Byron, the first British celebrity, was also a European poet and dramatist. Born in London, the only child of his mother Catherine Byron, and the son of his father Captain John Byron, he was quickly discovered to suffer from a deformity of the foot and lower leg, a disability that tormented Byron physically and psychologically throughout his life.[1] Travelling to Scotland, Catherine's home in 1789, Byron saw his father for the last time at two and a half, and was left with his mercurial mother. He inherited his title after the death of his great-uncle in 1798, after which he and his mother took possession of Newstead Abbey, Nottinghamshire. He began his schooling at Harrow in 1801 before going up to Trinity College, Cambridge in 1805. His first volume of poetry, *Fugitive Pieces*, was privately printed in 1806; its preoccupation with self-fashioning foreshadows his later poetry. His second collection, *Hours of Idleness*, released in 1808, attracted mixed reviews but also one well-aimed critique from the *Edinburgh Review*. Stung, Byron was provoked into his next work, *English Bards and Scotch Reviewers*, a satire on the literary scene that garnered strong reviews even though he would later disavow its attacks on figures he subsequently befriended.

Byron's Grand Tour of the Eastern Mediterranean (1809–11) inspired the poem that made him famous, *Childe Harold's Pilgrimage*. Attracting legions of fans, the poem's first two cantos, part romance, part travelogue, part lyric, were published in 1812, and Byron wrote and published the next two cantos between 1816 and 1818. Byron was captivated by the landscape and his experiences, and his travels were the bedrock of his poetry. His 'Turkish Tales' were composed and published between 1813 and 1816, and though Byron would later burlesque them, they contain the Byronic heroes on which his fame was built. He married Annabella Milbanke in 1815 and their

The Romantic Poetry Handbook, First Edition. Michael O'Neill and Madeleine Callaghan.
© 2018 John Wiley & Sons Ltd. Published 2018 by John Wiley & Sons Ltd.

short marriage produced their only child, Ada, before Annabella left Byron in 1816. Their separation led to Byron's self-imposed exile. The rumours circulating about their separation, particularly about his sexuality and his relationship with his half-sister, Augusta, dogged Byron, and his removal to Europe saw him attempt to outrun the speculation. A seminal meeting in his life also took place in 1816; Claire Clairmont, Mary Shelley's half-sister, with whom Byron had formed a relationship in England, contrived to introduce him to Shelley and Mary Shelley at Lake Geneva, and their immediate intimacy led to a lifelong friendship between Byron and Shelley. A daughter, Allegra, was born to Byron and Claire Clairmont in 1817. Moving to Italy, Byron plunged into Venetian life in 1818, and the city's impressions on him are recorded in *Beppo* and his extraordinary letters of the period. In 1819 he met Teresa Guiccioli with whom he remained in a relationship until his death. He began *Don Juan* in 1819, which eventually led to his break from his publisher, John Murray, and became increasingly involved in revolutionary activity with the Neapolitan Carbonari, but his ambivalent stance is reflected in his plays, *Marino Faliero* and *The Two Foscari*. Shelley's death in 1822 deeply affected Byron, and his subsequent decision to fight for Greek independence in 1823 led Roderick Beaton to claim that 'Byron's tribute to Shelley, finally, will be not a poem, but a war. His will be a tribute not of words but ... of deeds'.[2] Byron died in Missolonghi, Greece in 1824, partly owing to the ineptitude of his doctors, but the Byron legend lives on.

Notes

1 See Fiona MacCarthy, *Byron: Life and Legend* (London: Faber, 2003), p. 4.
2 Roderick Beaton, *Byron's War: Romantic Rebellion, Greek Revolution* (Cambridge: Cambridge University Press, 2013), p. 112.

Source

Fiona MacCarthy, *Byron: Life and Legend* (London: John Murray, 2002); Leslie A. Marchand, *Byron: A Biography* (London: John Murray, 1957); Jerome McGann, 'Byron, George Gordon Noel, sixth Baron Byron (1788–1824)', *Oxford Dictionary of National Biography*, Oxford University Press, 2004; online edn, May 2015 [http://www.oxforddnb.com/view/article/4279, accessed 3 June 2015]; George Gordon Noel Byron (1788–1824): doi:10.1093/ref:odnb/4279.

Biographies

Fiona MacCarthy, *Byron: Life and Legend* (London: John Murray, 2002).
Leslie A. Marchand, *Byron: A Biography*, 3 vols (London: John Murray, 1957).

John Clare (1793–1864)

Born 13 July 1793, John Clare was the son of Parker Clare, a thresher and local wrestler, and Ann in the village of Helpston, Northamptonshire. Clare mourned the death of his twin sister who had died only weeks after her birth. Keen that Clare should be literate (his mother was illiterate and his father had slight education), his parents sent him to school, when he wasn't required to work on the land, until he was twelve. His early meeting with Mary Joyce at school became, as did nature and his locale, a key subject of his poetry, as Clare fell deeply in love with the younger girl.

A keen devourer of poetry, chapbooks, and oral ballads and folklore, Clare began to write original poetry. Though apprenticed at fourteen to a local cobbler and then to a stonemason, Clare did not take to the work, and moved between various occupations before enlisting and serving briefly as a soldier during the Napoleonic Wars. Clare's earliest poetry was written informally on scraps of paper for his parents, but by 1814 he began to keep his poetry collected in a manuscript book. Though Clare entered into a publishing arrangement in 1817 to publish some of his poems by subscription, the project never took off, but meeting Edward Drury, a Stamford bookseller, changed his fortune. Soon the publishers Taylor and Hessey took up Clare's cause; they published his *Poems Descriptive of Rural Life and Scenery* in 1820, and its success propelled him to some celebrity. Feted by Lamb, Hazlitt, and Coleridge, and many others, Clare had every reason to assume that he had become a part of the literary establishment. He had recently married his pregnant girlfriend, Martha Turner, a milkmaid, and Clare's poetic success offered welcome income and fame to the young couple. His second collection, *The Village Minstrel*, was published in 1820 and went into a second edition in 1821, but it failed to achieve the acclaim of his first

The Romantic Poetry Handbook, First Edition. Michael O'Neill and Madeleine Callaghan.
© 2018 John Wiley & Sons Ltd. Published 2018 by John Wiley & Sons Ltd.

collection and sales were relatively low. However, it was the failure of *The Shepherd's Calendar*, published in 1827 after six years of silence, that devastated Clare. Father of a growing family (Clare and his wife would have nine children), he worked hard at his poetry and writing, but his work as a part-time labourer did not provide enough income and his health was increasingly poor. Despite the assistance of his friends, E. T. Artis and J. Henderson, in setting him up as an independent farmer, Clare's lack of business sense and declining mental and physical health saw this bid for financial improvement fail. His final poetry collection, *The Rural Muse*, came out in 1835 to little fanfare. By 1837, he took his publisher John Taylor's advice and chose to enter an asylum. He remained there until he escaped in 1841, but six months later, in Northborough, Clare was committed to Northampton General Lunatic Asylum. Possessed by delusions, depression, and insomnia, Clare imagined he was, in fact, Lord Byron, and also Robert Burns, among others, but continued to compose poetry. He wandered around Northampton by permission of his doctors, and died in the asylum in 1864. Clare is increasingly acknowledged as a fine lyric poet, whose poetry reveals an intense engagement with nature and, as our account in 'Readings' shows, with identity, emotion, and memory.

Source

Eric H. Robinson, 'Clare, John (1793–1864)', *Oxford Dictionary of National Biography*, Oxford University Press, 2004 [http://www.oxforddnb.com/view/article/5441, accessed 3 September 2015]; Duncan Wu, 'John Clare (1793–1864)', in *Romanticism: An Anthology*, ed. Duncan Wu, 4th edn (Oxford: Wiley Blackwell, 2012), p. 1271.

Biography

Jonathan Bate, *John Clare: A Biography* (London: Picador, 2003).

Samuel Taylor Coleridge (1772–1834)

Samuel Taylor Coleridge, one of the most significant figures of the Romantic period, was born in Ottery St Mary, Devon on 21 October 1772, the youngest of ten children of his father's (Reverend John Coleridge's) second marriage. Encouraged in his precocious reading by his father, who was the headmaster of the local grammar school (and died when his son was eight years old), Coleridge showed such promise that his mother chose to send him away to school at Christ's Hospital, London. Despite being marked out as gifted by being made a 'Grecian', and befriending Charles Lamb, who would be a lifelong friend, Coleridge's experience of school was mixed. Entering Jesus College, Cambridge in 1792, his university years were intellectually and emotionally turbulent. The terror of the French Revolution was under way, and Coleridge was also beset by debt and by an unfulfilled passion for Mary Evans. He became fascinated by the theories of Joseph Priestley and a supporter of William Frend, a fellow of Jesus College, who was being prosecuted for his advocacy of parliamentary reform and attack on the liturgy of the church. He began to live a dissipated life and moved to London to escape his difficulties before enlisting in the 15th light dragoons under the assumed name Silas Tomkyn Comberbache. Fortunately, his brother George bought him out of the army and Coleridge returned to Cambridge.

In 1794, Coleridge met Robert Southey, with whom he formed a plan to move to America and establish a pantisocracy (a settlement based on egalitarian living), marrying Sara Fricker in 1795 (Southey married her sister, Edith) despite their idea never coming to fruition. Though Sara features prominently in Coleridge's poetry of the time, their union was ultimately unhappy, and Sara never took part in Coleridge's intellectual life, to his despair. Moving to Bristol in 1795, Coleridge began to lecture on philosophy

The Romantic Poetry Handbook, First Edition. Michael O'Neill and Madeleine Callaghan.
© 2018 John Wiley & Sons Ltd. Published 2018 by John Wiley & Sons Ltd.

and religion and established a journal, *The Watchman*, to which he was the main contributor. He met Wordsworth and Dorothy in July 1797, and they all moved to Dorset and began an intense poetic and intellectual relationship that would alter the course of their lives. Coleridge and Wordsworth profoundly influenced one another, and Duncan Wu rightly points out that Coleridge's poetic appreciation of nature stems from their meeting.[1] Coleridge's conversation poems date from this period, and he also wrote *The Rime of the Ancient Mariner*, *Christabel*, and *Kubla Khan*, poems in a very different style. In December 1797, the Wedgwood brothers sent him £100, which Coleridge returned as he sought more stable employment, and he became a Unitarian minister. At his sermon in Shrewsbury, Coleridge met William Hazlitt and made a great impression on the youth, but, again, the Wedgwoods interceded, offering Coleridge an annuity of £150 per year if he would devote himself to writing rather than remaining a minister. He accepted, and then, with the Wordsworths, developed a plan to publish *Lyrical Ballads* and use the proceeds to fund a tour of Germany, a centre of intellectual life. Though Coleridge would not contribute nearly as many poems as Wordsworth, the trip to Germany proved fruitful for Coleridge's intellectual development. Learning the language, meeting with philosophers, reading German poetry, and pursuing biblical exegesis made a profound impression on him. Coleridge's second son, Berkeley, died while Coleridge was in Germany, and the physical separation of Coleridge and his wife created a breach between the pair that never healed. On returning to England, Coleridge fell in love with Sara Hutchinson, the sister of Wordsworth's future wife, Mary. Coleridge went to London to take the post of staff writer on the *Morning Post*. In April 1800, he went back to Keswick to work on the second edition of *Lyrical Ballads* and eventually moved back to Keswick to live in Greta Hall. Suffering health problems, Coleridge began to take laudanum to which he became addicted, and his marriage became still more troubled. Southey and his family moved to Keswick to join the Coleridges at Greta Hall, but Coleridge moved to Malta, working as a secretary for the British administration in 1804, to help his illness, but also to escape his domestic stress. After visiting Sicily and Italy, Coleridge returned to England in 1806. The relationship between Wordsworth and Coleridge became strained as the latter came to envy Wordsworth's domestic happiness and imagine an affair between Sara and Wordsworth. He began working on *The Friend*, a journal he wrote and published intermittently between 1808 and 1810, but his opium addiction was becoming difficult to manage along with his emotional problems. Coleridge and Wordsworth became estranged for a period after Basil Montagu informed Coleridge of Wordsworth's slighting remarks about him, remarks Wordsworth denied. However, in January 1813, *Remorse* was performed at Drury Lane to good notices, and Coleridge was pleased by Byron's support of his poetic activities. He published *Biographia Literaria* in 1817, and spent the rest of his life largely producing prose works, such as *Aids to Reflection* (1825), amongst many others. With the help of James Gillman and his wife, he sought to wean himself off laudanum. Increasingly religious in old age, Coleridge died on 25 July 1834 of longstanding cardiac problems. Coleridge's prose and poetry reveal him as a singularly gifted thinker whose poetry continues to enchant his readers.

Note

1 Duncan Wu, 'Samuel Taylor Coleridge (1772–1834)', in *Romanticism: An Anthology*, ed. Duncan Wu, 4th edn (Oxford: Wiley Blackwell, 2012), p. 613.

Source

John Beer, 'Coleridge, Samuel Taylor (1772–1834)', *Oxford Dictionary of National Biography*, Oxford University Press, 2004; online edn, October 2008 [http://www.oxforddnb.com/view/article/5888, accessed 7 September 2015]; Samuel Taylor Coleridge (1772–1834): doi:10.1093/ref:odnb/5888; Duncan Wu, 'Samuel Taylor Coleridge (1772–1834)', in *Romanticism: An Anthology*, ed. Duncan Wu, 4th edn (Oxford: Wiley Blackwell, 2012), pp. 611–18.

Biographies

Walter Jackson Bate, *Coleridge* (Cambridge, MA: Harvard University Press, 1987).
Richard Holmes, *Coleridge: Early Visions* (London: HarperCollins, 1998).
Richard Holmes, *Coleridge: Darker Reflections* (London: HarperCollins, 1998).

Felicia Hemans (1793–1835)

Felicia Hemans, *née* Felicia Dorothea Browne, was born in Liverpool where she was the fourth of six children in her family to survive infancy. The failure of her father's wine merchant business led the family to leave Liverpool when she was seven for Gwrych near Abergele in North Wales, and her father left the family to emigrate to Canada in 1810, dying two years later. Hemans's mother encouraged Felicia's budding poetic gift. She read avidly, studying several languages along with music and art, and her first collection of poetry (*Poems*) was released in 1808, when she was fourteen years old. The small financial success of the volume paid for her education, and foreshadowed Hemans's future need to support herself and her family. *Poems*, sold by subscription, was subscribed to by her future husband, Captain Alfred Hemans. The couple first met in 1810 and their relationship developed after he returned from the war in 1811. Hemans's second collection, *England and Spain; or, Valour and Patriotism* (1808), a long poem in heroic couplets, revealed her patriotic sense of national pride as she wrote, in part, in support of her brothers George and Henry, who were serving as officers in the Peninsular War. Hemans married in 1812, when her third collection, *The Domestic Affections &c*, was released.

Despite a disappointing lack of notice Hemans continued to write, and her poem, *The Restoration of the Works of Art to Italy* (1816), was praised by Byron, which attracted Murray to purchase it for a second edition. Murray became her publisher, and in 1817 *Modern Greece* met with some acclaim, but in 1818, for reasons that are unclear, Captain Hemans left behind his family (with Hemans pregnant with their fifth child) for Italy. His abandonment of his family echoed her father's, and became one of the most significant events of her life, as Susan Wolfson notes in her introduction

The Romantic Poetry Handbook, First Edition. Michael O'Neill and Madeleine Callaghan.
© 2018 John Wiley & Sons Ltd. Published 2018 by John Wiley & Sons Ltd.

to Hemans's poetry: '[t]he idealism of heart and home for which "Mrs. Hemans" would become famous was haunted by these desertions, even as the Captain's departure strengthened her determination to support her family with her writing.'[1] Hemans's writing went from strength to strength, with its promotion of domestic virtues balanced against melancholy and defiant strains.

By the 1820s, Hemans was beginning to establish herself as a major poetic voice. *The Siege of Valencia* enjoyed praise from many quarters, including the Tory journals that boosted her stature despite their distaste for female writers.[2] With work published in significant journals, magazines, and annuals, Hemans's fame spread, and *The Forest Sanctuary &c* (1825 and 1829), in which the titular poem focused on the Spanish Inquisition, also suggestively alluded to contemporary political events, such as Catholic Emancipation, an issue about which Byron had spoken to the House of Lords.[3] Her long poem, written in a variation of the Spenserian stanza, earned praise for its depictions of suffering, but it is *Records of Woman: With Other Poems* (1828) that is most widely praised by modern critics. *Songs of the Affections, with Other Poems* (1830) contains 'Corinne at the Capitol', in which Hemans hints at her own unhappiness despite her fame: 'Happier, happier far than thou / With the laurel on thy brow, / She that makes the humblest hearth / Lovely but to one on earth!' (45–8). Her late poems show Hemans becoming a still finer poet, as 'The Lost Pleiad' confidently alludes to Byron and Shelley's poetry. Hemans became seriously ill in 1834 and died within months, in 1835, at forty-one years of age, eight years after her beloved mother. Though Hemans's star began to wane in the late Victorian period, recent decades have seen critics re-exploring her poetic achievement.

Notes

1 Susan J. Wolfson, 'Introduction,' in *Felicia Hemans: Selected Poems, Letters, Reception Materials*, ed. Susan Wolfson (Princeton: Princeton University Press, 2000), p. xxii.
2 See the *British Critic* 20 (July 1823): 50–61, which claims 'We heartily abjure Blue Stockings'. Qtd in Wolfson, *Felicia Hemans: Selected Poems, Letters, Reception Materials*, p. 537.
3 His most important speech on Irish Catholic Emancipation was given on 21 April 1812.

Source

Nanora Sweet, 'Hemans, Felicia Dorothea (1793–1835)', *Oxford Dictionary of National Biography*, Oxford University Press, 2004; online edn, May 2008 [http://www.oxforddnb.com/view/article/12888, accessed 2 March 2015]; Felicia Dorothea Hemans (1793–1835): doi:10.1093/ref:odnb/12888; Susan J. Wolfson, 'Introduction,' in *Felicia Hemans: Selected Poems, Letters, Reception Materials*, ed. Susan Wolfson (Princeton: Princeton University Press, 2000), pp. xiii–xxvii.

Biography

H. F. Chorley, *Memorials of Mrs Hemans with illustrations of her literary character from her private correspondence*, 2 vols (London: Saunders and Otley, 1836).

(James Henry) Leigh Hunt (1784–1859)

Born on 19 October 1784 to British loyalists who moved back to England owing to their political opinions, Leigh Hunt was the youngest of nine children, and his parents' political and social views coloured his development as a poet, literary critic, and journalist. Hunt's father, Isaac, a Church of England minister, was frequently in debt, and Hunt grew up sickly and nervous. However, he began school at Christ's Hospital, London (Coleridge and Lamb had also attended) as a charity boy, and his fascination with mythology and fine arts led him to begin writing poetry, publishing his first original collection, *Juvenilia*, in 1801. He met his wife-to-be, Marianne Kent, in 1802 (they married in July 1809) and steadily continued to publish poetry in journals such as the *Morning Chronicle*, while also working as a clerk to his brother Stephen, a lawyer, for a spell in 1803, and from 1805 to 1808 in the War Office. However, his essays on the theatre, written from 1805, reveal Hunt's critical acumen and campaigning stance, and they were later collected as *Critical Essays on the Performers of the London Theatres* (published early 1808). 'This book', writes Nicholas Roe, 'has not received the attention it deserves as a formative statement of Romantic ideas of drama and theatre',[1] but it was with the immensely popular weekly newspaper, *The Examiner*, set up with his brother John in 1808, that Leigh Hunt made his name.

Hunt and his brother set themselves up in opposition to the abuses of power by the monarchy and the increasingly repressive government and its protracted war against Napoleon. They were successfully defended by Henry Brougham against three prosecution attempts between 1808 and 1812, but finally the government won, sentencing the Hunts to two years in prison and a hefty fine for libel in relation to Leigh Hunt's article of

The Romantic Poetry Handbook, First Edition. Michael O'Neill and Madeleine Callaghan.
© 2018 John Wiley & Sons Ltd. Published 2018 by John Wiley & Sons Ltd.

22 March 1812 which denounced the Prince Regent. Attracting sympathy from many quarters, including Shelley, Hazlitt, and Haydon, Hunt was allowed a great deal of liberty at Surrey Gaol, permitted by his gaoler to live with his family and receive visitors until 10 p.m., and to furnish his cell with luxurious fittings and his books. He and John continued to publish their paper from prison, and Hunt also continued to pursue his poetic ambitions. Once released in February 1815, Hunt completed *The Story of Rimini* and published his masque, *The Descent of Liberty*, which he had written while in prison. *The Story of Rimini* was appraised by Shelley as housing a story of 'a very uncommon & irresistible character, – tho it appeared to me that you have subjected yourself to some rules in the composition which fetter your genius',[2] a view suggestive of Hunt's distinctive poetics which empha-sized a jaunty liberality and freedom from Augustan decorum. Such poetics incited the rage of John Gibson Lockhart in *Blackwood's Edinburgh Magazine*, a Tory publication, and Lockhart repeatedly published attacks on Hunt and his 'Cockney School'.

Shelley showed warm affection for Hunt and made efforts to help his friend and literary patron, who was often in financial distress. It was Keats for whom Hunt's influence would be the most crucial to his poetic develop-ment. Though Keats later repudiated his mentor's assistance, Hunt made a lasting intervention in Keats's poetic development, one that Shelley would note in his elegy for Keats, *Adonais*. *Foliage*, published in 1818, was an ambitious collection that sought to create a poetic coterie in its sonnets addressed to Shelley and Keats. A three-volume *Poetical Works* (1819) and four issues of the *Literary Pocket-Book, or, Companion for the Lover of Nature and Art* (1819–22) showed Hunt fashioning himself as a literary rather than political writer. *The Examiner* had become gradually more liter-ary than political on Hunt's release from prison, and Hazlitt and Hunt collaborated on a series of 'Round Table' articles that would be reprinted in 1817 as a collection of essays. After repeated invitations from Shelley, the Hunts relocated to Italy on 15 November 1821, and they began to publish *The Liberal*, which contained work by Byron, Hunt, and Hazlitt. However, Shelley's death in July 1822 divided the group, with Byron moving to Greece and Mary Shelley going back to England. The Hunts were left in Florence until they returned to England in 1825. In the later decades of his life, Hunt remained an active writer, penning many works, including his grief-stricken *Lord Byron and some of his Contemporaries* (1828) and his well-judged *Imagination and Fancy* (1844), which stand as two of his most important achievements. Leigh Hunt, though hardly the most widely read poet of the Romantic period, is one of its central figures, uniting the disparate personages of Hazlitt, Shelley, Keats, and Byron, amongst others.

Notes

1   Nicholas Roe, 'Hunt, (James Henry) Leigh (1784–1859)', *Oxford Dictionary of National Biography*, Oxford University Press, 2004; online edn, October 2009 [http://www.oxforddnb.com/view/article/14195, accessed 6 September 2015].
2   *The Letters of Percy Bysshe Shelley*, ed. F. L. Jones, 2 vols (Oxford: Clarendon Press, 1964), 1.518.

Source

Nicholas Roe, 'Hunt, (James Henry) Leigh (1784–1859)', *Oxford Dictionary of National Biography*, Oxford University Press, 2004; online edn, October 2009 [http://www.oxforddnb.com/view/article/14195, accessed 6 September 2015]; Duncan Wu, 'James Henry Leigh Hunt (1784–1859)', in *Romanticism: An Anthology*, ed. Duncan Wu, 4th edn (Oxford: Wiley Blackwell, 2012), pp. 816–19.

Biography

Nicholas Roe, *Fiery Heart: The First Life of Leigh Hunt* (London: Pimlico, 2005).

John Keats (1795–1821)

John Keats's life, tragically curtailed when he died in Rome at age twenty-five, has spellbound his readers almost as much as his poetry has. Born in October 1795 (there is some debate as to whether he was born on 29 or 31 October), he was the son of the manager of a livery stable. His father died in 1804, after which his mother (*née* Frances Rawlings) swiftly remarried, prompting some familial consternation, before she died in 1810. Keats attended John Clarke's Enfield school from 1803, befriending Charles Cowden Clarke and J. H. Reynolds, who encouraged him in his literary efforts throughout his life. Apprenticed to a surgeon in 1811, Keats completed his training at Guy's Hospital in 1816, and passed his exams to become a licentiate of the Society of Apothecaries. Despite this achievement, which would have allowed Keats to practise as a surgeon, apothecary, or physician, he decided to dedicate his life to poetry rather than medicine, though his poetry retains some traces of his professional training.

Meeting Leigh Hunt in October 1816 was a vital stage of Keats's poetic development. Drawn into Hunt's circle, Keats met painter Benjamin Robert Haydon, Percy Bysshe Shelley, and Horace Smith, amongst others, and the heady political and literary conversations sparked him into creating increasingly ambitious poetry. C. and J. Ollier, Shelley's publishers, brought out his first volume, *Poems*, in 1817, but they quickly dropped him from their list. This misfortune did not leave Keats in the wilderness, as Taylor and Hessey elected to become his publishers within a month. Critics, notably *Blackwood's*, began to abuse his poetry, and such ignominy continued after the publication of his long romance, *Endymion*, in 1818; Shelley would explicitly blame the *Quarterly Review* for Keats's early death in *Adonais*. Yet Keats was seemingly unperturbed by such criticism, claiming instead to

The Romantic Poetry Handbook, First Edition. Michael O'Neill and Madeleine Callaghan.
© 2018 John Wiley & Sons Ltd. Published 2018 by John Wiley & Sons Ltd.

write for posterity rather than to obsess over his reception in his own era. His domestic life was proving increasingly difficult. His brother George, who had been a pragmatic source of strength for Keats, moved with his new bride, Georgiana, to America, and his other brother Tom became desperately ill with tuberculosis and died on 1 December 1818: Keats nursed him for the final months of his life. However, Keats also met the love of his life, Fanny Brawne, in November 1818, and his remarkable letters to her, to George and Georgiana Keats, and many other correspondents, testify to Keats's intellectual vigour despite his worsening health. Remaining formidably productive, between 1818 and 1820, Keats wrote *The Eve of St. Agnes, The Eve of St. Mark, Hyperion, Lamia, Isabella,* and his Odes, amongst many other poems. By July 1820, Keats was ordered by his doctor to go to Italy; despite the attention of his companion, the painter Joseph Severn, his tuberculosis made him gravely ill, and he died on 23 February 1821. His reputation steadily grew until, by the late nineteenth century, the general public began to recognize his rightful place amongst the great poets. As Shelley wrote in his elegy for Keats, he became part of 'the abode where the Eternal are'.

Source

Kelvin Everest, 'Keats, John (1795–1821)', *Oxford Dictionary of National Biography*, Oxford University Press, 2004; online edn, May 2006 [http://www.oxforddnb.com/view/article/15229, accessed 7 September 2015]; John Keats (1795–1821): doi:10.1093/ref:odnb/15229; Duncan Wu, 'John Keats (1795–1821)', in *Romanticism: An Anthology*, ed. Duncan Wu, 4th edn (Oxford: Wiley Blackwell, 2012), pp. 1384–96.

Biographies

Andrew Motion, *Keats* (London: Faber, 1998).
Nicholas Roe, *John Keats: A New Life* (New Haven, CT: Yale University Press, 2012).

Letitia Elizabeth Landon (1802–1838)

The eldest of three children, Letitia Elizabeth Landon was born in Chelsea, London to Catherine and John, a midshipman who, on retirement, became a partner in the army agent Adair's and Co. The family moved to Trevor Park, a country house in East Barnet, when she was five years old, but reduced circumstances owing to the end of the war and economic difficulties forced the family to return to Fulham, London in 1815, and then to Old Brompton in 1816. Landon showed great promise at an early age, with a prodigious appetite for books and writing, and the move to Old Brompton also brought her a powerful mentor, William Jerdan, the editor of the popular *Literary Gazette*. He began to publish her poetry, starting with 'Rome', on 11 March 1820, signed simply with the initial L. In August 1821, with the financial assistance of her grandmother, she published *The Fate of Adelaide: a Swiss Tale of Romance; and other Poems* under her full name, but despite favourable notices, the volume did not attract much public attention. Undaunted, she continued to publish in the *Literary Gazette*, now under the teasingly anonymous initials L. E. L., and Jerdan, who had several children by Landon, appointed her to the powerful position of chief reviewer. Carefully cultivating a fascinating image and gaining in literary fame, Landon intrigued her growing readership.

The Improvisatrice, and other Poems (1824) went into six editions, and her Byronic style attracted the public through its performative self-fashioning. Landon became a highly sought-after poet whose improvisatorial method lent itself to the rapid production of accomplished poetry. However, her father's death in late 1824 led her, like Felicia Hemans and Charlotte Smith, to write to support her remaining family as she contributed to her brother's education and her mother's living. A rift between mother and daughter led

The Romantic Poetry Handbook, First Edition. Michael O'Neill and Madeleine Callaghan.
© 2018 John Wiley & Sons Ltd. Published 2018 by John Wiley & Sons Ltd.

Landon to move in with her grandmother in 1825, but following her grand-mother's death, she moved into a room in Miss Lance's school for girls. However, this 'unusual independence cost the young L. E. L. dear, both in literary "drudgery" and eventually in reputation'.[1] Soon, scurrilous rumours began to circulate, particularly about Landon's relationship with three men: William Jerdan, William Maginn, and Edward Bulwer-Lytton. Landon was devastated by these attacks on her character, dismissing the rumours as cruel speculation about an impoverished female writer. The press enjoyed giving vent to such gossip even as Landon produced a tremendous amount of poetry and general writing for annuals and journals, with the annuals offer-ing highly lucrative remuneration for authors.

Landon's remarkable pace of work meant she published several volumes of poetry in quick succession – *The Troubadour* (1825), *The Golden Violet* (1826), *The Venetian Bracelet* (1829), *The Easter Gift* (1832), and *The Vow of the Peacock* (1835) – but none achieved the sensation of *The Improvisatrice, and other Poems*. Landon also published novels, *Romance and Reality* (1831), *Francesca Carrera* (1834), and *Ethel Churchill* (1837), which were very different from the poetry and reveal Landon as developing a sardonic voice for her social commentary. In 1834 her engagement with John Forster was broken off because of rumours about her romantic entan-glements, and her waning fame made her anxious to find domestic happi-ness. When she met Captain George McLean, Governor of the Cape Coast Castle in West Africa (now Ghana), in 1837, they quickly became engaged, and married on 7 June 1838. Only two months later, Landon was found dead in Africa with an empty bottle of prussic acid close to hand. Though the doctor declared it an accidental death, biographers remain uncertain as to whether her demise at thirty-six was the result of suicide or misad-venture. Her early and mysterious death meant that Landon's notoriety continued beyond the grave, and her story became a cautionary tale of the lot of female poets. But Landon's poetic achievement was far more considerable. Her arch and intelligently seductive poetry deserves the reconsideration it has recently begun to receive.

Note

1 Angela Leighton, *Victorian Women Poets: Writing Against the Heart* (Hemel Hempstead: Harvester Wheatsheaf, 1992), p. 49.

Source

Glennis Byron, 'Landon, Letitia Elizabeth (1802–1838)', *Oxford Dictionary of National Biography*, Oxford University Press, 2004; online edn, September 2011 [http://www.oxforddnb.com/view/article/15978, accessed 16 April 2015]; Letitia Elizabeth Landon (1802–1838): doi:10.1093/ref:odnb/15978; Alison Chapman, 'Laetitia Landon', *The Literary Encyclopedia*, first published 18 July 2002 [http://www.litencyc.com/php/speople.php?rec=true&UID=5142, accessed 9 April 2015].

Biography

Glennis Stephenson, *Letitia Landon: The Woman Behind L.E.L.* (Manchester: Manchester University Press, 1995).

Thomas Moore (1779–1852)

Though his reputation has seriously waned, Moore was considered one of the preeminent poets in his day. James Joyce caricatures Moore as a 'Firbolg in the borrowed cloak of a Milesian' in *A Portrait of the Artist as a Young Man*.[1] However, Moore was a far more complex figure than this description would suggest. Born in Dublin on 28 May 1779, Moore entered Trinity College, Dublin in 1795, where he became a good classicist and politically engaged thinker, and was a close friend of Robert Emmet. Moving to London to pursue a legal career in 1799, Moore continued to write poetry and his sociable bent proved an attraction to Francis Rawdon Hastings, Earl of Moira, whose patronage hastened Moore's literary success. *Poetical Works of the Late Thomas Little* (1801) sold well, and he was offered the position of Irish poet laureate, but refused owing to his political beliefs. However, in 1803, he accepted the post of registrar of the naval prize court in Bermuda, travelling in North America as well as in Bermuda. On returning to England, Moore published *Epistles, Odes, and other Poems* (1806), which was damningly reviewed by Francis Jeffrey, a key Romantic reviewer and essayist. Though Moore challenged him to a duel, the confrontation ended in farce with both men arrested, much to the amusement of the press. Byron's later recounting of the tale in *English Bards and Scotch Reviewers* (1809) earned Moore's rage and contempt, but they became firm friends on Byron's return from the continent, and Byron tried to suppress any later reissues of his early satire.

Moore moved back to Dublin in 1806–7 and met two composers who invited him to write his *Irish Melodies*. It was this series of *Irish Melodies* (1808–34) that caught the public's attention, as Moore's English recasting

The Romantic Poetry Handbook, First Edition. Michael O'Neill and Madeleine Callaghan.
© 2018 John Wiley & Sons Ltd. Published 2018 by John Wiley & Sons Ltd.

of Irish airs that drew on Irish history and culture found a large and sympathetic audience. Becoming involved in the theatre, even writing a play, *M. P., or The Blue-Stocking*, performed in London in 1811, Moore met and married an actress, Elizabeth (Bessy) Dyke, in the same year. He continued to write successful poems, and the *Intercepted Letters, or, The Twopenny Post-Bag* appeared in March 1813. John Murray and Longman competed to publish his much-trumpeted oriental romance, *Lalla Rookh*; Longman prevailed, buying it for £3,000 in December 1814. Finally published in 1817, the poem rewarded Longman's patience with Moore's extensive rewriting and editing, and went into multiple editions over years. Despite such literary success, Moore and his wife were devastated by the death of their first child, Barbara, at the age of six in 1817; further catastrophe struck when his deputy in Bermuda absconded, leaving him £6,000 in debt. Though his satirical political poem *The Fudge Family in Paris* (1818) was successful, Moore could not begin to repay the debt, and he was forced to move abroad to France and Italy to escape arrest. Byron gave Moore his memoirs when the latter visited him in Italy, paving the way for Moore's later role as Byron's biographer. However, in 1821, Moore's friend Lord Lansdowne managed to agree a settlement that allowed Moore to return to England, and he continued to write, publishing political satires such as *Fables for the Holy Alliance* (1823) and *Odes upon Cash, Corn, Catholics, and other Matters* (1828). Beginning as a biographer, Moore wrote *Memoirs of the Life of the Right Honourable Richard Brinsley Sheridan* (1825), managing to present a mostly sympathetic portrait of a difficult subject. This influenced John Murray, Byron's longstanding publisher, to offer him 4,000 guineas to publish Byron's biography (Byron had died in 1824 in the Greek War of Independence). Byron's memoirs were burned but Moore decided to write the biography. Moore's final works before his death turned more political in inflection. *Memoirs of Captain Rock* (1824), *The Life and Death of Lord Edward Fitzgerald* (1831), *Travels of an Irish Gentleman in Search of Religion* (1833), and *History of Ireland* (1835–46) reveal the depths of Moore's Irish patriotism. Suffering from senile dementia, Moore died on 25 February 1852, survived by his wife.

Note

1   James Joyce, *A Portrait of the Artist as a Young Man*, ed. Seamus Deane (London: Penguin, 1992), pp. 194–5.

Source

Geoffrey Carnall, 'Moore, Thomas (1779–1852)', *Oxford Dictionary of National Biography*, Oxford University Press, 2004; online edn, September 2013 [http://www.oxforddnb.com/view/article/19150, accessed 6 September 2015]; Thomas Moore (1779–1852): doi:10.1093/ref:odnb/19150.

Biography

Ronan Kelly, *Bard of Erin: The Life of Thomas Moore* (Dublin: Penguin Ireland, 2008).

Mary Robinson (1758–1800)

Mary Robinson (*née* Darby and also known as Perdita) was born in Bristol on 27 November 1758 to John Darby (a whaling captain) and Hester Vanacott, though the accuracy of the date is disputed. When her father attempted but failed to establish permanent cod, salmon, and seal fishing posts on the southern coast of Labrador in 1765, she was moved, on the separation of her parents, from her Bristol home to London in 1768. Taught by the talented dipsomaniac Merinah Lorington, Robinson was instructed in languages, mathematics, and sciences. When her mother set up her own school in Little Chelsea (around 1771), Robinson instructed the students in English before her father insisted that the school be shut, and she then attended a finishing school in Marylebone where her interest in acting brought her into David Garrick's sphere. Under pressure from her mother, she married Thomas Robinson, an articled clerk, on 12 April 1773 at St Martin-in-the-Fields, Westminster. However, his charm allowed him to conceal his real financial status, and the couple fell into penury, with Robinson nursing her first daughter (Mary Elizabeth, born 1774) in a debtor's prison cell where her husband was sent in 1775.

While in prison, Robinson wrote and published her first volume of poetry, *Poems*, in 1775, part funded by Georgiana Cavendish, the Duchess of Devonshire. David Garrick and Richard Brinsley Sheridan encouraged and facilitated her stage debut as Juliet in *Romeo and Juliet*, and Robinson became an overnight star, going on to play many of Shakespeare's heroines and several other roles in various productions. She also brought out *Captivity: A Poem* in 1777. In full public view, she became the mistress of the teenage Prince of Wales in 1779. Though promised a fortune, £20,000, she did not receive the money when he eventually tired of her. An ugly battle

The Romantic Poetry Handbook, First Edition. Michael O'Neill and Madeleine Callaghan.
© 2018 John Wiley & Sons Ltd. Published 2018 by John Wiley & Sons Ltd.

ensued between the Prince and Robinson, and she was showered in public ignominy. Despite managing to extract £5,000 from the royal family thanks to the intercession of her new lover, Lord Maldon, Robinson never went back on stage. Her 1781 visit to France confirmed her as both a woman of fashion and a notorious figure, and she was thought to have had a series of high-profile romances, including with Charles James Fox (who secured for her an annuity of £500). However, during the summer of 1783, she became paralysed from the waist down at the age of twenty-four, perhaps owing to a miscarriage. When she was partly recovered, she was forced abroad by her creditors and returned to France where she apparently assisted her lover, Colonel Banastre Tarleton, to write his *History of the Campaigns of 1780 and 1781 in the Southern Provinces of North America.*

She returned to London in January 1788, and by the autumn, writing under the *nom de plume* Laura, Robinson began a public poetry exchange with 'Leonardo' (Robert Merry) in *The World*, aligning herself with the increasingly influential group the Della Cruscans, writers marked by an emphasis on sentiment and a much-mocked rhetoric of affect. Though briefly lauded, the group swiftly fell from grace, but Robinson continued to write. Though her first volume of collected poems (1791) was a triumph, her second volume (1794) was far less successful. Despite this disappointment, Robinson was not without poetic admirers. Coleridge, in particular, exchanged letters and poetry with her, and Wordsworth admired her *Lyrical Tales* (1800). Robinson was close to her daughter, and died at her home in Englefield Green on 26 December 1800 of dropsy. Her short and eventful life made her a prominent and fascinating figure in her lifetime, and increasing critical attention has re-evaluated her significance as a poet, journalist, and writer.

Source

Claire Brock, 'Mary Robinson', *The Literary Encyclopedia*, first published 21 March 2002 [http://www.litencyc.com/php/speople.php?rec=true&UID=3820, accessed 9 September 2015]; Martin J. Levy, 'Robinson, Mary [Perdita] (1756/1758?–1800)', *Oxford Dictionary of National Biography*, Oxford University Press, 2004; online edn, January 2008 [http://www.oxforddnb.com/view/article/23857, accessed 9 September 2015]; Mary Robinson (1756/1758?–1800): doi:10.1093/ref:odnb/23857; Duncan Wu, 'Mary Robinson (1758–1800)', in *Romanticism: An Anthology*, ed. Duncan Wu, 4th edn (Oxford: Wiley Blackwell, 2012), pp. 250–3.

Biography

Paula Byrne, *Perdita: The Life of Mary Robinson* (London: HarperCollins, 2004).

Percy Bysshe Shelley (1792–1822)

Shelley's poetry, drama, and prose reveal his deep engagement with his own cultural epoch. Born in Horsham, Sussex to a wealthy family, he was the eldest child of Timothy Shelley (later Baronet in 1806), and was educated at Eton College. He published two Gothic novels in 1810, *Zastrozzi* and *St. Irvine*, and published and subsequently withdrew a collection of poetry, *Original Poetry by Victor and Cazire*, with his sister Elizabeth, and *Posthumous Fragments of Margaret Nicholson*. In the same year, Shelley went up to University College, Oxford, and was expelled in 1811 for publishing *The Necessity of Atheism* with his friend and fellow student, Thomas Jefferson Hogg. This was also the year he met and married Harriet Westbrook in Edinburgh when he was nineteen and she sixteen years old. The marriage and his expulsion from Oxford led his father to disown Shelley.

His political radicalism intensified, and, accompanied by Harriet, he went to Dublin and distributed copies of his political pamphlets on Catholic Emancipation and Irish political reform. On his return, he moved from Wales to Devon, and then back to Wales while composing *Queen Mab*. His first child, Ianthe, was born in 1813. However, Shelley's marriage had become strained, and his meeting with William Godwin not only brought him into the sphere of a political and philosophical thinker he deeply admired, but also introduced him to Godwin's and Mary Wollstonecraft's daughter, Mary Godwin, in 1814. Mary and Shelley fell in love, and the couple eloped. From 28 July they toured Europe accompanied by Claire Clairmont, Mary's half-sister, before returning to England on 13 September 1814. Mary and Shelley lost their first child (born on 22 February 1815), but their financial difficulties were alleviated by the death of Shelley's grandfather and his father's financial settlement with Shelley.

The Romantic Poetry Handbook, First Edition. Michael O'Neill and Madeleine Callaghan.
© 2018 John Wiley & Sons Ltd. Published 2018 by John Wiley & Sons Ltd.

Their first son (William Shelley) was born on 24 January 1816. The summer of 1816 saw Shelley and Byron meet in Geneva. Also present were Claire Clairmont, who had begun a sexual liaison with Byron in England, and Mary Shelley (or Mary Godwin as she then was). Claire discovered that she was pregnant by Byron; Mary began to write *Frankenstein*; and both Shelley and Byron wrote poetry inspired, in part, by their intellectual connection. After his return to England, life was deeply traumatic. Fanny Godwin, Mary's half-sister, committed suicide, as did Harriet Shelley in late 1816. Shelley lost custody of both Ianthe and Charles, his children by Harriet. Mary and Shelley married a month after Harriet's suicide, presumably so as to gain custody of the children. Their petition was overturned in March 1817, and in March 1818 they moved to Italy, for a complex set of personal, financial, and medical reasons.

If Italy initially improved Shelley's health, it could not prevent further tragedies. He and Mary lost Clara when she was a year old in 1818 and William when he was three years old in 1819, and their marriage suffered as a result of their loss. However, Shelley's work went from strength to strength, with 1819 often referred to as his *annus mirabilis*, when he wrote *Prometheus Unbound*, *The Cenci*, and *The Mask of Anarchy*, amongst others. His work was often critically neglected or poorly reviewed owing to his radically heterodox views and his friendship with Leigh Hunt, a notorious radical, but most reviewers recognized his poetic talent. In his elegy for John Keats, *Adonais*, which he referred to as 'perhaps better in point of composition than any thing I have written',[1] Shelley commemorated the death of a literary peer whom he held in high esteem. Planning to start *The Liberal* with Leigh Hunt and Byron, Shelley died in 1822, just after Hunt had arrived in Italy. Returning from meeting Hunt in Pisa, Shelley drowned when his boat, the *Don Juan*, sank. He died with his friend Edward Williams and a deckhand, Charles Vivian. Shelley's range of writing, encompassing poetry, philosophical and political prose, and novels and plays, attests to his radical and sympathetic world-view; his work remains alert to reality even as it aspires to glimpses of some 'unascended Heaven' (*Prometheus Unbound* 3.3.204).

Note

1   *The Letters of Percy Bysshe Shelley*, ed. F. L. Jones, 2 vols (Oxford: Clarendon Press, 1964), 2.294.

Source

James Bieri, *Percy Bysshe Shelley: A Biography*, 2 vols; vol. 1, *Youth's Unextinguished Fire, 1792–1816* (Newark, DE: University of Delaware Press, 2004); vol. 2,

Exile of Unfulfilled Reknown, 1816–1822 (Newark, DE: University of Delaware Press, 2005); Zachary Leader and Michael O'Neill, 'Introduction', in *Percy Bysshe Shelley: The Major Works*, ed. Zachary Leader and Michael O'Neill (Oxford: Oxford University Press, 2009 [2003]), pp. xi–xxiv; Michael O'Neill, 'Shelley, Percy Bysshe (1792–1822)', *Oxford Dictionary of National Biography*, Oxford University Press, 2004; online edn, January 2009 [http://www.oxforddnb.com/view/article/25312, accessed 9 September 2015]; Percy Bysshe Shelley (1792–1822): doi:10.1093/ref:odnb/25312.

Biographies

James Bieri, *Percy Bysshe Shelley: A Biography*, 2 vols; vol. 1, *Youth's Unextinguished Fire, 1792–1816*; vol. 2, *Exile of Unfulfilled Renown, 1816–1822* (Newark, DE: University of Delaware Press, 2004–5).
Ann Wroe, *Being Shelley: The Poet's Search for Himself* (London: Jonathan Cape, 2007).

Charlotte Smith (1749–1806)

Born Charlotte Turner into a genteel and affluent family, Smith experienced early tragedy, with her mother dying when Charlotte was a young child. Smith's life was also marked by her father's extravagance with money. In 1765, at nearly sixteen years old, she was married off to a wealthy though profligate and abusive husband, Benjamin Smith, a marriage she soon came to see as a hideous error, referring to herself as 'sold, a legal prostitute,' in a letter to Sarah Rose.[1] Her husband's mounting debts landed him in debtor's prison in 1783 where Smith joined him. Her first self-funded collection, *Elegiac Sonnets, and Other Essays by Charlotte Smith of Bignor Park, Sussex* (1784), proved a great success, and the profits from the collection secured her husband's release from prison. However, he was unable to reform, leading the couple to leave for France in October 1784. Returning in 1785, Smith legally separated from her husband in 1787, leaving her with sole responsibility for their eight surviving children (the union had produced twelve). Highly influential and popular, Smith's collection revived the sonnet form in the Romantic period, and went through many editions owing to its instant acclaim.

Despite her success as a poet, Smith turned to novel writing, producing eleven novels which represent, as Stuart Curran claims, 'the major achievement in English fiction during those years [1788–1798]'.[2] The novels and the poetry share preoccupations, most notably Smith's fascination with representing heroines beset by strife. Though drawing on circumstances from her own life, Smith's oeuvre reveals her ability to blur the line between biography and artistry in a way that anticipates how Romanticism would develop from Wordsworth to Byron. Having experienced the vicissitudes of the legal system after the death of her father-in-law, Richard Smith, she was

The Romantic Poetry Handbook, First Edition. Michael O'Neill and Madeleine Callaghan.
© 2018 John Wiley & Sons Ltd. Published 2018 by John Wiley & Sons Ltd.

well placed to represent its injustice. Her politicized vision is notable in all her novels, but particularly evident in her final novel, *The Young Philosopher* (1798), whose protagonist leaves the crumbling *ancien régime* of England in hopes of a better life in an idealized vision of the American republic.

The greatest loss of Smith's life was the death of her much-loved daughter, Anna Augusta, in 1795. Once again Smith created art out of adversity, and the second volume of *Elegiac Sonnets* is suffused with mourning for her loss. *The Emigrants* (1793) shows Smith's poetic range as well as recalling her novels' political undertones; it suggests, only to refuse, epic grandeur. Smith focuses on the suffering of French émigrés reeling from the loss of their country, friends, and family in the aftermath of the violence of the French Revolution, and their British counterparts, such as the poor and the poet herself, whose victimhood mirrors the dispossessed French émigrés. Smith draws little distinction between the French and the British victims, emphasizing the powerlessness of her subjects in the poetry. Her final volume of poetry, *Beachy Head and Other Poems*, was unfinished but offers, as Curran shows, 'an alternate Romanticism that seeks not to transcend or to absorb nature but to contemplate and honor its irreducible alterity'.[3]

Notes

1 Charlotte Smith to Sarah Rose, 15 June 1804. Qtd in Loraine Fletcher, *Charlotte Smith: A Critical Biography* (Houndmills: Macmillan, 1998), p. 25.
2 Stuart Curran, 'Introduction', in *The Poems of Charlotte Smith* (Oxford: Oxford University Press, 1993), pp. xix–xxix (at p. xxiii).
3 Curran, 'Introduction', p. xxviii.

Source

Stuart Curran, 'Introduction', in *The Poems of Charlotte Smith* (Oxford: Oxford University Press, 1993), pp. xix–xxix; Loraine Fletcher, *Charlotte Smith: A Critical Biography* (Basingstoke: Macmillan, 1998); Sarah M. Zimmerman, 'Smith, Charlotte (1749–1806)', *Oxford Dictionary of National Biography*, Oxford University Press, 2004; online edn, October 2007 [http://www.oxforddnb.com/view/article/25790, accessed 9 August 2015]; Charlotte Smith (1749–1806): doi:10.1093/ref:odnb/25790.

Biography

Loraine Fletcher, *Charlotte Smith: A Critical Biography* (Basingstoke: Macmillan, 1998).

Robert Southey (1774–1843)

Frequently grouped as a Lake poet along with William Wordsworth and Samuel Taylor Coleridge, Southey never enjoyed the reputation of his exceptional peers, but he was a significant influence on the second-generation Romantic poets (as is brought out in the section on him under 'Readings'), despite their hostility to his later politics and personal, poetic, and political attacks on their work. Shelley, in particular, rapturously received Southey's epics, especially his *The Curse of Kehama* and *Thalaba the Destroyer*, with echoes of and allusions to them spanning his career. Known as a poet and prominent reviewer, Southey was born in Bristol to a genteel mother and a merchant father. His maternal aunt, Elizabeth Tyler, took pains to insulate him from what she perceived to be the less salubrious influences of his childhood, but she imbued him with a love of the theatre that would persist throughout his life. Despite unhappy experiences at school, when he entered Westminster School in 1788, Southey made some enduring friendships and wrote precocious poetry influenced by Ariosto, Tasso, and Spenser. He was expelled from Westminster for his subversive views and his expulsion, combined with his father's bankruptcy and death in 1792, left him in a despairing state. At Balliol College, Oxford, he began his epic, *Joan of Arc*. Initially drawn to medicine, Southey was horrified by the realities of the operating theatre, and his radical political views barred him from government work. On meeting the Bristol seamstress Edith Fricker, Southey fell in love with her, and he began to consider emigration as a way out of his difficulties, a course of action galvanized by meeting Coleridge in 1794. Together they contemplated setting up a pantisocratic community in America, and Coleridge married Edith's sister, Sara. The pantisocratic scheme came to nothing, and Southey married Edith in 1795 before moving

The Romantic Poetry Handbook, First Edition. Michael O'Neill and Madeleine Callaghan.
© 2018 John Wiley & Sons Ltd. Published 2018 by John Wiley & Sons Ltd.

to Lisbon, Portugal, leaving his new wife with the bookseller Joseph Cottle, a longtime supporter of both Southey and Coleridge. His stay in Portugal (and Spain) proved fertile for his writing, and he produced *Letters Written during a Short Residence in Spain and Portugal* (1797) to modest success.

Pleased by the favourable notices of *Joan of Arc*, Southey began work on his epic projects, *Madoc* and *Thalaba the Destroyer*, before straitened financial circumstances and ill health forced him and his wife to move to Portugal. Returning after over a year in 1801, Southey undertook translation work and began to write for the *Annual Review*, with the latter providing much needed financial support. Southey's mother died in 1802, prompting the couple's return to Bristol, but following the death of his daughter, Margaret, in her first year, Southey succumbed to Coleridge's pressure to move to Keswick and live in Greta Hall. Despite Coleridge's proximity to the Wordsworths, his increasingly troubled marriage led him to leave Keswick for Malta, leaving Southey to care for Coleridge's wife and children along with his own. Southey continued writing, publishing *Letters from England* (1807) that drew on his Spanish and Portuguese knowledge, and Walter Savage Landor encouraged Southey to write *The Curse of Kehama* (1810) by offering to subsidize his epics.

Southey was growing increasingly conservative, and this burgeoning political perspective gained force from his well-remunerated employment with the new journal, the Tory *Quarterly Review*. He became poet laureate in 1813, and took the opportunity to expound his conservative and nationalistic views, much to the amusement and fury of his political opponents. The pirated republication in 1817 of his early radical work *Wat Tyler* caused him serious embarrassment, despite his claim to be professing the same principles in favour of human progress as he had in his youth. However, to younger poets, such as Shelley and Byron (who had been attacked by Southey in the periodical press), Southey had become a symbol of fatuous poetry at the service of political oppression. When *A Vision of Judgement* (1821) was published, Byron lost no time in writing a magisterial parody, *The Vision of Judgement* (1822), that lampooned Southey's patriotic and monarchist poem; references to Southey in *Don Juan* parade the loathing Byron felt for Southey's 'turn[ing] out a Tory' (*Don Juan*, 'Dedication', 1.3). Southey's later publications reveal a greater calm, with *A Tale of Paraguay* (1825), *Colloquies of Society* (1829), *History of Brazil* (1810–19), *History of the Peninsular War* (1823–32), *Lives of the British Admirals* (1833–7), and his final published poem, *Oliver Newman: a New-England Tale* (1845), offering a quieter world-view. After the death of his wife, Southey married Caroline Anne Bowles in 1839; he began to lose his faculties before dying on 21 March 1843.

Source

Geoffrey Carnall, 'Southey, Robert (1774–1843)', *Oxford Dictionary of National Biography*, Oxford University Press, 2004; online edn, January 2011 [http://www.oxforddnb.com/view/article/26056, accessed 6 September 2015]; Robert Southey (1774–1843): doi:10.1093/ref:odnb/26056.

Biography

W. A. Speck, *Robert Southey: Entire Man of Letters* (New Haven, CT: Yale University Press, 2006).

William Wordsworth (1770–1850)

Wordsworth was a major poet whose work profoundly influenced his peers and poetic descendants. Born in Cockermouth, Cumberland, on 7 April 1770, Wordsworth was the second of five children in an affluent household. Losing his mother in 1778, Wordsworth was sent to Hawkshead grammar school, where he thrived as sympathetic teachers nurtured his taste for poetry, but the death of his father when Wordsworth was thirteen had far-reaching consequences. Now orphans, his siblings were separated and he was thrown on the mercy of his extended family, who encouraged him to seek financial independence by becoming a clergyman. Precociously brilliant, Wordsworth began to write startlingly fluent poetry by fifteen, and had a poem, 'On Seeing Miss Helen Maria Williams Weep at a Tale of Distress', published under a pseudonym in *European Magazine* at sixteen. Arriving at St John's College, Cambridge in late October 1787, Wordsworth did not excel academically at university, owing at least in part to his feelings of antipathy towards the university structure. Choosing to embark on a walking tour in France in 1790 with Robert Jones, a college friend, Wordsworth shrugged off his family's ambition for him to take holy orders. The pair also visited Switzerland, Italy, and Germany before returning to England. Reunited with his sister Dorothy in Forncett, near Norwich, the pair reminisced about his travels and the detailed letters he had sent to her, before Wordsworth moved to London in late January 1791. In London Wordsworth was thrown into a whirl of political debate that excited and inspired the young poet, and he chose to return to France, this time to Paris, on 30 November 1791. This visit proved life changing for Wordsworth, as, following his tourist activities, he met and fell in love with Annette Vallon.

The Romantic Poetry Handbook, First Edition. Michael O'Neill and Madeleine Callaghan.
© 2018 John Wiley & Sons Ltd. Published 2018 by John Wiley & Sons Ltd.

He followed his now pregnant lover to her hometown, Blois, where he met Captain Michel de Beaupuy, who features in *The Prelude* and influenced the English poet's political views. Annette gave birth in December 1792 to a daughter, Caroline, but Wordsworth had already been forced to return to London, where he published his poems, *An Evening Walk* and *Descriptive Sketches*. Longing to return to Annette, he was barred from doing so by the British declaration of war on France in February 1793 following the execution of Louis XVI.

Such distress compounded Wordsworth's revolutionary fervour, and his pamphlet, *A Letter to the Bishop of Llandaff*, with its principled defence of regicide, would have created serious trouble for the poet had it been published (it eventually appeared in 1876). Heading on foot to visit Robert Jones, Wordsworth was then reunited with Dorothy in 1794 in the north of England. Returning to the south of England in February 1795, Wordsworth began to associate with the most prominent radicals in the country, including William Godwin. However, by 1796, Wordsworth was increasingly disillusioned by Godwin's anti-emotional brand of rationalism. When he moved away from London, John and Azariah Pinney offered Wordsworth the chance to stay at one of their father's properties, Racedown Lodge in Dorset. By September 1795 Wordsworth and Dorothy had moved in together. The environment was excellent for Wordsworth to begin composing some of his most important poetry, such as the earliest draft of *The Ruined Cottage*; he also redrafted what would become *Adventures on Salisbury Plain*, and wrote *The Borderers*. Coleridge's visit in 1797 (after Wordsworth had visited him at Nether Stowey in the same year) was vital for his poetic development.

Coleridge's visit sparked a plan to travel to Germany for Wordsworth, Dorothy, and Coleridge, and *Lyrical Ballads* was designed as a means of funding the trip. Arriving in Germany in autumn 1798, the Wordsworths and Coleridge parted company, and the Wordsworths headed for Goslar. Lacking language skills and money, they were confined to their quarters during a harsh winter, and Wordsworth wrote the first draft of what would become *The Prelude*, before returning to England in April 1799 and deciding to remain in the Lake District. Marrying Mary Hutchinson in 1802, Wordsworth put down roots in Grasmere, close to Greta Hall, Keswick, where Coleridge and his family had moved in 1800 and where Southey and his family joined them in 1803. The first child, John, was born in 1803, Dorothy (known as Dora) in 1804, Thomas in 1806, Catharine in 1808, and the last child, William, in 1810. Domestic tensions grew between Coleridge and the Wordsworth family, and Coleridge left their circle in 1804.

The death of John Wordsworth, Wordsworth's sailor brother, on 5 February 1805 was a heavy tragedy for the family, and the years between 1806 and 1813 proved difficult for Wordsworth. He struggled with financial issues, his disintegrating relationship with Coleridge, and fears about the direction of his poetic vocation. His *Poems, in Two Volumes* of 1807 received many negative notices, particularly from Francis Jeffrey. Two of his children, Catherine and Thomas, died within months of each other in 1812, the year in which the family moved again, this time to a permanent home, Rydal Mount. Lord Lonsdale made Wordsworth the Distributor of Stamps for Westmorland and the Penrith area of Cumberland in 1813, easing his financial concerns. *The Excursion* (1814) announced his continued poetic ambition to the world, and enlarged his audience. Touring the continent in the early 1820s allowed Wordsworth to reacquaint himself with his daughter Caroline, and he also devoted himself in 1820 to work on a four-volume set of his collected works, which he oversaw. Further complete works were issued in 1827, 1832, 1836, 1845, and 1849–50. *Yarrow Revisited*, published in 1835, succeeded commercially, with new editions in 1836 and 1839. *Poems, Chiefly of Early and Late Years* (1842) was Wordsworth's final original collection. He was made poet laureate in 1843, but he continued to revise his poetry until his death in 1850, after which *The Prelude* was first published.

Source

Stephen Gill, 'Wordsworth, William (1770–1850)', *Oxford Dictionary of National Biography*, Oxford University Press, 2004; online edn, May 2010 [http://www. oxforddnb.com/view/article/29973, accessed 7 September 2015]; William Wordsworth (1770–1850): doi:10.1093/ref:odnb/29973; Duncan Wu, 'William Wordsworth (1770–1850)', in *Romanticism: An Anthology*, ed. Duncan Wu, 4th edn (Oxford: Wiley Blackwell, 2012), pp. 420–5.

Biographies

Stephen Gill, *William Wordsworth: A Life* (Oxford: Clarendon Press, 1989).
John Worthen, *The Life of William Wordsworth* (Oxford: Wiley Blackwell, 2014).
Duncan Wu, *Wordsworth: An Inner Life* (Malden, MA: Blackwell, 2002).

Ann Yearsley (1753–1806)

Ann Yearsley was born Ann Cromartie in Clifton Hill, Bristol, and she was also known as 'Lactilla' and 'the Bristol Milkwoman'. Her mother, a milk-woman like Yearsley herself, encouraged her daughter's education, ensuring that Yearsley learned to read and helping her to borrow books from travelling libraries so as to expand her daughter's range of knowledge. In June 1774, she married John Yearsley who, despite being listed as a yeoman in an administrative document, lost his status as a yeoman and worked as a day labourer. Yearsley bore him seven children between 1775 and 1790, and the family fell into destitution in the winter of 1783–4. They refused parish charity and ended up living in a disused farm building where Yearsley's mother died before charitable individuals offered alms to the struggling family. Yearsley was already writing poetry, and Hannah More's cook showed Yearsley's writing to her mistress, who then sought to help Yearsley publish her work.

Hannah More, a successful writer, was highly impressed by Yearsley's poetry, and sought to help her to make an entrance into literary society. Her first volume, *Poems on Several Occasions* (1785), was published by subscription, and More's vigorous efforts to secure subscribers through her connections made it an economic success. However, More's emphasis on Yearsley's impoverished background was suggestive of condescension towards her protégée, and when the profits came in, More refused to allow Yearsley to have control over her earnings, claiming to be concerned about how Yearsley's husband might dispose of the capital of around £600. This caused a rift between More and Yearsley that was never mended. Yearsley broke completely from More in 1786 once More ended the trust and Yearsley gained access to the money.

The Romantic Poetry Handbook, First Edition. Michael O'Neill and Madeleine Callaghan.
© 2018 John Wiley & Sons Ltd. Published 2018 by John Wiley & Sons Ltd.

Yearsley continued to write, publishing *Poems, on Various Subjects* in 1787, with the assistance of new patrons, in particular Frederick Augustus Hervey, Earl of Bristol and Bishop of Derry, and she continued to enjoy the support of many prominent figures. 'A Poem on the Inhumanity of the Slave-trade' (1788) typifies Yearsley's strongly impassioned political poetry. She also began to write for the stage, and one of her plays, *Earl Goodwin: an Historical Play* (performed 1789 and printed 1791), was staged in her lifetime at Bristol and Bath. Her four-volume historical novel, *The Royal Captives: a Fragment of Secret History, Copied from an Old Manuscript* (1795), reportedly received a £200 advance, and Kerri Andrews argues that the novel grew out of Yearsley's connection with radical writers and literature.[1] *The Rural Lyre* (1796) showed Yearsley continuing to write poetry despite her diverse literary interests. Containing poems on local matters, such as 'Bristol Elegy', and works that display her broader range, her final collection reveals the proto-Romanticism noted by many critics. Publishing no further collections after *The Rural Lyre*, Yearsley focused on managing a circulating library at the Colonnade, Hotwells. Her husband died in 1803. As Moira Ferguson shows, '[t]hrough refusing class collusion and publicizing her altercation with Hannah More, Ann Yearsley fashioned a subversive multiple identity that was both liminal and culturally acceptable'.[2] Yearsley's oeuvre suggests the difficulty of pigeonholing her as a particular type of political or social poet; she eludes definition in such terms.

Notes

1   Kerri Andrews, *Ann Yearsley and Hannah More: Poetry and Patronage* (London: Pickering & Chatto, 2013), p. 101.
2   Moira Ferguson, *Eighteenth-Century Women Poets*, SUNY Series in Feminist Criticism and Theory (New York: State University of New York Press, 1995), pp. 73–4.

Source

Stephen Van-Hagen, 'Ann Yearsley', *The Literary Encyclopedia*, first published 3 March 2007 [http://www.litencyc.com/php/speople.php?rec=true&UID=4830, accessed 9 September 2015]; Mary Waldron, 'Yearsley, Ann (*bap.* 1753, *d.* 1806)', *Oxford Dictionary of National Biography*, Oxford University Press, 2004 [http://www.oxforddnb.com/view/article/30206, accessed 2 May 2015]; Ann Yearsley (*bap.* 1753, *d.* 1806): doi:10.1093/ref:odnb/30206.

Biography

Mary Waldron, *Lactilla, Milkwoman of Clifton: The Life and Writings of Ann Yearsley, 1753–1806* (Athens, GA: University of Georgia Press, 1996).

Part 4 Readings
First-Generation Romantic Poets

Anna Laetitia Barbauld, 'Epistle to William Wilberforce, Esq., on the Rejection of the Bill for Abolishing the Slave Trade'; 'The Rights of Woman'; *Eighteen Hundred and Eleven, A Poem*

Indicating the scope of Anna Laetitia Barbauld's achievement, Emma Major refers to her as 'poet, essayist, political pamphleteer, and educationalist'.[1] A committed Rational Dissenting writer, Barbauld was a highly educated poet devoted to the Enlightenment principles of the innate goodness of humanity, reason, and the importance of education.[2] Praised by Wordsworth and Coleridge, she occupies a position on the cusp of Romanticism while speaking with the even and mannered tones of eighteenth-century poetry. Brad Sullivan notes that 'Barbauld's rhetorical strategies as a poet often aim to create a "Dissenting frame of mind" in her readers',[3] and her poetry seeks to stimulate a thoughtful response that moves and educates the reader. Her 'persona is formed in no small part by Barbauld's careful and intelligent response to the work of her predecessors, notably Milton and James Thomson (the poet most closely associated with Milton's legacy in the eighteenth century)',[4] but her poetry remains studiedly individual.

Despite a range of critical responses to her achievement, her contemporaries and much current criticism have primarily tended to evaluate her status as a female poet.[5] Though Barbauld has been maligned for her apparent antagonism to feminism, recent critics have shown her stance to be far more nuanced than her difference from Mary Wollstonecraft's *Vindication of the Rights of Woman* would suggest.[6] Barbauld's learned and often prophetic poetry draws on various models from Milton to Elizabeth Singer Rowe, and it is her 'confident assumption of the mantle of the female prophet during this period [1790s]' that impels her poetry.[7] 'Epistle to William Wilberforce,

The Romantic Poetry Handbook, First Edition. Michael O'Neill and Madeleine Callaghan.
© 2018 John Wiley & Sons Ltd. Published 2018 by John Wiley & Sons Ltd.

Esq. on the Rejection of the Bill for Abolishing the Slave Trade,' 'The Rights of Woman', and *Eighteen Hundred and Eleven* reveal the breadth of Barbauld's political and cultural concerns and her poetic versatility.

In 'Epistle to William Wilberforce', Barbauld coolly traces the deceit that allows slavery to continue. Written in carefully formed heroic couplets, the insistent regularity of the lines suggests that Barbauld is recalling Pope's decorous tone as she corrects the erring ethical character of the age. Despite the arguments urged by 'Preacher, Poet, Senator' (3),[8] 'Still Afric bleeds / Uncheck'd, the human traffic still proceeds' (15–16). Prophesying African rage turning on Britain owing to 'minds deprav'd by bondage known' (47), Barbauld's poetry presents horrified images of coming turbulence, where the polished form clashes with the brutal content. The unearned luxury and ease created by slavery's fruits destroy British virtue, as Barbauld curtly states: 'By foreign wealth are British morals chang'd, / And Afric's sons, and India's, smile aveng'd' (104–5). Such bleakness goes unmitigated by the close of the poem, as Barbauld urges Wilberforce to 'seek no more to break a Nation's fall' (116). Comfortless, the speaker reassures Wilberforce that his efforts have earned his salvation, but asserts that, for Britain, he 'strove in vain' (123). Barbauld anatomizes Britain's venal tyranny, offering no salving note to mitigate her vision.

'The Rights of Woman', despite its description in the seminal edition of Barbauld's work as an 'outburst of anger at Wollstonecraft',[9] has been compellingly re-evaluated by Penny Bradshaw, who argues that 'it functions only ironically in its relegation of women to the non-public realm of blushes and tears, a realm which was certainly not occupied by Barbauld in her own life'.[10] There is no firm evidence that Barbauld's poem attempted to respond to Wollstonecraft's *Vindication of the Rights of Woman, With Strictures on Political and Moral Subjects*, and Barbauld's poem seems, on the surface, to advocate that women should behave as feeling rather than rational creatures, against Wollstonecraft's essay. If read without recourse to irony, the poem seems to contradict much of Barbauld's other work, particularly where Barbauld implies that feeling rather than reason wins the day. Advocating 'Soft melting tones' (11) and 'Blushes and fears' (12) in place of war, Barbauld's witty detachment becomes easy to overlook. The poem is written in cross-rhymed quatrains, and the speaker aligns herself with neither women nor men, even if the highly structured style seems more appropriate for 'male' reason rather than 'female' sentiment. Applauding women as the 'courted idol of mankind', Barbauld is apparently content with women as other than men. Yet, as Adeline Johns-Putra points out with reference to *Washing-Day*, 'Barbauld's mock-heroic mode always possesses the potential to mock – not heroicise – the domestic',[11] and in 'Rights of Woman', Barbauld seems more tongue in cheek than didactic in her advice to her own gender in a short but complicated poem. The appeal to Nature's 'soft maxims' (31) serves not to promote rights but endanger them, and the silenced and softened female, imprisoned by the restrictive patriarchal view in the poem, is prevented from speaking. Surrendering her own gender in the poem, Barbauld's silent refusal to write from the first-person perspective witnesses her need to resign her femininity in order to speak; this subtle poem suggests restrictions placed on the female voice that it does not name.

Despite her high reputation, Barbauld's *Eighteen Hundred and Eleven* marked the end of her career as a poet as 'reviewers were quick to chastise her for abandoning her proper feminine realm'.[12] Published in 1812 to sneers from John Wilson Croker, who would also famously demolish Keats's *Endymion*, Barbauld's heroic couplets offer an unsparing critique of the state of Britain. Composed and printed during political crises, including the Napoleonic Wars (which had been raging since 1793), and a miserable economic situation, the opening of the poem succinctly captures the desolation suffered by the country,[13] before Barbauld moves into her favoured prophetic mode. *Eighteen Hundred and Eleven* is often referred to as a jeremiad as its verse prophecy imagines a future in which Britain's dominance has sunk. Sternly informing Britain that 'thy Midas dream is o'er' (61), the poem gives no sense that the British Empire is either undeserving of its ruin or that prosperity was its natural state. Refusing to be numbered with its 'flatterers', Barbauld writes: 'but, Britain, know, / Thou who hast shared the guilt must share the woe' (45–6), the couplet typically twinning knowledge and sorrow.[14] Offering no solutions, the poem is thorough in its condemnation of what it reveals to be an empire on the cusp of decline, telling Britain, 'Yes, thou must droop' (61), despite the speaker's avowed patriotism. In Barbauld's vision, America inherits culture and freedom, with American visitors going to tourist sites with 'duteous zeal' (129) just as British tourists visited the ruins of Rome and Greece.

Yet, despite the gloom of the poem, 'Barbauld's cosmopolitan jeremiad implies the possibility of recovering a reformed Enlightenment faith in historical progress and undermines narrowly nationalist and partisan views'.[15] Though sorrowful for London's and Britain's 'faded glories' (158), Barbauld places her faith in continued progress facilitated by Western domination, as Francesco Crocco notes: '[u]nderstood by her contemporaries as unpatriotic for her anti-war beliefs, Barbauld in fact reifies colonial ideology in *Eighteen Hundred and Eleven*'.[16] Rooted in her Dissenting beliefs, Barbauld's poetry is poised and self-contained, moving between ironized domestic notes to searing political comment, while remaining united by 'her confident assumption of an authoritative *feminine* voice'.[17] A product and proponent of the Enlightenment, Barbauld retains the detached balance of Pope's poetry alongside her Miltonic condemnation of 'Enfeebling Luxury and ghastly Want' (*Eighteen Hundred and Eleven*, 64).[18]

Notes

1   Emma Major, 'Nature, Nation, and Denomination: Barbauld's Taste for the Public', *ELH* 74.4 (2007): 909–30 (at 909).

2   See Orianne Smith, *Romantic Women Writers, Revolution and Prophecy: Rebellious Daughters, 1786–1826* (Cambridge: Cambridge University Press, 2013), p. 159.

3   Brad Sullivan, 'Cultivating a "Dissenting Frame of Mind": Radical Education, the Rhetoric of Inquiry, and Anna Barbauld's Poetry', *Romanticism on the Net* 45 (2007): http://www.erudit.org/revue/ron/2007/v/n45/015817ar.htm.

4   Robert W. Jones, 'Barbauld, Milton, and the Idea of Resistance', *Romanticism* 9.2 (2003): 119–40 (at 119–20).

5   'What this range of responses to Barbauld's work has in common is that for all of them it is the gendered character of her writing that is at issue: it is her willingness or failure to appear properly feminine that is the central focus of their criticism.' Harriet Guest, *Small Change: Women, Learning, Patriotism, 1750–1810* (Chicago: University of Chicago Press, 2000), p. 226.

6   See, in particular, Penny Bradshaw, 'The Limits of Barbauld's Feminism: Re-reading "The Rights of Woman"', *European Romantic Review* 16.1 (2005): 23–37, which casts serious doubt on readings of 'The Rights of Woman' as a reaction to Wollstonecraft by showing that such readings are conjectural and do not fit with the rest of Barbauld's rhetorical strategies adopted elsewhere in her work.

7   Smith, *Romantic Women Writers*, p. 169 and p. 158.

8   'Epistle to William Wilberforce, Esq. on the Rejection of the Bill for Abolishing the Slave Trade', in *The Poems of Anna Letitia Barbauld*, ed. William McCarthy and Elizabeth Kraft (Athens, GA: University of Georgia Press, 1994), p. 114.

9   'The Rights of Women', in *The Poems of Anna Letitia Barbauld*, p. 289.

10 Penny Bradshaw, 'Gendering the Enlightenment: Conflicting Images of Progress in the Poetry of Anna Lætitia Barbauld', *Women's Writing* 5.3 (1998): 353–71 (at 368, n.2).

11 Adeline Johns-Putra, 'Satire and Domesticity in Late Eighteenth-Century Women's Poetry: Minding the Gap', *Journal for Eighteenth-Century Studies* 33.1 (2010): 67–87 (at 75).

12 Evan Gottlieb, 'Fighting Words: Representing the Napoleonic Wars in the Poetry of Hemans and Barbauld', *European Romantic Review* 20.3 (2009): 327–43 (at 336).

13 See William Keach, 'A Regency Prophecy and the End of Anna Barbauld's Career', *Studies in Romanticism* 33.4 (1994): 569–77 (at 573).

14 Barbauld admitted the 'gloomy' quality of her poem. See the letter to Judith Beecroft, 19 March 1812, quoted in *Anna Barbauld: Selected Poetry and Prose*, ed. William McCarthy and Elizabeth Kraft (Peterborough, Ont.: Broadview, 2001), p. 160.

15 William Levine, 'The Eighteenth-Century Jeremiad and Progress-Piece: Traditions in Anna Barbauld's "Eighteen Hundred and Eleven"', *Women's Writing* 12.2 (2005): 177–86 (at 178).

16 Francesco Crocco, 'The Colonial Subtext of Anna Letitia Barbauld's *Eighteen Hundred and Eleven*', *Wordsworth Circle* 41.2 (2010): 91–4 (at 91).

17 Angela Keane, 'The Market, the Public and the Female Author: Anna Laetitia Barbauld's Gift Economy', *Romanticism* 8.2 (2002): 161–78 (at 164).

18 As Jacqueline Labbe shows, 'she brings to much of her writing an Enlightenment perspective of detachment and impartiality, but occasionally sparks into a more personalized style'. Jacqueline Labbe, 'Communities: Mary Robinson, Charlotte Smith, Anna Letitia Barbauld, and Romanticism', *Literature Compass* 1 (2004): 1–12 (at 3).

Charlotte Smith, *Elegiac Sonnets*

As sardonically witnessed by Byron in *English Bards and Scotch Reviewers*, the Romantic period saw 'Sonnets on sonnets crowd'[1] into the literary arena. Charlotte Smith was a major innovator of this poetic trend, with her *Elegiac Sonnets* of 1784 running into ten editions. Her poetry earned praise from Wordsworth, who heralded her as late as 1833 as 'a lady to whom English verse is under greater obligations than are likely to be either acknowledged or remembered'.[2] Increasingly, critics have attempted to rescue Smith from this gloomy prognosis, re-evaluating her and many of her female peers as central figures in the formation of some of Romanticism's most important innovations, such as the rehabilitation of the sonnet form and the metrical tale.[3] Smith's mastery of the formal possibilities open to the poet, alongside the personal quality of her sonnets, enraptured contemporary readers. As Jacqueline Labbe writes, 'Smith does not simply enact or represent the pressures attendant on being a woman writer in the Romantic period; she exploits them'.[4] By underscoring her femininity even as she challenges its limitations within contemporary society, Smith performs her status as a female poet while refusing to allow it to stifle her creative freedom. This poetic self-confidence coexists with her mournful subject matter as her sonnets display artistic independence even as they bemoan her emotional state. By combining allusions to Petrarch, Milton, and Metastasio (amongst others) with her individual voice, Smith's sonnets seemed 'utterly personal' even as they spoke to her educated appreciation of poetic tradition.[5]

Stuart Curran's pithy analysis of Smith's poetry suggests the importance of self as a theme of her writing: 'Charlotte Smith made a virtual career out of self-pity. She rises from it in her novels, but it is the obsession of her poetry and, to judge by her letters, of her life.'[6] Yet, as the same critic points

The Romantic Poetry Handbook, First Edition. Michael O'Neill and Madeleine Callaghan.
© 2018 John Wiley & Sons Ltd. Published 2018 by John Wiley & Sons Ltd.

out in the introduction to his edition of her poetry,[7] of Smith's ninety-two sonnets, thirty-six are spoken by other voices, embedded into the sonnet sequence nearly seamlessly. Smith's use of other voices questions the boundaries of selfhood, subsuming the difference between self and other as all speakers are united in grief. The opening sonnet of the collection immediately sets the tone sustained throughout, as Smith determinedly individualizes her grief: 'Ah! then, how dear the Muse's favours cost, / *If those paint sorrow best—who feel it most!*' ('Sonnet I', 13–14).[8] Alluding to the private pain of the speaker, Smith performs a double gesture: she writes herself into her poem, even as the line recalls Pope's 'Eloisa to Abelard', as she points out in her footnote. Rather than presenting herself as overshadowed or silenced by her poetic predecessors, Smith capitalizes on their work to deepen and enrich the self.

Sonnet III, 'To a nightingale', shows Smith uniting with her predecessors, notably Milton and Petrarch, by addressing the nightingale. Yet Smith is not content to rehearse the same themes as her poetic forefathers, instead addressing three sonnets to the nightingale (Sonnets III, VII, and LV) that underscore a troubling identification between the 'songstress sad' ('Sonnet III', 13) and the poet herself. In the case of Sonnet III, as Luca Manini argues, Smith departs sharply from Petrarch's emphasis,[9] choosing to spotlight the suffering self over Petrarch's meditation on the vanity of mortal things. Opening with questions that seek to discover the cause of 'this mournful melody of song' (III.4), the octave, though divided into two, shows the poet seeking to decipher, or translate, the causes and meanings of the bird's distress.

> Pale Sorrow's victims wert thou once among,
>   Tho' now released in woodlands wild to rove?
>   Say—hast thou felt from friends some cruel wrong,
> Or died'st thou—martyr of disastrous love?
> Ah! songstress sad! that such my lot might be,
> To sigh, and sing at liberty—like thee!   (III.9–14)

Drawing on the biographical knowledge she placed before the reader in the prefaces to the sixth edition and volume II of her *Elegiac Sonnets*, the reader is offered tantalizing clues to the cause of Smith's woes. The questions seem less speculative than leading, each intensifying the sense that Smith's personal circumstances spark her 'song'. Smith does not use the content alone to suggest the 'domestic and painful nature' ('Preface to the Sixth Edition', 6) of her difficulties. Her careful use of form is calculated to direct the reader to reach the correct conclusions; the off-rhyme of 'rove' and 'love' is deliberately jarring, reinforcing the implication that Smith herself is the 'martyr of disastrous love'. But Smith is careful to demonstrate that such domestic vulnerability does not breed artistic weakness. The inclusion of a sestet suggests that she keeps her sonnet consistent with the Petrarchan model, yet the rhyme scheme departs from his example. Incorporating the couplet into a sonnet which was almost modelled on the Petrarchan sonnet, Smith builds in a surprising and snapped-shut ending, where the poet subtly claims in her work the longed-for liberty of the nightingale. Sonnet VII, 'On the departure of the nightingale', and Sonnet LV, 'The return of the nightingale. Written in May 1791', show Smith ridding the sonnet of the Petrarchan octave in favour of using the Shakespearean form throughout. Having refashioned Petrarch's sonnet in her own image in her first sonnet to the nightingale, Smith confidently anglicizes the following two poems, making Shakespeare's form seem Smith's choice.

Smith's statement of her artistic autonomy clashes with the sense of fate as immovable curse that she conjures throughout her sonnets. Yet Smith's choice of the sonnet form comes to complement her content. The restrictions inherent to the sonnet form become limitations that mirror the poet's entrapment by the immutable laws governing her life. Sonnet XII, 'Written on the sea shore.—October, 1784', shows Smith using the enclosed Petrarchan octave to enact the claustrophobic solitude that moves throughout the poem. Pathetic fallacy creates the sense of the poet as, in Seamus Heaney's words, 'lost, / Unhappy and at home':[10] Smith's nature poetry does not offer nature as a palliative cure for despair, but rather represents nature as a fellow sufferer. Its 'tempestuous howl' (XII.4) and 'deep and solemn roar' (XII.5) resemble her human despair without blending with it. Smith insists on nature not as auxiliary to the self, but as a fitting Other which mirrors rather than depends on the 'mournful temper' (XII.8) of the self. Expecting no rescue, with 'From whence no succour comes—or comes too late' (XII.12), Smith predicts an anguished and exhausted end despite the 'feeble cries' (XII.13) of her sonnets.

Though Smith often alludes to the 'artless' quality of her sonnets, artlessness suggestive of her influence on Wordsworth's sense of poetry as 'the spontaneous overflow of powerful feelings',[11] she balances artlessness against an oblique affirmation of her poetic power. Sonnet XIX, 'to Mr. Hayley, on receiving some elegant lines from him', though careful to praise the dedicatee of her volumes, seems equally intent on declaring her own importance as a poet. The first line states, without feigned modesty, that 'For me the Muse a simple band design'd', and despite its appearance as 'A garland form'd as artless as my song', there is little doubt that the Muse herself has bestowed a gift upon the poet, a gift that seems more deserved than questioned. Despite the poem's ostensible praise for Hayley as a poet, Smith draws attention to

William Hayley as patron rather than poet, performing a similar move in her suppressed dedication to *The Emigrants* to William Cowper.[12] Such esteem for her unique sonnet sequence, which saw her consciously embrace the 'illegitimate' Shakespearean model (three quatrains followed by a couplet) more frequently than the traditional 'legitimate' Petrarchan version (with its division into octave and sestet), allowed Smith the freedom to contend with her poetic peers, appropriating and rewriting their themes and forms to fit her own brand of personal poetry. Smith's sonnets, which draw on predecessors from Metastasio to those 'Supposed to be written by Werter' (Sonnets XXI to XXV), evince a potent sense of her poetic power despite her personal sorrows.[13] Merging with her alternate speakers, Smith takes over their voices, using Werter's longing for death to combine with her own despair, asking the North Star to 'leave me to despair and die!' (XXIII.14). Despair becomes a guarantor of her status as a poet, and her apostrophe to Melancholy in Sonnet XXXII, like Milton's 'Il Penseroso', sees it as a spur to creativity. Where Milton reflects on Melancholy, claiming that 'These pleasures Melancholy give, / And I with thee will choose to live' ('Il Penseroso', 175–6),[14] Smith affirms the 'magic power' (XXXII.12) of Melancholy with more unmixed worship than her predecessor.

The death in 1795 of her daughter Anna Augusta, whom Smith refers to as 'The loveliest, the most beloved of my daughters, the darling of all her family', who was 'torn from us for ever',[15] is a haunting loss referred to throughout the entire second volume of the *Elegiac Sonnets* (the sonnets are divided at LX). Though the sonnets rarely become overt elegies, the sadness that suffuses the volume seems still deeper as her memory refuses to fade, as 'still to *me* Oblivion is denied, / There's no Nepenthe, now, on earth for me' (LXXXVIII, 'To Nepenthe', 13–14). Milton's elegies become models for Smith as she alludes to his Sonnet 23 in 'To the Sun' (Sonnet LXXXIX) to draw a parallel between his loss and her own. The Shakespearean octave, with its forward momentum, initially seems to suggest the regenerative and recuperative powers of nature, but Smith, like Milton, refuses to feign consolation.

> Celestial lamp! thy influence bright and warm
>   That renovates the world with life and light
> Shines not for me—for never more the form
>   I loved—so fondly loved, shall bless my sight;
> And nought thy rays illumine, *now* can charm
>   My misery, or to day convert my night!   (LXXXIX.9–14)

Mixing rhyme schemes as the Shakespearean octave passes into a Petrarchan sestet, Smith refuses any solving couplet in favour of Milton's desolation.

Smith is cut off from the mortal world by her status as mourner, haunted by visions that can never be realized by the poet. Neither Milton nor Smith can use poetry to alter their states. Inconsolable despite her poetic power, Smith goes beyond 'reiterated sorrows [that] are somewhat numbing'[16] to achieve an intensely personal music while suggesting her status as Miltonic inheritor. The final sonnet in the sequence (Sonnet XCII, 'Written at Bignor Park in Sussex, in August, 1799') sustains and furthers her self-presentation as a poet in nature, consigned to a misery that can never be mitigated despite her will. The 'old paternal trees' (XCII.4) that she views anchor her into both the specific moment and the location, Bignor Park, her childhood home, but the 'dark shadows' (XCII.5) gathering point up the continued threats to any hope for equanimity. Smith is already 'crush'd' (XCII.11), but, still more painfully, it is the absence of hope that marks the poetry:

> ...—Lo! the radiant star of day
> Lights up this lovely scene anew—My fate
>   Nor hope nor joy illumines—Nor for me
>   Return those rosy hours which here I used to see!   (XCII.11–14)

The repeated negatives reinforce the blank misery the poet must face, a misery that contrasts sharply with the early happiness she had felt. Adela Pinch's observation that Smith's sonnets are built around 'the artful, pathetic phrase' seems apt,[17] but Smith's ability to reinvigorate despair in each of the sonnets reveals the sustained artfulness which unites the *Elegiac Sonnets* into a coherent and impressive artistic whole.

Notes

1 Lord George Gordon Byron, *English Bards and Scotch Reviewers*, l. 147, in *Byron's Poetry and Prose*, ed. Alice Levine, Norton Critical Edition (New York: Norton, 2010).

2 William Wordsworth, note to 'Stanzas, Suggested in a Steamboat off St. Bees' Heads, on the Coast of Cumberland', in *Poetical Works*, ed. Thomas Hutchinson, rev. edn Ernest de Selincourt (New York: Oxford University Press, 1936), p. 724n.

3 Stuart Curran, 'The "I" Altered', in *Romanticism and Feminism*, ed. Anne K. Mellor (Bloomington: Indiana University Press, 1988), pp. 185–207 (at p. 189).

4 Jacqueline M. Labbe, *Charlotte Smith: Romanticism, Poetry and the Culture of Gender* (Manchester: Manchester University Press, 2003), p. 3.

5 Luca Manini, 'Charlotte Smith and Petrarch', in *British Romanticism and Italian Literature: Translating, Reviewing, Rewriting*, ed. Laura Bandiera and Diego Saglia (Amsterdam: Rodopi, 2005), pp. 97–108 (at p. 105).

6 Curran, 'The "I" Altered', p. 199.

7 Stuart Curran, 'Introduction', in *The Poems of Charlotte Smith*, ed. Stuart Curran (Oxford: Oxford University Press, 1993), pp. xix–xxix (at p. xxvi).

8   In *Poems*, ed. Curran. All poetry by Smith will be quoted from this edition unless otherwise indicated.

9   Manini, 'Charlotte Smith and Petrarch', 105.

10   Seamus Heaney, 'The Tollund Man', III, in *Opened Ground: Poems 1966–1996* (London: Faber, 1998).

11   William Wordsworth, 'Preface to Lyrical Ballads, with Pastoral and Other Poems (1802)', in *William Wordsworth: The Major Works*, ed. Stephen Gill, Oxford World's Classics (Oxford: Oxford University Press, 2011), pp. 595–615 (at p. 611).

12   *Poems*, ed. Curran, pp. 132–3. See Labbe's discussion, *Charlotte Smith*, pp. 30–1.

13   'Even where the perspective of the poet seems radically self-denying, it is balanced by the self-confidence of its art.' Curran, 'The "I" Altered', p. 205.

14   John Milton, 'Il Penseroso', in *John Milton: The Complete Poems*, ed. with preface and notes by John Leonard (London: Penguin, 1998).

15   Charlotte Smith, 'Preface to Volume II', in *Poems*, ed. Curran, p. 7.

16   Curran, 'Introduction', p. xxv.

17   Adela Pinch, 'Sentimentality and Experience in Charlotte Smith's Sonnets', in *Strange Fits of Passion: Epistemologies of Emotion, Hume to Austen* (Stanford, CA: Stanford University Press, 1996), pp. 51–72 (at p. 60).

Charlotte Smith, *Beachy Head*

Beachy Head, Smith's last poem, was published in 1807, after her death, as the first poem in a collection entitled *Beachy Head, Fables, and Other Poems*. Smith had lived near Beachy Head for a large part of her life, as is apparent from her clear affinity with its landscape. This affinity is coupled with an alertness to the place as a potentially dangerous one by virtue of its vulnerability to any potential attack by Napoleon's French forces and its reputation as the site of many suicides.[1] Smith also uneasily balances natural and nationalist histories along with personal and political meditations. Smith's 'compelling and baffling poetic experiment' reveals her significance to the Romantic period as a whole;[2] the fractured versions of the self and the fragmentary conclusion to the work show her experimenting with Romantic selving in a way that anticipates and guides her inheritors.

Beachy Head's double vision insists on maintaining an ambitious balancing act where antitheses never collapse into an artificial union. 'Wandering sublime thro' visionary vales, / Where bright pavilions rise, and trophies, fann'd / By airs celestial; and adorn'd with wreaths' (86–8),[3] Smith also tracks 'The fishermen, who at set seasons pass / Many a league off at sea their toiling night' (100–1). Smith conjures a scene 'when the Omnipotent / Stretch'd forth his arm, and rent the solid hills' (6–7), even as she resists the lure of such myth-making by her attention to the local and the particular. Though Smith occasionally mouths the patriotic words required by contemporary fears of a potential French invasion, with her affirmation that England, unlike the 'enervate sons of Italy' or the 'Iberian' (146, 147), would never 'put on / Degrading fetters' (149–50), *Beachy Head* mostly frees itself from such nationalistic restraints, concerning itself with juggling of multiple perspectives, jostling selves, and competing representations of the landscape.

The Romantic Poetry Handbook, First Edition. Michael O'Neill and Madeleine Callaghan.
© 2018 John Wiley & Sons Ltd. Published 2018 by John Wiley & Sons Ltd.

Despite frequent criticism from scholars who consider Smith's autobio-graphical laments to 'border on the unseemly',[4] her apparently self-referential interlude in *Beachy Head* earns its place in the poem. Anticipating Wordsworth, Smith reveals an adept use of the confessional mode cloaked in contemplative blank verse. Contrasting her country past with her urban present, the poem uses memory to reclaim the 'Haunts of my youth! / Scenes of fond day dreams, I behold ye yet!' (297–8), in a triumphant stay against the pain of exile from her untroubled infancy. Asking and stating

> who *is* happy? Happiness! a word
> That like false fire, from marsh effluvia born,
> Misleads the wanderer, destin'd to contend
> In the world's wilderness, with want or woe—
> Yet *they* are happy, who have never ask'd
> What good or evil means. (255–60)

Smith celebrates ignorance, looking ahead to Wordsworth's later and more equivocal reminiscence of his 'glad animal movements all gone by' ('Lines Written a Few Miles above Tintern Abbey', 75),[5] but the accumulated pathos of Smith's speaker uttering such words comes from her earlier *Elegiac Sonnets* and their sustained lament about her speaker's troubled life.[6] Mourning, however plangent, does not take over the poem for long. Celebrating the landscape, Smith's speaker styles herself 'An early worshipper at Nature's shrine', recalling how 'I loved her rudest scenes—warrens, and heaths, / And yellow commons, and birchshaded hollows' (346–8), bearing out Jacqueline M. Labbe's characterization of Smith as shaping 'a poetic self [who] is always outdoors, always unhoused, always seeking shelter'.[7] Anticipating Shelley's 'Mont Blanc', Smith's earlier prospect poem rings with questions and intuitions as she absorbs and reflects on nature. Smith questions both material facts and nature's design.

Magisterially condemning human aspiration, she demands: 'Hither, Ambition, come! / Come and behold the nothingness of all / For which you carry thro' the oppressed Earth, / War, and its train of horrors' (419–22). Defying any potential nihilism, Smith's dedication to nature lends power to her disdain for 'Ambition'. Declining to expound upon this theme, Smith passes to a portrait of the hermit, completing her movement from the wide frame of the historical vision to a localized portrait of his life and death. Smith intimates how this portrait of the hermit verges on self-portraiture, where his doomed love combined with his love of nature forms the mainstay of his song. Hastening to remind the reader that 'The visionary, nursing dreams like these, / Is not indeed unhappy' (655–6), Smith's poetic self-consciousness wins out, rescuing her sketch of the hermit from seeming unwittingly autobiographical or mawkish. Despite his suffering, Smith insists on his continued sympathy with society as 'he still acutely felt / For human misery' (690–1) notwithstanding his chosen exile from the world. Painting her hermit as one who had saved people from their suicidal impulses, people who 'liv'd to bless the hermit of the rocks' (709), Smith stops short of fleshing out her presentation of the hermit, writing no elegy for his death. Offering no more than the certainty 'That dying in the cause of charity / His spirit, from its earthly bondage freed, / Had to some better region fled for ever' (729–31), the speaker closes the poem with an affirmation, but one that does not memorialize or eulogize the dead man. Estranging rather than enchanting, Smith's final poem closes with a haunting ambiguity that sidesteps consolation or closure.

Notes

1   Loraine Fletcher, *Charlotte Smith: A Critical Biography* (New York: St Martin's Press, 1998), p. 330.
2   Theresa M. Kelley, 'Romantic Histories', *Nineteenth-Century Literature* 59.3 (2004): 281–314 (at 289).
3   *Beachy Head*, in *Poems*, ed. Curran, pp. 217–47 (at p. 220).
4   Kelley, 'Romantic Histories', p. 283.
5   William Wordsworth, 'Lines Written a Few Miles above Tintern Abbey', in *Lyrical Ballads, 1798 and 1802*, ed. with intro. and notes by Fiona Stafford, Oxford World's Classics (Oxford: Oxford University Press, 2013), p. 89.
6   Kari Lokke sees Smith constructing *Beachy Head* as 'a complex tribute to herself'. Kari Lokke, 'The Figure of the Hermit in Charlotte Smith's *Beachy Head*', *Wordsworth Circle* 39.1–2 (2008): 38–43 (at 39).
7   Labbe, *Charlotte Smith*, p. 143.

Ann Yearsley, 'Poem on the Inhumanity of the Slave-trade'; 'Bristol Elegy'

Ann Yearsley, or Lactilla as she named herself in a reference to her profession as a milkwoman, was a labouring-class Bristol poet and author writing at the outset of Romanticism. Kerri Andrews argues: 'Having been neglected for nearly two centuries, Yearsley's later poetry ought now to be recognized as a crucial bridge between the work of late eighteenth-century poets, and the new generation of soon-to-be Romantic writers.'[1] Yearsley's earlier work also evinces a proto-Romantic energy and self-consciousness that she refines in her later work. Producing three collections of poetry, *Poems, on Several Occasions* (1785), *Poems, on Various Subjects* (1787), and *The Rural Lyre* (1796), she also wrote plays, one of which, *Earl Goodwin: an Historical Play* (performed 1789 and printed 1791), was staged in her lifetime at Bristol and Bath, and a four-volume historical novel entitled *The Royal Captives: a Fragment of Secret History, Copied from an Old Manuscript* (1795).

Yearsley's career reflects her socially, financially, and poetically precarious position in the literary landscape of the period. Her writing came to the attention of Hannah More, a distinguished writer and social commentator in her own right, whose zeal and dedication to finding subscribers to Yearsley's first volume of poetry launched her protégée's career. Despite her esteem for Yearsley, More refused to grant her any control over the profits of her poetry, even writing to her co-patron, Elizabeth Montagu, to justify her decision to refuse Yearsley financial agency, and Yearsley and More never reconciled after Yearsley took possession of her own earnings. Yearsley's poetic career as a whole tends to be sidelined in favour of discussion of this early event.[2] Yet, Yearsley's poetry is hardly amenable to any simple political labelling. As Dustin Griffin points out, 'Her politics, while

The Romantic Poetry Handbook, First Edition. Michael O'Neill and Madeleine Callaghan.
© 2018 John Wiley & Sons Ltd. Published 2018 by John Wiley & Sons Ltd.

they may disappoint some contemporary critics looking for a working-class ideology of resistance to authority, reflect the reformist beliefs of the broad political middle ground, neither radical nor high-flying Tory, in the 1790s'.[3] Her poetry spans a range of possible political positions, witnessing Yearsley's unique place in the literary landscape.

Passionate and energetic, both of the poems discussed here reveal Yearsley's profound political engagement with the social issues of the period. 'A Poem on the Inhumanity of the Slave-trade', published in 1788 separately from Yearsley's volumes of poetry, was, in Moira Ferguson's arresting phrase, an 'assault against slavery'.[4] The Society for the Abolition of the Slave Trade had been established in 1787 in London, and Yearsley's poem followed a year later, coming out only a day after her former mentor Hannah More's poem on slavery, 'Slavery, A Poem'.[5] The *Bristol Gazette*'s anonymous poem compared 'More's polish'd muse, [with] Yearsley's muse of fire',[6] linking the two women as Bristol's poets despite their public enmity. Yearsley's untaught quality which fuelled her 'muse of fire' was self-proclaimed in the poem. Her readers are challenged to engage with her natural tenderness and elevate her ideas from their wild state into articulate and focused outrage against slavery.

'A Poem on the Inhumanity of the Slave-trade' is pitched between anger and pity. As J. R. Oldfield notes, Yearsley draws on Aphra Behn's *Oroonoko* (1688), which relates the cruelty suffered by the eponymous hero at the hands of corrupt slavers,[7] but makes Luco, her own hero's character, less ambiguous than Behn's protagonist. Opening with an address to the city, Yearsley endeavours to shake her readers out of complacency:

> Custom, Law,
> Ye blessings, and ye curses of mankind,
> What evils do ye cause? We feel enslav'd,
> Yet move in your direction.   (18–21)

Yearsley's baffled sadness and anger challenge shibboleths, revealing the paradox of a society's chosen enslavement. Directly addressing Bristol, Yearsley asks that the denizens of her home city 'snatch her rustic thought / Her crude ideas, from their panting state, / And let them fly in wide expansion' (10–12).[8] Making reference to her position in the popular imagination as 'Lactilla' or 'the Bristol Milkwoman', the sentiment of these lines belies Yearsley's confident wielding of her blank verse and her choice to weigh in on this vexed national issue. Lamenting the fallen state of society and the suffering of the slaves, Yearsley's empathy where 'My soul with sorrow bends' (48) seeks to stir the same virtue in her reader.

Anne K. Mellor links such defiance of the norm in the name of virtue to a female poetic mode: 'Again and again, the female poet insisted that she spoke on behalf of Virtue, a virtue that she consistently gendered as female, a virtue that in a Christian nation must govern both the private and the public sphere, thus taking precedence over all merely expedient considerations of government policy or commercial advancement.'[9] Yet Yearsley's appeal against the status quo is equally grounded in her economic status and her poetic preference for mingling confrontation with any straightforward panegyric or emotional complaint.[10] Protected by powerful patrons yet unable to ascend to the safety of middle-class affluence,[11] Yearsley's poetry is both radical and conservative as it moves between political positions rather than committing itself to a single ideological formula. The poem's confrontational style employs both empathy and challenge. In an attempt to shock the reader into empathy with the enslaved, Yearsley demands that the 'moody' (81) Christian slaver sell his own family. Her rhetorical question, 'Is it *Nature* strains / Thine heart-strings at the image?' (89–90), draws attention to the unnatural cruelty of the slave trade. Lingering on a depiction of Luco's bereft family and his lost love, Incilanda, some of Yearsley's descriptions err towards creating images of the noble savage. She condemns Christian slavers who are unmoved by the sufferings undergone by their slaves. Her notes to the poem spell out her political and moral affiliations, and reveal her knowledge of the practice of slavery. Closing with lines reminiscent of Thomson, 'Hail social love! true soul of *order*, hail' (389), she moves to heal the turbulence of the poem, replacing rage with promise of 'future glory' (402). Powerful in her anger, Yearsley closes the poem with sympathy and hope.

'Bristol Elegy' commemorates the 1793 Bristol Bridge Riots, where Bristolians were murdered by soldiers for protesting against the renewal of an act levying tolls on Bristol Bridge, despite the offers by Quakers to liquidate arrears. Pleading with the readers and authorities to notice and finally end the struggle in the city, the poem despairs of finding the empathetic response it craves. Written in cross-rhymed couplets, Yearsley's poem uses the form to police content as the demands of the quatrain prevent the content spilling beyond the limits of the stanza form. As Claire Knowles notes of Yearsley's self-presentation, 'The poet is presented to her readers (by herself, by her patrons and by reviewers) explicitly as a figure of feminine distress'.[12] 'Bristol Elegy' shows Yearsley using this self-portrait at the opening of her poem as she cries, 'In vain I plead' (21). Refraining from self-representation in the main, Yearsley turns the reader's attention to the suffering of the murdered people that she traces in the poem. From the father of seven who dies within the second stanza, to the murder of a heavily pregnant woman, Yearsley relentlessly shows the privation and pain suffered. The children of the murdered father are left 'to a world too rude' (16), where the death of a young man leaves behind an aged mother to mourn for him. Despite the agonies suffered, Yearsley does not encourage or even countenance revolution:

> Then nurse not dark revenge.—The peaceful mind
> > Can the true value of existence prove;
> In contemplation ev'ry blessing find;
> > Calm in its joy, expanded in its love. (97–100)

Though her poem reveals the horror of the murders, choosing evocative exemplary figures to develop a sense of the cruelty and injustice of these government agents, the close of the poem insists on her readers embracing Christian mildness. The lamenting poem never gives way to wildness thanks to the discipline required by the quatrains; without irony or decorous restraint, Yearsley fashions the poem into a troubling 'fearful scream' (65). Refusing the Satanic route of revenge, Yearsley rhymes 'prove' and 'love' and 'peaceful mind' with 'blessing find' to emphasize the healing power she hopes to claim in her poetry. Despair must be mitigated by belief, and, turning back to God at the close of the poem, Yearsley mournfully trusts to the mystery of faith. In asking the victims to 'pardon all who wrong'd you' (117), the poem's agonized opening notes give way to sad acceptance.

Though writing with reference to 'A Poem on the Inhumanity of the Slave-trade', Moira Ferguson's remark that 'Yearsley offered insights beyond the reach and desire of her middle-class peers' has resonance beyond this single poem.[13] However, her insights are more complex than merely a class-based situational vantage point suggests. Ann Yearsley's poetry is explicitly aligned by some of her critics with an 'emergent Romanticism',[14] and this is suggestive of the use of nature, self, and marginalized voices in her work. Certainly Yearsley's relationship with contemporary culture, poetic mores, and political ideas renders her a complex figure in her own right.

Notes

1 Kerri Andrews, '"No more than as an atom 'mid the vast profound": Conceptions of Time in the Poetry of William Cowper, William Wordsworth, and Ann Yearsley', in *Class and the Canon: Constructing Labouring-Class Poetry and Politics 1780–1900*, ed. Kirstie Blair and Mina Gorji (Houndmills: Palgrave Macmillan, 2013), pp. 95–115 (at p. 114).

2   Kerri Andrews, *Ann Yearsley and Hannah More: Poetry and Patronage* (London: Pickering & Chatto, 2013), p. 3.

3   Dustin Griffin, *Patriotism and Poetry in Eighteenth-Century Britain* (Cambridge: Cambridge University Press, 2002), p. 288.

4   Moira Ferguson, 'Resistance and Power in the Life and Writings of Ann Yearsley', *The Eighteenth Century* 27.3 (1986): 247–68 (at 254).

5   J. R. Oldfield reads Yearsley's poem as 'intended as a direct challenge'. J. R. Oldfield, *Popular Politics and British Anti-Slavery: The Mobilisation of Public Opinion against the Slave Trade, 1787–1807* (Manchester: Manchester University Press, 2008), p. 136.

6   E. D. in the *Bristol Gazette*, 29 May 1788, qtd in Andrews, *Ann Yearsley and Hannah More*, p. 89.

7   Oldfield, *Popular Politics and British Anti-Slavery*, p. 136.

8   'A Poem on the Inhumanity of the Slave-trade', in *The Collected Works of Ann Yearsley*, ed. Kerri Andrews, 3 vols (London: Pickering & Chatto, 2014), 1.109.

9   Anne K. Mellor, 'The Female Poet and the Poetess: Two Traditions of British Women's Poetry, 1780–1830', *Studies in Romanticism* 36.2 (1997): 261–76 (at 264).

10 'Her origins among the ranks of the dispossessed and the fact that she made a life of disadvantage and struggle the heart of a hard-won (and quickly forgotten) art further enhances her importance.' Ferguson, 'Resistance and Power', 247.

11 Frank Felsenstein points out the continuing importance of patronage through-out Yearsley's career: 'Although Ferguson is aware that, following her break with Hannah More, the poet found a second benefactor in Frederick Augustus Hervey, Earl of Bristol and Bishop of Derry (1730–1803), to whom *The Rural Lyre* (1796) was dedicated, she chooses to ignore this in her championing of Yearsley's independence.' Frank Felsenstein, 'Ann Yearsley and the Politics of Patronage. "The Thorp Arch Archive: Part I"', *Tulsa Studies in Women's Literature* 21.2 (2002): 346–92 (at 351).

12 Claire Knowles, 'Ann Yearsley, Biography and the "Pow'rs Of Sensibility Untaught!"', *Women's Writing* 17.1 (2010): 166–84 (at 173).

13 Moira Ferguson, *Subject to Others: British Women Writers and Colonial Slavery, 1670–1834* (London: Routledge, 1992), p. 172.

14 Knowles, 'Ann Yearsley', p. 179.

William Blake, *Songs of Innocence and of Experience*

Both the publication and the relationship with history of these limpid, distilled illuminated poems are complex. *Songs of Innocence* was published in 1789, *Songs of Experience* in 1794, the same year in which Blake appears to have combined separate copies of the two sets of songs into one collection; in 1795, he first printed the poems as a single work. The poems transcend historical specifics; they are the products of a man who, as T. S. Eliot put it, possessed 'a profound interest in human emotions, and a profound knowledge of them'.[1] Yet the initial publication dates of the separate volumes coincide with the initial rapture associated with the French Revolution, 'that glad dawn of the day-star of liberty', in Hazlitt's movingly retrospective phrase, and with the horrors of the Revolution's descent into massacre and state-sponsored terror.[2]

So to phrase the matter, however, is to impose a false symmetry on 'innocence' and 'experience', and their supposed historical coordinates. Three of the songs in *Innocence* appear in the 1785 satirical work *An Island in the Moon*, where the presence of irony directed at the speaker of, say, 'Holy Thursday', leads David V. Erdman to believe that 'Blake had both contraries [Innocence and Experience] in mind all along'; moreover, notebook evidence suggests that the *Songs of Experience* were composed in 1792–3, 'in the Year One of Equality', as Erdman has it, 'in the time of the birth of the French Republic and the London Corresponding Society'.[3] On such a reading, *Songs of Experience* expresses disillusion, not with the course of the Revolution, but with the fact that 'the revolutionary spring torrent ... is still in England dammed and frozen'.[4] Looking at the issue in a different way, however, the poetry's refusal to preach straightforwardly can mean that historical messages are difficult to identify reliably.

The Romantic Poetry Handbook, First Edition. Michael O'Neill and Madeleine Callaghan.
© 2018 John Wiley & Sons Ltd. Published 2018 by John Wiley & Sons Ltd.

In what follows particular attention is given to the poetry's manipulated shifts of perspective, one aspect of which was that, as Blake went on printing separate copies of the two sets, individual poems such as 'The School Boy', 'The Voice of the Ancient Bard', 'The Little Girl Lost', and 'The Little Girl Found' were switched from *Innocence* to *Experience*.[5] Relevant here is Blake's mode of production, described thus by Joseph Viscomi:

> Blake drew a design on a copper plate with an acid-resistant varnish and etched away the unprotected metal to bring the design into relief. He printed the plates on an etching press and colored the impressions by hand; each copy of each book is unique.[6]

Thanks to the 'Blake Archive' (www.blakearchive.org), it is now possible for anyone with an internet connection to take on board the implications of Viscomi's final clause. Pictorial values vary from copy to copy and require the reader to engage continually in the process of interpretation. Sometimes the design is seemingly at odds with the text, notoriously so in the case of 'The Tyger', for which the designs are mainly unintimidating, even cuddly, save for one copy. The text depicts a creature who calls into question the nature of his creator. 'Did he who made the Lamb make thee?' (20), the speaker asks, as though the contraries of gentle innocence and an awe-inspiring energy 'burning bright, / In the forests of the night' (1–2) were impossible to imagine as coexisting. The mounting intensity of the poem's pounding rhythms, the newly forged power and suggestiveness of its images, and an air of inscrutable mystery are all impressively to the fore. Harold Bloom argues with attractive nonchalance that the poem ironizes its hysterical speaker.[7] However, Blake's imaginative suggestions, as in the lines, 'When the stars threw down their spears / And water'd heaven with their tears' (17–18), remain unglossed, hauntingly so. Erdman reads these lines as a 'synoptic vision of the defeat of royal armies, as at Yorktown and at Valmy'.[8] Yet such criticism seeks to hold a symbolic wind in the meshes of its historicist net. The poem defeats paraphrase, reductivism, or easy visualization; it exists as a visionary performance to its fearfully symmetrical fingertips, and Blake's designs seem wryly to concede as much.

Blake's generation of what Stephen C. Behrendt calls 'a "third text", a meta-text that partakes of both the verbal and the visual texts, but that is neither the sum of, nor identical with either of, those two texts',[9] prompts the reader's enquiring involvement with his poetic works. Such involvement bears witness to Blake's way of working on the reader's consciousness and, not infrequently, conscience. How should one read, for example, the 'Introduction' to *Songs of Experience*? The text begins confidently enough, asserting bardic authority: 'Hear the voice of the Bard!' (1). But a trailing syntax, postlapsarian in its appositional ensnarings, makes it hard to erase the sense that the Bard, 'The Holy Word' (4), and 'the lapsed Soul' (6) are all toppling over into an abyss of fallenness. Thus the second stanza reads:

> Calling the lapsed Soul
> And weeping in the evening dew:
> That might controll,
> The starry pole;
> And fallen fallen light renew!   (6–10)

One assumes that it is the 'Holy Word' that is 'Calling' and 'weeping', but the fact that the poem begins by referring to the Bard's voice, plus the slippage created by the 'apparently chaotic punctuation', makes it possible to hear the Bard as also calling and weeping.[10] Further ambiguities surround the following lines: 'Is it', ask the Norton editors appositely, 'the Soul or the Word who could reverse the fallen state if only it chose to?'[11] Robert Gleckner argues that the last stanzas should be heard as doubly voiced, spoken by a corruptly repressive Holy Word and by the 'Bard, mortal but prophetically imaginative', and yet the poem seems unready to supply what he calls 'the all-important point of view'.[12] The reader has to enter the labyrinth of doubt and uncertainty. Narrative plots deriving from Genesis and Milton haunt the poem; in a reworking of Miltonic epic, the lyric seeks to justify to itself the ways of Blake's imaginative search for authority.

The very form of the poem, with its four five-line stanzas and contrapuntal rhyming (*abaab*), establishes it as a stay against chaos and, potentially, as a form of entrapment. The poem's addressee, the Earth, interprets the final appeal as a patriarchal trick. In the subsequent poem 'Earth's Answer' she refers to herself as 'Prison'd on watry shore' (6). In 'Introduction' the 'watry shore' (19) 'Is giv'n thee till the break of day' (20), serving as a stabilizing boundary. In 'Earth's Answer' the same rhyme scheme and images are used (though the poem has an extra stanza), but the tone has changed from poignant appeal ('O Earth O Earth return!', 'Introduction', 11) to angry, anti-repressive assertion ('Selfish father of men / Cruel jealous selfish fear', 'Earth's Answer', 11–12). What the bardic speaker of 'Introduction', possibly in a state of self-aggrandizing delusion, may view as a proffer of help is regarded by Earth in 'Earth's Answer' as a means of imposing the 'bondage' (25) of restraint.

In the design for 'Introduction', we see a naked figure, back to the viewer, on a couch or robe, itself supported by what looks like cloud; she is surrounded by a few stars and has a rising sun behind her head, but the image, partly because of its coldly blue tonalities, may suggest not so much the imminent approach of 'the break of day' (20) as a posture of resigned waiting. 'Introduction' expresses a mood of longing for a voice that 'might controll, / The starry pole; / And fallen fallen light renew!' (8–10), but the purity of lyric yearning coexists with a complexity of perspective. Although Blake may have been 'a man without a mask', in Samuel Palmer's memorable phrase,[13] his songs are engaged in 'Shewing the Two Contrary States of the Human Soul', as the subtitle to *Songs of Innocence and of Experience* has it. They are often mini-monologues, provoking the reader to question the speaker's view. At the same time, and herein lies a major source of their hypnotic force, the songs always invite us to enter into the 'State of the Human Soul' that is being explored: whether it is the speaker's savagely exultant delight in 'A Poison Tree' that his 'Christian forbearance' (a draft title) has destroyed his enemy, or his chagrin in 'My Pretty Rose Tree' at being unrewarded by his partner for his resistance to temptation, it is the human mind's psychological workings that capture Blake's most immediate interest. The poems stop before moral judgement starts. Should we prefer the clod's seeming selflessness or the pebble's gleeful selfishness in 'The Clod & the Pebble'? Crystalline in their phrasing, assertive in their syntax and use of statement, Blake's poems manage continually to stir up a variety of jostling responses.

These are poems that read the reader. They expose assumptions and underlying biases. Easy to misread as simplistic, *Songs of Innocence* may suggest how hard it is to re-enter a state to which children often seem to have access, a state marked by trust, acceptance, kindness, mercy. Blake's speakers are sometimes children (a 'two days old' (2) child in 'Infant Joy'), sometimes adults. They delight in a world seen as providentially arranged and structured, whatever its apparent realities or ills. Those realities or ills impinge on a number of poems in which an element of social protest seems on the verge of voicing itself, but only to subside in favour of an affecting mood of acceptance. Arguably, this subsiding only makes the social point more strongly.

The little black boy in the poem of that name guilelessly exposes the cruelly hierarchical binaries associated with attitudes to skin colour. The poem links these binaries to a Christian ideology that promises those who suffer on earth a compensatory reward in heaven. That said, this Christian ideology is voiced by the mother who speaks, consolingly, with gentle affection and concern for her son. The poem works as an ideological critique of racism and slavery (a word never mentioned in the poem), of the indoctrination that leads the speaker to say, 'But I am black as if bereav'd of light' (4). That critique entwines itself with and emerges from the poem's engagement with the boy's innocent perspective. Thus, Blake explores in the final stanza the boy's sense of supposed inferiority. In heaven, says the black boy, he will 'be like' (28) the 'little English boy' (22) 'and he will then love me' (28).

Here as so often, Blake cuts below the abstractions of protest poetry and evokes a complicated response; we may detect the presence of what a Marxist would call 'false consciousness', but we hear the catch of hopeless hope in 'and then'; critique coexists with pity and even – and here the poetry has an uncomfortable force – a kind of admiration for the boy's innocent acceptance. The little black boy could have been indignant; instead, he is continually loving, innocent in that he is unaware of the exploitative ideology of which he is the victim, but innocent, too, in that his gentleness and capacity for love shine out radiantly from the poem. As Northrop Frye argues, the *Songs of Innocence* 'satirize the state of experience', as much as experience ironizes innocence.[14] This is not to say that the poem satirizes the would-be protester against social injustice; rather, it brings radiantly alive a refreshed understanding of a value that the social protester is likely to view with caution, that of innocent trust: easily manipulated and exploited, but still a form of rebuke to more worldly-wise perspectives. Indeed, that subtle form of rebuke may well disturb readers more deeply than the angrily sincere anti-slavery rhetoric which was widespread in the period.

Blake's attention to the speakers of the poems, their contrary states of soul, occurs in a number of poems which have the same title in each collection. 'Holy Thursday' (*Innocence*) invites us to question whether the speaker (originally Obtuse Angle in *An Island in the Moon*) is myopically delighted to see 'the annual regimented singing of London charity-school children as evidence that the flogged and uniformed boys and girls are angelically happy'.[15] Erdman, whose sarcastic description has just been quoted, sees the contrary poem in *Experience* as bringing out explicitly the irony latent in the *Innocence* version.[16] Yet the *Innocence* poem seems both to acknowledge the speaker's delight in 'these flowers of London town' (5) and to suggest perspectives beyond the speaker's scope, though touched on almost inadvertently by his language. An example is the line, 'Now like a mighty wind they raise to heaven the voice of song' (9); the long, flowingly cadenced line paints a quasi-biblical picture in which the children are able to pierce the ears of heaven with the 'voice of song'; it also suggests how, without complaining of their lot, the children might be heard as reserving a right of complaint amidst their jubilation. On this reading, the last line's prudential moral, 'Then cherish pity, lest you drive an angel from the door' (12), is well intentioned yet an unconscious indictment of a system that might, indeed, bring a poverty-blighted 'angel' to 'your door'. The design shows regimented children 'walking two & two' (2), as if to bring out the reality of the children's condition, dependent on charity and authority figures, 'beadles' with 'wands as white as snow' (3). Yet in this song of innocence we weigh in the balance a keen sense of adult complacencies and an even fuller recognition of the children's innocence and 'radiance' (6). That is, irony and protest, so evident in the *Experience* counterpart, are neither absent from, nor the only or last words in, the *Songs of Innocence*.

As Erdman notes of the *Songs of Innocence*, 'There is woe in this world', citing among a number of examples the fact that 'the chimney sweeper has been sold to hard labor'.[17] 'The Chimney Sweeper' illustrates the subtlety of *Songs of Innocence*, partly because of its layering of voices and perspectives. The chimney sweeper is aware of horrific social realities, yet he is, humblingly, unembittered by them; the movement of the opening – 'When my mother died I was very young, / And my father sold me' (1–2) – is uncomplaining. Only a fleeting trace of sharpness can be felt in the 'your' of 'So your chimneys I sweep & in soot I sleep' (4).[18] The poem's metrical deftness suggests an awareness that is grave, non-accusatory, even as the child's exploited state is made painfully clear, the more so because of the absence of protest. In this world the brutal is accepted as normal, leaving the sweeper to comfort a younger boy, Tom Dacre, when 'his head / That curl'd like a lambs back, was shav'd' (5–6). Blake brings out the sweep's care for another in writing of restraint and poignancy; much work is done, for instance, in the just-quoted lines by the controlled rhythmic movement that dwells on 'curl'd like a lambs back' and then comes up sheer against the shearing in 'shav'd'. Blake's meanings inhere in the play of voice and stress, in, for instance, the subsequent and quickly responsive 'so I said' (6) which introduces the hushing consolation given by the speaker to the younger child.

Tom's ensuing dream of the boys' release by an 'Angel' (13) from 'coffins of black' (12) is clearly wish-fulfilment. The older sweep seems to approve of the dream, yet not to share in it; 'they run' (15) in the retelling of Tom's fantasy, not 'we run', just as when the dream fades and the sweeps wake up to go to work, the speaker says: 'Tho' the morning was cold, Tom was happy & warm' (23), a way of putting it that shows the older sweep's reticence and concern for Tom. Yet in its vigour and vitality – the boys are imagined 'leaping laughing' (15) – the dream embodies an innocence captured in the poem and yearned for, the more so when Blake brings out the repressive effects of doctrinal teaching, first on Tom (19–20), and then on the older sweep, who concludes with a moral – 'So if all do their duty, they need not fear harm' (24) – that brings chilly comfort.

Blake suggests differing feelings within as well as between *Songs of Innocence* and *Songs of Experience*. The theme of poetic authority may, as suggested, loom large in the Introduction to the later book. But it is present in the piper's song in the 'Introduction' to *Songs of Innocence*; after the child instructs the piper to 'write / In a book that all may read' (13–14), hints of loss, faint intimations at best, but present all the same, enter the poetry. The child vanishes; the piper plucks a 'hollow reed' (16) and 'stain'd the water clear' (18), where 'clear' may be adjective or adverb, pulling in negative or positive directions, respectively, and the series of strong active verbs concludes with a conditional 'may': 'And I wrote my happy songs, / Every child may joy to hear' (19–20). Does Blake imply that giving form to the idea of innocence involves, necessarily, loss of some pre-verbal harmony or vision? 'The Echoing Green' switches in its final line from 'Ecchoing Green' (10, 20) to 'darkening Green' (30), and a shadow cast by the imminence of experience seems to pass over the calmly accepting joyfulness of the poem. Inexorably time enters the poem, stealing in with the past tense of the old people's memories, 'Such such were the joys' (17), and the final effect is one of mingled acceptance and muted foreboding, even as – in a further twist – the beautiful illustrations extend a joyous welcome to process and sexuality. The second design has a reclining youth handing grapes down to a girl in a red-pink bonnet; she is at the end of a procession of youthful figures guided by 'Old John' (11).

In *Songs of Experience* Blake does not give his prophetic ambitions an easy time. Even in 'London', when he hears 'In every cry of every Man' (5) 'mind-forg'd manacles' (8), he is part of what he reports, as Bloom notes: '"Every man" includes the Londoner William Blake, whose voice also must betray the clanking sound of "mind-forg'd manacles".'[19] And yet the poem does not simply deconstruct the speaker's passionate vision. The poem persuades one by allowing for the speaker's involvement in what he sees, an involvement that heightens and does not nullify its force. The poet may have to 'wander', to be in exile, but his vision proves its validity through the power of metaphor. Blake's metaphors in the poem work to expose startling connections, as he turns from sight to sound and hears 'How the Chimney-sweepers cry / Every blackning Church appalls, / And the hapless soldier's sigh [:]/Runs in blood down palace walls' (9–12). The verb 'appalls' suggests hypocritical dismay (one imagines an unctuous sense of being 'appalled'), but it also implies that the church wears the cries like the soot that the chimney sweepers are made to clean. The soldier's 'sigh' implies expiration of breath on a battlefield, yet it turns, as in some biblical omen, into a sign of coming retribution as it 'Runs in blood down palace walls'.

Marriage and prostitution are yoked together in the final stanza, violently but also with visionary insight, and, as with many of Blake's *Songs*, with variously ponderable suggestions:

> But most thro' midnight streets I hear
> How the youthful Harlots curse
> Blasts the new-born Infants tear
> And blights with plagues the Marriage hearse.   (13–16)

Powerfully mixing trochaic and iambic feet, making full use of the poetry's stress system to bring the voice of the poet down with maximum impact on key verbs, and packing their language with menacingly yoked-together opposites, these tetrameters represent some of the most searing lines written by a Romantic poet. They root themselves in the grim realities of Blake's London; they speak for all time as a nightmarish account of how 'all best things', to draw on the Fury's word in *Prometheus Unbound* 1.628, can be 'confused to ill'. In the poem's design, depicting an old man being guided by a young boy, however, one senses that innocence still has a role to play in leading Blake beyond the impasse often presented by experience.

Notes

1   T. S. Eliot, 'William Blake', in *The Complete Prose of T. S. Eliot*, vol. 2, *The Perfect Critic*, ed. Anthony Cuda and Ronald Schuchard (Baltimore: Johns Hopkins University Press, 2014), p. 189.

2   William Hazlitt, *Complete Works*, ed. P. P. Howe (London: Dent, 1930–4), 4.116.

3   David V. Erdman, *Blake: Prophet against Empire: A Poet's Interpretation of the History of His Own Times* (Princeton: Princeton University Press, 1954), p. 118; David V. Erdman, 'Blake: The Historical Approach', in *Modern Critical Views: William Blake*, ed. Harold Bloom (New York: Chelsea House, 1985), p. 21.

4   Erdman, *Blake: Prophet against Empire*, p. 250.

5   See *Blake's Poetry and Designs: Illuminated Works, Other Writings, Criticism*, sel. and ed. Mary Lynn Johnson and John E. Grant, 2nd edn (New York: Norton, 2008), p. 9. All quotations from Blake are taken from this edition.

6   Joseph Viscomi, '[Blake's Relief Etching Process: A Simplified Account]', in *Blake's Poetry and Designs*, ed. Johnson and Grant, p. 542.

7   Harold Bloom, 'Introduction', in *Modern Critical Views*, ed. Bloom, p. 14, where Bloom asks, 'What does it mean for a major lyric never to deviate from its own hysterical intensity?'.

8   Erdman, 'Blake: The Historical Approach', p. 21.

9   Stephen C. Behrendt, '[The "Third Text" of Blake's Illuminated Books]', in *Blake's Poetry and Designs*, ed. Johnson and Grant, p. 549.

10   Robert Gleckner, 'Point of View and Context in Blake's Songs', in *Modern Critical Views*, ed. Bloom, p. 39.

11   *Blake's Poetry and Designs*, ed. Johnson and Grant, p. 29n.

12 Gleckner, 'Point of View and Context', p. 40.

13 Samuel Palmer, 'Letter to Alexander Gilchrist', in *Blake's Poetry and Designs*, ed. Johnson and Grant, p. 515.

14 Northrop Frye, *Fearful Symmetry: A Study of William Blake* (Princeton: Princeton University Press, 1969 [1947]), p. 237.

15 Erdman, *Blake: Prophet against Empire*, p. 110.

16 Erdman, *Blake: Prophet against Empire*, pp. 111–12.

17 Erdman, *Blake: Prophet against Empire*, p. 117.

18 For a valuable discussion of the poem's interpretation of Innocence as 'a state, not of ignorance but of knowledge, though not a state of being "knowing" (which is characteristic of Experience)', a discussion which comments on 'the dignified, patient (and "unpoetic") first line', see D. G. Gillham, *Blake's Contrary States: The 'Songs of Innocence and of Experience' as Dramatic Poems* (Cambridge: Cambridge University Press, 1966), pp. 38–44 (at pp. 39, 40).

19 Bloom, 'Introduction', in *Modern Critical Views*, ed. Bloom, p. 11.

William Blake, *The Marriage of Heaven and Hell*; *The Book of Urizen*; 'The Mental Traveller'

'Exuberance is Beauty', one of the Proverbs of Hell in William Blake's *The Marriage of Heaven and Hell* (1790), hereafter *MHH*, is an equation validated by the work itself. In it Blake combines an array of genres and tones; what results is an artistic creation that is vibrant with apocalyptic hope and contrarian life. Mainly composed in sharply witty and provocative prose, *MHH* consists of 'An Argument' (a poem in tautly cadenced free verse), 'The voice of the Devil', scintillatingly immoderate proverbs, and several memorable fancies mocking the 'Memorable Relations' told by Emanuel Swedenborg (1688–1772), a Swedish visionary whom Blake had once admired.[1] It concludes with 'A Song of Liberty', written in the form of pseudo-biblical verses. *MHH* recalls so-called Lucianic or Menippean satire, typified by an inclusive medley of forms, and redeploys Swiftian techniques in places.[2] But, as it leaps with verve from aphorism to fable, jousting with 'All Bibles or sacred codes' (4; references are to plate numbers), with Milton, Swedenborg, and the Authorized Version, *MHH* shapes, through the interplay of word and richly coloured image, a work that is uniquely itself.

Throughout, Blake mingles satirical and revolutionary notes. What gives *MHH* its electrifying charge of newsness is a revolutionary readiness to think the unthinkable in moral, religious, political, and artistic terms, to reject and revalue tradition and orthodoxy. Blake is out to shock the meekly compliant believer. The new millennium 'will come to pass by an improvement of sensual enjoyment' (14), a statement belonging to a group of plates that the Norton editors gloss as commending 'expanded sense perception'.[3] The gloss is true, but Blake's phrases honour and release a libidinal sexual energy, too, as his designs reveal with their bodies bathed in flames. An example is the

The Romantic Poetry Handbook, First Edition. Michael O'Neill and Madeleine Callaghan.
© 2018 John Wiley & Sons Ltd. Published 2018 by John Wiley & Sons Ltd.

sexually explicit frontispiece, featuring a 'nude couple' exchanging a 'frankly erotic embrace'.[4] Blake makes clear, with playful zest, that his own methods of printing are central to the dismissal of the notion that 'man has a body distinct from his soul'. Blake will disprove this falsehood 'by printing in the infernal method, by corrosives, which in Hell are salutary and medicinal, melting apparent surfaces away, and displaying the infinite which was hid' (14). Blakean printing methods, involving the acidic 'melting' of 'surfaces' and subsequent 'displaying' of the 'infinite', confer a positive value on 'Hell' and locate the 'infinite' in the actual seen anew, not in some misty beyond.

In a Memorable Fancy that follows this assertion, Blake finds himself 'in a Printing house in Hell' where he 'saw the method in which knowledge is transmitted from generation to generation' (15). The narrative that ensues describes five chambers in each of which some stage of the 'method' is carried out, culminating in the fifth chamber in which 'Unnam'd forms' 'cast the metals into the expanse' before they 'took the forms of books' (15). Punning on 'formes' as meaning both shapes (yet to be given a name) and a printer's 'forms', the bed that holds the type,[5] Blake fuses the material conditions of his individual mode of book production and the ways in which 'the doors of perception' might be cleansed (14). He produces a Romantic version of Spenser's Cave of Mammon, revalued so as to suggest an imaginative redemption.[6] The Memorable Fancy does not preach a doctrine; instead, 'Numerous intriguing combinations and permutations demand the reader's mental energy'.[7]

The work's central proposition, 'Without Contraries is no progression', leads Blake to redefine Good and Evil as, respectively, 'the passive that obeys Reason' and 'the active springing from Energy' (3). Living with and accepting 'Contraries' is a buoyant but troubled ideal in the work: buoyant because Blake convincingly embodies in his sharp but good-humoured sallies the notion that creativity thrives on the 'Opposition' that is 'True Friendship' (20);[8] troubled because one side of the paired contraries – namely the 'active' or 'Evil' – continually enjoys the rhetorical upper hand in the work. Blake has little time for 'the passive that obeys Reason'. What, then, does Blake understand by the term 'Contraries'? Martin K. Nurmi distinguishes Blake's idea of contraries from apparent parallels in Hegelian thought. Whereas Hegel sees thesis and antithesis as a dialectic continually resolved by a progression of syntheses, Blake's 'only "progression" … is that of continued creativeness'.[9] In its ideal form, a 'Contrary' is a positive, complementary coupling 'between', as the idea is exemplified by Nurmi, 'the creative imagination and the ordering reason, or between idea and form'.[10]

At points in *MHH*, however, 'Contraries' include as one term of a binary pair an attitude that Blake rejects. In the voice of the Devil passage, as

Harold Bloom notes, contraries 'have ceased strictly to be contraries, for Blake declares one set to be error and the other to be true'.[11] The Devil's propositions do not so much exist in creative tension with dualistic orthodoxy as seek to overthrow it. The errors castigated by the Devil are threefold: that human beings consist of 'a Body & a Soul', that Good comes from the latter, Evil from the former, and 'That God will torment Man in Eternity for following his Energies'. 'But', asserts Blake, assuming a diabolic voice hard to distinguish from his own, 'the following Contraries to these are True', namely that 'Man has no Body distinct from his Soul', that 'Energy is the only life and is from the Body, and Reason is the bound or outward circumference of Energy', and that 'Energy is Eternal Delight' (4).

A partial solution to the conundrum is that Blake's credal trinity of 'Contraries' contain 'Contraries' within themselves, not simply in their relationship to that which they critique. The interplay between energy and reason, for example, will dominate Blake's poetic practice for many years, undergoing sombre complications in the major prophetic books. The emergence of Urizen, whose name suggests 'Your reason' or 'horizon', as a major anti-hero in works such as *The Book of Urizen* and *Milton* bears witness to Blake's wrestle with the problem posed by reason. Reason, at its best, supplies the necessary 'bound or "outward circumference" of Energy' (4), and Blake himself uses 'Reason' in *MHH* to anatomize what is wrong with the erroneous reasonings enshrined in 'sacred codes'. Possibly the closest that the poem comes to adumbrating a genuine 'Contrary' is this coupling of Energy and Reason, rephrased in plate 16 as the dynamic tension between 'the Prolific' and 'the Devourer', the former initially identified with creative 'Giants', the latter with cunningly restraining agents. Yet when he gives the 'two classes of men' their titles of Prolific and Devourer, Blake gives a role to the latter class that is not merely negative; the active receptivity of the Devourer is vital for the two classes to enjoy the productive enmity which is Blake's notion of 'True Friendship'.

From the opening 'Argument', Blake's own combination of energy and reason is exhilaratingly present. The poem tells an elliptical fable in which the 'just man' finds himself mimicked by the 'villain', who usurps the domain of the just man, until a present state is reached in which anger and rage are the only legitimate forms of expressing authentic selfhood. Yet though Blake finds a typically obscure, self-mythologized other in the 'Rintrah', a figure of the poet-prophet in the wilderness, who begins and ends the poem as he 'roars & shakes his fires in the burden'd air' (2), his own tone is coolly playful rather than fiery. It is his ideological enemy and subsequent friend, the Angel, who turns various colours before 'mastering himself' as a result of hearing a very Blakean Devil assert that 'The worship of God is, Honouring his gifts in other men, ... for there is no other God' (22–3). The way in which this Memorable Fancy concludes characterizes Blake's creative insouciance in the work; the Angel, after being persuaded by the Devil that 'Jesus was all virtue, and acted from impulse, not from rules', embraced fire, 'was consumed and arose as Elijah'. Becoming Blake's 'particular friend', he and the author read 'the Bible together in its infernal or diabolical sense which the world shall have if they behave well'. With high good humour, Blake dominates the Angel and patronizes the 'world' – then he intensifies his provocation: 'I have also: The Bible of Hell: which the world shall have whether they will or no' (24). In little, the tones here establish *MHH* as a visionary, revolutionary performance, not, for all its acuteness of thought, a philosophical treatise.

MHH mounts a challenge to religious systems, retelling in trenchant fashion a revolutionary story that Shelley will also narrate in *A Defence of Poetry* in which he praises poets such as Dante and Milton who 'have conferred upon modern mythology a systematic form';[12] 'modern mythology' would appear, in context, to be Christianity. It seeks, as the editors of the *Early Illuminated Books* point out, a 'redirection of attention from religion, which is cast as derivative, external, and oppressive, to art, cast as original, internal, and liberating'.[13] A series of plates culminating in Blake's account of his own creative activity (discussed earlier) brings this theme fully to the fore. In plate 11 he mordantly describes the process by which the imaginings of 'The ancient Poets' were turned into 'a system' presided over by a 'Priesthood'. Initially poets 'animated all sensible objects with Gods or Geniuses'. But this originating impulse was subsequently repressed until 'men forgot that All deities reside in the human breast'. This formulation does not deny deity, but it insists that Gods were created by and reside within human beings. Then in an entertaining yet strangely unsettling Memorable Fancy, Ezekiel presents himself as an early believer in 'the Poetic Genius (as you now call it)' (12). The passage is unsettling because Ezekiel, answering Blake's question about the efficacy of a 'firm perswasion' (12), comes perilously close to proving such efficacy through the fact that 'we so loved our God, that we cursed in his name all the deities of surrounding nations' (13). Persuasion sounds dangerously close to conquest here. Blake, one senses, claims for Hebrew religion a prophetic, poetic quality, yet Ezekiel's talk of consequent 'subjection' seems momentarily to deconstruct itself. Brio and reckless fun are part of the mixture, and Blake does not mind subjecting his own persuasions to the possibility of critique. It is in the following passage, discussed above, that he makes clear his use of the 'infernal method' of printing, as if to state his own role as a poet capable of announcing, even bringing about, the new millennium: 'The ancient tradition', Blake writes as though he were coming to fulfil it, 'that the world will be consumed in fire at the end of six thousand years is true, as I have heard from Hell' (14).

At such moments Blake seems to voice the revolutionary energies of his age. He does so in a work that is *sui generis*, but has a swift, sharply etched sense of purpose. Error after error is exposed; possibilities of redemption assert themselves in the substance and manner of the work's impudent riposte to orthodoxy. The marriage imagined in the title and suggested by *MHH* is very much on hell's terms.[14] In one of the period's major rewritings of *Paradise Lost*, Blake claims Milton as author, against his conscious will, of a subversive epic that shows the folly of attempts to 'restrain desire' (5). Blake mocks Milton's depiction of God, adding a rider, after which Milton criticism would never be quite the same: 'Note. The reason Milton wrote in fetters when he wrote of Angels & God, and at liberty when of Devils & Hell, is because he was a true Poet and of the Devil's party without knowing it' (6). Impishly inflected with condescension, the praise insists that Milton should be read on Blake's terms. Milton, indeed, is caught up in the irresistible but pointed flow of a work that reaches its triumphant climax in 'A Song of Liberty' (and Chorus) with its anti-imperialist assertion that 'Empire is no more!' and its ontological belief that 'every thing that lives is Holy' (27).

Blake would rarely sound so rapturously if open-mindedly sure again. In *The Book of Urizen* (1794) the outlook is almost unmitigatedly bleak. The poem is a parody of a sacred text in word and design. In the frontispiece, Urizen, white-bearded, eyes closed, copies with both hands into books on each side; behind him are two tablets of stone. The image mocks the Mosaic law, commandments written on tablets of stone; but it also incriminates the process of writing itself, as if to suggest a connection between Urizen and his creator. Fundamental to this first book of the 'Bible of Hell' unnervingly promised in *MHH*, set out in double columns that mimic the traditional way in which the Bible is printed, is the idea that creation involves a fall. Whereas creation in Genesis is a work of wonder, benignly approved by its all-powerful author (see Genesis 1:31), creation in *The Book of Urizen* involves a continual sundering, self-division, and falling away from an original plenitude. Blake's techniques for rendering this tearing apart include short, tersely phrased lines gathered together in convoluted syntaxes, mirroring the confusion and chaos at the heart of every attempt to define, to restrain, to bound. Urizen is 'A self-contemplating shadow, / In enormous labours occupied' (3: 21–2), determined to separate himself from the 'Eternals', at whose behest Blake claims to write (see 2: 5). What results is a terrifying update of Genesis and *Paradise Lost*. Urizen sees himself in heroic terms, a cross between Milton's God and Satan, yet he is at one with what his confused pronouncements suggest that he sees himself as confronting, namely 'A wide world of solid obstruction' (4: 23).

Los, whose role as blacksmith-artist and surrogate of Blake is greatly expanded in later works such as and especially *The Four Zoas*, *Milton*, and *Jerusalem*, seeks to give boundaries to Urizen's collapse into formlessness. Yet the imposition of form leads to a description of the making of the human body, and subsequently the division into male and female, that suggests, from the Eternals' perspective, and indeed Blake's, catastrophe, anguish, and woe. Los and his partner or Emanation, in Blake's word, Enitharmon, have a child, Orc, whom they chain 'to the rock / With the Chain of Jealousy / Beneath Urizen's deathful shadow' (20: 23–4). The relentless unfolding of 'dark visions of torments' (2: 7) gives the work a nightmarish force, one apparent in some of the full-length designs, full of foreboding and terror, of cramped, constricted figures, as though the creation were viewed as an aberration, and everything that lived in a Urizenic universe was unholy.

Orc's chaining marks the inauguration of what Blake critics refer to as the 'Orc cycle', the process by which Urizenic repression gives rise to Orc's rebellion in an endless cycle that bears on the progress of the French Revolution and the repression of radical ideas in Britain during the 1790s.[15] The only positive that emerges from *The Book of Urizen* is the candour, audacity, and artistic brilliance of the work itself. Or, to put it another way, Blake tests and validates the strength of 'mind-forg'd manacles' ('London', 8), yet the ferocity of his delineation creates a wish that the poet's 'swift winged words' (2: 6) will propel a breakthrough. Hints of such a breakthrough come at the joyous endings of the major prophetic books, as in the gravely celebratory chant at the close of *Jerusalem* where the poet writes of 'All Human Forms identified' (99). There, the long line flows, not with exhaustion, but with delight in a truly human 'living going forth & returning'. It makes clear that Blake's pursuit of what in his most famous lyric he calls 'Mental Fight' (*Milton* 1: 13) aims at a transvaluation of the present.

Yet it remains the case that Blake is often at his poetically finest when confronting all that opposes his will to affirm. Above all, he wishes to break from temporal cycles without rejecting the world in which human beings live. 'The Mental Traveller', a lyric from the so-called Pickering manuscript, presents, in a ballad of twenty-six quatrains, a seemingly inexorable process of sexual warfare, carried out between the generations: a 'Woman Old' (10) binds a young boy; when he grows up she 'grows young' (20) and he 'binds her down for his delight' (24). As the youth grows old he looks after 'A little female Babe' (44), who seems to offer comfort and beauty, yet the 'fire' of which she is made is disquietingly 'solid' (45), indicating that 'hers is not the free, exuberant flow of Energy'.[16] The grim cycle repeats itself until the Orc-like young man reappears only for the 'Woman Old' (102) once more to nail 'him down upon the Rock' (103). 'And all is done', the balladeer signs off, with a bitter flourish, 'as I have told' (104). Throughout, the poem manages, especially through repeated rhyme sounds (on the word 'old') and a controlled, strong rhythmic beat, to convey the sense of a cycle marked by stages and station, but always heading back inexorably to its starting point.

The poem 'pivots upon two births' as Morton Paley notes,[17] that of the boy at the start and the female babe halfway through, and two cycles result. The theme of the first cycle is the fate of energy at the hands of the world that the boy enters (hence the echoes of Christ's crucifixion); the theme of the second cycle spins round the entrance of a female counterpart. Fallenness in Blake often shows itself through failures in relationships between men and women; sexual identity is at the very heart, for Blake, of human desire. Over and over in the poem, remorselessly conveyed through the conjunction 'till,' possible episodes of happiness turn out to be illusory, leading, at best, into 'Labyrinths of wayward Love' (83) and, at worst, into the violent impulse to dominate and repress signalled by the ending's brutally matter-of-fact return to the crucifixion motif. But the poem remains a masterpiece, possibly Blake's greatest song of experience.

The three poems show how for Blake the poet's role was, respectively, energizing, conflicted, near-tragic. In *MHH*, enacting his belief that 'All deities reside in the human breast', he employs a satirical-cum-visionary voice to unleash beautifully exuberant heterodoxies; in *The Book of Urizen*, he shows the poet as one who believes with Thomas Hardy (in 'In Tenebris II') that 'if way to the Better there be, it exacts a full look at the Worst' (14);[18] in 'The Mental Traveller', the speaker he visits as from another cosmos, almost nonchalantly outraged by 'such dreadful things / As cold Earth wanderers never knew' (3–4), but reminding us always that 'the Eye altering alters all' (62). Though it carries a pessimistic freight in the poem, it reminds us, implicitly, as Blake's work often does, that visionary poetry can alter our outlook; can 'open the Immortal Eyes / Of Man inwards into the Worlds of Thought: into Eternity / Ever expanding in the Bosom of God, the Human Imagination', as he put it in *Jerusalem* (5: 18–20). Fittingly, that last line, in true Blakean fashion, identifies 'God' with the 'Human Imagination'.

Notes

1   For detailed discussion of Blake's response to Swedenborg in *MHH*, see William Blake, *The Early Illuminated Books: 'All Religions Are One', 'There Is No Natural Religion', 'The Book of Hell', 'The Marriage of Heaven and Hell', 'Visions of the Daughters of Albion'*, ed. with intro. and notes by Michael Eaves, Robert N. Essick, and Joseph Viscomi (Princeton: Princeton University Press, in

conjunction with the William Blake Trust, 1993), pp. 118–28, which discusses Blake's 'complex rhetorical and intellectual feat of mastering, expanding, and redirecting Swedenborgian discourse' (p. 126).

2 For Menippean satire, see Blake, *The Early Illuminated Books*, p. 118. For relations between Blake and Swift's *Tale of a Tub* and *Gulliver's Travels*, see *Blake's Poetry and Designs*, ed. Johnson and Grant, pp. 66, 74.

3 *Blake's Poetry and Designs*, ed. Johnson and Grant, p. 67.

4 Blake, *The Early Illuminated Books*, p. 130.

5 See 'Introduction' to *Unnam'd Forms: Blake and Textuality*, ed. Nelson Hilton and Thomas A. Vogler (Berkeley: University of California Press, 1986), p. 4.

6 See Robert F. Gleckner, 'Edmund Spenser and Blake's Printing House in Hell', *South Atlantic Quarterly* 81 (1982): 311–22.

7 Blake, *The Early Illuminated Books*, p. 215.

8 Obliterated in the Norton source text (hence in square brackets there) and in half of the copies of *MHH*: *Blake's Poetry and Designs*, ed. Johnson and Grant, p. 78n.

9 Martin K. Nurmi, '[On *The Marriage of Heaven and Hell*]', in *Blake's Poetry and Designs*, ed. Johnson and Grant, p. 556.

10 Nurmi, '[On *The Marriage of Heaven and Hell*]', p. 557.

11 Harold Bloom, *The Visionary Company: A Reading of English Romantic Poetry*, rev. and enlarged edn (Ithaca, NY: Cornell University Press, 1971), p. 66.

12 Percy Bysshe Shelley, *The Major Works*, ed. Zachary Leader and Michael O'Neill, Oxford World's Classics (Oxford: Oxford University Press, 2003), p. 692.

13 Blake, *The Early Illuminated Books*, p. 124.

14 See Blake, *The Early Illuminated Books*, p. 122.

15 For discussion, see Northrop Frye, *Fearful Symmetry: A Study of William Blake* (Princeton: Princeton University Press, 1947), pp. 227–9.

16 Morton D. Paley, *Energy and the Imagination: A Study of the Development of Blake's Thought* (Oxford: Clarendon Press, 1970), p. 127.

17 Paley, *Energy and the Imagination*, p. 124.

18 Thomas Hardy, *Selected Poems*, ed. Tim Armstrong (London: Longman, 2009).

Mary Robinson, *Sappho and Phaon*

Mary Robinson's sonnet sequence *Sappho and Phaon: In a Series of Legitimate Sonnets* (1796) appears in the wake of much experimentation by other poets with a form revived in the years leading up to and in the Romantic period, the sonnet. (See the discussion of Charlotte Smith's *Elegaic Sonnets*, above.) The sequence presents in lyrical form Sappho's feelings about her love for the young man, Phaon, and deploys the strict rhyme scheme of the Petrarchan form in cunning tension with the depiction of a 'mind, enlightened', as Robinson puts it in her address 'To the Reader', 'by the most exquisite talents, yet yielding to the destructive control of ungovernable passions'.[1] Robinson, quoting Milton's 'O Nightingale, that on yon bloomy spray' as 'an example of the measure' (p. 144) in which she composes, obliges the reader to look hard at the word 'legitimate' and the claim for poetic authenticity and authority that it enforces; she 'is', in Daniel Robinson's words, 'bolder than that of any of the eighteenth-century poets in explicitly asserting her poetic legitimacy as both a woman and a poet'.[2]

The sequence shows Robinson's roots in an idiom of sensibility, dominated by consideration of the rival claims of passion and reason, moving between abstraction, image, personification, and intense feeling. The sequence is rightly said by Jerome McGann to 'explore the ambiguous significance of passion and reason, chastity and pleasure, feeling and thought'.[3] Sonnet XXIV typifies Robinson's ability to make poetry out of contrast. The moon is addressed in the opening quatrain as 'Sublimely still, and beautifully pale' (4), an adept conflation of Burke's categories of the sublime and the beautiful. Yet immediately a question undermines its

The Romantic Poetry Handbook, First Edition. Michael O'Neill and Madeleine Callaghan.
© 2018 John Wiley & Sons Ltd. Published 2018 by John Wiley & Sons Ltd.

emblematic authority and opens up a wholly different picture, that of the passion-disrupted self:

> What can thy cool and placid eye avail,
>   Where fierce despair absorbs the mental sight,
>   While inbred glooms the vagrant thoughts invite,
> To tempt the gulph where howling fiends assail?   (5–8)

The sequence finds its true subject in that phrase 'inbred glooms', an inward unhappiness that is generated through the 'mental' operations suggested by 'invite'. Placed in the rhyme-position at the line-ending, the verb is seemingly restricted, before the real nature of the invitation extended to 'the vagrant thoughts' is brought out by the final line of the octave. The poetry may risk melodrama, but its concern with 'vagrant thoughts' is aesthetically redemptive, especially since the phrase catches up and internalizes the earlier mention of Phaon's 'vagrant heart' (IX.13). And in its approach towards a 'gulph' the poem cleverly prefigures Sappho's final suicidal 'leap of Leucata' (p. 154), the subject of Sonnets XLI to XLIII. The sestet illustrates Robinson's control of tone, as it steals away from 'fierce despair' and 'inbred glooms' to reaffirm 'the temper'd power' (9) of 'Night'. And yet its long melodious invocation of that 'power' concludes in a subtle and affecting recognition of nature's and poetry's inadequacy: 'Yet, vain is ev'ry charm! and vain the hour, / That brings to madd'ning love, no soothing dream!' (13–14). The last two lines are part of the sestet's interlacing triple rhymes, but they have the adversative kick of a final couplet resistant to what has preceded it. The reader is left grasping at what the poetry wants but cannot supply: a 'soothing dream' to provide solace for 'madd'ning love'.

The poetry manages to avoid self-pity through its adroit handling of abstractions, as here, as though 'madd'ning love' were an incurable illness to be diagnosed in the moment of being felt.[4] Mere effusiveness is checked, too, by the poetry's technical polish. For one thing, words that on their own may seem to risk over-emphasis, such as 'madd'ning', take on nuanced meanings through the fact of skilful repetition: the same word occurs in XLI as emotion colours landscape and 'madd'ning billows combat with the skies!' (4). For another, the metrical control is impressive. So in XXVII Sappho asserts, this time looking, in an anticipation of Keats's famous sonnet, at 'ye bright Stars' (1): 'Love strikes the feeling heart with ruthless hand, / And only spares the breast which dullness shields' (7–8). The elegant phrasing uses the iambic pulse of the metre to shape a clarity that is both 'feeling' and 'ruthless'. The idea that anyone with sensitivity will suffer the pangs of love is offered wryly as evidence of nature's way of being 'capricious' (9) since it 'but bestows / The fine affections of the soul, to prove / A keener sense of desolating woes' (9–11); the rhyme delivers 'woes' with a 'fine' inevitability.

That said, Robinson is often at her most persuasive when she portrays her speaker as least in control of her feelings. Sonnet VI uses a series of anaphoric questions governed by 'Is it' to ask about the nature of love and gives a credible sense of love's obsessiveness:

> Is it to chant *one* name in ceaseless lays,
>   To hear no words that other tongues can say,
>   To watch the pale moon's melancholy ray,
> To chide in fondness, and in folly praise? (5–8)

Coleridge admired Mary Robinson, and she him, as 'To the Poet Coleridge' reveals, with its series of dazzled and dazzling references to *Kubla Khan*,[5] as when she writes intertextually: 'I'll mark thy *sunny dome*, and view / Thy *Caves of Ice*, thy fields of dew!' (13–14). The above lines conclude with a possible source of his 'Words of unmeant bitterness' (665) in the Conclusion to Part 2 of *Christabel*. Simpler here than elsewhere, Robinson is also nuanced, as she implies through the near-chime of her two rhymes the concern of the lover with the '*one* name' of her beloved. The sonnet sustains itself with great skill until it concludes: 'Is it to loath the light and wish to die? / For these I feel, – and feel that they are Love' (13–14). The poem gives the impression of feeling what might be called generic emotions with a vivid subjectivity.

The sequence is remarkable for its inwardness. It studies with poise a 'mind' – the word is central to Sonnet XI, among others – that is aware it is not master over its own unruly household. This poem pays ironic homage to 'Reason! vaunted Sov'reign of the mind' (1), as the very rhyme words prompted by 'mind' indicate: it is asked mockingly whether it can 'the vagrant fancy bind' (4), where 'vagrant' again serves as a marker of an instability that cannot be stilled; it has to reckon with 'sighs of Love' (6) that are 'capricious as the wav'ring wind' (5) and with the sobering fact that 'Pleasure's hands the sheaves of Truth unbind' (8). The cumulative effect of the poem is to subvert the very idea of rational control, even as the poem's idiom maintains an air of analytic grasp. There is a proto-Shelleyan quality to this duality, and the poem ends with lines that would not be out of place in some of Shelley's more disenchanted writing: 'Then, what wert thou? O! Idol of the wise! / A visionary theme! – a gorgeous shade!' (13–14). Certainly, in her blend of precision and passion, Robinson offers in *Sappho and Phaon* one of the Romantic period's most compelling delineations of the clash between sensibility and the bitter facts of experience.

The *English Review* sorrowfully regretted the presence of 'the contortions and dislocations of Della Crusca' in the sequence, opining that 'If she had followed nature, seldom more justly and elegantly represented than in her own mind, free from the shackles of imitation, she would have produced sonnets nearer akin to the natural, pathetic, and passionate Sappho'.[6] Ironically, the reviewer wanted Robinson to be more 'natural', 'free from the shackles of imitation', more, as we might say loosely, 'Romantic', closer to the example of Smith in her *Elegiac Sonnets*. But Romantics are also poets who need a mask to say what they think and feel, and the adoption of the persona of Sappho gives Robinson access to a forebear that makes possible her own commitment to rhetorical intensities of feeling and complexities of figuration. Sonnet XXXV is an example of how 'imitation' licenses an extreme yet artful language of despair and anguish: 'Phaon is false! and hopeless Sappho dies!' (8), writes Robinson, as she goes on to imagine what Phaon might have said to take the edge off his alleged falsity. As often in Romantic poetry, 'passion' is not simply expressed; it is psychologized, subjected to reflective 'dislocations', so that the speaker's emotions analyse themselves in the process of expression. This poem's sestet reads as follows:

> 'Farewell! my Lesbian love, you might have said,'
> Such sweet remembrance had some pity prov'd,
> 'Or coldly thus, farewell, Oh! Lesbian maid!'
> No task severe, for one so fondly lov'd!
> The gentle thought had sooth'd my wander'ing shade,
> From life's dark valley, and its thorns remov'd!   (9–14)

The exclamation marks hardly suggest the presence of a cool presiding intelligence, but such an intelligence is, indeed, present. The quoted lines are from Pope's *Sappho to Phaon*, involving a further layer of intertextuality.[7] Robinson makes them part of a dialogic, internalized drama, one in which the artifices of poetry serve affective self-exploration. The speaker enters a realm of conditional reprieve: the 'had' of the penultimate line means 'would have' and the final rhyme suggests a knowingly futile wish to be 'remov'd' from the struggles involving love and proof articulated earlier in the poem and in the sequence as a whole. The reader is made doubly aware of 'life's dark valley and its thorns' as the speaker expresses her wish to escape them. Through such double motions of poetic art and affective recoil the sequence establishes its claims upon us.

Notes

1   *Mary Robinson: Selected Poems*, ed. Judith Pascoe (Peterborough, Ont.: Broadview, 2000), p. 149. Robinson's poetry is cited from this edition.

2 'Reviving the Sonnet: Women Romantic Poets and the Sonnet Claim', *European Romantic Review* 6 (1995): 98–127 (at 117).

3 Jerome McGann, *The Poetics of Sensibility: A Revolution in Poetic Style* (Oxford: Clarendon Press, 1996), p. 109.

4 McGann reads the sequence, through the implicit feminism and exaltation of a 'Sapphic' perspective, to be 'finally a political and republican work' (*The Poetics of Sensibility*, p. 114). But its emphasis on desolation and loss suggests that Robinson's republican ideal, if that is what it is, is no Utopia from which suffering has been banished.

5 See Daniel Robinson, 'From "Mingled Measure" to "Ecstatic Measures": Mary Robinson's Reading of "Kubla Khan"', *The Wordsworth Circle* 26 (1995): 4–7.

6 See *Mary Robinson*, ed. Pascoe, p. 385.

7 As pointed out in *Mary Robinson*, ed. Pascoe, p. 175n.

Robert Burns, Lyrics

Robert Burns is a poet who calls into question periodicizing decisions made with respect to Romantic poetry. There is a strong case for regarding his collection, *Poems, Chiefly in the Scottish Dialect* (1786), as inaugurating Romantic poetry proper. The volume uses devices such as personification familiar in eighteenth-century poetry, but in its radical sympathies, subversive ironies, and pursuit of greater conversational naturalness it is a companion as well as forerunner of the poetry of Blake, Wordsworth, and Coleridge. Above all, it is written in a newly original style, at once skilfully artful and eloquently demotic, fusing formal skill with colloquial vigour, standard English and Scottish dialect. This section looks at a handful of his poems.

With the novels of Scott, Burns's poetry represents the best of what Murray Pittock calls 'Scottish Romanticism', even as regionalism has living commerce with a wider universalism, evident in 'Man Was Made to Mourn, A Dirge'. Unlike Wordsworth's poems of encounter, this meeting between narrator and 'rev'rend Sage' (10) begins with questions from the person encountered, whose speech is less one of counsel than of saddened awareness that 'Man was made to mourn', words whose calculated ambiguity concludes stanzas 3 to 6 (24, 32, 40, 48): the speaker implies both that man is created in such a way that he will inevitably be forced to mourn and that man is treated in such a way by his fellow man that he will be compelled to mourn.[1] 'Mourn' appears as the final word from the third stanza to the concluding eleventh stanza, and the monorhyming displays Burns's virtuosic skills, as in the famous conclusion to stanza 7:

> And Man, whose heav'n-erected face,
>   The smiles of love adorn,
> Man's inhumanity to Man
>   Makes countless thousands mourn!   (53–6)

The stanza captures the accents of incredulous speech, its opening two lines failing to resolve into a sentence, as they pass into the memorable aphorism that follows, obliging us to hold in suspension the fact that the same creature whose 'face, / The smiles of love adorn' can be relied upon to demonstrate, illogically but inexorably, 'inhumanity' to his fellows. Written in standard English, the poem is bitingly intelligent in its reflectiveness: if, asks the speaker, I was meant to be 'yon lordling's slave' (65), 'Why was an independent wish / E'er planted in my mind?' (67–8). If such social subjugation is not an inherently intended part of the scheme of things, it goes on, 'why am I subject to / His cruelty, or scorn? / Or why has Man the will and pow'r / To make his fellow mourn?' (69–72). The cast of mind is one of Enlightenment universalism; the trenchant compassion and inquiring mind informing the sharply turned phrases is Burns's own. The questions asked by the poem add up to a revisiting of the traditional *unde malum*: whence evil? Is it innate or conditioned? Can it be explained or eradicated? Burns's phrasing is deftly turned across the line-ending so that 'will' and 'power' each, with driven near-sadistic intent, govern the imperative (grammatical and seemingly instinctual) 'To make his fellow mourn'. The poem reminds us that Romantic poetry, for all its hopeful yearnings and affirmations, dwells on and is haunted by the problem of evil.

Shelley is likely to have remembered that stanza in *The Triumph of Life*, when the narrator laments that 'power and will / In opposition rule our mortal day' (228–9); his variation pits ineffectual idealistic 'will' against hegemonic 'power'. Burns is an immediate forerunner of and a significant presence in the work of other Romantics. He features, with Chatterton, as an exemplar of the plunge from 'gladness' (48) to 'despondency and madness' (49) that Wordsworth fears in 'Resolution and Independence' is the virtually inevitable lot of the poet. When Wordsworth thinks of Burns as 'Him who walk'd in glory and in joy / Behind his plough, upon the mountain-side' (45–6), he does more than celebrate Burns as a peasant or labouring-class poet; his rhythms mime the steady tread of the ploughman and the poet's steadfast capacity to walk 'in glory and in joy'. (There is in the lines a possible half-echo of Vaughan's 'I see them walking in an air of glory'.)[2]

Keats finds himself troubled with complicated feelings in his sonnet 'On Visiting the Tomb of Burns'. Something interferes with the full expression of homage to the poet he names in the second-to-last line as 'Great shadow' (13), something projected by 'Fickly imagination and sick pride' (11). Yet he responds to greatness, as does Coleridge in his repeated singling out of the image of pleasure's transience from Burns's comic narrative masterpiece 'Tam o' Shanter': 'Like snow that falls upon a River / A moment white then gone for ever—'.[3]

The image's poignancy derives from its proto-Byronic refusal to be either wholly serious or merely playful. It follows the mock-heroic yet democratically vigorous account of Tam as 'glorious, / O'er a' the ills o' life victorious' (57–8). 'Kings may be blest' (57), but Tam is in touch with the essence of happiness, as Burns wryly sees that elusive condition: good fellowship while drunk. The lines that follow move from Bruegel to Mozart, from the fuggy, illusory warmth of the alehouse to snow shivering into blank non-being down a falling river. They move, too, for a moment into standard English, a supple shift that reveals how Burns can code-switch to eloquent effect, as he offers images of vanishing pleasure that anticipate effects in Shelley, Byron, and Keats: pleasures are 'like the borealis race, / That flit ere you can point their place', where the flitting outruns the attempted pointing, 'Or like the rainbow's lovely form / Evanishing amid the storm' (63–6), where the 'form' precedes the obliterating 'storm' and 'Evanishing', through its polysyllabic length, makes us see the process of fading.

There are aspects of Byron's later practice in the poem's deft handling of humorous rhyme, as when Burns's narrator, prurient eyes on a stalk, imagines that, had the women Tam sees been 'queans, / A' plump and strapping in their teens' (151–2), 'I wad hae gi'en them off my hurdies, / For ae blink o' the bonie burdies!' (157–8). Again, the horrors of the scene were so 'awefu' (141) that 'even to name' them 'wad be unlawfu'' (142): a rhyme which in full English form occurs in *Don Juan*, canto 3, when the narrator teasingly mocks the prudish reader with a sidelong glance at where 'unlawful' reading led Dante's ill-fated lovers, Paolo and Francesca: 'Then if you'd have them wedded, please to shut / The book which treats of this erroneous pair, / Before the consequences grow too awful; / 'Tis dangerous to read of loves unlawful' (93–6).

For Wordsworth, Coleridge, Byron, and Keats, then, Burns is a 'great' poet who is associated with complexities of feeling. In Shelley he has a frank candour about the erotic that makes Wordsworth (or Peter Bell) seem 'A solemn and unsexual man' (551) in one of his developing and diminishing guises. At the heart of his greatness as a poet is his poetry's ability to move between opposites, often embodied in the poetry's diction. A remarkable feature of his work, as already suggested, is its linguistic code-switching.

Burns is the poet of Scottish dialect and a more elevated, standard English. 'Duan Second' of 'The Vision' opens in the second manner, with just a suspicion of mock-heroic mimicry, as the Muse Coila appears reassuringly:

> With musing-deep, astonish'd stare,
> I view'd the heavenly-seeming *Fair*;
> A whisp'ring *throb* did witness bear
>   Of kindred sweet,
> When with an elder Sister's art
>   She did me greet.   (133–8)

Latinate, on its stilts, this adapts the standard 'Habbie' stanza favoured by Burns to the demands of a polished literary performance.[4] Yet the fact that the Muse has a Gaelic name, Coila, suggests a wish to tweak the nose of London-centred norms, and Burns has already set the stylistic cat among the pigeons with his vigorous, funny, and dialect-packed self-recrimination for wasting his time writing poetry:

> I started, mutt'ring blockhead! coof!
> And heav'd on high my wauket loof,
> To swear by a' yon starry roof,
>   Or some rash aith,
> That I henceforth would be *rhyme-proof*
>   Till my last breath—
>
> When click! the *string* the *snick* did draw;   (31–7)

The 'wauket loof' (thickened palm of the hand) speaks of hard toil; 'coof' has been glossed by 'blockhead' already (Burns sometimes yokes dialect and translation together). Bound together by rhyme, they zip with exhilarating exasperation off the page. Burns gives dramatic body to his 'rash aith', even as he is amused by the spectacle of his own self-censure, neatly exposing its would-be '*rhyme-proof*' condition as impossible by using the word as the fourth *a*-rhyme in the stanza. One might pause, too, to admire the transition at the start of the next stanza: 'When click!' changes the mood and alerts the ear. Overall, the poem manages to blend expressive lyric, one indebted to the *aisling* mode in which a muse in the guise of a beautiful young woman appears to a poet, with an address on the state-of-the-Scottish (and English) poetic nation.

    Burns delights in splicing high and low cultural references. His 'Address to the Deil' is among the most memorable Romantic-period responses to Milton, lines from whose *Paradise Lost* supply the poem with its epigraph: 'O Prince, O chief of many thronèd pow'rs, / That led the embattl'd Seraphim to war'. What follows put solemn elevation to flight: 'O Thou, whatever title suit thee! / Auld Hornie, Satan, Nick, or Clootie' (1–2). The poem's rhymes and diction have a zestful, high-spirited inventiveness, raiding the lexicon of Scottish dialect to retell the old story with impish delight. Adam and Eve are 'youthfu' lovers' 'pair'd' (86) 'Lang syne in *Eden*'s bonie yard' (85), a way of putting it that suggests the fall was into Calvinist castigation of 'love'. Satan, the humorous villain of the piece, spoils the lovers' pleasure: 'Then you, ye auld, snick-drawing dog! / Ye cam to Paradise incog, / An' played on man a cursed brogue, / (Black be your fa'!)' (93–6): suddenly Satan's incursion into Paradise is brought down to earth and close to home, 'a snick-drawing dog', a crafty, sneaky operator working mischief in disguise.

The poet's commitment to an uncensorious mode of looking at life and love shows in his diction – the slangy casualness (that clinches a rhyme) of 'incog', for example. Burn's retelling of *Paradise Lost* is done self-mockingly. He imagines Satan 'thinkan, / A certain *Bardie's* rantin, drinkin' (115–16). At the same time there is a quality of perfect balance between self-assurance and humour as Burns, in effect, does what he says cannot be done, namely to speak of Satan's doings in '*Lallan* tongue, or *Erse*, / In Prose or Rhyme' (113–15), the last phrase an allusion to Milton's Ariosto-inspired claim to sing of 'Things unattempted yet in prose or rhyme' (*Paradise Lost* 1.16). The poem's ethics reside in its 'devil-may-care' verbal devilry, Burn capturing with unpatronizing glee and energy the stuff of popular superstition:

> When twilight did my *Graunie* summon,
> To say her pray'rs, douse, honest woman!
> Aft 'yont the dyke she's heard you bumman,
>   Wi' eerie drone … (31–4)

The effect is not simply to mock 'my *Graunie*', partly because of the homespun diction: 'heard you bumman' has a downrightness that catches out Satan rather than '*Graunie*'.

'To a Mountain-Daisy, On Turning One Down, with the Plough, in April—1786' spans close observation with semi-humorous allegorizing. The poet has cut down a daisy with his ploughshare, and if he treats this incident with incomparable delicacy, it is because his delicacy is not self-regarding in the 'sentimental tradition', even if that tradition sponsors his act of contrition. Burns's tenderness towards the daisy, caught in the run of adjectives with which the poem opens, 'Wee, modest, crimson-tipped flow'r' (1), is self-aware, controlled, and wry. The line quoted humanizes the flower, in part through the address to it as a 'thou', and yet it brings a botanical accuracy to the description. Burns concedes the flower's toughness, its ability to withstand the lark's springy weight and 'the bitter-biting *North*' (13), using the repeated rhymes of the 'Habbie' stanza to suggest the daisy's resilience as it 'Adorns the histie *stibble-field*, / Unseen, alane' (23–4).

The poem makes its way along a tightrope, managing not to fall into the clutches of sentimentality or jocoseness. Again, diction does much to convey Burns's fresh perspective; 'Adorns', in the lines just quoted, could have been a tired poeticism, but in the context of 'the histie *stibble-field*' it recovers a brave allure. Rhyme is a marker of modulating feeling and retained control at the moment describing how 'now the *share* uptears thy bed, / And low thou lies!' (29–30). The allegorizing moral – when the daisy's plight is compared to 'the fate of artless Maid' (31), 'simple Bard' (37), and '*suffering worth*' (43) – works easily and effectively, as Burns slides into standard English, maintaining his sympathy through an unshowy extension of compassion. And the poem's conclusion is both prepared-for and surprising, as the poet addresses, not the daisy, but himself as 'thou', probably recalling the close of Gray's 'Elegy Written in a Country Churchyard' in which the elegist turns to elegize a version of himself, but also anticipating Romantic recognitions of the way in which the self is inextricable from any train of meditation:

> Eve'n thou who mourn'st the *Daisy's* fate,
> *That fate is thine*—no distant date;
> Stern Ruin's *plough-share* drives, elate,
>   Full on thy bloom,
> Till crush'd beneath the *furrow's* weight,
>   Shall be thy doom!   (49–54)

Burns's command of pathos and his artistic power, in evidence here, help to explain his importance for the Romantic period.

Comparable sympathies and skills are at play in 'To a Mouse, on Turning Her Up in Her Nest with the Plough, November, 1783'. Burns addresses the mouse with heartfelt if serio-comic tenderness as 'Wee, sleekit, cow'rin, tim'rous beastie' (1), the initial spondee slowing down the line and ensuring attention is paid to the 'beastie'. The procession of adjectives moves from noticing the mouse's tiny size and sleekness to empathizing with its fear. The poet rises to his subject; makes us see a small incident from a different perspective. His tone is genuine yet mock-heroic as he apologiszs in the second stanza:

> I'm truly sorry Man's dominion
> Has broken Nature's social union,
> An' justifies that ill opinion
>   Which makes thee startle
> At me, thy poor earth-born companion,
>   An' *fellow-mortal*!   (7–12)

'Nature's social union' is a phrase that bridges attitudes to nature in James Thomson and in Wordsworth, compacting a quasi-metaphysical understanding and a deeply felt apprehension. The syntax spins round in a circle as the speaker, apologizer for and representative of 'man's dominion', enacts recognition of the 'startling' fact that he is an 'earth-born companion / An' *fellow-mortal*' of the mouse. What that rhyme between 'startle' and 'mortal' springs into being is the startling sense that man and mouse are fellow-mortals. What follows builds on this recognition with witty dismay, until the poet is able to utter the aphoristic statement that 'The best laid schemes o' *Mice* an' *Men* / Gang aft agley' (39–40) and to end with a final discovery of difference that centres the poem on its speaker's anxiety about the past and the future:

> Still thou art blest compared wi' *me*!
> The *present* only toucheth thee:
> But Och! I *backward* cast my e'e
> > On prospects drear!
> And *forward*, tho' I cannot *see*,
> > I *guess* an' *fear*!   (43–8)

There's wry humour here in the sharp, crisp wording; yet there's an overt cry too, as Burns seems to speak from his and to the reader's heart, as he – simply, memorably – encapsulates the human condition as it invests itself in him, unable to 'see' into the future, only too vulnerable to the impulse to '*guess* an' *fear*'. The result of such rhetorical control is a body of work enlisted for many different causes, but clearly a current in the mainstream of Romantic poetry.

Notes

1. Robert Burns, *Complete Poems and Songs*, ed. James Kinsley (Oxford: Oxford University Press, 1969).
2. For a thought-provoking critique of these lines, see Robert Crawford, *Robert Burns and Cultural Authority* (Iowa: University of Iowa Press, 1997), pp. 175–6.
3. See *Coleridge on Shakespeare: The Text of the Lectures of 1811–12*, ed. R. A. Foakes (Abingdon: Routledge, 2005 [1971]), p. 34. Burns's lines are quoted as given in Foakes.
4. A six-line stanza, as Wikipedia notes, rhyming *aaabab*, with tetrameter *a* lines and dimeter *b* lines, named after the sixteenth-century piper Habbie Simpson.

William Wordsworth and
S. T. Coleridge, *Lyrical Ballads*

Lyrical Ballads ushered in a revolution in Romantic poetics despite its understated 'Advertisement' describing the majority of the poems in the collection as 'experiments' on the public's taste.[1] The volume was first published in 1798. The second edition of 1800 included a second volume of poetry largely by Wordsworth, and 1802 saw a revised and expanded Preface and minor revisions made to the existing poetry. The first edition was published anonymously as a joint enterprise between Wordsworth and Coleridge, and this decision helped to speed its critical success. But the sales were slow, and led to Sara Coleridge's disconsolate though inaccurate sense that 'The Lyrical Ballads are laughed at and disliked by all with very few excepted'.[2] Although Robert Southey, a close friend of both poets, offered a disappointing response to the volume in the *Critical Review*,[3] it garnered some excellent reviews. Despite the apparent tentativeness of describing the poems in the collection as 'experiments', even the first edition seems sure of its artistic principles, warning the reader to expect 'feelings of strangeness and aukwardness [*sic*]' ('Advertisement', *Lyrical Ballads*, p. 3).

The focus on marginalized, impoverished, and rustic figures in the poetry was both revolutionary and unsettling. Wordsworth and Coleridge took aim at accepted subject matter and ideas of poetic diction that they refused to merely inherit. Marrying moral and aesthetic beauty in the poetry, the 1802 Preface defines the poet as 'the rock of defence of human nature; an upholder and preserver' ('Preface', *Lyrical Ballads*, p. 106). Rather than cementing the view of Wordsworth as propounding his 'egotistical sublime',[4] as Fiona Stafford points up, 'Wordsworth is talking here of Poetry in the grandest and widest sense'.[5] The *Lyrical Ballads* is a manifesto for the new kind of poetry typical of the Romantic period.

The Romantic Poetry Handbook, First Edition. Michael O'Neill and Madeleine Callaghan.
© 2018 John Wiley & Sons Ltd. Published 2018 by John Wiley & Sons Ltd.

The 1798 single-volume edition of *Lyrical Ballads* opens with *The Rime of the Ancyent Marinere*, Coleridge's chilling and estranging ballad that deepens rather than solves its poetic enigma. The 1800 and 1802 editions, however, begin with 'Expostulation and Reply' and 'The Tables Turned', magnifying the combative tone of some sections of the Preface where Wordsworth takes aim against the 'gaudiness and inane phraseology of many modern writers' ('Preface', *Lyrical Ballads*, p. 96) as he asserts that 'Poetry is the image of man and nature' ('Preface', *Lyrical Ballads*, p. 105). What 'Expostulation and Reply' terms 'wise passiveness' ('Expostulation and Reply', 24) where the poet contemplates nature rather than looks for descriptions of nature in books, enacts, in miniature, the principles on which *Lyrical Ballads* rests. Wordsworth and Coleridge emphasize the immersion of poetry in nature without advocating any anti-intellectual rejection of the poetic tradition. The simple metre and rhymes of 'The Tables Turned' are suggestive of the ballad metre without quite employing it, as in Spenser's July eclogue from *The Shepheardes Calender*.[6] The naturalness of the stanza lends itself to speech as Wordsworth calls upon poetic tradition to defend Nature as a means of moral guidance:

> One impulse from a vernal wood
> May teach you more of man;
> Of moral evil and of good,
> Than all the sages can.   ('The Tables Turned', 21–4)

The poem becomes a kind of 'impulse from a vernal wood'; the elegant simplicity of the diction underlines the naturalness promoted by the content.

Form and content work hand in hand in *Lyrical Ballads* as the preoccupations of the 'Preface' echo throughout the collection. 'Goody Blake and Harry Gill: A True Story', praised by contemporary reviewers, traces the genesis of a curse similar to that of *The Rime of the Ancient Mariner*, but here, Wordsworth removes the mysterious quality of Coleridge's poem, opting instead to make explicit the warning against greed and disdain for one's fellow man. The tetrameter adds verve and pace to the poetry, where the narrative and didactic quality of the poem is supported by its strong rhythms and rhyme. Goody Blake's poverty and Harry Gill's wealth and greed, and her revenge at God's hands, are gleefully related by the narrator. This sense of social justice burns equally strongly in many poems in the collection, but 'Simon Lee: The Old Huntsman', while lacking the persecuting figure in 'Goody Blake and Harry Gill', dwells on the misery of life for Simon and Old Ruth, the 'poorest of the poor' ('Simon Lee', 60), in contrast to Simon's earlier life as a huntsman, 'full of glee' ('Simon Lee', 18). Slyly sending up his responsibilities as a narrator, the speaker mock-apologetically comments, 'How patiently you've waited' ('Simon Lee', 70), going on to tell the story-greedy reader to engage in more 'silent thought' ('Simon Lee', 74) so as to find 'A tale in every thing' ('Simon Lee', 76). The responsibility falls to the reader, with Wordsworth including a single incident for the reader to consider. Watching Simon Lee struggle to chop the root of an old tree, the narrator takes over and with one blow, cuts through the root which had caused the older man so much trouble. The final stanza affectingly describes Simon Lee's thanks and praise and their effect on the narrator:

—I've heard of hearts unkind, kind deeds
With coldness still returning:
Alas! the gratitude of men
Hath oftner left me mourning. ('Simon Lee', 100–3)

The opposition of unkind and kind points up the possible callous response to kindness, but here, as Andrew Griffin writes, Wordsworth makes 'an oblique, sad discovery of tragedy in gratitude'.[7] Closing with a note of pathos after what promised to be a narrative poem thrusts the reader into an emotional situation that demands their engagement with Simon Lee's and the broader situation. As Wordsworth affirms, 'we have all of us one human heart' ('The Old Cumberland Beggar: A Description', 146).

Despite Wordsworth's and Coleridge's often positive view of nature and the countryside, *Lyrical Ballads* does not present rural life as entirely without problems. In 'The Thorn', Wordsworth reveals the claustrophobic nature of small town life. In his preface to the poem, Wordsworth offers a highly detailed account of the speaker who is introduced as a superstitious character who creates or magnifies an air of mystery in any given story. The poem itself, as narrated by such a character, is built on conjecture and questioning, where the almost neurotic speaker punctuates his insinuations with breathless asides such as "Tis said' ('The Thorn', XIII.137) and 'some remember well' ('The Thorn', XV.163). The almost pathological curiosity of the speaker suggests that the story reveals more about the psychological state of Martha Ray's watchers than Martha Ray herself. Lacking sympathy and understanding beyond a thirst for knowledge, the speaker seems to be a poor interpreter who pieces together gossip even while pretending that he refuses to engage in such habits: 'I cannot tell how this may be' ('The Thorn', XXIII.243). Such lack of sympathy is not confined to 'The Thorn'. The speaker of 'We are seven', in his attempt to reason with the little girl, reveals his lack of imagination in comparison to the richness of her inner world. Quizzing her on her family in the hopes of forcing her to recognize that 'ye are only five' ('We are seven', 36), the small girl's responses are touching for her insistence that 'we are seven' ('We are seven', 63) despite the adult's upbraiding tone. As she attempts to involve her dead siblings when she sings to them and plays by the side of their graves, death is a part of life in her imaginative framework.

The poems in *Lyrical Ballads* hold communion with one another; ideas, distinct poetic forms, and voices move from poem to poem as if to bind the collection. 'The Nightingale, a Conversational Poem', renamed 'The Nightingale, written in April, 1798' in the 1802 edition of *Lyrical Ballads*, is written in blank verse that wittily overturns poetic conventions in favour of poetic observations of nature. Quoting Milton's description of the nightingale ('"Most musical, most melancholy!"' 13), Coleridge is less intent on mocking Milton (as his footnote makes clear) than poets who merely echo tired tropes. Turning to his son at the close of the poem, Coleridge hopes to 'make him Nature's playmate' ('The Nightingale, a Conversational Poem', 92), one that will hear the nightingale's natural joy rather than its famed melancholy. Coleridge's fatherhood forms the theme for many of his poems, from 'Frost at Midnight' (not collected in *Lyrical Ballads*) to 'Anecdote for Fathers', which was collected in all editions.

The larger sense of using humour to challenge and remould perceptions is taken up by Wordsworth's 'The Idiot Boy' where the love between parent and child is represented as the poem's gentle wit celebrates rather than laments Johnny's difference. The close of the poem, where Betty Foy, her son Johnny, and her ill neighbour, Susan Gale, are reunited, shows Johnny adopting a triumphal tone:

'The Cocks did crow to-whoo, to-whoo,
And the Sun did shine so cold.'
—Thus answered Johnny in his glory,
And that was all his travel's story.   ('The Idiot Boy', 460–3)

Wordsworth refers to 'Idiots' in his letter to John Wilson defending his poem with a scriptural expression, '*their life is hidden with God*' (*Lyrical Ballads*, p. 319). Though Susan and Betty cannot understand Johnny fully, Johnny is glorious in the moment of his explanation of his travels. Betty's maternal love for Johnny shines from the poem, connecting it with 'The Mad Mother' and 'The Complaint of a Forsaken Indian Woman'. 'The Complaint of a Forsaken Indian Woman', shot through with the pain of separation from her son and the lack of understanding from her peers, offers a pitiful portrait of the woman. However, 'The Mad Mother' and its empathy with its subject make the poem seem almost a personal lyric in its intimacy. 'The Mad

Mother' melts into the first person after the opening stanza establishes her appearance and linguistic identity. The poem's sudden move into her voice reveals the terrifying disorientation of the woman, with her obvious adoration of her child juxtaposed with the delusions she suffers, where she imagines 'fiendish faces' ('The Mad Mother', 23) and even 'wicked looks' ('The Mad Mother', 86) from her own son. As Hale Roberts points out, 'no other poem in the 1798 *Lyrical Ballads* is so regular',[8] and such forced formal regularity, compared with the other, more natural and irregularly rhymed poetry in the volume, creates a dangerous sense of artificiality.

Such formal alertness is revealed in Wordsworth's use of the Spenserian stanza in 'The Female Vagrant'. Eschewing Spenser's Faery Land, Wordsworth purges ornaments and its sometimes luxuriant artificiality from his stanzas to make the form serve down-to-earth, if often mysterious, narrative purposes. Avoiding the free enjambment preferred by later Romantic experimenters with the form, such as Byron in *Childe Harold's Pilgrimage* or Shelley in *Adonais*, Wordsworth makes his use of the form seem effortlessly natural. With a social conscience reminiscent of Oliver Goldsmith's *The Deserted Village*,[9] Wordsworth keeps aesthetic beauty firmly in play as he transfers the 'nakedness and simplicity' ('Preface', *Lyrical Ballads*, p. 109) of his style onto the difficult Spenserian stanza. The effect of the changing countryside and urbanization obliges the speaker to travel to the New World, where her family dies of the privations they suffer. On return to England, she is unfit to work, condemning her to vagrancy. Poverty, owing to the new order of a society that does not respect the importance of the 'old hereditary nook' ('The Female Vagrant', 17), claims her for a victim despite her inability to speak 'the beggar's language' ('The Female Vagrant', 153). The distress of poverty in 'The Last of the Flock' makes the speaker, a father, become unnatural: 'God cursed me in my sore distress; / I prayed, yet every day I thought / I loved my children less' ('The Last of the Flock', 86–8). Insistently exposing the human cost of penury and war, Wordsworth's attention to marginal figures forces the reader to feel with his speakers.

'Lines Composed [originally 'Written'] a Few Miles above Tintern Abbey, On Revisiting the Banks of the Wye during a Tour. July 13, 1798' (hereafter 'Tintern Abbey') is the final poem in the 1798 edition of *Lyrical Ballads* and the final poem of the first volume of the two-volume 1800 and 1802 editions. Containing many of the themes that had driven the collection as a whole, 'Tintern Abbey' seems suspended between the past and the future, backward looking in its emphasis on the importance of memory which connects to Wordsworth's sense of poetry as 'emotion recollected in tranquillity' ('Preface', *Lyrical Ballads*, p. 111) and facing the future in its moving address to Dorothy which closes the poem. In 'Tintern Abbey', Wordsworth relates his maturation from his boyish 'glad animal movements' ('Tintern Abbey', 75) to his adult 'sense sublime' ('Tintern Abbey', 96) of the power of nature. Reaching a climax where he affirms his relationship with nature, the visionary yet democratic quality of the poem shines through with the strategic use of 'we', suggestive of every person's capacity to feel that which the poet feels, to experience valuable moments when 'We see into the life of things' (50), a seeing made almost corporeal through the poem's remarkable, pulse-slowing control of rhythm:

> Therefore am I still
> A lover of the meadows and the woods,
> And mountains; and of all that we behold
> From this green earth; of all the mighty world
> Of eye and ear, both what they half create,
> And what perceive; well pleased to recognize
> In nature and the language of the sense,
> The anchor of my purest thoughts, the nurse,
> The guide, the guardian of my heart, and soul
> Of all my moral being.   ('Tintern Abbey', 103–12)

The stately blank verse sounds the accents of passionate speech as the poetry affirms the influence of nature on Wordsworth's life. The repeated phrase 'of all' emphasizes the bounty of nature which forms the centre and circumference of the poet's moral sense. The 'language of the sense' subtly suggests nature as a poet, speaking to the poet and informing the poetry that Wordsworth creates. Jerome McGann argues that 'Abundant recompense' is a 'cherished madness of [Wordsworth's] heart'.[10] Yet here the conviction of nature's importance and its changing role in Wordsworth's life brings out both the poem's pathos and maturity.

'Nutting' and *Michael: A Pastoral Poem*, also written in blank verse, show how, by volume two, Wordsworth had understood the power of the form for uniting narrative and lyric elements. 'Nutting' paints a darkly potent portrait of a boyish vandal. Opening with the beauty of the day in question, 'One of those heavenly days which cannot die' ('Nutting', 3), the poem's speaker engages in a 'merciless ravage' ('Nutting', 43) of what was a 'virgin scene' ('Nutting', 19) only to end the poem on a note of pain as he realizes that 'there is a Spirit in the woods' ('Nutting', 54). The uneasy eroticism that gives way to violence and then to empty pain offers a Fall like to Adam and Eve losing paradise, but Wordsworth keeps possible analogies implied rather than explicitly stated in 'Nutting'. Such lightness of touch is vital to *Michael: A Pastoral Poem*, which relates the tale of Michael and his wife, Isabel, when they send their son, Luke, to work in London to raise money to avoid selling the land. As in *The Brothers* and 'The Female Vagrant', Wordsworth is concerned with the loss of land that divides families and fragments villages. Leading the reader to feel for Michael, the humble shepherd, Wordsworth's poem has serious moral ends: 'The two poems [*The Brothers* and *Michael*] that I have mentioned were written with a view to show that men who do not wear fine clothes can feel deeply' (Letter to Charles James Fox, *Lyrical Ballads*, p. 308). But Wordsworth does not simply create poetry to propound a didactic message. Tracy Ware suggests the importance of the biblical story of Abraham and Isaac to *Michael*,[11] as noted in our Introduction, and Wordsworth's artistry builds empathy throughout the poem as the reader learns to feel deeply for Michael.

Critics have labelled *Lyrical Ballads* as either revolutionary or reactionary,[12] but the poetry itself remains morally and aesthetically charged through its focus on marginalized figures, the self as half-created by the natural world, and the sustained attention to form and metre and their effect on the reader. Wordsworth's and Coleridge's new vision for poetry spoke to both the contemporary moment and future generations of reader; the 'certain colouring of the imagination' ('Preface', *Lyrical Ballads*, p. 97) that suffuses *Lyrical Ballads* continues to inspire.

Notes

1 William Wordsworth and Samuel Taylor Coleridge, 'Advertisement', in *Lyrical Ballads, 1798 and 1802*, ed. with intro. and notes by Fiona Stafford, Oxford World's Classics (Oxford: Oxford University Press, 2013), p. 3. All quotations from *Lyrical Ballads* in this section are from this edition.

2 Sara Coleridge, from a letter to Thomas Poole, March 1799, qtd in *Wordsworth: The Critical Heritage*, vol. 1, *1793–1820*, ed. Robert Woof (London: Routledge, 2001), p. 58.

3 Robert Southey, Unsigned review, *Critical Review* (October 1798): xxiv, 197–204. *Wordsworth: The Critical Heritage*, ed. Woof, p. 65.

4 John Keats, *The Letters of John Keats, 1814–1821*, ed. Hyder E. Rollins, 2 vols (Cambridge, MA: Harvard University Press, 1958), 1.387.

5 Stafford, 'Introduction', in *Lyrical Ballads*, p. xlvi.

6 As pointed out in Brennan O'Donnell's study, *The Passion of Meter: A Study of Wordsworth's Metrical Art* (Kent, OH and London: Kent State University Press, 1995), p. 137.

7 Andrew L. Griffin, 'Wordsworth and the Problem of Imaginative Story: The Case of "Simon Lee"', *PMLA* 92.3 (1977): 392–409 (at 392).

8 Robert Hale, 'Wordsworth's "The Mad Mother": The Poetics and Politics of Identification', *Wordsworth Circle* 39.3 (2008): 108–14 (at 109).

9 As suggested by Janet Sorensen, 'Literature of the Ocean', in *Transatlantic Literary Studies: 1660–1830*, ed. Eve Tavor Bannet and Susan Manning (Cambridge: Cambridge University Press, 2012), pp. 124–38 (at p. 135).

10 Jerome McGann and James Soderholm, 'Byron and Romanticism, a Dialogue', in Jerome J. McGann, *Byron and Romanticism*, ed. James Soderholm, Cambridge Studies in Romanticism 50 (Cambridge: Cambridge University Press, 2002), p. 299.

11 Tracy Ware, 'Historicism Along and Against the Grain: The Case of Wordsworth's "Michael"', *Nineteenth-Century Literature* 49.3 (1994): 360–74 (at 366).

12 See Yu Liu, 'Revaluating Revolution and Radicalness in the *Lyrical Ballads*', *Studies in English Literature, 1500–1900* 36.4 (1996): 747–61, for a discussion that considers the degree of revolutionary content in *Lyrical Ballads*.

William Wordsworth, 'Resolution and Independence'; 'Ode: Intimations of Immortality'; 'Elegiac Stanzas, Suggested by a Picture of Peele Castle in a Storm, Painted by Sir George Beaumont'; 'Surprized by Joy'

This section considers a sample of Wordsworth's finest lyric poems after *Lyrical Ballads*, poems that entwine memory and imagination, loss and fortitude. In 'Resolution and Independence', Wordsworth stages a crisis in his career as a poet and a man. After initially evoking a scene of natural beauty and harmony, the poet-speaker finds himself subject to 'fears, and fancies' (27), 'Dim sadness, and blind thoughts' (28), chilling thoughts of what the future might hold: 'Solitude, pain of heart, distress, and poverty' (35). In this dejected state of mind, reflecting the intense dialogue with Coleridge begun by the first four stanzas of 'Ode: Intimations of Immortality' and continued in Coleridge's 'Dejection: An Ode', he describes an encounter with an old leech gatherer (in its original form the poem was called 'The Leech Gatherer'). As a result of this encounter, one that is at once ordinary and uncanny, the poet is able to resolve the agitation and confusion of his 'untoward thoughts' (54). The old man's courage and sense of purpose inspire the poet to conclude as follows: '"God", said I, "be my help and stay secure; / I'll think of the Leech-gatherer on the lonely moor!"' (146–7).

As is hinted, even in that seemingly cheerful close, the poem combines tones and effects. It gives the continual impression of accommodating disparate feelings and thoughts. Prayer and resolution join hands here, and a key word in the self-admonishing last line is 'lonely'. The adjective takes

The Romantic Poetry Handbook, First Edition. Michael O'Neill and Madeleine Callaghan.
© 2018 John Wiley & Sons Ltd. Published 2018 by John Wiley & Sons Ltd.

the reader back to the previous stanza in which Wordsworth indicates how the leech gatherer's prosaic words ('Yet still I persevere, and find them where I may', 134) affect him:

> While he was talking thus, the lonely place,
> The Old Man's shape, and speech, all troubled me:
> In my mind's eye I seemed to see him pace
> About the weary moors continually,
> Wandering about alone and silently ...   (134–8)

Wordsworth's response is characteristically internal. What matters to him and gives force to the poetry is that this response opens a window onto another 'lonely place': the imaginative mindscape conjured up after the crucial verb 'troubled'. To be 'troubled' in the way evoked in the next three lines, where each line pushes through newly expanded frames of awareness, might frighten another poet. Indeed, the passage contains an element of fear, especially in the image of the old man as a figure 'Wandering about alone and silently': both the strong stress on 'Wandering' and the evocation of a lonely silence prove haunting. For Wordsworth, however, the moment bears witness to the sublime capacity of his own imagination.

In its use of the seven-line, rhyme royal stanza employed by Chaucer in *Troilus and Criseyde*, and by Thomas Chatterton in 'An Excelente Baladc of Charitie', from whom the Romantic poet borrows the alexandrine in the final line, Wordsworth's poem employs to the full possibilities offered by the form of developments, diversion, 'wanderings', processes of imaginative 'resolution and independence'. The poem aims to synthesize, but it is honest about the tendency of its materials to pull apart, as in the ruefully awkward rhyme that closes stanza VII. The stanza has brooded on predecessors such as Thomas Chatterton, 'the marvellous Boy' (43), and Robert Burns, before it concludes: 'We Poets in our youth begin in gladness; / But thereof come in the end despondency and madness' (48–9). 'Gladness' tips over into its rhyme partner 'madness' with a wry sense of inconsequential necessity.

Again, in the elaborate comparison between leech gatherer, stone, and sea-beast, discussed in Wordsworth's 'Preface to *Poems* (1815)' (610–11) as illustrating 'the conferring, the abstracting, and the modifying powers of the Imagination' (610), the writing makes us as much aware of the labour involved in triangulating the three elements implicated in the simile as in the 'just comparison' which Wordsworth claims his words achieve. It is a self-conscious process, and yet one alert to the degree to which writing evades complete rationalizing. The clinching line, 'Such seemed this Man, not all alive nor dead' (71), both builds on and holds in suspension the account of the 'huge Stone' (64) as seemingly 'a thing endued with sense' (68). Indeed, the process of comparison brings out the poet's need to validate his imagination's life. It is a later simile that suggests that the poet's imagination really is alive, when the old man is said to stand 'Motionless as a Cloud … / That heareth not the loud winds when they call; / And moveth all together, if it move at all' (82–4). There, the old man's stillness is conveyed through a rhythm that seems to face obstacles in the way of forward movement and momentum, before, having scaled the caesura of the final line, the cloud and the man do coalesce and the resulting figurative compound 'moveth all together'.

As Coleridge saw, though not with complete sympathy, the poem is typical of Wordsworth in its movement between tones and styles.[1] It is at every moment open to the accidental, to changes of direction that can feel like graspings after hope or meaning, yet it reveals a shape and an order that correspond to the poet's attempted journey towards greater comprehension of his predicament and vocation. Paradoxically, greater comprehension involves recognition of a visionary troubling that brings about its own 'incomprehension'. From the start, the poem reveals an openness to the uncertain, even the unsettling, but the fact that natural harmony is restored after the storm at night suggests an initial faith in a cyclical order of things and a capacity to be delighted by the present. Yet almost as a reflex reaction against both those objects of faith emerges the fear that the cyclical will give way to a despondency-inducing linearity and that the present will darken into an unhappy future.

At the heart of the poem is Wordsworth's ability to do justice to the accidental and chancey in life ('But, as it sometimes chanceth' (22) is how he heralds the onset of burgeoning fears for the future), and to his sense that design of a kind, possibly design intuited or shaped by the poetic imagination, is at work in the experiences that make possible his poems. So, here, though he introduces the encounter with the old man as if there were varying possibilities of understanding it – it might be 'a peculiar grace, / A leading from above, a something given' (50–1) – all three options suggest a gift beyond the poet's will, made available to him in the act of writing a poem. The poem does not despise the work of the will: fortitude and resolution are clearly prized and reaffirmed as virtues. But with great delicacy it rehearses the workings of a consciousness that realizes that its form of control must accommodate awareness of much that resists the will.

The poem's capacity to stage a journey, then, to turn and return, is central to its status as a major lyric. A small example concerns the hare, which appears three times in the poem. All three moments involve varying angles of vision. Wordsworth first mentions the hare in stanza 2; skilfully, his rhythms run their own races as he renders the creature's exuberant, lithe vivacity:

> The grass is bright with rain-drops; on the moors
> The Hare is running races in her mirth;
> And with her feet she from the plashy earth
> Raises a mist; which, glittering in the sun,
> Runs with her all the way, wherever she doth run.   (10–14)

The language shows to advantage Wordsworth's descriptive gifts. Much has to do with the language's ability to be a medium for movement; it has its own 'running' vigour, demonstrating sharpness of attention to what is physically rehearsable, the hare's springing across the bouncily firm yet squelchy 'plashy earth'. It is, at the same time, potentially symbolic. In the words 'Raises a mist', Wordsworth suggests the aureole, the halo of lit-up steam that the hare's darting run generates and, also, the 'glittering' that may be conferred as well as discerned by the poet's eye. It is a remarkable image, both kinetic, in its suggestion of energy, and holistic, in its marrying of delighted poet and self-delighting creature. If we are to believe the poet's descent into dejection we need to trust his capacity for joy.

The second mention of the hare in the third stanza abruptly shifts tenses: 'I was a Traveller then upon the moor, / I saw the Hare that raced about with joy' (15–16). 'I saw': the brief phrase renarrates the poet's response to the hare. It turns out to have been in the past; we have shifted to a retrospective state, one in which the hare is ceasing to be a creature and is becoming an emblem as the poet, in his third mention of it, makes clear his willed desire to be happy: 'I heard the Sky-lark singing in the sky; / And I bethought me of the playful Hare: / Even such a happy Child of earth am I' (29–31). The movement back into the present tense in that last quoted line sounds (calculatedly) over-asserted, and inaugurates the drama of poetic consciousness staged in the remainder of the poem. Part of that drama, it might be noted as a clue to the peculiarly objective nature of Wordsworthian subjectivity, is a recognition that there is more to the world than the poet's sense of it.

In 'Ode: Intimations of Immortality', begun before the composition of 'Resolution and Independence', but not finished until two years later in 1804, Wordsworth produces his major lyric poem about the mind and the world, about human beings and their spiritual aspirations, about memory, about poetic vision, about death and birth, about the human heart, about God. The themes are huge, and Wordsworth implies the ambition of the poem in the epigraph he attached to it in 1807, the Virgilian phrase *Paulò majora canamus* (Let us sing a somewhat loftier strain). Yet the poem is not on its stilts; it is no mere copy of eighteenth-century odes on large abstractions. From the start, the poet's involvement is first-hand, personal and felt on the rhythm's often monosyllabic pulses. The initial note is elegiac: 'There was a time when meadow, grove, and stream, / The earth and every common sight, / To me did seem / Apparelled in celestial light' (1–4). The lines are in touch with lost wonder, as is brought out by 'Apparelled' where the word implies a clothing now inexplicably gone. Instead, the poet's condition is one in which lost vision is dominant: 'The things which I have seen I now can see no more' (9).

The line is affecting as few other lines in English poetry manage to be. It is a mode distinctly Wordsworthian, in its almost stumbling honesty, unignorable depth, restraint, and heart-piercing directness – all controlled by a poetic intellect aware that words such as 'see' and 'things' have resonances. The poem's refusal to give over completely to mourning is evident in the wording of the line in which, as Oliver Clarkson points out, 'I now can see' has a residually affirmative suggestion, allowing us to 'catch a glimpse ... of the shimmering world that is "no more"',[2] and in the minimally positive suggestion of 'I have seen'. It will emerge, as the poem stages various twists and turns, including the attempted rallying of stanzas 3 and 4 after the numb restatement of loss in stanza 2, that the very fact of having once 'seen' 'things' is enough for the poet to construct a compensating answer to the questions which conclude stanza 4: 'Whither is fled the visionary gleam? / Where is it now, the glory and the dream?' (56–7).

Those questions have significantly different meanings. The first asks, with a superb rhythmic mimicry of yearning (a consequence, in part, of the opening trochee and the subsequent re-establishment of expected iambic stress in 'fled'), about the fading of the 'visionary gleam'; the second enquires, less heart-brokenly, about the present dwelling place of 'the glory and the dream'. 'Where is it now' suggests the significance of the poem itself as a space whose 'now' accommodates utterances of absence and compensatory recreations. It is, after all, through language that the poem has been able to speak powerfully of what reminds the poet of loss, doing so with special vividness in the dramatic transition that takes place just before stanza 4's concluding questions. Here Wordsworth turns away from his attempt to affirm current pleasure in natural joy and asserts, 'But there's a Tree, of many one, / A single Field which I have looked upon, / Both of them speak of something that is gone' (51–3). The focus on the 'one' tree, the 'single Field', is typical of Wordsworth, a poet who values singleness, uniqueness, the unreplaceable nature of the experience.

Yet as tree and field 'speak of something that is gone', they serve as tactful forerunners of the poet's own labour in the poem. Wordsworth's ability to 'speak of something that is gone' forms the basis of his hope that loss is not absolute. In stanza 5, he draws, by way of a Christianized Platonism, on the idea of the soul's pre-existence and imperishable spiritual destiny. Thus, he is able to assert:

> Our birth is but a sleep and a forgetting:
> The Soul that rises with us, our life's Star,
>   Hath had elsewhere its setting,
>   And cometh from afar.   (58–61)

The image lends the underlying idea the flavour of a 'conceit' in Metaphysical poetry. Wordsworth entertains the idea vividly, even magisterially, and he elaborates the sustaining image with great assurance. Yet the poem seems to operate here differently, less urgently than in the opening four sections, more rhetorically. This is not to impugn Wordsworth's religious sincerity, but to note how, in order to solve the enigmas mooted at the close of stanza 4, he has recourse to an idiom that allows him to use the first-person plural and to conquer distress through metaphor and assertion.

The art of the poem, indeed its beating heart, is that figurative devices never conquer experiential distress in any facile way. Even here the initial grandeur gives way to the reappearance of anxiety, sensed as it is repelled: 'Not in entire forgetfulness,' writes Wordsworth, 'And not in utter nakedness, / But trailing clouds of glory do we come / From God, who is our home' (62–5). That may seem confident enough, but the opening lines curve towards the conditions they outlaw (that is, 'entire forgetfulness' and 'utter nakedness'), while the phrase 'God, who is our home', seems more pious statement rather than uplifting promise. The rest of the section dwells on the inevitable encroachment by 'the light of common day' on 'the vision splendid' which accompanies the young man, still 'Nature's Priest' (72), even though beset by 'Shades of the prison-house' (67). Cleverly and sadly, the image of 'clouds of glory' passes into an account of its banishment. Wordsworth uses the image of a light extinguishing a greater light which will be crucial to Shelley's poetry, especially in *The Triumph of Life*.[3]

Stanzas 6 to 8 maintain this emphasis on the loss involved in growing up. Stanza 6 sees the 'Earth' as a foster-parent, determined with mistaken kindness to 'make her Foster-child, her Inmate Man, / Forget the glories he hath known, / And that imperial palace whence he came' (82–4). The 'imperial palace' comes across as emptily sonorous, and the stress is on Earth's determination to make her 'Foster-child' 'Forget'; even the span of lines between 'known' and its rhyme partner ('own' at the end of the stanza's first line) speaks to the erasure of memory taking place. Stanzas 7 grieves with affectionate mockery over the way in which a child of six throws himself into the roles played by human beings, 'As if his whole vocation / Were endless imitation' (106–7). Conceit is now charged with fantastical seriousness, as Wordsworth laments in 7 that the child, a 'best Philosopher' (110) and 'Eye among the blind' (111), should 'provoke / The Years to bring the inevitable yoke' (126–7). Those opening apostrophes to the child are lines derided by Coleridge for being absurd, but the reader senses that Wordsworth means every word of it, that he does believe in the child's near-wordless access to a vision denied to the adult.

At the same time, it is the adult poet who is able to articulate such a belief in a poem of great generic inventiveness, one that reworks the irregular stanzas of the Pindaric form and the tripartite structure common to that form. Wordsworth's very praise of the child communicates an almost agonized sense that his own perspective stands outside that of the 'Mighty Prophet! Seer blest! / On whom those truths do rest, / Which we are toiling all our lives to find' (114–16). It is this subliminal awareness that precipitates the final movement of the poem, begun in stanza 9, when Wordsworth breaks away from despair to voice a 'joy' possible only to the remembering adult:

> O joy! that in our embers
> Is something that doth live,
> That nature yet remembers
> What was so fugitive!   (132–5)

The lines effect a movement towards grave joy, a joy that is no less persuasive for being minimal, residual, a question of 'embers' kept from turning into ash only because of 'something' still living, because of the fact that 'nature', human nature it would seem, 'yet remembers'. 'What was so fugitive', the last line implies in its use of 'was', is no longer quite so 'fugitive', and yet the 'something' and the 'What' are hardly manifest in any clear way, as the following lines bring out, enacting the poet's investigation of the 'intimations' present in childhood. These intimations unsettle confident poetic utterance, and Wordsworth's appositional phrasing goes about and about, redefining, reformulating as he speaks of

> obstinate questionings
> Of sense and outward things,
> Fallings from us, vanishings;
> Blank misgivings of a Creature
> Moving about in worlds not realized,
> High instincts, before which our mortal Nature
> Did tremble like a guilty Thing surprised.   (144–50)

What incites 'Perpetual benedictions' (137), it turns out, are trauma-like experiences associated in adult life with the earliest stirrings of poetic imagination. Wordsworth's lines are themselves 'Fallings' and 'vanishings', not least in the way they appear to search for words to describe experiences that defeat words; but his 'questionings / Of sense' might be glossed by his episodes such as his mental state after the boat-stealing recounted in Book I of *The Prelude* (*1805*), when he knew a 'blank desertion' (422). These are moments when he felt 'Blank misgivings', misgivings he attributes to the fact that he was 'a Creature / Moving about in worlds not realized'. 'Creature' reminds us that he is the product of a Creator, 'God, who is our home', and the 'worlds not realised' suggest, hauntingly, that 'the light of common day' had yet to endow all it fell upon with structures of reality. The 'worlds', and the plural indicates the world-making which the child engages in, had yet to assume a falsely sturdy objectivity.

The later poet rejoices in these earlier experiences that have bequeathed 'shadowy recollections, / Which, be they what they may, / Are yet the fountain light of all our day, / Are yet a master light of all our seeing' (152–5). The second line makes clear that these experiences are unknowable; 'shadowy' associates them with the insubstantiality of vision. But uncertainty is the basis of confident declaration; those 'shadowy recollections' serve, with conscious paradox, as 'the fountain light' and 'a master light'. The passage gives way to an extended image of what 'our seeing' and hearing are still capable of in adult moments of vision when 'Our Souls have sight of that immortal sea / Which brought us hither' (166–7).

The poem is, throughout, able to move convincingly and with affecting eloquence between doubt and assertion. The final affirmation of stanza 9 is the more convincing for the note of despondency that has been warded off in previous lines that speak of 'truths that wake, / To perish never; / Which neither listlessness, nor mad endeavour, / Nor Man nor Boy, / Nor all that is at enmity with joy, / Can utterly abolish or destroy' (158–63). There, threats to the 'truths that wake' are given full scope in the writing, which brings into play, as it explicitly seeks to send packing, the fear that the truths may 'perish', or be the objects in human beings of an impulse to 'abolish or destroy'. Wordsworth stages a central conflict in the stanza when he rhymes 'joy' and 'destroy'.

Comparable interplays of feeling animate the concluding two stanzas, 10 and 11, the first of which returns to the spring morning addressed in stanza 4, only this time doing so 'in thought', a recognition of the journey travelled since childhood and in the course of the poem itself. Movingly Wordsworth reasserts the living, ongoing reality of loss, accepting that 'nothing can bring back the hour / Of splendour in the grass, of glory in the flower' (180–1), yet articulating an acceptance, at once stoic and compensatory, of his newly found, precarious equipoise: 'We will grieve not, rather find / Strength in what remains behind' (182–3). The stanza refers to 'the faith that looks through death' (188) yet the poem does not settle for easy piety. It is grounded in the human, all-too human reality of a poet who loves the natural world, but knows quietly it is insufficient to sustain the visionary intimations whose guarantee is ultimately their own reincarnation in this poem. Finally, though, in stanza 11, after re-establishing his bond with natural things ('Think not of any severing of our loves', 191), Wordsworth concludes, not simply with a reassertion of the imagination's power, but also with a restatement of the common humanity in which he shares, without which that power would be worthless:

> Thanks to the human heart by which we live,
> Thanks to its tenderness, its joys, and fears,
> To me the meanest flower that blows can give
> Thoughts that do often lie too deep for tears.   (203–6)

Those 'thoughts' are the final use of a word crucial in the poem; that they lie 'too deep for tears' opposes the weight of 'custom' which is 'deep almost as life' at the close of stanza 8.[4] Wordsworth links the 'human heart by which we live' to his individual capacity for grief-inflected vision, 'To me the meanest flower'. Throughout, 'to me' has been the signature of the poet's authenticity of response. That it surfaces at the end brings out how Wordsworth's Ode thrives on and owes its authority to its ability to speak profoundly both in personal and in general terms.

A fusion of the personal and the general occurs in two overtly elegiac poems by Wordsworth: his 'Elegiac Stanzas, Suggested by a Picture of Peele Castle in a Storm, Painted by Sir George Beaumont' and his sonnet 'Surprized by Joy'. 'Elegiac Stanzas', sparked into being by the death at sea of Wordsworth's brother John in 1805, is written in alternating rhymed quatrains in iambic pentameters, a metre suited to the poem's theme: the poet's previous association of Peele Castle with a calm, untroubled sea, and his new recognition that Sir George Beaumont's picture of the Castle surrounded by a 'sea in anger' (44), is valuable because it is a representation of 'what is to be borne' (58).

The poem hinges on a majestically sorrowful key-change. It spends a good while lovingly evoking the calm idyllic picture the poet would have produced, 'if mine had been the Painter's hand' (13), were he to have sought to capture his original response to the Castle and its surrounding sea. As the poet approaches the present, he begins to establish his distance from any sense of life as being 'Elysian quiet, without toil or strife' (26): a vision now recognized, in exquisitely melodious rhythms, to be seductive and unreal, the product of 'the fond delusion of my heart' (29). Then comes the key-change, one that involves the stoical acceptance of loss:

> So once it would have been, – 'tis so no more;
> I have submitted to a new control;
> A power is gone, which nothing can restore;
> A deep distress hath humanized my Soul.   (33–6)

In these lines the hiding places of Wordsworth's power make themselves manifest: the articulation of breakthrough moments of recognition, the entwining around one another of loss and recompense, the ability to breathe fresh resources of feeling into ordinary English words. Here the revitalized energy lent to 'new', 'gone', 'nothing', and 'deep' are examples. Above all, his poetry associates itself with permanent human states in a uniquely personal way, as is shown by the movement from 'humanized' – that is, the poet is made to realize his kinship with what he will call 'the Kind' (53) – to 'my soul'. The poem bids farewell to 'the Heart that lives alone' (53), yet it does so with the authority of a poet who knows all about the lure of proud alone-ness, even as he finally speaks uncoercively on behalf of instincts his readers will find themselves wishing to acknowledge, if only for the duration of the poem: 'Not without hope', the poem concludes, with an affecting use of a double negative, 'we suffer and we mourn' (60). The repetition of 'we' lends a wholly convincing nobility to our suffering and our mourning, conjoined activities, so the line persuades us, that are accompanied by a bare but tangible inkling of hope.

In 'Surprized by Joy', Wordsworth writes a sonnet in response to the death of his daughter Catharine, who had died at the age of three. The poem is a modified Petrarchan sonnet, with alternating rhymes in the octave, which matches the poem's fascination with 'vicissitude', a long Latinate word that attracts a great deal of attention to itself in the arresting opening quatrain:

> Surprized by joy – impatient as the Wind
> I wished to share the transport – Oh! with whom
> But Thee, long buried in the silent Tomb,
> That spot which no vicissitude can find?

'Vicissitude' comes from a Latin word *vicis* meaning 'turn, change', and in context Wordsworth's usage comes closest to *OED* 3 ('a change or altera-tion in condition or fortune; an instance of mutability in human affairs') or 4 ('alternating succession of opposite or contrasted things'). Wordsworth's rhyming captures the 'alternating succession' of feelings that is central to the poem – which operates both by registering the surprise of 'joy' (presumably a surprise because infrequently experienced by the poet after his daughter's death) and its saddened aftermath, the poet wishing to turn to his dead daughter to 'share the transport' with her. It works, too, by coupling with those feelings the sense of surprised but stoically anguished repetition. The sestet suggests that the 'pang' (10) he subsequently felt, after realizing it was impossible for his daughter to 'share the transport' with him, was equalled only by the time when the poet 'stood forlorn, / Knowing my heart's best treasure was no more; / That neither present time, nor years unborn / Could to my sight that heavenly face restore' (11–14).

Miltonic resonances from 'Methought I saw my late espoused saint' contribute to the effect of this ending. Milton imagines re-seeing his late espoused saint, only to be cruelly disillusioned: 'Her face was veiled, yet to my fancied sight / Love, sweetness, goodness in her person shin'd / So clear, as in no face with more delight' (10–12) only for his waking to mean that 'she fled, and day brought back my night' (12).[5] Wordsworth, taken back at the poem's close to a point implicitly worse than 'the worst pang that sorrow ever bore' (10), knows that nothing can 'restore' his daughter's lost 'face', and yet the poem remains both cleanly surgical in its evocation of grief's muddled vicissitudes and deeply affecting in its irrational, powerful intuition that his daughter, 'long buried in the silent Tomb', in some way survives, if only through the fact of poetic memorialization.

Notes

1 See Seamus Perry, *Coleridge and the Uses of Division* (Oxford: Clarendon Press, 1999), p. 274 ff. for an excellent discussion.
2 See Oliver Clarkson, 'Wordsworth's Negative Way', *Essays in Criticism* 67 (2017): 116–35 (at 131).
3 See Mark Sandy, '"Lines of Light": Poetic Variations in Wordsworth, Byron, and Shelley', *Romanticism* 22 (2017): 260–8.
4 For more on repetitions of words in the poem as forming a 'powerfully plotted succession … of "wounds" and "cures"', see Helen Vendler, 'Lionel Trilling and Wordsworth's Immortality Ode', in her *The Music of What Happens: Poems, Poets, Critics* (Cambridge, MA: Harvard University Press, 1999), pp. 93–114 (at p. 107).
5 *The Poems of John Milton*, ed. John Carey and Alastair Fowler (London: Longman, 1968).

William Wordsworth, *The Prelude*

The Prelude (1805) – on which this section concentrates and from which version the poem is quoted unless stated otherwise – grew out of the so-called *Two-Part Prelude* of 1799. In the longer thirteen-book form arrived at in 1805 (though the poem was not published – or given its title – until after Wordsworth's death, in 1850, and then in a much-revised form), it builds on the evocation of childhood experiences to the fore in the 1799 version. It is a poem about the growth of the poet's mind. While poetic identity is a mystery that cannot be fully explained, the plot of the poem is something like this: 'Fostered alike by beauty and by fear' (I.306) during childhood, by, that is, the Burkean complementarities of the beautiful and the sublime, the poet grew up, his imagination nurtured by nature.[1] In three places and stages of his life there were interruptions to this nurturing: while he was a student at Cambridge (Book III); when he went to London (a kind of underworld in Wordsworth's epic of the self, Book VII); and crucially his involvement in the French Revolution (Books IX and X) – first, as an ardent supporter; then as a continued supporter of the Revolution's ideals but a disenchanted spectator of its descent into bloodshed and violence, and of the belligerent responses to it of liberty-denying governments, including that of his own country; then as a would-be Godwinian rationalist, utterly losing his way, until saved from his fall into self-division by nature, his sister Dorothy, and his soulmate as a poet, Coleridge. Reconfirmed in his vocation as a poet, he describes himself and Coleridge as 'joint labourers in a work' (XIII.439) of general 'redemption' (XIII.441); as 'Prophets of nature' (XIII.442), they will preach a secularized creed based on the twin yet complexly interrelated doctrines of nature and imagination, speaking 'A lasting inspiration' (XIII.443) to others.

The Romantic Poetry Handbook, First Edition. Michael O'Neill and Madeleine Callaghan.
© 2018 John Wiley & Sons Ltd. Published 2018 by John Wiley & Sons Ltd.

The poem traces a circular journey: if its theme is Wordsworth's poetic growth, the evidence that he is, indeed, a poet is the poem which we are reading about his growth as a poet. From the beginning, in its echo in 'The earth is all before me!' (15) of the close of *Paradise Lost*, when, expelled from Eden, our first parents find that 'The world was all before them, where to choose / Their place of rest, and Providence their guide', Wordsworth challenges comparison with Miltonic epic.[2] He is offering less a justification of the ways of God to men than a vindication of the importance of what Jonathan Wordsworth calls 'inner consciousness', a theme the poet claims is 'heroic argument' (III.182), echoing and competing with Milton when the older poet, comparing himself with classical predecessors, says of his Christian 'argument' that it is 'Not less but more heroic' than theirs.[3]

Wordsworthian epic allows for contingency, true to a work that, for many years, the Romantic poet regarded as 'The Poem to Coleridge',[4] as the forerunner to his never-completed *Recluse*, which would include, in addition to *The Prelude*, 'a narrative poem of the epic kind' (3 June 1805).[5] Its structure is hospitable to the significance of external circumstances, even as it centres on the importance of the self; at one affecting moment, Wordsworth suggests the hidden quality of what spurs him on when he writes, after the assertion, 'I am lost' (XI.329), 'the hiding-places of my power / Seem open' (XI.335–6). As Joshua Wilner argues, the poem's episodes 'participate in and intimate a more enigmatic mode of totality'.[6]

Wordsworth himself, in the immediate aftermath of completing the 1805 version of the point, expresses disappointment: 'it seemed to have a dead weight about it, the reality so far short of the expectation'.[7] Yet that statement rehearses one of the themes of the poem, the gap between 'reality' and 'expectation'. Book I of *The Prelude* is not long under way before a note of self-reproach enters, as Wordsworth speaks of having 'a mind that every hour / Turns recreant to her task' (259–60); alluding to Matthew 25:14–30, about the steward who fails to use his 'talents',[8] he sees himself as 'Unprofitably travelling towards the grave / Like a false steward who has much received / And renders nothing back' (269–71). He goes on to ask, 'Was it for this', and, in the act of lamenting his unfulfilled promise, he apparently yet artfully stumbles on his great theme: childhood experience and the way in which it nurtured his creativity: 'Was it for this', the sentence unfurls, in a rearranged use of the poem's 'starting-point',[9] 'That one, the fairest of all rivers, loved / To blend his murmurs with my nurse's song' (I.271–3) and 'sent a voice / That flowed along my dreams' (275–6). That phrasing, 'flowed along my dreams', makes 'my dreams' a channel for the river's 'voice', a voice that helped to sponsor the poet's own voice.

This mingling of the physical and the metaphorical is among Wordsworth's major achievements as a poet. In the so-called Glad Preamble, at the poem's start, he moves from an actual wind, 'the sweet breath of heaven' (41) that 'Was blowing on my body' (42), to a figurative account of poetic inspiration (whose etymology means 'in-breathing'). This passage illustrates the unpredictability that animates Wordsworth's poetry. The state of inspiration starts as a harmonious response to the external, as 'A corresponding mild creative breeze' (43); within a few lines, it has become 'A tempest, a redundant energy / Vexing its own creation' (46–7). The breeze has turned into a tempest; the creative state now vexes itself, as if overwhelmed by its own energies. What emerges is a central theme of *The Prelude*: is there any object adequate to explain or to accommodate the mind's creative powers?

A key passage in this regard occurs in Book VI when Wordsworth describes crossing the Simplon Pass. More precisely, it centres on Wordsworth's belated discovery, via 'tidings' given by a 'peasant' (618), that he and his companion had already crossed the Alps. In the process of reflection, even, it almost seems, composition (especially in *1850* with its reference to 'here'), Wordsworth comes face to face with 'Imagination', apostrophized in the following way in the *1850* version, quoted here:

> Imagination – here the Power so called
> Through sad incompetence of human speech,
> That awful Power rose from the mind's abyss
> Like an unfathered vapour that enwraps,
> At once, some lonely traveller. (*1850*, 592–6)

Imagination asserts its all-governing primacy for the poet; it is 'unfathered', a quasi-deity, an 'awful Power', as Shelley's unknown ultimate would be called in the first line of 'Hymn to Intellectual Beauty'. It 'enwraps' the poet who is, for all his love of nature, a 'lonely traveller' in this world, driven on, as Wordsworth will go on to say, in a passage of great eloquence, by the pursuit of 'something evermore about to be' (608). Imagination is the origin of the mind's capacity for hope and expectation, which in turn is demonstrated by his continuing to suppose the Alps had still to be crossed even though he had already crossed them. Wordsworth here values the imagination's 'strength / Of usurpation' (599–600), a weighty line-ending pointing up the mind's capacity to supplant the 'real', moments when 'the light of sense' (600), our ability to form sense-impressions, 'Goes out' (601), but does so in 'a flash' (601) that 'has revealed / The invisible world' (601–2). The relationship between imagination and nature is less evidently harmonious here than in other parts of the poem (such as the Climbing of Snowdon at the start of Book XIII, discussed at the end of this section), though Wordsworth goes on to evoke, in his account of the subsequent descent down a 'narrow chasm' (621), a natural world revelatory of what might be called a humanist 'Eternity, / Of first, and last, and midst, and without end' (639). In *Paradise Lost*, Milton speaks of God in comparable terms (V.165). Wordsworth, as Jonathan Wordsworth notes, is 'Dealing in the numinous, not the specifically Christian'.[10]

Imagination and nature are at once allies and rivals in the poem. At its core are the 'spots of time' to which Wordsworth first refers in the 1799 *Prelude*. These visionary intimations speak of Wordsworth's longing to experience a kind of permanence that is rooted in the temporal. Significantly he prefaces explicit discussion of these spots in the 1799 *Prelude* by writing of tragic rural incidents to which 'other feelings' are later 'attached', along with 'forms' – undying mental impressions – 'That yet exist with independent life, / And, like their archetypes, know no decay' (*1799*, I.284, 285–7). The 'archetypes' are, one senses, 'forms' of nature that correlate with deep sources of strength within the poet's mind, and the wording is sure yet riddling, inviting philosophical glosses without wholly responding to them, hinting at an underlying knowledge of poetic nourishment. As revised in 1805, the passage describing and explaining 'spots of time' reads:

> There are in our existence spots of time
> Which with distinct pre-eminence retain
> A vivifying virtue, whence, depressed
> By false opinion and contentious thought,
> Or aught of heavier or more deadly weight
> In trivial occupations and the round
> Of ordinary intercourse, our minds
> Are nourished and invisibly repaired—   (XI.257–64)

'Such moments' (273), Wordsworth continues, 'in which / We have had deepest feeling that the mind / Is lord and master' (269–71), are seen as 'taking their date / From our first childhood' (274–5). These moments of imaginative restoration bring to mind the revelations of 'Tintern Abbey' when 'the heavy and the weary weight / Of all this unintelligible world / Is lightened' (40–2); in both cases, through a mood of austere affirmation created by diction and rhythm, the poetry evokes all that is antagonistic to the imagination (one notices the unignorable weight of 'unintelligible', for example), even as it asserts the epiphanic power of rekindled memory. Often, as in the two passages that follow – the experience of 'visionary dreariness' (310) when the young Wordsworth was 'Disjoined' (285) from his 'encourager and guide' (283), and the so-called 'Waiting for the Horses' episode – the content of the memory is close to trauma; what consoles the adult poet is the imaginative intensity and power of which his mind was and is capable.

In the second passage, Wordsworth associates a particularly bleak day when he waited for the horses which would take him home from school with the subsequent death of his father. Feeling chastised for his 'anxiety of hope' (371) by the father's death, Wordsworth evokes, as though strangely restorative, a composite blend of sights and sounds from which he 'would drink / As at a fountain' (383–4). Wordsworth at once catalogues and solemnly invokes

> the wind and sleety rain
> And all the business of the elements,
> The single sheep, and the one blasted tree,
> And the bleak music of that old stone,
> The noise of wood and water, and the mist
> Which on the line of each of those two roads
> Advanced in such indisputable shapes ...   (375–81)

In his 'Letter to Lord Byron', W. H. Auden describes Wordsworth as a 'most bleak old bore',[11] but even his insult bears involuntary witness to the unusual way in which Wordsworth uses words. Caught up in the 'business of the elements', Wordsworth's language is elemental, able to value what is 'single' and solitary, at the core of our diurnal existence yet seeming to encroach upon it from another world. The passage amounts to an unanalysable, symbolic hymn to what, elsewhere, Wordsworth calls 'the mystery of words' (V.621).

In the first 'spot of time' in the passage in Book XI under discussion, Wordsworth stumbles into a scene of terror, a place where 'in former times / A murderer had been hung in iron chains' (288–9). Described in the utterly bare way typical of Wordsworth when he is trying to drill down to the bedrock of his imagination, a combination of sights composes what Thomas De Quincey calls memory's 'involutes'. 'I have been struck with the important truth', De Quincey writes, 'that far more of our deepest thoughts and feelings pass to us through perplexed combinations of concrete objects, pass to us as *involutes* (if I may coin that word) in compound experiences incapable of being disentangled, than ever reach us directly and in their own abstract shapes.'[12] Wordsworth presents such 'perplexed combinations of concrete objects' with an uncanny force; 'ordinary' words conduct an electric charge:

> It was in truth
> An ordinary sight, but I should need
> Colours and words that are unknown to man

To paint the visionary dreariness
Which, while I looked all round for my lost guide,
Did at that time invest the naked pool,
The beacon and the lonely eminence,
The woman and her garments vexed and tossed
By the strong wind.   (XI.307–15)

The 'visionary dreariness' is an entranced ghostliness that is able to 'invest' – to clothe and to endow – an 'ordinary sight' that defeats representation. Sublimity boldly declares itself; the poet would 'need / Colours and words that are unknown to man'. It persuades us, too, of its presence through the way in which the poetry's repetition with variations imbues pool, beacon, and woman with significance. Mixing predominantly simple words with a few that are more complicated ('visionary dreariness', 'invest', 'eminence', 'garments'), the diction directs us to the work of the 'investing' mind as well as to the irreducibly 'naked' thisness of what lies outside the mind. The final image of the 'strong wind' takes us back to the opening of the poem and the image of the 'corresponding mild creative breeze' discussed above.

Originally that 'spot of time' was close to others that are widely distributed in 1805. A famous instance is the boat-stealing episode from the first book. The poetry depends for its effectiveness on its ability to reproduce the physical reality of the experience. So the rhythms dip and heave in sympathy with the boy's rowing in the lines: 'And as I rose upon the stroke the boat / Went heaving through the water like a swan' (403–4). As the boy rows, the 'huge cliff' (409) begins to loom, chastisingly, into view; the further away from the shore he rows, the more the horizon changes, bringing into prominence more distant objects. Hence the almost nightmarish quality of lines in which the boy struggles to flee from the menacing cliff which strides towards him:

I struck, and struck again,
And, growing still in stature, the huge cliff
Rose up between me and the stars, and still
With measured motion, like a living thing
Strode after me.   (I.408–12)

Wordsworth is at once experiencing child and remembering adult. As the cliff materializes, its presence is more than nightmarish: an august presence, it strides 'With measured motion, like a living thing', two Coleridgean echoes (from Kubla Khan and 'This Lime-Tree Bower My Prison') underscoring a sense of design and pantheism.

The idea of nature as 'living' gives power to the writing; we see Wordsworth's concern with what F. R. Leavis calls 'the living connexions between man and the extra-human universe'.[13] This universe remains both 'extra-human' and vitally akin to the human, a blend caught in the lines which conclude the episode. Wordsworth writes: 'after I had seen / That spectacle, for many days my brain / Worked with a dim and undetermined sense / Of unknown modes of being' (I.417–20). The lines eloquently struggle to comprehend difficult experience. Wordsworth's language lets us witness the struggle. The strong verb, 'Worked', and the receding syntax of the phrases that follow, seem arduously to pursue barely articulable feeling. A phrase such as 'dim and undetermined' is not simply vague; it means that something has challenged what Wordsworth calls a state 'In which the eye was master of the heart' (*1805*, XI.171) and that the experience has brought the poet into contact with the illimitable (that which cannot be given an end or defined, cannot be 'determined'). William Empson comments on the part played by 'The apparently flat little word *sense*', placed suggestively at the end of the line, meaning 'intuition' but reminding us of the role performed by sensation.[14] As he points out, Wordsworth's 'whole position depends on some rather undeveloped theory about how the mind interprets what it gets from the senses'.[15] The very lack of philosophical precision allows Wordsworth to be faithful to the experience of groping for 'sense'. In pinning down the way in which those 'unknown modes of being' make themselves felt, Wordsworth goes on to evoke how 'huge and mighty forms that do not live / Like living men moved slowly through my mind / By day, and were the trouble of my dreams' (425–7). The line-endings, used superbly, create a wealth of suggestions: the forms do not live; they do not live like living men (implying that they live in some way appropriate for 'huge and mighty forms'); and though they do not live, they still move like living men. Uncannily they do and do not exist within the boy's mind.

In one of its aspects, the huge cliff is a projection from a guilty child's mind of a stern parent. Wordsworth speaks of 'The self-sufficing power of solitude' (II.78) as a strength. Yet, at times, solitude seems close to alienation. In the woodcock-snaring episode, Wordsworth anticipates his use of 'trouble' in the boat-stealing passage, when he describes his former childish self as conspicuously alone in and at odds with a surrounding scene of natural harmony: 'Moon and stars / Were shining o'er my head; I was alone, / And seemed to be a trouble to the peace / That was among them' (I.321–4). The child discovers his isolation, his 'aloneness', as he grows sensitive to 'Moon and stars' that were, in both senses, 'o'er my head'. In retrospect, Wordsworth is able to give thanks to Nature for being a willing accomplice in this experience of being a 'trouble' to her. Nature has helped him discover a power within himself at odds with simple submission to natural beauty. As often in the poem, there is a strong impression, never wholly confronted in the commentary that follows the spots of time, of a transgressive, guilt-ridden quality in the poet's dealings with nature. This impression is vivid at the close of the woodcock-snaring episode:

> and when the deed was done
> I heard among the solitary hills
> Low breathings coming after me, and sounds
> Of undistinguishable motion, steps
> Almost as silent as the turf they trod.   (328–32)

Earlier, Wordsworth has made fun of his childhood self as a self-dramatizing fantasist, a 'fell destroyer' (318).[16] Now the heightened diction slows down the line in the long word 'undistinguishable', making us pause over this state of charged awareness, before we are moved on by the tiptoe-like lightness of 'steps', placed at the line's end. The passage takes us from an account of ordinary if intense experience to 'Low breathings' that are at once wholly explicable (projections from the child's guilt-ridden mind) and semi-supernatural (imagining nature as though it were humanly alive).

Throughout *The Prelude*, Wordsworth modulates between evocation and meditation. The most intense passages tend to be evocations. But Wordsworth's commentary makes the heightened moments more convincing; above all, it is often acutely aware that the growth of a poet's mind which, in one sense, it tries to explain, cannot be explained. So, a little after the woodcock-stealing episode, Wordsworth remarks in a passage in which abstract meditation assumes dramatic force:

> The mind of man is framed even like the breath
> And harmony of music; there is a dark
> Invisible workmanship that reconciles
> Discordant elements, and makes them move
> In one society.   (I.351–5)

Wordsworth might be describing other Romantic-period masterpieces apart from his own here: given the reference to 'the breath / And harmony of music', one might think of Beethoven's *Fifth Symphony* in its winning of ultimate victory out of turbulent orchestrations. Here the poetry preserves a sense of mystery even as it seeks to explain. The 'workmanship that reconciles / Discordant elements' is 'dark' and 'Invisible'. *The Prelude* as a whole tries to reconcile 'Discordant elements' while remaining aware of darker forces.

Even when politics and history are his subject, Wordsworth is always foregrounding the work of his imagination, and compelling our interest through the imaginative force of the writing. This force can result from the way in which narrative order is subverted. The famous lines recounting Wordsworth's delight in the onset of the Revolution – 'Bliss was it in that dawn to be alive, / But to be young was very heaven' (X.692–3) – ironize their delight by occurring after the traumatic inner upheaval that Wordsworth suffered as a result of the violence and slaughter into which the Revolution descended. The sense of 'Bliss' is still undeniable, but so, too, is the tragic awareness that the dawn proved to be a false dawn. The reader has already encountered a passage such as the following when, a month after the September massacres, Wordsworth experiences a near-apocalyptic nightmare in which 'I wrought upon myself, / Until I seemed to hear a voice that cried / To the whole city, "Sleep no more"' (X.75–7). Echoing Macbeth, Wordsworth experiences guilt, terror, and something close to prophetic vision; the circularity of history makes itself evident to him as a voice takes him over, impressing upon him a darker meaning of revolution, and he finds himself chanting:

> 'The horse is taught his manage, and the wind
> Of heaven wheels round and treads in his own steps;
> Year follows year, the tide returns again,
> Day follows day, all things have second birth;
> The earthquake is not satisfied at once!'   (X.70–4)

The lines are an incantation that summons up a vision of history as cyclical portent and fulfilment. Few passages convey as effectively as this and others in *The Prelude* what living through the Revolution must have been like at the time. Wordsworth was in France for much of 1792, where he met and had a daughter by Annette Vallon, returning to England in November of that year. As England fought against France, Wordsworth experienced divided loyalties, 'A conflict of sensations without name' (X.265), as he calls it in one place. The ebb and flow of feeling, Wordsworth struggling to remain loyal to the ideal of the Revolution even as he sees it besmirched and assaulted by alleged supporters and hostile antagonists, is sustained throughout; there are switchbacks of emphasis, subversions of narrative linearity, a constant ricocheting between positions. The result is among the finest instances of the fidelity to what experience feels like as it is re-entered through recollection that characterizes *The Prelude*.

That fidelity is present in the Climbing of Snowdon passage, placed climactically at the start of the epic's final book. The poetry's effectiveness owes much to its rootedness in believably rendered experience as the climbers negotiate their ascent on 'a summer's night, a close warm night' (10), 'Hemmed round on every side with fog and damp' (16). There is 'a touch of mock-heroic humour' in the evocation of the dog finding a hedgehog and making a Miltonic 'barking turbulent,'[17] before the writing uses its fluid rhythms, precise words, and images to recreate the speaker's ordinary yet visionary apprehension when 'instantly a light upon the turf / Fell like a flash!' (39–40). Wordsworth cunningly manipulates vowel sounds to lend force to the alliterative crescendo of 'Fell' (a strong stress reversal) 'like a flash' (picking up and consolidating the dawning sense conveyed by 'instantly a *light*'). The poet moves from 'turf' to universe; he experiences, in a single moment of poetic seeing and sensing, the moon 'Immense above my head' (42) and, 'at my feet' (44), 'a huge sea of mist' (43). This image of the mist as a sea then passes into an interplay between the metaphorical sea and the 'sea – the real sea, that seemed / To dwindle and give up its majesty, / Usurped upon as far as sight could reach' (49–51). With serious wit, Wordsworth suggests how notions of the 'real' can be transformed, and, through associations with power, majesty, and usurpation, he prepares for the subsequent allegorizing gloss that interprets the physical scene as an analogy for the mind's transformative powers: 'it appeared to me', writes Wordsworth, 'The perfect image of a mighty mind, / Of one that feeds upon infinity' (68–70). The blank verse is eloquently expressive here: the rhythms are regular, and yet each line sounds a new note, the balanced phrasing of line 69 giving way to the inexhaustible feeding of line 70 that keeps the poem open to 'infinity'.

Throughout, Wordsworth suggests that nature is alive and animate, and that that life is, in part, responsive to and an echo of the imaginative life we experience in the writing. All comes to a focus and yet to a vanishing point in the final discovery of 'a blue chasm, a fracture in the vapour' (56). This 'chasm' tears a rent in the poetry's verbal texture, even as it supplies a 'breach / Through which the homeless voice of waters rose' (62–3). There is power and a subdued plangency here, as though the 'homeless voice' arose, not in protest, but in insistence that it should be acknowledged, since it bears witness to and is an analogue of the poet's shaping imagination. Homelessness is ultimately the imagination's abiding city in *The Prelude*, which often thrives on unexpected movements beyond the describable, the known, and the local in the direction of 'infinity'. Yet mind and world seem rapturously in touch with one another's deepest longings in the passage; it is in 'That deep dark thoroughfare', Wordsworth asserts, that 'nature' had 'lodged / The soul, the imagination of the whole' (63–4). Nature lodges the imagination, even as the poet's imagination supposes that nature is capable of such a lodging. The gloss that follows lays emphasis on the scene as a revelation of the mind's power; the scene itself sustains a balance between what can be discerned and intuited, and the poetic faculty that articulates such a process of discernment and intuition. And the control of image, stress, word-choice all ensure that the poetry embodies what it describes: the imagination's delighted discovery of its own workings, a major theme of one of Romantic poetry's major works.

Notes

1 Qtd, as are all references to the *Prelude* in this chapter, from William Wordsworth, *The Prelude: The Four Texts (1798, 1799, 1805, 1850)*, ed. Jonathan Wordsworth (London: Penguin, 1995).
2 Echo pointed out and discussed in *The Four Texts*, ed. Wordsworth, p. 556.
3 See *The Four Texts*, ed. Wordsworth, p. lv, from which *Paradise Lost* IX is quoted.
4 See *The Four Texts*, ed. Wordsworth, p. xxv.
5 Qtd in *The Four Texts*, ed. Wordsworth, p. xli.
6 Joshua Wilner, 'Autobiography', in *William Wordsworth in Context*, ed. Andrew Bennett (Cambridge: Cambridge University Press, 2015), p. 148.
7 *The Four Texts*, ed. Wordsworth, p. xl.
8 *The Four Texts*, ed. Wordsworth, p. 559.
9 *The Four Texts*, ed. Wordsworth, p. 541.
10 *The Four Texts*, ed. Wordsworth, p. 596.
11 W. H. Auden, *Letter to Lord Byron, Part One, The English Auden: Poems, Essays and Dramatic Writings 1927–1939*, ed. Edward Mendelson (London: Faber, 1977).
12 Qtd from *The Four Texts*, ed. Wordsworth, p. 648, which points out that De Quincey 'had read the 1805 *Prelude* in MS'.
13 F. R. Leavis, *Revaluation: Tradition and Development in English Poetry* (London: Chatto & Windus, 1936), p. 165.
14 William Empson, *The Structure of Complex Words* (London: Chatto & Windus, 1951), p. 289.
15 Empson, *Structure*, p. 289.
16 See the superb discussion in Jonathan Wordsworth, *William Wordsworth: The Borders of Vision* (Oxford: Clarendon Press, 1982), pp. 41–4.
17 See *The Four Texts*, ed. Wordsworth, p. 656.

William Wordsworth, *The Excursion*

Wordsworth was known to his contemporaries as the author of a major long poem. But this poem was not *The Prelude*, first published only in 1850 after his death that year. Instead, it was *The Excursion*, one of the 'three things to rejoice at in this Age', according to Keats in a letter.[1] It seemed to many contemporary readers such as Hazlitt and Byron to involve a retreat from sympathy with radicalism into conservatism. Later commentators have found it to be lacking the poetic intensity and flair of the greatest writing in *The Prelude*. More recently, however, there has been renewed interest in and admiration for a poem that can be thought of as powerfully dramatic.[2] Involving a narrator and an encounter with a disillusioned Solitary, whose 'despondency' is the object of attempted 'correction' through the advice and often sympathetic admonitions of two other characters, the Wanderer and the Pastor, the poem engages the reader in and through its depiction of different moods and perspectives.

Formally, Wordsworth takes over the nine-book form favoured by eighteenth-century meditative poems such as Edward Young's *Night Thoughts*, a form also used by Blake in *The Four Zoas* and by Shelley in *Queen Mab*. *The Excursion* begins after an important manifesto-like Prospectus, intended for the philosophical poem *The Recluse*, which Wordsworth never completed, but of which *The Excursion* was intended as a part. In this Prospectus Wordsworth, in a majestic and resonant blank verse, claims '*the Mind of Man*' as '*My haunt, and the main region of my Song*' (40, 41).[3] He claims, as already noted in the Introduction, that this subject creates more '*fear and awe*' (37) than Miltonic subjects such as '*Chaos*' (35) and '*The darkest pit of lowest Erebus*' (36), or than the '*blinder vacancy – scooped out / By help of dreams*' (37–8). The language, there, is responsive to the '*vacancy*' it affects to despise,

The Romantic Poetry Handbook, First Edition. Michael O'Neill and Madeleine Callaghan.
© 2018 John Wiley & Sons Ltd. Published 2018 by John Wiley & Sons Ltd.

partly an effect of the vigorous phrase, '*scooped out*', and alerts us to the tensions that give dynamic energy to the long poem that follows.

Those tensions come into view towards the close of Book I, in which Wordsworth first published material relating to the sufferings of a woman called Margaret, whose husband is driven by economic need to desert her and join the army. At the end of Book I the reader is presented with the problem of how to respond to the tale, which ends with the death of Margaret and attempted solace offered to the narrator and the reader. It was first conceived as a poem called 'The Ruined Cottage'.[4] In *The Excursion* it is told to a narrator by the Wanderer (the Pedlar in the earlier version) whose formation is described in language and rhythms that are alert to the influences exercised by nature upon his developing imagination. Wordsworth mingles inner and outer in wording that blends 'deep feelings' (152) and 'Great objects' (153); the physical and the mental form a composite form and force that 'on his mind' (154), a phrase repeated from the previous line, 'lay like substances, and almost seemed / To haunt the bodily sense' (155–6). The passage captures the forming power of experience, as it impresses itself upon the young boy's mind and imagination, through enjambments, lineation, and images that are all imbued with a vital responsiveness.

Wordsworth conveys the story of Margaret with restraint, economy, and tragic simplicity, but also with attention to the involvement of teller and listener. The poem deploys a blank verse of an unusual bareness and capacity; it serves, quite unsentimentally, to evoke strong emotion. This capacity is evident in the Wanderer's outcry, picked up by Shelley at the end of his Preface to *Alastor* (possibly turning Wordsworth's words against him): 'the good die first, / And they whose hearts are dry as summer dust / Burn to the socket' (531–3). Internal rhyme ('die' and 'dry') combines with a blank verse of expressive strength (apparent in the stress on 'Burns') to communicate the speaker's half-embittered state of distress. Elsewhere, Wordsworth implies a parallel between the increasingly ramshackle cottage and Margaret's inability to care for herself or her child. Or he charges words such as 'changed' with heart-stopping power: 'Her face was pale and thin, her figure too / Was changed' (786–7).[5] As often in Wordsworth's poetry, forms of the verb 'to be' – here the word 'was' – insist on a condition that is what it is, ungainsayably itself.

And yet, though much is unignorable, much remains to be revealed. On two occasions Margaret speaks as though fulfilling the Wanderer's apprehensions on her behalf, as in the chiastic, 'I have slept / Weeping, and weeping I have waked' (804–5). However, his preoccupation with her sadness, his sense that he is seeming 'to muse on One / By sorrow laid asleep' (820–1), must contend with the rather stranger implication of her words later on, when she says of a tree, 'I fear it will be dead and gone / Ere Robert come again' (880–1), with its affecting hint, supported by the fact that she keeps his clothes and staff 'undisturbed' (889), that what torments Margaret is not despair but the desperate hope, communicated through the last four words, that Robert will 'come again'.[6] Indeed, returns, real and imagined, are vital to the poem's success. Margaret endures 'A sore heart-wasting' (910) before her death, seen by the Wanderer in a further image of sleep as a merciful release into the care of nature: 'She sleeps in the calm earth, and peace is here' (971), he tells the narrator, offering the solace of a pantheistic intuition and gently rebuking his auditor for giving way to grief. Nature absorbs Margaret back into itself, putting a stop to her 'sore heart-wasting' by arresting her status as a living person. This absorption may seem faintly ominous, but the Wanderer seeks to reassure the narrator through an exquisitely meditative account of grasses 'By mist and silent rain-drops silvered o'er' (974) that conveyed to him 'So still an image of tranquillity' (976) that it seemed momentarily to nullify 'all the grief / That passing shews of Being leave behind' (980–1). The passage comforts and discomforts in equal measure. The writing carries us along on an eloquent tide of rhythmic and figurative conviction, yet we may protest at the suddenly long-angled view that includes the experiential data of Margaret's endurance among 'the passing shews of Being'. Wordsworth is at pains to suggest that the Wanderer's feelings of contentment and solace are just that, feelings that do not exclude what the tale as a whole has made clear, that human suffering has about it an irreducible reality.

The story of Margaret is probably the finest passage in *The Excursion*. But the poem contains much else that is worth close attention, especially when it seeks both to provide solace and to recognize the human need for consolation. An example occurs in a passage from Book IV, a book much admired by Keats, in which the Wanderer explains the source of mythological imaginings as deriving from the need to foster and cherish 'A thought / Of Life continuous, Being unimpaired' (IV.750–1). Expertly using the resources of blank verse, especially its ability to accommodate qualifications extending across a long sentence, Wordsworth goes on to describe what such a thought surmounts. In doing so he brings into play a powerful sense of the human condition, one that left its mark upon Keats's 'Ode to the Nightingale' and his 'Ode on a Grecian Urn':

> From diminution safe and weakening age;
> While Man grows old, and dwindles, and decays;
> And countless generations of Mankind
> Depart, and leave no vestige where they trod.   (756–9)

The writing dwells here on all that the 'thought' of 'Life continuous, being unimpaired' holds at bay. It finds an idiom that achieves a grave authority as it articulates the sorrowful truths of mutability, transience, and oblivion. It serves as a small instance of an impulse at work in *The Excursion*. At war with the merely or tediously prescriptive and didactic, this impulse is in tune with the realities of ordinary human suffering and able to endow those realities with a persuasive grandeur. Wordsworth's writing here and elsewhere in the poem has about it a subdued visionary power. This power can flare into sublime vision, as in the account of the sky and cloudscape towards the close of Book II as a New Jerusalem. The passage has something of the sudden revelation typical of a spot of time in *The Prelude*, but its vision in the sky of 'a mighty City' (870) has, if anything, a bolder, more transcendental, more architecturally shaped grandeur. Wordsworth captures, his fluid syntax flowing, it would seem, in all directions, 'an unimaginable sight' (886), a sight imagined as composed of 'Clouds of all tincture, rocks and sapphire sky, / Confused, commingled, mutually inflamed, / Molten together' (889–91). Effects of confusion, commingling, and molten fusion happen at once in a poetry of rare visionary richness. The language suggests that political confusions have been displaced onto a vista of the heavens, and the sense throughout the passage that, despite the elaborated metaphors of structure and building, the vision is about to dissolve gives it, in the context of the poem as a whole, an almost unnerving tonal blend, one made up of wonder, resilience, imaginative comfort, and a quiet, self-aware quality of resignation.

Again, the poetry compels when it gives full scope to the Solitary's story of personal happiness and sadness (the loss of a child and wife), exaltation at the sense of liberation when France embarked on its Revolution, and subsequent disillusion at the behaviour of both France and its enemies, especially Britain. All existence heads towards nothingness in the powerful close of his speech in this book, the third, in which he expresses 'a hope / That my particular current soon will reach / The unfathomable gulph, where all is still!' (996–8). There, much work is performed by the interplay of indeterminate adjective and homeless noun.

More of the poem's finest moments, however, derive from a complex doubleness of perspective that challenges the Solitary's near-nihilistic pessimism as expressed at the end of Book III. In Book IV, for example, the image of the sea heard in a shell communicates the Wanderer's conviction that it is possible to hear 'Authentic tidings of invisible things; / Of ebb and flow, and ever-during power; / And central peace, subsisting at the heart / Of endless agitation' (1138–41). Here, one is in touch with the poem's ability to intuit the possibility of 'central peace' while allowing for the pervasive experience of 'endless agitation'. Yet, cunningly and truthfully, the syntax gives such 'agitation' the last word; peace shines out from a structure that is endlessly folded over on itself and responsive to 'agitation'. At such moments, one is aware that the poem contains some of Wordsworth's finest achievements as a writer of blank verse, that it embodies his mature response to the problems posed by ordinary human suffering, those presented by ageing, loneliness, disease, and poverty, and that it seeks, often with much success, to dramatize inner debates and conflicts.

Notes

1 John Keats, *The Letters of John Keats, 1814–1821*, ed. Hyder E. Rollins, 2 vols (Cambridge, MA: Harvard University Press, 1958), 1.203.
2 See essays published in the bicentenary year of the poem's publication and gathered in a special issue of *The Wordsworth Circle* devoted to the poem, 45.2 (2014).
3 Qtd as is *The Excursion* from *The Excursion*, ed. Sally Bushell et al. (Ithaca, NY: Cornell University Press, 2007).
4 See *Wordsworth*, ed. Gill, pp. 740–1 for a succinct account of relevant textual complications.
5 For commentary on 'changed', see Jonathan Wordsworth in his indispensable analysis of 'The Ruined Cottage' version of the poem in *The Music of Humanity: A Critical Study of Wordsworth's 'Ruined Cottage'* (London: Nelson, 1969), p. 137. The present account of the poem (or Book) is indebted to this work.
6 The point is Jonathan Wordsworth's in *The Music of Humanity* where he writes: 'It is in the moment of apparently total despair that one becomes aware of the greatness of Margaret's hope', p. 142.

Samuel Taylor Coleridge, Conversation Poems: 'The Eolian Harp', 'This Lime-Tree Bower My Prison', 'Frost at Midnight', and 'Dejection: An Ode'

Influenced by the 'divine Chit chat' of William Cowper,[1] and by other eighteenth-century poets such as James Thomson whose immensely popular *The Seasons* related lyrical descriptions of nature to moods of consciousness, Coleridge in the poems discussed in this section effectively patented a new genre of poem: the conversation poem. Richard Holmes includes nine poems under this heading in his thematically arranged selection of Coleridge's poems and argues provocatively that 'the Conversation Poems can be read as a single sequence, exploring an extending pastoral vision of friendship and family life, rooted in the countryside'.[2] Holmes is a persuasive advocate for the ambition as well as the pleasingness of the poems, yet it may be more accurate to see Coleridge as inventing a form able to deal with very different challenges, less a planned 'sequence' than a series of seemingly improvised performances. These performances shape themselves, often after arduous revision, into achieved coherences that are the more impressive for continually threatening to undo their hard-won sense of order and wholeness.

In most of the conversation poems, there is a trajectory described by M. H. Abrams:

> The speaker begins with a description of the landscape; an aspect or change of aspect in the landscape evokes a varied but integral process of memory, thought, anticipation, and feeling which remains closely intervolved with the outer scene. In the course of this meditation the lyric speaker achieves an insight, faces up to a tragic loss, comes to a moral decision, or resolves an emotional problem. Often the poem rounds upon itself to end where it began, at the outer scene, but with an altered mood and deepened understanding which is the result of the intervening meditation.[3]

The Romantic Poetry Handbook, First Edition. Michael O'Neill and Madeleine Callaghan.
© 2018 John Wiley & Sons Ltd. Published 2018 by John Wiley & Sons Ltd.

'The Eolian Harp' answers to this description, even as its movement is more fluid than Abrams's generic account allows. The poem, first published as 'Effusion XXXV', went through many adjustments before it reached its final form, effectively in the errata slip to *Sibylline Leaves* (1817), where Coleridge added lines that seem to distil the essence of his most joyously affirmative thinking in the 1790s:

> O! the one Life within us and abroad,
> Which meets all motion and becomes its soul,
> A light in sound, a sound-like power in light,
> Rhythm in all thought, and joyance every where – (26–9)[4]

These lines not only define Coleridge's understanding of the 'One Life', but also recreate his sense of what it might be like to experience it. This recreative quality has much to do with the poetry's balanced caesural pauses and phrasing, so that 'light' and 'sound', for example, fold round one another. It is evident throughout 'The Eolian Harp', which locates itself in the particular and local. Coleridge, addressing 'My pensive Sara!' (1), immediately provokes our interest: why is Sara 'pensive'? The answer to that question follows after the reference to 'our Cot, our Cot o'ergrown / With white-flower'd Jasmine, and the broad-leav'd Myrtle' (3–4), where the repetition caresses without coddling, and is double: Sara, like the poet, is attuned to the coming of evening and able to imagine a liminal space between sound and silence, precisely rendered in the sonically exquisite last line and a half of the first paragraph: 'The stilly murmur of the distant Sea / Tells us of silence' (11–12).

However, she is also 'pensive', we might surmise, because she does not share in the poet's surmises, rendered in the next three paragraphs, in which the poet's voyaging, associative thoughts are set going by the Eolian harp placed in the casement. If the initial suggestion of a breeze playing on and over the harp is erotic, the subsequent 'witchery of sound' (20) is more evidently self-reflexive, related to the effect produced by the poem Coleridge is writing and we are reading. Coleridge strikes a subtly nuanced balance between 'half yielding' (15) and an active process in which the mind is part of the 'one Life within us and abroad, / Which meets all motion and becomes it soul'. The poem follows yet urges on the mind's associative instincts, one of which is to recur to the trope of silence and music begun in the first paragraph; at the end of the second paragraph, 'the mute still air / Is Music slumbering on her instrument' (32–3), a potent image of inspiration's imminence that draws its power from the interplay of vowels and short and longer words.

The third and fourth paragraphs pursue the poet's adventure of thought, repeating, as Max F. Schulz remarks, 'the same sequence': 'the note of tranquillity ..., the sudden sound of the wind harp, ... the mounting exaltation of his thought'.[5] Coleridge first makes explicit the analogy between breeze and harp, and 'idle flitting phantasies' (40) and 'indolent and passive brain' (41), then suggests how that mental passivity is capable of speculative daring, as he pushes the analogy one step further, imagining 'all of animated nature' (44) as 'organic Harps' (45) swept over by 'one intellectual breeze, / At once the Soul of each, and God of all' (47–8). Though framed as a question, the speculation verges on a brilliantly moving pantheism that allows for difference – the harps are 'diversely fram'd' (45) – but seeks out a benignant, all-influencing 'intellectual breeze'. It marks, this section, a highpoint of the poem as a vehicle for philosophical investigation, one carried out without strain, reaching rarefied heights yet staying in touch with ordinary experience, apprehended with extraordinary deftness, agility, and depth.

Here Sara's pensiveness comes to the fore. Coleridge's unbounded flight of fancy receives a check from 'a mild reproof' (49) that a look of hers gives him, as though she were reading his thoughts and rejecting them as 'shapings of the unregenerate mind' (55). Coleridge's rejection of his beautiful skein of analogous thoughts seems self-destructive, yet it has humorous aspect as it catches one dynamic of his relationship with Sara. Charles and Mary Lamb certainly thought this was the case. It figures, too, his sense of being isolated from an audience, an admission with its own pathos given that he goes on to pay homage to 'The Incomprehensible' (59), an altogether darker conception of God. God is, within a few lines, the supreme poet, passing over 'animated nature' like an 'intellectual breeze', and a guilt-inducing presence beyond comprehension, leaving Coleridge to experience a lurch into self-debasement as 'A sinful and most miserable man, / Wilder'd and dark' (62–3). The poem finishes on a more positive note, returning to 'this Cot, and thee, heart-honour'd Maid!' (64), but its poet is no purveyor of saccharine pastoral trifles. Thought is delight but also danger in 'The Eolian Harp'. Speculations about the 'one life' mirror the very process of meaning-making in the poem. They may also, the poet guiltily fears, cost him his soul.

'This Lime-Tree Bower My Prison' starts with deprivation and loss, the poet unable, because of 'an accident, which disabled him from walking' (p. 136), to join his friends, including the poem's addressee, Charles Lamb, on an exploration of the countryside; it concludes with an enhanced sense of the beauty both of what the friends are imagined as having experienced and what the poet himself, looking from his bower, has found. Lamb, the poem speculates, 'Struck with deep joy may stand, as I have stood, / Silent with swimming sense' (38–9), intuiting what Humphry House calls Coleridge's

'Theistic Metaphysic of Nature' in the possible vicinity of 'such hues / As cloath the Almighty Spirit, when yet he makes / Spirits perceive his presence' (41–3).[6] The 'hues' that inhere in the 'bodily' (41) join hands with the world of spirit in this deftly intermingled dance of terms. In a comparable way, Coleridge respects Lamb's otherness ('may stand') and shares in his experience. His own personal response to nature is attuned to the interplay of light and shade, sound and silence, an interplay that seems to tremble on the verge of a covert theology, as does the subsequent rehabilitation of a rook which here is no *Macbeth*-like harbinger of evil, but is delighted in as it 'Flew *creeking*' (74; Coleridge's italics); the poem articulates the doctrinal views that 'Nature ne'er deserts the wise and pure' (61) and that 'No sound is dissonant, which tells of Life' (76), yet it manages to allow these statements of provisional belief to emerge from the poem's imaginative journey, one marked by great assuredness in the handling of diction (kept close to sensuous response), enjambments, pauses, and emphases.

'Frost at Midnight' takes its point of departure from the fourth book, 'A Winter Evening', of Cowper's *The Task*, in which the poet pictures himself looking into a fire, 'myself creating what I saw' (290) and associating the 'sooty films' (292) with 'some stranger's near approach' (295).[7] The work of others was often a spur to Coleridge, even as his own conversation poems prompted poets such as Wordsworth in 'Tintern Abbey' to experiment with a new form.[8] Cowper is content to see his experience as merely involving 'fancy ludicrous and wild' (284); such self-ironizing detachment gives way in Coleridge to a poem that trusts its associative apprehensions and where they may lead. The poem contains four verse-paragraphs. In the first, the poet imagines how 'The Frost performs its secret ministry, / Unhelped by any wind' (1–2).[9] In the clipped, withheld wording the poet communicates his sense of beginning a 'secret ministry' of his own, initially 'Unhelped by any wind' of inspiration. Yet the poem's delicacy of suggestion shows in the way in which Coleridge avoids explicit analogies. Instead, we find him, in his cottage, everyone else asleep, including his infant son, detecting a 'calm' that 'disturbs / And vexes meditation with its strange / And extreme silentness' (8–10). Such vexing disturbance will prove an incitement to poetic exploration; it is among the poem's indications that the self exists in a large universe. Movements of imagination and memory through space and time begin to dominate the poem. At first, the poet, Cowper-like, half mocks the need felt by 'the idling Spirit' (20) to find 'a companionable form' (19), 'every where / Echo or mirror seeking of itself' (21–2). The poem, that is, gets in its deconstruction at the outset. But soon the speaker discovers that these processes of echo- and mirror-seeking are not arbitrary; they are the means by which an intelligible structure can be shaped and discerned.

The second paragraph begins with the recollection of the poet as a boy at school watching the 'fluttering *stranger*' (26), the film on the hearth, hoping it would portend the arrival of someone known to him, 'Townsman, or aunt, or sister more beloved, / My playmate when we both were clothed alike' (42–3). That final reference takes the poet right back to his earliest infancy, and the transition to the 'Dear Babe, that sleepest cradled by my side' (44) feels inevitable, as does the speaker's parental hopes for his child, anticipating that Hartley Coleridge will, unlike his father who had been 'reared / In the great city' (51–2), 'wander like a breeze' (54). The natural description here involves a cunningly circular syntax that has the 'clouds' (56) imaging 'both lakes and shores / And mountain crags' (57–8), itself an intimation in its harmony of 'The lovely shapes and sounds intelligible / Of that eternal language, which thy God / Utters' (59–61). Nature becomes 'intelligible', a 'language' spoken by God, reinterpreted by Coleridge as poet-priest in the effortlessly interlinked blank-verse movements of the poem. The final paragraph brings the poem back to the initial scene in the context of assuring the child that 'all seasons shall be sweet to thee' (65), including moments such as the present, transformed in imagination, when 'eave-drops fall / Heard only in the trances of the blast' (70–1), mirroring, as Schulz points out, the earlier hearing of the baby's 'gentle breathings' (45) in 'interspersed vacancies / And momentary pauses of the thought' (46–7),[10] and ushering in the great conclusion:

Or if the secret ministry of frost
Shall hang them up in silent icicles,
Quietly shining to the quiet Moon. (72–4)

These lines were followed in the first printing by a further six lines describing the baby's 'eagerness', which were subsequently cut by Coleridge as spoiling the poem's 'rondo, and return upon itself'.[11] In effecting a 'return upon itself', the poem invites us to read 'the secret ministry of frost' differently, now seen as benign if still inscrutable and having deep affinities with the poetic mind of its observer. The three lines are full of words describing forms of soundlessness: a state intimated by 'secret', rephrased in the perception of 'silent icicles', where the adjective impresses because of its very redundancy (has anyone ever expected icicles to speak?), as if inviting a full look at what is usually taken for granted,[12] and culminating in an image of reciprocity for mind and nature, poet and moon, one of a mute and mutual shining and caught in the nearness of 'Quietly' and 'quiet'.[13]

'Dejection: An Ode', composed in 1802, in dialogue with the first four stanzas of Wordsworth's 'Ode: Intimations of Immortality', and revision of a longer verse letter to Sara Hutchinson, stands as the culmination of and near-valediction to the Coleridgean conversation poem.[14] There would be later ventures, such as 'To William Wordsworth', but 'Dejection: An Ode' takes the conversation poem into a changed generic and experiential dimension, one in which the colloquial if measured style rises to and plumbs impassioned heights and depths associated with the form of the ode and in which the affirmations of earlier poems encounter a crisis. This crisis has to do with the poet's state of mind, named in the title as 'dejection' and evident in the way in which the apparently confident accents of the opening, 'Well! If the Bard was weatherwise, who made / The grand old ballad of Sir Patrick Spence' (1–2), slide by means of the expressive syntax of the opening stanza into the poet's confession of his altered condition. Coleridge speculates that the Eolian harp in his window, emblem here of his poetic stagnation in the 'dull sobbing' (6) it produces, might be awakened to something livelier by 'The coming-on of rain and squally blast' (14) forecast by the 'New Moon, / With the old Moon in her arms', as the epigraph from the 'grand old ballad' has it. He hopes, almost as though referring back to earlier inspirations commemorated in previous conversation poems, that such 'sounds' (17) – always important in Coleridge, alongside their close companion, silence – 'Might now perhaps their wonted impulse give, / Might startle this dull pain, and make it move and live!' (19–20). The rhyme cuts to the heart of the poem's concerns; who or what is the source of the giving that makes life worth living?

The allusion to Paul's account of God, 'in whom we live and move and have our being' (Acts 17:28) is at once ironic and implicitly devout. Coleridge is not proclaiming a general principle of life-endowing goodness; he is asking to be shaken out of the condition that envelops him, the condition that stanza 2 will call 'A stifled, drowsy, unimpassioned grief' (22). As the poem develops, it achieves a force and eloquence of utterance that means it can at least give expression to the feeling of being 'stifled'; it shows a keen sensitivity to natural appearance and inner feeling that is the reverse of 'drowsy', and in its evocation of the poet's own distress and its recognition of the value of joy, it rises beyond the 'unimpassioned'. If this results in a poetic victory, it is won at the cost of emotional defeat. Coleridge defines his predicament in different ways, but possibly the central word in the poem is 'heartless' in the phrase 'wan and heartless mood' (25): the poet is without heart, without conviction; he can 'see, but not feel, how beautiful' (38) natural objects are. His 'genial spirits fail' (39), he goes on to say, echoing Milton's Samson, who asserts, in *Samson Agonistes*, 'My genial spirits droop' (594), that is, his inner source of inspiration falters.

Much of the poetic power of 'Dejection: An Ode' derives from the gap between the poet's capacity for lucid analysis and the anguishing consequences for him of his reasoning. If it is true that 'we receive but what we give, / And in our life alone does Nature live' (47–8), not only do the near-pantheist ideas of 'The Eolian Harp' get their comeuppance, but the poet realizes that his inability to 'give' means that 'nature' cannot 'live' for him as it did formerly. As he describes the condition from which he is exiled, Coleridge produces memorable accounts of what a marriage between mind and Nature might produce, 'A new Earth and new Heaven' (69), something close to an apocalyptic transformation. As it is, he can only recommend the 'beautiful and beauty-making power' (63) of 'Joy' to his poem's addressee, a 'Lady' in the poem's final form, one to whom Coleridge turns in the final stanza to wish her well. Touchingly, he does so after describing an imaginative response to the storm after it finally arrives, rousing in him less a rediscovery of a 'beauty-making power' than images of war's horrors and the cries of a lost child, one of the most piteously unsentimental images through which a major English poet has projected feeling.

From that image, in an early version first attributed to Wordsworth, then later to Otway, of a 'little child' (121) who 'now screams loud, and hopes to make her mother hear' (125), Coleridge offers, in a final transition of great poignancy, a line chastened by reserve and 'stifled' restraint: ''Tis midnight, but small thoughts have I of sleep' (126). The rest of this last stanza dwells on the 'Joy' that the poet hopes the Lady will experience, a flood of harmony entering the poem through interlaced and couplet rhymes. One line, however, remains unrhymed, as though defeating Coleridge's best efforts: it is the apostrophe, 'O simple spirit, guided from above' (137). The transcendental 'above', in this poem, finds no answering verbal partner, no 'love', to use the word one expects to find, obliquely reminding the reader of Coleridge's nearness to the group from which he seeks to distinguish himself in the poem: 'the poor loveless ever-anxious crowd' (52).

Notes

1 *The Collected Letters of Samuel Taylor Coleridge*, ed. Earl Leslie Griggs, 6 vols (Oxford: Clarendon Press, 1951–71), 1.279.
2 See Samuel Taylor Coleridge, *Selected Poetry*, ed. with intro. and notes by Richard Holmes (London: Penguin, 1996), p. 31. The nine poems included by Holmes are 'To a Friend (Charles Lamb)', 'The Eolian Harp', 'Reflections on Having Left a Place of Retirement', 'To the Rev. George Coleridge', 'This Lime-Tree Bower My Prison', 'Frost at Midnight', 'Fears in Solitude', 'The Nightingale' (which Coleridge subtitled 'A Conversation Poem'), and 'To William Wordsworth'. To this group critics such as George M. Harper, who coined the term 'conversation poem' in his 1925 essay, 'Coleridge's Conversation Poems', collected in *English Romantic Poets: Modern Essays in Criticism*, ed. M. H. Abrams, 2nd edn (Oxford:

Oxford University Press, 1975), pp. 188–201, sometimes add, as does this section, 'Dejection: An Ode' as having qualities in common with the other works.

3   M. H. Abrams, 'Structure and Style in the Greater Romantic Lyric' (1965), in *Romanticism: Critical Concepts in Literary and Cultural Studies*, ed. Michael O'Neill and Mark Sandy, 4 vols (London: Routledge, 2006), pp. 197–224 (at p. 197).

4   Qtd from *Romantic Poetry: An Annotated Anthology*, ed. Michael O'Neill and Charles Mahoney (Malden, MA: Blackwell, 2008), which takes the poem's 1834 printing as its copy text.

5   Max F. Schulz, *The Poetic Voices of Coleridge* (Detroit: Wayne State University Press, 1963), p. 83.

6   Humphry House, *Coleridge*, The Clark Lectures, 1951–2 (London: Hart-Davis, 1953), p. 80.

7   For valuable discussions, see House, *Coleridge*, pp. 78–9, and Jonathan Wordsworth, *The Invisible World*, ed. Richard Haynes (Createspace, 2015), pp. 173–201.

8   In a copy of *Sibylline Leaves*, Coleridge wrote at the poem's close: 'Let me be excused, if it should seem to others too mere a trifle to justify my noticing it – but I have some claim to the thanks of no small number of the readers of poetry in having first introduced this species of short blank verse poems – of which Southey, Lamb, Wordsworth, and others have since produced so many exquisite specimens', qtd from Mary Lynn Johnson, 'How Rare Is a "Unique Annotated Copy" of Coleridge's *Sibylline Leaves*?', *Bulletin of the New York Public Library* 78 (1975): 451–81 (at 472).

9   Qtd from *Romantic Poetry*, ed. O'Neill and Mahoney, as is 'Dejection: An Ode'.

10 Schulz, *Poetic Voices*, p. 94.

11 See *Coleridge's Poetry and Prose*, ed. Nicholas Halmi, Paul Magnuson, and Raimonda Modiano (New York: Norton, 2004), pp. 122–3.

12 See Schulz for the view that 'the silent formation of icicles has become an emblem of the eternal processes of life in man and in nature', *Poetic Voices*, p. 94.

13 For a more politically explicit reading of the poem, which was first published in 1798 with two overtly political poems, 'Fears in Solitude' and 'France: An Ode', see Paul Magnuson, *Reading Public Romanticism* (Princeton: Princeton University Press, 1998), which argues that the poem presents Coleridge both as 'a loyal patriot' and 'devoutly religious man' and as a continued supporter of 'Jacobin ideals of liberty', p. 78.

14 For a succinct summary of the revisions involved, see the note to the poem in *Coleridge's Poetry and Prose*, ed. Halmi et al., p. 155.

Samuel Taylor Coleridge, *The Rime of the Ancient Mariner*; *Kubla Khan*, 'The Pains of Sleep'; *Christabel*

William Hazlitt describes Samuel Taylor Coleridge as 'too rich in intellectual wealth, to need to task himself to any drudgery: he has only to draw the sliders of his imagination, and a thousand subjects expand before him, startling him with their brilliancy, or losing themselves in endless obscurity'.[1] Hazlitt's insight, though negative in this characterization, is suggestive of the nature of Coleridge's achievement in *The Rime of the Ancient Mariner*, *Kubla Khan*, 'The Pains of Sleep', and *Christabel*. Imaginative and experimental, Coleridge's intellect informs the moral and aesthetic universes created and uncreated in the poetry. Deftly generating images and impressions, Coleridge immediately undercuts any certainty, favouring sublime 'obscurity' in his innovative and evanescent poetry.

The Rime of the Ancyent Marinere, featuring in the 1798 edition of *Lyrical Ballads* as the first poem in the collection, and in volume one of the 1802 edition, breathes new life into the ballad. *The Rime* encompasses religious and supernatural themes along with travel and scientific elements, uniting them via the ballad's capacious form. *Biographia Literaria*, Coleridge's literary memoir, recollects the poem as based on strict poetic principles developed by Wordsworth and Coleridge,[2] where Wordsworth explains *The Rime* as an attempt at a collaborative project from which he removed himself after realizing the creative differences between the pair.[3] The Advertisement to the 1798 edition of *Lyrical Ballads* claims that 'The Rime of the Ancyent Marinere was professedly written in imitation of the *style*, as well as of the spirit of the elder poets';[4] but this gloss of the poem deliberately declines to discuss the innovative quality of a poem which estranges as it intrigues the reader. *The Rime of the Ancient Mariner*

The Romantic Poetry Handbook, First Edition. Michael O'Neill and Madeleine Callaghan.
© 2018 John Wiley & Sons Ltd. Published 2018 by John Wiley & Sons Ltd.

has attracted critical attention, in part, for the perplexing moral universe created in the poem. William Empson observes that Coleridge seems to be playing a trick on the reader, implying a Christian framework and 'using it to teach moral truths which were not its own' by having the only practical moral as 'Don't pull poor pussy's tail, because God loves all His creatures'.[5] But Edward E. Bostetter points out the chilling quality of the poem's ethical dimension: 'The moral conception here is primitive and savage – utterly arbitrary in its ruthlessness ... it is the Old Testament morality of the avenging Jehovah.'[6] However, *The Rime of the Ancient Mariner*, though often discussed as a poem primarily concerned by morality, indulges in digression, archaisms, and inexplicable shifts to complicate any sense of straightforward didacticism. Evading easy answers, the poem heightens rather than dispels the tension embedded in the poem, courting the reader's attempt to discover significance only to refuse it. The menacing brutality of the *Rime*, despite the comforting rhymes of the mariner at the close of the poem, suggests the continuing impulse in Coleridge's poetry to complicate. Fissure and doubts shadow the poetry despite the outward 'impulse for unity'.[7]

Kubla Khan develops the poet as a bard-like figure who encapsulates an almost pure kind of poetry. The Preface immediately creates a series of problems that work to distance the reader from the poetry. The reader is offered not the vision experienced by the disoriented and rudely awoken poet, but 'a fragment of a very different character, describing with equal fidelity the dream of pain and disease'.[8] The poem is characterized not as an aesthetic achievement, but as a 'psychological' curiosity. But the poem seems to free itself from pathologized constraints, focusing on the creative imagination as a force:

> But oh! that deep romantic chasm which slanted
> Down the green hill athwart a cedarn cover!
> A savage place! as holy and enchanted
> As e'er beneath a waning moon was haunted
> By woman wailing for her demon-lover!   (*Kubla Khan*, 12–16)

The passionate energy of the speaker, where exclamation marks repeatedly underscore the ecstatic vision experienced, take the focus away from any notion of a record of 'the dream of pain and disease'. The preface seems disconnected from the poem as the imagination, the synthesizing faculty, creates an excitement that propels the poetry forwards after the initial description of the 'stately pleasure-dome' (2) and its surroundings. The irregular rhymes that deploy cross-rhyme and couplets bolster the savage and enchanting beauty of the scene. The wailing woman's cry becomes the song that the poet would revive, the song that seems impossible to articulate in poetry:

> Could I revive within me
> Her symphony and song,
>   To such a deep delight 'twould win me,
> That with music loud and long,
> I would build that dome in air,
> That sunny dome! those caves of ice!
> And all who heard should see them there,
> And all should cry, Beware! Beware!
> His flashing eyes, his floating hair!
> Weave a circle round him thrice,
> And close your eyes with holy dread
> For he on honey-dew hath fed,
> And drunk the milk of Paradise.   (*Kubla Khan*, 42–54)

The leap from the wailing woman's cry to the symphony and song of the 'damsel with a dulcimer' (37) suggests the increasing complexity of the poet's vision. In the act of retelling, the poet deepens and refines his vision, as the excitement increases from line to line. The poet's dream, though apparently foiled as he cannot rebuild 'that dome in air', is far from lost. The power and mystery of poetic creation ripple through this implicit avowal of creative limits. Kathleen Wheeler argues that 'the narrator is symbolically the imagination itself, or the ideal poet, the ideal creator, omniscient, mysterious, and unknown'.[9] While this insight is suggestive, Coleridge keeps the narrator resolutely human. Though the power of the poetry and vision transfigures him, as in Shelley's 'Hymn to Intellectual Beauty', such divine inspiration cannot last. Poetic inspiration inspires 'holy dread' as the poet is both elevated and maddened by the vision and 'milk of Paradise'.

Heightened states form the focus of much of Coleridge's poetry, with 'The Pains of Sleep' painting an affecting portrait of the tormented poet. Though composed in 1803, Coleridge published the poem alongside *Kubla Khan* and *Christabel* in 1816. Though it has been read as a record of Coleridge's opium-fuelled dreams, the poem carefully evades such simplistic interpretations by its arresting structure, which moves from the calm of the poet composing himself for sleep in 'reverential resignation' ('The Pains of Sleep', 7) to the brawl of his recollected dream, to self-accusing guilt and self-exculpation. Yet the opening sets up the uneasiness that will descend into nightmare in the second stanza. Choosing submission, Coleridge's poem immediately positions the poet as a supplicant. Though 'not unblest' ('The Pains of Sleep', 11) with the negatives shadowing the sense that he has almost descended to such a state, he senses that he is surrounded, within and without, by 'Eternal strength and wisdom' ('The Pains of Sleep', 13). Yet the focus of the poem is not the submission he now feels, but the agony of the preceding night:

> But yester-night I prayed aloud
> In anguish and in agony,
> Up-starting from the fiendish crowd
> Of shapes and thoughts that tortured me:
> A lurid light, a trampling throng,
> Sense of intolerable wrong,
> And whom I scorned, those only strong!
> Thirst of revenge, the powerless will
> Still baffled, and yet burning still!   ('The Pains of Sleep', 14–22)

Surrounded by a 'fiendish crowd' of torturing demons, Coleridge is oppressed by 'Life-stifling fear, soul-stifling shame' (32). The rhyme of 'agony' and 'me' makes suffering the poet's identifying feature. Yet the emotions chosen, the thirst for revenge and the powerless will, present the poet as imprisoned by the same vices that consigned Satan and the fallen angels to Hell in *Paradise Lost*. Horrified by these tormenting visions, the poet cannot discern whether these horrors are things 'I suffered, or I did' (29). The vision overwhelms and terrifies the poet who suffers without recourse to knowledge or certainty. If *Kubla Khan* made vision a triumph that cannot quite be sustained and fully articulated by the human poet, 'The Pains of Sleep' makes vision a degrading horror that offers a window into hell. The final, solving stanza shows such vision to be no aberration; three nights are cursed by such torments as 'Sleep, the wide blessing, seemed to me / Distemper's worst calamity' (35–6). Denied the sustenance of rest, the poet attempts to find a reason for such torment:

> I wept as I had been a child;
> And having thus by tears subdued
> My anguish to a milder mood,
> Such punishments, I said, were due
> To natures deepliest stained with sin,—
> For aye entempesting anew
> The unfathomable hell within
> The horror of their deeds to view,
> To know and loathe, yet wish and do!
> Such griefs with such men well agree,
> But wherefore, wherefore fall on me?
> To be beloved is all I need,
> And whom I love, I love indeed.   ('The Pains of Sleep', 40–52)

The poet's tears, a kind of catharsis, offer a new perspective on the baffling suffering experienced over that night and the previous two nights. In explicitly Christian terms, he affirms that misery is appropriate agony for 'natures deepliest stained with sin', yet this apparent moral is undermined by the insertion of 'I said' partway through his explanation of nightmarish torment. Coleridge appears to be grasping for a rationale for his suffering rather than discovering an unassailable truth. The 'hell' within once again recalls Milton's Satan's torments in Book IV of *Paradise Lost* as he discovers that 'myself am Hell',[10] but moral reasoning seems undermined by the suffering falling on the poet himself. If the poet's explanation for such misery is correct, then it follows that Coleridge is one of Satan's men, imprisoned by the 'unfathomable hell within'. Or, as in *The Rime of the Ancient Mariner*, such agonies are arbitrary, unjust, and nightmarish, borne undeservedly by morally upstanding men even as the vicious go unpunished. The repeated 'wherefore' agonizingly reveals the depth of the poet's pain, where the broken sense that his question will never be answered pervades the poetry. The final couplet seems a solving gesture, but one that deliberately fails to provide the answer that he needs. Uncertainty assails the poet even as he attempts to close 'The Pains of Sleep' with some semblance of an affirmation.

Omitted from the second edition of *Lyrical Ballads* (1800) for which it was written, Coleridge did not publish *Christabel* until 1816, including it in his collection with *Kubla Khan* and 'The Pains of Sleep'. Having survived through recital for many years, the poem had earned many plaudits before its publication, most notably from Byron, who requested that John Murray publish the poem. *Christabel*'s relationship with the *Rime of the Ancient Mariner* is revealed through both poems' preoccupation with the problem of evil while creating ambiguity through sustained focus on the limits and possibilities of interpretation. Geraldine and Christabel's relationship opens up many critical possibilities, with Coleridge implying vampiric, lesbian, and Christian overtones to the poem. 'Christabel', a portmanteau of Christ and Abel, announces her as a good victim, with Coleridge retaining Christ's suffering rather than his power. The 'Abel' element immediately suggests a missing sisterly presence that should mimic Cain's role; the reader is primed to expect Geraldine and her seductive darkness even before her arrival into the poem. More fascinated with formal experimentation than the *Rime*, Coleridge announces a new metrical system 'of counting in each line the accents, not the syllables' ('Preface to *Christabel*', p. 69). The consequence is that, as O'Neill and Mahoney suggest, 'each line seems like a stealthy event'.[11] Ostensibly relating Christabel's encounter with the most fair and fatal Geraldine, the narrator continually questions and suggests readings of Geraldine that shroud her in mystery that deepens with every line. As in

'The Thorn', the questioning and doubt experienced by the speaker destabilize the poem, deliberately undermining any narrative simplicity. Suggestive rather than overt, Coleridge makes the poem whisper its discomfiting statements, as in the line 'Some say, she sees my lady's shroud', and make possibly innocuous events, such as the mastiff's howls, seem prescient and eerie. This oddly questioning mode adds a metapoetic dimension to the poem, as the narrator asks: 'Is the night chilly and dark? / The night is chilly, but not dark' (*Christabel* 1.14–15). Going over his gothic checklist, the narrator is forced to admit that the scene does not quite conform to the genre, just as the story deliberately fails to pinpoint Geraldine as entirely evil. *Christabel* creates the impression that it knows not what it is; its mystery becomes the centre and circumference of the poetry.

Christabel's first encounter with Geraldine sees the former almost overcome by the otherworldly beauty of the 'damsel bright' (*Christabel* 1.58):

> There she sees a damsel bright,
> Drest in a silken robe of white,
> That shadowy in the moonlight shone:
> The neck that made that white robe wan,
> Her stately neck, and arms were bare;
> Her blue-veined feet unsandl'd were,
> And wildly glittered here and there
> The gems entangled in her hair.
> I guess, 'twas frightful there to see
> A lady so richly clad as she—
> Beautiful exceedingly!   (*Christabel* 1.58–68)

This passage, inspirational for Keats's 'La Belle Dame Sans Merci' and Shelley's supernatural female 'Upborne by her wild and glittering hair' (46) in 'The Two Spirits: An Allegory', shows Coleridge playing with symbolism as aesthetic pleasure threatens to overwhelm moral judgement. Geraldine, as yet unnamed, is clothed in dazzling white outshined only by her skin. Her bare and blue-veined feet are both beautiful and vulnerable, and the 'wildly' glittering jewels in her hair are the only suggestion of her possible danger. The inclusion of 'I guess' attempts to explain Christabel's recoil from Geraldine, but rather than her gorgeous appearance seeming to hypnotize Christabel, it seems that she instinctively avoids evil, praying that 'Mary mother, save me now!' (*Christabel* 1.69). Christabel, orphaned, is vulnerable and motherless, in the moment of encounter with the beautiful and dangerous Geraldine.

The narrator repeatedly implies Geraldine's sinister qualities, such as where the 'mastiff old' (*Christabel* 1.147) moans angrily as Geraldine passes, and the almost coy suggestion, 'Perhaps it is the owlet's scritch' (*Christabel* 1.152), serves only to increase the reader's sense of Geraldine's danger. Seeming possessed, Geraldine attempts to expel Christabel's mother from her protective role, bidding her ghost: '"Off, wandering mother! Peak and pine! / I have power to bid thee flee"' (*Christabel* 1.205–6). The narrator even wonders: 'Why stares she with unsettled eye? / Can she the bodiless dead espy?' (*Christabel* 1.208–9). Despite such leading commentary, the narrator can still seem to sympathize with her, even referring to her as 'poor Geraldine' (*Christabel* 1.207). Unsettling in both her beauty and her ambiguous moral position, the sensual encounter between the two women shows Geraldine take a dominant, even maternal role with regards to Christabel. Here, the narrator explicitly associates beauty with danger:

> Her silken robe, and inner vest,
> Dropt to her feet, and full in view,
> Behold! her bosom and half her side—
> A sight to dream of, not to tell!
> O shield her! shield sweet Christabel!   (*Christabel* 1.250–4)

Reminiscent of Spenser's Acrasia and Duessa, Geraldine's beauty has a power to destroy those who look upon her. 'Behold!' enjoins the reader to imagine Geraldine's naked frame. The narrator resists any lingering description, eschewing the blazon in favour of a terrified series of exclamation marks that suggest fear for Christabel at Geraldine's hands, but the fear is tinged by erotic desire. Rather than making Geraldine simply evil, the narrator presents her as troubling and troubled:

> Ah! what a stricken look was hers!
> Deep from within she seems half-way
> To lift some weight with sick assay,
> And eyes the maid and seeks delay;   (*Christabel* 1.256–9)

Geraldine is seemingly compelled to be the seductress, and the narrator records a flicker of doubt in her performance. Desperately attempting to lift the 'weight' that forces her to continue with the destruction of Christabel, the triplet rhymes agonizingly lengthen Geraldine's trial. Though later, Geraldine will seem arrogantly proud of the spell cast on Christabel, as she 'tricks her hair in lovely plight, / And nothing doubting of her spell' (*Christabel* 2.365–6), Coleridge refuses to allow the reader to simply align Geraldine with evil without thinking more deeply of the forces working upon her.

The plot, following Christabel's enchantment, seems almost Shakespearean in its development. Christabel's father, Sir Leoline, after Geraldine informs him that her father is an old and estranged friend of his youth, vows to protect her in his name. Overlooking his daughter's stunned behaviour and her plea that Geraldine be sent from court, Sir Leoline decides to follow his resolution to protect the woman he believes to be his former friend's daughter. Explained by the narrator as an overcompensation for the enmity sprung up between the two men – 'And to be wroth with one we love, / Doth work like madness in the brain' (*Christabel* 2.412–13) – the psychological acuity developed in the poem balances the supernatural elements carefully.

It is Bracy the bard who dreams the symbolic vision of the snake crushing the dove, a vision that has him dismissed from court as he seeks to defend Christabel against her serpentine enemy, Geraldine. The poet, as in *Kubla Khan*, has the power to see deeply into the life of things, but here, such power can only be frustrated by the audience, unwilling to partake in the vision offered to them. Coleridge creates a poetry of blurred boundaries, where art and life, the supernatural and the natural, become not two separate things, but amorphous and entwined.[12] If, as Seamus Perry persuasively writes, Coleridge's work pivots on the tension between unity and division, these split allegiances bubble under the surface, creating a strain that the poet aims to unify despite his talent for division.[13]

Notes

1   William Hazlitt, *The Spirit of the Age*, in *The Complete Works of William Hazlitt*, ed. P. P. Howe, 21 vols (London and Toronto: J. M. Dent and Sons, 1930–4), 11.30.

2   See Samuel Taylor Coleridge, *Biographia Literaria, or Biographical Sketches of My Literary Life and Opinions*, ed. and intro. George Watson (London: J. M. Dent, 1975), 14, pp. 168–9.

3   William Wordsworth, *The Fenwick Notes of William Wordsworth*, ed. Jared Curtis (London, 1993), 3, qtd in Fiona Stafford, 'Introduction,' in *William Wordsworth and Samuel Taylor Coleridge, Lyrical Ballads 1798 and 1802*, ed. with intro. and notes by Fiona Stafford, Oxford World's Classics (Oxford: Oxford University Press, 2013), p. xxvii.

4   William Wordsworth and Samuel Taylor Coleridge, 'Advertisement,' in *Lyrical Ballads, 1798 and 1802*, ed. Fiona Stafford (Oxford: Oxford University Press, 2013), p. 4.

5   William Empson, *Coleridge's Verse: A Selection*, ed. William Empson and David Pirie (Manchester: Carcanet, 1989), p. 78.

6   Edward E. Bostetter, 'The Nightmare World of "The Ancient Mariner,"' *Studies in Romanticism* 1.4 (1962), 241–54 (at 245).

7   Seamus Perry, *Coleridge and the Uses of Division*, Oxford English Monographs (Oxford: Clarendon Press, 1999), p. 63.

8   Samuel Taylor Coleridge, 'Preface to *Kubla Khan: Or, A Vision in a Dream, A Fragment*,' in *The Major Works, including Biographia Literaria*, ed. with intro.

and notes by H. J. Jackson, Oxford World's Classics (Oxford: Oxford University Press, 2000), p. 102. All quotations from Coleridge's poetry in this section are from this edition.

9   Kathleen M. Wheeler, *The Creative Mind in Coleridge's Poetry* (London: Heinemann, 1981), p. 25.

10 *Paradise Lost* 4.75, in *John Milton: The Complete Poems,* ed. John Leonard (London: Penguin, 1998).

11 'Christabel', in *Romantic Poetry: An Annotated Anthology,* ed. Michael O'Neill and Charles Mahoney (Oxford: Blackwell, 2008), p. 207.

12 Kathleen M. Wheeler, '"Kubla Khan" and the Art of Thingifying', in *Romanticism: A Critical Reader,* ed. Duncan Wu (Oxford: Blackwell, 1995), p. 132.

13 Perry, *Coleridge and the Uses of Division,* p. 4.

Robert Southey, *Thalaba the Destroyer* and *The Curse of Kehama*

Thalaba the Destroyer (1801) and *The Curse of Kehama* (1810) are metrical romances with quasi-epic scope. Mingling fascination with fable and accumulation of cultural lore (evident in the long notes added to the poems, indicating provenance and sources), they bring into English poetry a resource that resonated with the period's interest in other cultures. They orchestrate narrative and poetic motifs of power and richness in themselves, and are highly influential for later poets. One main example must suffice. Shelley, a great admirer of the poems, shows the impact of their situations and wording in many places. To consider the effect on the younger poet of just the earlier poem by Southey: when Thalaba goes on a boat-trip 'Without an air, without a sail' (11.376),[1] he anticipates the voyage undertaken by the protagonist of *Alastor*; and when he descends to the Domdaniel, the realm of the evil sorcerers at the close of *Thalaba*, he anticipates the descent of Asia, Panthea, and Ione into the cave of Demogorgon in the second act of *Prometheus Unbound*.

Moreover, the Green Bird (embodied soul of the slain Laila) that 'Woke wonder while he gazed / And made her dearer for her mystery' (11.285–6) contributes to the way in which Shelley celebrates Intellectual Beauty's effects as kin to that which is 'Dear, and yet dearer for its mystery' ('Hymn to Intellectual Beauty', 11). The bird's voice has a feminine influence of a kind that anticipates effects not just of plot in Shelley but also of technique, since Southey delights in effects of varying, incremental repetition. In the lines, 'It cheered his heart to hear / Her soft and soothing voice; / Her voice was soft and sweet' (11.272–4), Southey, like Wordsworth and Coleridge in *Lyrical Ballads*, or Shelley in many passages, successfully surmounts the

The Romantic Poetry Handbook, First Edition. Michael O'Neill and Madeleine Callaghan.
© 2018 John Wiley & Sons Ltd. Published 2018 by John Wiley & Sons Ltd.

risks of mawkish simplicity or mere redundancy as he invites us to trace Thalaba's kindling response to Leila's presence. *The Curse of Kehama* leaves multiple traces on Shelley's work: the germ of the 'Ode on the West Wind', with its figuration of the wind as a Vishnu / Seeva-like 'Destroyer and pre-server' (14), can be located in Book 19 when the Glendoveer prays to Seeva: 'Thou who art every where, / Whom all who seek shall find, / Hear me, O Seeva! hear the suppliant's prayer!' (183–5). For his part, Keats's evocation of the sorrowful beauty of Thea's countenance close to the start of *Hyperion* is indebted to Southey. 'How beautiful,' writes Keats, 'if sorrow had not made / Sorrow more beautiful than Beauty's self' (35–6), reworking with elaborate stylishness Southey's elegant lines in *Thalaba*, 'She seemed sorrow-ful, but sure / More beautiful for sorrow' (11.383–4).[2]

The plot of *Thalaba* is episodic, and yet effectively coherent as a whole, recalling in this aspect as in others the impact of Spenser's *The Faerie Queene*. Whereas Spenser takes us into a hypnotically relevant dream-world, however, Southey, for all his poetry's fascination with the strange-ness of event, rarely lingers over the symbolic wealth that the reader suspects lurks within his materials. This absence of poetic self-concern is not always to the poem's disadvantage. *Thalaba* supplies the driven plot-line of Romantic quest; for symbolic and inward glosses on such questing we might wish to go to Coleridge's earlier *Kubla Khan* or Shelley's later *Alastor*. Thalaba seeks to avenge the death of his father Hodeirah; he has an ambiguous relation with enchantment himself, deploying yet finally casting aside the power of a magical ring he has taken from an enemy sorcerer. The tale has an Islamic colouring, but Thalaba's virtues seem preeminently those of a pious, self-denying English Protestantism, not incompatible with the sense of moral superiority that accompanied ongoing imperialist expansion at the time.

There are frequent complications of incident, yet recurrent events help bind the poem together, as does the emphasis on the hero's pure, unyielding intensity of purpose as Thalaba embarks on his avenging quest. The poem involves a continual battle between masculine firmness and an alternately yielding and tempting that is gendered female. Such yielding is first apparent in the attitude and subsequent death of Thalaba's mother Zeinab, with her piously acquiescent mantra 'Praise to the Lord our God, / He gave, he takes away!' (1.172–3), and then in the deaths of the mother substitutes and lover figures, Oneiza and Laila; the tempting is evident in the hero's need to resist various seductive females, notably Maimuna, the witch-like spell-caster who finally converts to good. Yet even here Southey is not merely stereotypical: Thalaba's final submission to the voice of the 'Prophet of God!' (12.486) he addresses at the close, when he says to it, 'Do with me as thou wilt! thy will is best' (12.489), shows him to be very much his mother's son. And to the degree that he seems to be more obedient automaton than morally taxed hero, Thalaba is a protagonist who raises questions in the reader's mind about the meanings that Southey attaches to what he calls 'the chariot-wheels of Destiny' (11.2). Is this a poem exhorting or interrogating, for example, a British sense of imperial sway as it undertook its forays into the east? Such a political reading can be extracted from the poem, but the poem remains cunningly guileless, as though its one purpose were simply to narrate its tale.

For all the unambiguous moral clarity of his poem's design, Southey excels at suggesting the inexplicable power of evil. The description (turning into evocation) of Maimuna's beguiling spell is one example, where the writing's use of monosyllabic nouns and verbs masks as it implies her sinister intent, 'And then again she spake to him / And still her speech was song' (8.332–3), where 'to him', omitted in printings from 1809, points up the fact that she has Thalaba in her thrall, even as he 'knew not the words' (8.303). Another is the dialectical argument shaped by the 'sophist speech' (9.145) of the arch-enemy Morareb, arguing enticingly for a relativist view of 'Evil and Good ... / What are they Thalaba but words?' (9.169–70; ellipses are Southey's); there, the hero's name is used with an almost chummy familiarity, as though Thalaba's high moral air were merely an act. Southey manages well, too, his hero's haughty, unhasty response: 'know ye not / That leagued against you are the Just and Wise / And all Good Actions of all ages past, / Yea your own Crimes, and Truth, and God in Heaven!' (9.219–22). As in an X-ray, one sees at this textual moment a flaring into eloquent being of the Romantic defiance to be heard in Byron and Shelley: a defiance at once proudly individualist yet calling on the past for support, even as it is, arguably, more religiously orthodox in inflection than the later poets ever manage or want to be.

A key to the poetic effect of *Thalaba* is Southey's choice of a metre that avoids rhyme and varies in line length; based, he tells us in the Preface, on the 'dramatic sketches of Dr. Sayer[s]' (p. 3), it is among the most significant prosodic experiments undertaken by the first-generation Romantic poets. Sayers was the author of *Poems, Containing Sketches of Northern Mythology* (1792), and, as Tim Fulford notes, Southey admired in Sayers his 'abandonment of the neo-classical couplet'.[3] The metre Southey uses seeks to avoid either the mechanically regular rhythm of the iambic pentameter or the merely improvised. What Southey wants is a measure that supplies both 'the sense of harmony' and 'the accent of feeling', a metre that does not chop lines 'which could be read as one', but allows each line its own life, even as the overall effect is intended to be harmonious. For Southey, metre is the soul of poetry. The metre of *Thalaba* 'suits', he claims, 'the varied subject' and is 'the *Arabesque* ornament of an Arabian tale' (Preface, p. 3).

An '*Arabesque* ornament' twists, undulates, and interweaves through a design, and Southey's metre adapts itself particularly well to the expression of interwoven events, descriptions, and transitions, and to the questioning which Southey introduces in order to nuance the predominantly declarative, active force of his poem's syntax. Typically a character is introduced in a place; we learn his or her history later and, indeed, history as fallen narrative is a powerful force in the poem. We meet characters who exist in their own imaginative space like figures from Spenser, and the poem, for all its awareness of the hurts of memory and its near-apocalyptic anticipation of a final contest, enjoys a continual emphasis on a narrative immediacy: spaces in which acts of will and moral choice have to be confronted and imaginatively undertaken all over again. To take just one instance, more or less at random, the following lines typify the startling thereness of Southey's narrative technique, as though each instant contained a quality of the potentially marvellous: 'The song of many a bird at morn / Aroused him from his rest. / Lo! By his side a courser stood!' (6.19–21). The effect is both to delight in the particular 'courser' standing by him and to suggest the hero's larger function, continually to be arisen from 'rest'. The consequence, overall, is a highly significant and unfairly neglected example of poetic narrative in the period.

The Curse of Kehama thrives on the episodic, dividing its twenty-four books into a number of sections and employing rhyme with as much virtuosity as *Thalaba* dodges it. In *Kehama* Southey often rhymes and occasionally avoids rhyme with extraordinary skill. An example occurs in Book 2 in which Kehama curses Ladurlad, preventing him from sleeping or from the release of death, or from the effects of time, by taking him out of nature – and thus inadvertently conferring the capacity for heroic status on him (Ladurlad will be able to save his daughter from burning to death – apparently her only way of escaping rape – because of his invulnerability to fire). The curse is a powerful incantation, mingling intensifying triplet rhyme (161–3) and a line, 'With a fire in thy heart' (164), that stands expressively alone, without a rhyme partner. In the passage that ensues (170–84), describing the impact on Ladurlad of the terrifying curse, Southey eschews rhyme, an eschewal that, in context, reinforces inability to believe what has just happened, as his hero stands 'with loose-hanging arms, / And eyes of idiot wandering' (172–3). The control of mood and pace effected by Southey's handling of rhyme effects is highly impressive throughout the poem.

The poem's story is once again Manichean in import and inflection, as it adapts Indian mythology to a tale of good versus evil, coming to a focus in Kehama's drinking of 'The Amreeta-cup of immortality' (24.131), another Southeyan detail which Shelley seems to have remembered in *The Triumph of Life*:

> He did not know the holy mystery
> Of that divinest cup, that as the lips
> Which touch it, even such its quality,
> Good or malignant: Madman! and he thinks
> The blessed prize is won, and joyfully he drinks.   (24.214–18)

The lines illustrate the declarative terseness and lucid compression of Southey's writing, with its sharp rhymes and enjambments. The poem strikes a fine balance between sketching the possibly Napoleon-like power of Kehama,[4] exemplified by his acts of sudden brutality (and Southey doesn't shrink from a considerable degree of physical horror), and the believable courage of Ladurlad and Kailyal, 'Sufferers from tyranny' (23.283), whose champion is the Glendoveer, half angelic Sir Galahad, half Popean sylph. The division of the poem into a series of encounters and dramatic high-points allows Southey to maintain tension and offer a virtual tour round the domain of his mythological learning. Gods are depicted with solemnity and respect, yet with a strong sense of the limitations placed upon their exercise of absolute power. The resemblance is more with classical than Christian narrative since the idea of plural deities holds sway in the poem, even as the notion of 'omniscience' and 'omnipotence' (24.208, 209) warrants the narrator's fulminating interest. In his 1838 Preface, Southey depicts himself as an adventurous mythographer, explaining the poem as produced by the desire 'of exhibiting the most remarkable forms of Mythology which have at any time obtained among mankind, by making each the ground work of a narrative poem' (Preface, p. 3). The poem has a conflicted nature; it has 'radical elements' in its hatred of despotism and sympathy for ordinary, lower-caste people that appealed to Shelley, as the editor of the Pickering edition notes (p. xviii), and it attempts to do justice to the benign and more fearsome aspects of Hindu mythology in (for example) the material about Baly and the Juga-Naut (see vol. 4, p. xxvii). The argument that it promotes a Christianizing, proto-imperialist view of its subject-matter is fashionable, yet it ignores Southey's responsiveness to his materials. What he achieves in *The Curse of Kehama* is a poem that finds in Hindu mythology more than an exotic other and not merely a serviceable mirror of Western concerns; there is a passion of narrative invention and immersion in episodic intensity that gives the poem a continuing life.

Notes

1 Southey's poetry is quoted from Robert Southey, *Poetic Works 1793–1810*, gen. ed. Linda Pratt, 5 vols (London: Pickering & Chatto, 2004); *Thalaba the Destroyer* qtd from vol. 3, ed. Tim Fulford, with the assistance of Daniel E. White and Carol Bolton; *The Curse of Kehama* qtd from vol. 4, ed. Daniel Sanjiv Roberts; copy texts for both texts in the Pickering edition are the original printed editions.

2 Echo noted in *The Poems of John Keats*, ed. Miriam Allott (London: Longmans, 1970), p. 399n.

3 *Thalaba*, ed. Fulford, p. xii.

4 See Simon Bainbridge, *Napoleon and English Romanticism* (Cambridge: Cambridge University Press, 1995), p. 121.

Second-Generation Romantic Poets

Thomas Moore, *Irish Melodies*

Thomas Moore is a poet of great versatility, producing satires, epistles, romances, and many other forms, but it is as a major exponent of the Romantic song or lyric that his significance chiefly resides. Famous in his day, a popular poet of Irish descent and concerns, a friend and mostly amiable rival of Byron, taken up by the Whig party and its fashionable coteries, Moore has often been dismissed as a purveyor of largely nostalgic and sentimental poems about 'Erin' (Ireland), a mawkish entertainer pandering to the hypocritical sympathies of an imperialist ruling class. 'Mr. Moore', writes Hazlitt with some savagery in *The Spirit of the* Age, 'converts the wild harp of Erin into a musical snuff-box!'[1] In fact, that 'musical snuff-box' contained heady poetic substances. Moore cannot simply be dismissed as an elegant weathervane, reflecting changes in contemporary poetic taste. Seamus Deane comes closer to the truth when, acknowledging Moore's cultural importance and invention of 'Irish nationalism', he argues that the Irish poet 'was a minor poet but a major phenomenon'.[2]

We need to allow for the way in which the tag 'minor poet' can get in the way of close inspection of what a poet manages to do. Moore wrote lyrics in an idiom that has been called 'Anacreontic', after the ancient Greek poet Anacreon, who wrote lyrics in praise of love and wine. In her illuminating essay on Moore's early *Odes of Anacreon*, Jane Moore notes that 'The structural economy of Anacreontic verse is one of imitation, rather than innovation'.[3] Yet as she herself remarks, Moore's mode of imitation is often one that 'modifies' the 'Anacreontic ethos' and this blend of respect for tradition and capacity subtly to make it new pervades Moore's lyrics.

His *Irish Melodies* (ten numbers between 1808 and 1834) are among the major products of the period's interest in poetic nationalism, in the idea that

The Romantic Poetry Handbook, First Edition. Michael O'Neill and Madeleine Callaghan.
© 2018 John Wiley & Sons Ltd. Published 2018 by John Wiley & Sons Ltd.

ballads and songs derive from the ancient sources of a culture, often one deserted, abandoned or subjected to tyrannical rule. The political subtext of Moore's poems, with their hints of protest against current English government policy, is no less strong for being shrouded in lyrical veils, as in his lament for his friend Robert Emmet, hanged and beheaded after the failed 1803 Irish uprising:

Oh! breathe not his name, let it sleep in the shade,
Where cold and unhonour'd his relics are laid;
Sad, silent, and dark be the tears that we shed,
As the night-dew that falls on the grass o'er his head.

But the night-dew that falls, though in silence it weeps,
Shall brighten with verdure the grave where it sleeps;
And the tear that we shed, though in secret it rolls,
Shall long keep his memory green in our souls.[4]

The kind of poem that led Byron to refer to Moore 'as the Burns of Ireland',[5] these lines make an eloquent lyricism out of what cannot be spoken, the name of the fallen freedom-fighter; they 'breathe' the name in the act of letting it 'sleep in the shade'. The lines appear to allude to Emmet's own supposed speech in the dock in which in one version he asked for the 'charity of silence' until his country had taken 'her place among the nations of the earth'.[6] Moore's lyricism, with its alliteration, vowel music, and anapaestic lilt, may lull, but the poetry's velvety form conceals a steely content apparent in the way in which 'grass' sets going a train of associations which culminate in the patriotic 'green' of the last lines, or in the turn effected from 'night-dew' as merely symbolic of forlorn lament to its use as a symbol of renewal.[7] There may be an element of the 'unfulfilled proposition', in Jane Moore's words, about the final image, but Moore's swaying, rounding on itself lyricism is not inhospitable to the kind of far gaze into futurity found in other Romantic works such as Shelley's *Prometheus Unbound*: these gazes can be dismissed over-hastily as idealistic to a fault or, more sympathetically, they can be seen as courageously sustaining the reader's vision. Deane is right to single out Moore's commitment to 'the fidelity of the tender heart' in the face of 'The treachery of time',[8] but one needs to add that his pledge to steadfast commitment has toughness in it as well as tenderness. Certainly there's an honesty and a cunning in the writing: a deep latent anger coexists with a refusal to commit itself to any political position other than reverential respect and grief.

Moore did not wholly disclaim political motives: he mockingly takes the fight to those prejudiced against his native country in his 'Prefatory Letter on Music', added to the third number of the *Irish Melodies* (1810): 'it was not to be expected that those touches of political feeling, those tones of national complaint, in which the poetry sometimes sympathizes with the music, would be suffered to pass without censure or alarm' (p. 194). But Moore deftly parts company with 'those who identify nationality with treason, and who see in every effort for Ireland a system of hostility towards England' (p. 195), and his shrewdly balanced position is evident in a poem such as 'Oh! blame not the bard' which continues:

> if he fly to the bowers
> Where Pleasure lies, carelessly smiling at Fame,
> He was born for much more, and in happier hours
> His soul might have burn'd with a holier flame   (p. 208)

In his preface Moore wrote that 'as [the *Melodies*] are intended rather to be sung than read, I can answer for their sound with somewhat more confidence than their sense; yet it would be affectation to deny that I have given more attention to the task, and that it is not through want of zeal or industry if I unfortunately disgrace the sweet airs of my country by poetry altogether unworthy of their taste, their energy, and their tenderness' (pp. 193–4). In the above poem 'sound' and 'sense' cooperate and interact: the run of long *i* sounds suggests the pleasure theme before the 'born for much more' series of echoing vowels backs up the sense of promise wasted, the various feelings mingling in the wistfulness of 'might', recalling but offsetting the depiction of 'Pleasure'.

Through its attention to sound, indeed, Moore's poem is alert to the political difficulties facing an Irish poet at a time when, as Kelly puts it, 'all hopes of Irish independence had been destroyed'.[9] The smoothly tripping metre is dexterously supportive of and at odds with the matter: the attitude includes an oblique mixture of self-reproach and self-justification on Moore's part, even as the poem offers itself a part of a volume of traditional 'melodies' and a note ironically portrays the bard as 'one of those wandering bards whom Spenser so severely, and perhaps truly, describes in his State of Ireland' (p. 208n). The bard may appear to be blameworthily hedonistic in reaction to political disappointment. But the poem finally offers something close to a reaffirmation of the poet's role in difficult times, as the maintainer of the flame of Irish memory:

> But though glory be gone, and though hope fade away,
> Thy name, lovèd Erin, shall live in his songs;
> Not even in the hour, when his heart is most gay,
> Will he lose the remembrance of thee and thy wrongs.   (p. 209)

A poet's 'remembrance' is not merely personal; it serves here to name a cultural function, the poet as storer and recorder of Ireland's 'wrongs'.[10] Loving, living on, and not losing link alliteratively. In such work, Moore evolves a mode and style that allowed him to fly below the censorious radar of Regency England and to ensure that 'Erin' and her 'wrongs' were in the 'remembrance' of the culture at large, as is shown by Shelley's reference to him in *Adonais* as sent to by 'Ierne' (Ireland) as 'The sweetest lyrist of her saddest wrongs' (269, 270).

Arguably, the very fame of *Irish Melodies* has led to their critical under-estimation. Often they take the note of lament found in much late eighteenth-century poetry, such as Hugh Macpherson's *Ossian*, and lift it to a pitch of near-incantatory, memorable speech, bearing witness to the way in which memory keeps intruding into consciousness, both the source of pain and a sign that an ideal still seeks baffled expression. Thus, 'The Harp that Once through Tara's Halls' sustains its tightly worked iambic tetrameters and trimeters into its concluding second stanza in the following way:

> No more to chiefs and ladies bright
>   The harp of Tara swells:
> The chord alone, that breaks at night,
>   Its tale of ruin tells.
> Thus Freedom now so seldom wakes,
>   The only throb she gives
> Is when some heart indignant breaks
>   To show that still she lives   (p. 197).

This passage suggests that in the past the bard's role was traditional, to sing to an aristocratic elite of 'chiefs and ladies bright', but that now it is played by an individual who speaks of a 'tale of ruin'. If it is normally now 'mute', it is also the witness to a residual impulse to protest. Poetry's role, the lines suggest, has changed for the poet – and not necessarily in the way, the con-cluding glossing lines intimate, for the worse. It may be Freedom is a broken heart whose 'only throb' is the moment that it 'breaks', but that breaking speaks of indignation and of the fact that 'still she lives', where 'still' means 'always' as well as 'even now'. The poem's melody is mournful but also surprisingly defiant. The fact that all but one rhyme in the stanza involves a verb speaks of conflict, latent struggle, the remaining if desperate hope that Freedom 'lives'.

Other lyrics espouse an artful credo of complementary feeling, as in 'Erin! The Tear and the Smile in Thine Eyes', in which the mingled affect typical of lyrics by Shelley and Byron is itself the subject of the song. The tear and the smile are worked up into a conceit of the rainbow uniting various lights that may smack of contrivance but reveals a light yet yearning strain of political hope.[11] In 'Erin, O Erin!' (pp. 207–8) he anticipates the political force attaching to the central metaphor of Shelley's 'Ode to the West Wind', that winter will give way to spring: 'Thus Erin, O Erin!', the poem concludes, '*thy* winter is past / And the hope that lived through it shall blossom at last'. The versification is again attuned to the matter at hand, the last line moving with a more regular march and beat than its predecessor. Moore's lyricism inspired responses from Berlioz[12] and Emily Brontë, who derives the first line of her complexly inflected 'Remembrance' from Moore's 'When Cold in the Earth'.[13] He is able continually in *Irish Melodies* to move between and fuse feelings with an art that veils but finally points up a rare and influential poise and depth of engagement.

Notes

1   Qtd in Linda Kelly, *Ireland's Minstrel: A Life of Tom Moore: Poet, Patriot and Byron's Friend* (London: Tauris, 2006), p. 150.

2   Seamus Deane, *A Short History of Irish Literature* (London: Hutchinson, 1986), p. 65.

3   Jane Moore, 'Thomas Moore, Anacreon and the Romantic Tradition', *Romantic Textualities* 21 (Winter 2013), qtd from romtext.org.uk.

4   *The Poetical Works of Thomas Moore* (London: Warne, 1891).

5   Qtd in Jeffrey Vail, *The Literary Relationship of Lord Byron and Thomas Moore* (Baltimore: Johns Hopkins University Press, 2001), p. 83.

6   The text as elaborated in the most famous received version reads: 'I have but one request to ask at my departure from this world – it is the charity of its silence! Let no man write my epitaph: for as no man who knows my motives dare now vindicate them. Let not prejudice or ignorance asperse them. Let them and me repose in obscurity and peace, and my tomb remain uninscribed, until other times, and other men, can do justice to my character; when my country takes her place among the nations of the earth, then, and not till then, let my epitaph be written. I have done.' For a text see www.robertemmet.org and for discussion of the different versions see, among others, Timothy Webb, 'Coleridge and Robert Emmet', *Irish Studies Review* 8 (2000): 304–24.

7   See Carmen Casaliggi and Porscha Fermanis, who write that the poem is 'far from being a fatalistic and sentimental portrait of Gaelic defeat', but 'can be read as gesturing towards a clandestine revolutionary solidarity that draws strength from Emmet's memory'. *Romanticism: A Literary and Cultural History* (London: Routledge, 2016), p. 103.

8   Deane, *Short History*, p. 65.

9   *Ireland's Minstrel*, p. 33.

10 For a balanced discussion that takes issue with Thomas Kinsella's critique of Moore for allegedly 'withholding his talents from the service of the oppressed

and choosing to entertain the oppressor' (qtd p. 186), see Mary Helen Thuente, *The Harp Re-strung: The United Irishmen and the Rise of Irish Literary Nationalism* (Syracuse, NY: Syracuse University Press, 1994), pp. 171–92.

11 As Deane remarks, pointing up the fact that Irish identity had to be made, constructed, 'The synthetic and artificial element in his work is its most important feature'. *Short History*, p. 65.

12 See Kelly, *Ireland's Minstrel*, pp. 77–8.

13 As noted in *The Poems of Emily Brontë*, ed. Janet Gezari (London: Penguin, 1992), p. 229.

Leigh Hunt, *The Story of Rimini*

Leigh Hunt's *The Story of Rimini* was first published in 1816. Parts of it (canto 3 and a 'small part' of canto 4) were written while Hunt was in Surrey Gaol for allegedly libelling the Prince Regent. In its stylistic mannerisms, which emphasize freedom from conventional handling of the couplet and in its opposition to hierarchical pride and its advocacy of the affections, the poem exemplifies what John Strachan calls Hunt's 'literary avant-gardism'.[1] It is preceded by a dedicatory letter to Byron, who is addressed with egalitarian want of ceremony as 'MY DEAR BYRON', an '(over-) familiarity much-criticised in the Tory press' (p. 323). That defiant address is suggestive of the poem's mainly genial assault on the hidebound and hierarchical, and its preference for the natural and the free, words used in the Preface, each carrying a considerable ideological freight.

Jane Stabler puts the matter well when she depicts 'Hunt's ideal of his own literary persona' as 'extravagantly and yet gently set against cold custom'.[2] Hunt argues in the Preface that his 'endeavour' is 'to recur to a freer spirit of versification' and to deploy 'a free and idiomatic cast of language' (p. 167). One notices 'recur': Hunt's attempt is to recover freedoms he feels have been lost as a result of the regularity favoured by 'Pope and the French school of versification' (p. 167). Hunt wishes freedoms that are excluded from Pope's practice, the freedom to vary the position of the caesura, to extend the unit of sense beyond the couplet boundary, to depart from linguistic decorum in the interests of freshness, novelty, up-to-dateness, to use feminine rhymes frequently. He presents himself as a slicker, more urban version of the Wordsworth who sought to return to 'a selection of the language really used by men' (Wordsworth's use of 'selection' allows him to avoid identifying the poet with a mere transcriber of daily speech).[3] At the

The Romantic Poetry Handbook, First Edition. Michael O'Neill and Madeleine Callaghan.
© 2018 John Wiley & Sons Ltd. Published 2018 by John Wiley & Sons Ltd.

same time Hunt is aware of the dangers inherent in 'exaggerations of simplicity'. Indeed, the Preface to *The Story of Rimini* is a fascinating piece of critical writing as it positions Hunt between extremes of 'the artificial style' and 'the natural' (p. 168).

A touchstone cited in the Preface is Lear's 'I am a very foolish fond old man, / Fourscore and upward' (qtd p. 168): lines said to exhibit 'all that criticism can say, or poetry can do'. But in his narrative expansion of the Paolo and Francesca episode from Dante's *Inferno*, canto 5, Hunt's idiom is brisker, more aggressively intent on challenging ideas of decorum. Siding with the lovers and opposed to Dante's understanding of sin, 'the whole melancholy absurdity of his theology', as he characterizes the matter in the Preface, Hunt deploys an idiom in sympathy with what he calls 'one genuine impulse of the affections' (p. 165).

This 'genuine impulse' is the subject of the third canto, a remarkable study of the growing attraction between Francesca and Paolo, her husband's brother and the man whom she was led, mistakenly, to suppose would be her husband. Without vulgarizing Dante's incomparable depiction of erotic obsession and consequent damnation, Hunt transposes it into the key of the novel of sentiment: a work such as Rousseau's *Julie*, pored over by Shelley in the year in which *Rimini* was published, might be a distant progenitor of Hunt's poem, with its attention to the intricate ethical issues raised by love. Hunt captures well the 'conscious' quality of the lovers' response to one another at the outset of their fatal meeting, where 'conscious' means 'aware, co-knowing in a slightly guilty way':

> There's apt to be, at conscious times like these,
> An affectation of a bright-eyed ease,
> An air of something quite serene and sure,
> As if to seem so, were to be, secure ...   (3.585–8)

The jauntiness of 'apt to be' and 'bright-eyed ease' speaks less of Hunt's inability to match Dante's tragic pathos than of his good-humoured aware-ness that his poem is itself seeking to be 'quite serene and sure', even as it must confront pain and suffering. The subsequent moment of passion, when Paolo 'felt he could no more dissemble, / And kissed her, mouth to mouth, all in a tremble' (603–4), uses its feminine rhyme to create a sympathetic image of the lovers driven by 'one genuine impulse of affection'. Hunt understates the achievement of canto 3 when in the fourth and last canto, as if in reaction to the feelings that the lovers' plight creates in him, he defines 'Sorrow' (17) as 'but the discord of a warbling sphere, / A lurking contrast' (18–19). His discomfort with his story's sadness offers itself as the source of the vigour with which he turns his attention to the response of spectators to Francesca's death – 'They saw her tremble sharply, feet and all, — / Then suddenly be still' (4.408–9); there 'tremble' contrasts mordantly with its earlier use (quoted above). But this discomfort also suggests his own affecting wish not to dwell exclusively on the darker side of experience.

The thrust of the poem, from the start, is a sympathy with impulse, affection, naturalness. The first paragraph in this poem of very unPopean rhymed couplets is a case in point, with its vivid investment in all the goings on of the present: 'The sun is up, and 'tis a morn of May / Round old Ravenna's clear-shewn towers and bay' (1–2) is how the poem opens, locating the poem in the here and now. In accord with the poem's resistance to Augustan practice, the opening couplet does not endstop its unit's sense after line 2, but allows it to flow on into a description of 'A morn, the loveliest which the year has seen' (3). The unashamed use of the intensifying 'loveliest' accompanies an alertness to the visual and physical that makes Hunt's diction surprisingly reinvigorating rather than pert or hackneyed. So, we're told that 'A balmy briskness comes upon the breeze; / The smoke goes dancing from the cottage trees' (9–10). Hunt's verbs 'comes' and 'goes' along with 'briskness' and 'dancing' prevent the rhyme of 'breeze' and 'trees' from being merely banal; it, too, participates in a shared sense of vitality, 'nature, full of spirits' (15). There's a comparable energy of observation in the account of how

> the far ships, lifting their sails of white
> Like joyful hands, come up with scattery light,
> Come gleaming up, true to the wished-for day,
> And chase the whistling brine, and swirl into the bay. (21–4)

The passage shows Hunt's ability to turn narrative into momentary lyric and it makes one think of Tennyson's lines, in 'Tears, Idle Tears': 'Fresh as the first beam glittering on a sail, / That brings our friends up from the underworld' (6–7):[4] lines that add a sadder, more sombre tinge to Hunt's, but a tinge that is present in Hunt's lines precisely because it is potently absent. A poem about transgressive love and its fatal consequences wishes also to hymn the essential goodness of life. In that sense, Hunt's moment of lyric intensity, in which narrative seems to be interrupted in favour of description and comparison, has a bearing on the overall story: 'joyful hands', his fine simile, is a phrase that suggests what should be possible in life, but, because of custom and human malevolence, too often isn't. The repetition of 'come up' suggests a freshness deep down things always ready to emerge, while the final alexandrine illustrates the poem's readiness to

214

experiment in the interests of stylistic variety; 'scattery light', toned down in 1832 to 'scatter'd light' in deference no doubt to the criticisms of indecorum heaped on the poem (see p. 324) is leapingly exuberant and prepares us for Hunt's central moral, uttered in the course of his analysis of Giovanni, Francesca's proud husband:

> He lost the sight of conduct's only worth,
> The scattering smiles on this uneasy earth   (3.71–2)

It's not a moral that would have satisfied Dante. But in its robust defence of sexual attraction and the virtues of sympathy and love, and in its generous response to natural beauty, *The Story of Rimini*, a poem of great significance for Keats among others, is still a Romantic poem deserving of the closest study.

Notes

1   *The Selected Writings of Leigh Hunt*, vol. 5, *Poetical Works, 1801–21*, ed. John Strachan (London: Pickering & Chatto, 2003), pp. 161, 162. The poem is quoted from this edition.
2   Jane Stabler, 'Leigh Hunt's Aesthetics of Intimacy', in *Leigh Hunt: Life, Politics, Poetics*, ed. Nicholas Roe (London: Routledge, 2003), p. 112.
3   *William Wordsworth*, ed. Stephen Gill, 21st-Century Oxford Authors (Oxford: Oxford University Press, 2010), p. 53.
4   *Poems of Tennyson*, ed. Christopher Ricks (London: Longman, 1969).

Lord Byron, *Lara*; 'When We Two Parted'; 'Stanzas to Augusta'; *Manfred*

This section looks at four poems – one tale, two lyrics, and a 'dramatic poem' – to illustrate the range of Byron's generic experimentation between 1814 and 1816. *Lara*, written in May and June 1814 and published in the same year, belongs to Byron's so-called 'Turkish Tales', in which he created the 'masterful, moody outlaws' that became known as Byronic heroes.[1] Byron sardonically claimed the action was meant to take place on the moon.[2] His advertisement to the 1814 edition implied that *Lara* could be read as a sequel to *The Corsair*, but Leslie Brisman points out that this does not shed much light on the poem.[3] Rather, Byron's Tales represent his interest in the psychological aftershocks of trauma, as Bernard Beatty summarizes: '[Byron] is interested in pain as consequential in some sense and, above all, in its recognitions and acknowledgement by those who endure it'.[4] This interest spurs his work into the explorations of repression, looming secrets, and the damaging effects of love. The hero is a vehicle for Byron to explore these ideas as the poet shrouds his hero with mystery, with every detail of his Tale suggesting that there is another 'tale untold' (*Lara* 2.25.627).[5]

In *Lara* Byron creates a profoundly ambiguous moral universe that makes the reader aware that what we know is always subject to what the speaker tells us; any pretence at the objective is continually thwarted and deferred, with the Tale acting both to 'invite moral judgement and make that judgement impossible'.[6] Paraphrase suggests the narrative intricacy of the work. The poem opens with Lara returning to his ancestral lands with his foreign page, Kaled, to take possession of his estates. It soon becomes apparent that Lara fails to share 'The common pleasure or the general care; / He did not follow what they all pursued' (1.4.102–3) and his isolation from his peer group renders him the topic of general discussion as 'Lara's vassals

The Romantic Poetry Handbook, First Edition. Michael O'Neill and Madeleine Callaghan.
© 2018 John Wiley & Sons Ltd. Published 2018 by John Wiley & Sons Ltd.

prattled of their lord' (1.9.154). After an unexplained confrontation with Ezzelin, Lara arranges to fight a duel with his adversary, only to fight Otho successfully in the stead of the absent Ezzelin, who disappears to rumours of Lara's involvement. Such rumours and dissatisfaction with the rule in the region lead to Lara entering into open warfare with his fellow feudal chiefs. Lara becomes the aristocrat who would fight for the rights of his serfs, as 'that long absence from his native clime / Had left him stainless of Oppression's crime' (2.8.170–1). After initial success, soon Lara's forces are decimated by the superior strength of the armies of the other chiefs. Wounded by an arrow, Lara lies dying, cared for by Kaled, his foreign page, to whom he addresses his dying words in a foreign language despite Otho's presence. Kaled then reveals that he is a woman, and chooses to die by Lara's grave.

Despite the apparently comprehensible plot, the story is far from simple owing to its style of narration. The reader pivots from tacit support of Lara, to anger and condemnation of his seeming lack of care for his men and his needlessly antagonistic attitude to Otho. Nor does it seem that we learn anything about the inner life of Lara, or Kaled, or Ezzelin, or Otho. Nigel Leask points to Byron's poetic skill in this narrative poem where the poet's aesthetic power and control become part of the poem's action: '*Lara* shows Byron as a master of suspense, and there is considerable power in his handling of narrative deferral and chilling denouement.'[7] Byron, from the beginning, makes the reader aware of the many fissures, and the power of the unexpressed and the unsaid, in the work:

> The Serfs are glad through Lara's wide domain,
> And Slavery half forgets her fuedal chain;
> He, their unhop'd, but unforgotten lord,
> The long self-exiled chieftain, is restored: (1.1.4)

With 'half forgets', Byron suggests the joy of forgetting the painful ties that bind the people to their masters while remembering how impossible such forgetfulness would be. He holds open a hope only to half-undercut it with a darker understanding of the dehumanizing effect of slavery. Equally, the negative prefixes attached to 'hoped' and 'forgotten' cancel even as they suggest the states he conjures. *Lara* ripples with a tension between the tale told and what could be said as Byron makes emotional, physical, and mental states difficult to define. This uneasiness means that the tale told becomes something scrutinized rather than accepted.

Lara forces the reader to enter into the poem's maze of interpretation as Byron underscores the impossibility of assigning moral judgements, doing so by the perspective shifts he makes in the poem. This is a vital component of *Lara*'s challenging two-part design, which, as Jerome McGann argues, was part of his insistence on how his reader must engage closely with his poetry: 'Byron taught his public how to read his poetry, led them to see (for example) that more was meant in *The Giaour* and the other tales than met the eye of one who simply read them as exotic tales of adventure.'[8] *Lara*'s themes become dangerously relevant to Britain, and more universally, as class, dangerous rumours, guilt, and uncertainty pervade the text. The French Revolution, with its initial optimistic removal of the aristocrats from power by the people, degenerated into a bloody killing spree, and Byron's poetry retains this tortured ambiguity. Rather than Lara becoming a symbol of liberation, Byron explicitly complicates Lara's freeing of his slaves: 'And cared he for the freedom of the crowd? / He raised the humble but to bend the proud' (2.9.252–3). The careful, polished couplets, the twists and turns, and digressive sections of the plot, all ensure that the reader must concentrate on the tale told through 'textual digressions within a tightly controlled formal patterning'.[9] The couplet form, though less challenging than Byron's later *ottava rima*, is deceptively simple. The text ripples with discontinuities and evasions created, at least in part, through Byron's judicious use of form. *Lara* exerts a hold on the reader through such disruptive tactics as we move through the couplets, trying to catch a glimpse of his hero.

Lara, though possessing a mysterious past, is intriguing because of the teller's skill, not by virtue of being the subject of the tale. The narrative is broken by our incomplete understanding of what has actually happened. Lacking the precise content of Lara's past, or Kaled's identity, or of the grounds of Ezzelin's complaint, or if we should support Lara's fight, the reader is left to follow the meandering tale. The narrator creates Lara's intrigue, guessing at rather than observing his character:

> There was in him a vital scorn of all:
> As if the worst had fall'n which could befall,
> He stood a stranger in this breathing world,
> An erring spirit from another hurled;
> A thing of dark imaginings, that shaped
> By choice the perils he by chance escaped;
> But 'scaped in vain, for in their memory yet
> His mind would half exult and half regret: (1.3.313–20)

Though apparently offering information, the lines heighten rather than dispel mystery. The 'As if' of line 314 undoes the sense that this speculation is based on fact and the narrator introduces the idea that Lara is both more than and separate from the greater mass of humanity. Aesthetic beauty sings through the lines; 'breathing world' shocks with both its obvious yet original strength and 'erring spirit' carefully reminds us of Milton's Satan while refusing to commit to the identification. Lara's 'inexplicably mixed' (1.289) character defies categorization as his silence becomes the vacuum that must be filled by all observers: 'His silence formed a theme for others' prate— / They guess'd—they gazed—they fain would know his fate' (1.17.293–4). If, for Nigel Leask, 'the poem's subject is *repression*',[10] here Byron suggests that for Lara's observers, the common theme is obsession. The dashes scored across the page suggest the tantalizing longing to classify Lara comfortably within the bounds of their understanding as Byron almost pathologizes their speculative mania for answers. *Lara*, a highly accomplished narrative poem, becomes almost a psychological exploration of its eponymous hero and its narrator as it leaves its reader with more questions than answers.

'When We Two Parted', composed between August and September 1815, feigns a confessional simplicity even as it misdirects the reader. Showcasing Byron's superb ability with metre and rhyme, the poem is divided into four sections of eight alternate rhymed lines in tightly compressed trimeter with varying stresses. Roughly speaking, each of the eight lines is broken into an iamb, followed by an anapaest, with the odd-numbered lines containing a final unstressed beat:

> Thy vows are all broken,
>   And light is thy fame;
> I hear thy name spoken,
>   And share in its shame.   ('When We Two Parted', 13–16)

Trailing his bleeding heart across its stanzas, Byron cleverly positions himself as standing brooding and apart from the group as he deals with his secret love and secret betrayal. Though 'When We Two Parted' belonged to a collection published in 1816, Byron labels it 1808, and Jerome McGann rightly points out that the dating of the poem is a deliberate attempt to mislead his readers: 'But the lines were not written in 1808 – that was a ruse of Byron's – they were written in 1815; and their immediate subject was Lady Frances Wedderburn Webster. Byron manipulated his 1816 text in order to hide that fact. But he was also manipulating another, altogether invisible text – a poem which he wrote in 1812 to Lady Caroline Lamb.'[11] Though Byron might claim that he wrote these lines earlier, many in Byron's London social milieu would be aware of the poem's true context, and the 1812 poem to Lady Caroline Lamb that had formed part of 'When We Two Parted'.[12] Byron creates groups of the 'knowing' and uses his poetry to signal indirectly to their members in a deliberate manipulation of the concept of lyric. Lyric poetry fashions a relationship with its reader based on sincerity. Byron undermines this fragile trust and, with great care and skill, transforms the lyric.

'Stanzas to [Augusta]' was written July 1816 and published that year. It complements the 'Epistle to Augusta' (written August 1816 and published 1831) in being addressed to Augusta Leigh (Byron's half-sister). The lines move between using three anapaestic feet and an unstressed final syllable, and combining iambs and anapaests, and exhibit subtle metrical flexibility. The eight-line stanzas consist of alternate rhymes, mixing feminine and masculine rhymes to shape and disrupt the sense of set patterning. Byron allows his voice freedom to fall into rhymes without the rhymes seeming over-determined. Sharing its themes with the 'Epistle to Augusta', 'Stanzas' repeatedly isolates the poet and his addressee. It asserts that its addressee, ostensibly Augusta, shares his grief with a loyalty and love that his heart 'never hath found but in *thee*' ('Stanzas to [Augusta]', 8). Here it echoes the language of Byron's letter to Augusta in 1816, where he writes tenderly to her: 'What a fool I was to marry—and you not very wise—my dear— [...] I shall never find any one like you—nor you (vain as it may seem) like me. We are just formed to pass our lives together, and therefore—we—at least—I—am by a crowd of circumstances removed from the only being who could ever have loved me, or whom I can unmixedly feel attached to.'[13] The poem mingles both the confessional and the artificial as Byron makes poetry out of pain rather than simply transcribing it.

> Though human, thou didst not deceive me,
>   Though woman, thou didst not forsake,
> Though loved, thou forborest to grieve me,
>   Though slander'd, thou never could'st shake,—
> Though trusted, thou didst not betray me,
>   Though parted, it was not to fly,
> Though watchful, 'twas not to defame me,
>   Nor, mute, that the world might belie.   ('Stanzas to [Augusta]', 25–32)

The patterning of stanza 4 is relentless in its anaphora as it dramatizes Augusta's uniqueness. Dividing each line into two, Byron embodies the separation between himself and Augusta and the negatives serve to emphasize his treatment at the hands of 'the world' (33) from which he attempts to separate Augusta and himself. Isolation from the world and his beloved became a recurrent theme in Byron's poetry and drama, and though Byron suffered from this alienation, it proved the spark that set his poetry alight.

Manfred, written in 1816 and 1817, represents an early foray into what Byron calls his 'mental theatre',[14] and Byron wrote it as a dramatic poem not intended for performance. The play centres on Manfred, the play's ambiguous aristocratic hero, a late version of the Cain type, mingled with Prometheus. Byron explored various versions of these types throughout his career.[15] It opens with Manfred invoking 'Ye spirits of the unbounded Universe!' (1.1.29) as he demands of the seven assembled spirits that he should be granted forgetfulness, but will not name that which he wishes to forget, telling the spirit 'Ye know it, and I cannot utter it' (1.1.138). The spirits cannot grant him this, nor death, but appear to him in the shape of Astarte, the beautiful dead woman who seems strongly connected to Manfred's unnamed guilt. Bemoaning the conflict of the flesh and the spirit, Manfred laments later that we are 'Half dust, half deity, alike unfit / To sink or soar' (1.2.40–1). A chamois hunter saves Manfred from a suicide attempt, and in their subsequent conversation, Manfred sheds some light on Astarte, implying an incestuous relationship between the pair before the chamois hunter counsels Manfred to be stoical in the face of existence. When Manfred encounters the Witch of the Alps, he reveals the depths of his torment as he claims of Astarte that 'I loved her, and destroy'd her!' (2.2.117). The Witch demands his submission, but Manfred refuses to grant it, keeping his autonomy despite the temptation to surrender to her will. Likewise, when he meets Arimanes, 'Sovereign of Sovereigns!' (2.4.23), he will not kneel before him, and his refusal leads them to grant him the boon of seeing her. But the vision of her, and her words, which do not grant him the forgiveness he begs, convulse him. Having been promised by Astarte that his woes would end the next day, Manfred becomes calm ahead of his encounter with the Abbot of St Maurice. The Abbot attempts to convert Manfred to Christianity, asking him to show penitence and beg pardon. Manfred reads his overtures as requiring him to submit to a higher power, and refuses, telling him, 'The lion is alone, and so am I' (3.1.123), as the Abbot laments that 'This should have been a noble creature' (3.1.160) and decides to follow him in secret. Following Manfred into the tower, the Abbot makes a final attempt to save Manfred, and the spirits appear to bid him to follow them. Defying both the Abbot and the spirits, Manfred insists on his own will, and his final words, 'Old man! 'tis not so difficult to die' (3.4.151), underscore a sense of self-mastery that endures from the beginning to the end of the play.

For Jerome McGann, '*Manfred* is a nakedly autobiographical piece in which Byron tries to represent what sort of life can remain for a man once he knows not only that his soul is a sepulchre, but that he himself has made it so'.[16] Yet *Manfred* seems another attempt at dealing with 'the inadequacy of [man's] state to his Conceptions',[17] a task that preoccupied Byron throughout his poetic and dramatic career. Manfred openly challenges everything, attempting to command spirits, explore the limitations and freedom of the self, and remain imperiously in charge of his own destiny.

While it might be a form of self-mastery, it is a bitterly broken form of heroism where the self comes up against its own destruction, leading Frederick Garber to argue: 'At the dead end there is only himself, those closed-in walls and that bitter kingdom of the mind in which he is lord and subject and, he argues, his own destroyer.'[18] This emphasis on human, fragile power based on the will rather than divine strength means that Byron keeps human vulnerability in play. Despite the commanding tone of Manfred's speeches to the spirits, there is a desperation beneath the lines as Manfred struggles with his guilt for the unnamed crime. As noted above, the crime itself revolves around Astarte, where Byron hints at an incestuous relationship with this now dead figure. But the crime is only in the eyes of the world; Manfred adopts a pose of splendid isolation from the opinions of society. His rejection of the social order should create a new relationship of self and world, new boundaries, and new standards of value. Yet this new relationship never truly emerges. Manfred might be an isolated hero but he never adopts a tantalizing potential freedom. Although he seemingly could choose to be otherwise, Manfred still appears to feel sinful as he remains tormented by guilt. He may insist that he creates his own rules, and appears powerful in commanding the spirits, but he punishes himself through his adherence to the rules of a society he struggles to reject. While asserting the power of the individual's mind to create its own heaven and its own hell in the manner of Milton's Satan, his own mind punishes him for a crime defined by society.

In the conclusion of the final Act, Manfred banishes the Spirits with great authority:

> *Thou* didst not tempt me, and thou couldst not tempt me;
> I have not been thy dupe, nor am thy prey—
> But was my own destroyer, and will be
> My own hereafter.—Back, ye baffled fiends!
> The hand of death is on me—but not yours!
> > [*The Demons disappear.*   (*Manfred* 3.4.137–41)

Manfred describes himself as a 'destroyer' and asserts his potency through his choice of wording in 'I have not been thy dupe', assuming that he holds the power to choose not to be a pawn in their game. Yet there is an implicit fear on his part that he was never in control. Instead, society, the spirits, and religion continue to exert power no matter how hard Manfred tries to disavow their importance. But Byron also points up Manfred's defiant self-control. The stage direction, 'The Demons disappear', shows Byron subtly changing Manfred's interlocutors from the earlier description as a singular 'spirit' into multiple 'Demons'. The change and distortion confirms Manfred's power, and the commanding nature of the speech reaffirms the power of his mind to choose his own fate, even if that fate is death. Yet the play's tragedy is to show that such a display of titanic defiance and self-determination only leads Manfred to his death. Heroism, self-determination, and overweening strength end up destroyed. Here, 'There woos no home, nor hope, nor life, save what is here' (*Childe Harold's Pilgrimage* 4.105.945). The problem becomes something so deep as to be unalterable, and as Peter Manning writes: 'Society does not need redemption; Manfred alone, like Milton's Satan, is cut off from joy.'[19] In *Manfred* Byron created the epitome of his own blasted and wasted hero type whose triumph must be his destruction.

Notes

1   Marilyn Butler, *Romantics, Rebels and Reactionaries: English Literature and its Background 1760–1830* (Oxford: Oxford University Press, 1981), p. 118.
2   Byron to Murray, 24 July 1814; *BLJ* 4.145–6.
3   Leslie Brisman, 'Byron: Troubled Stream from a Pure Source', *ELH* 42.4 (1975): 623–50 (at 632).
4   Bernard Beatty, 'Fiction's Limit and Eden's Door', in *Byron and the Limits of Fiction*, ed. Bernard Beatty and Vincent Newey (Liverpool: Liverpool University Press, 1988), pp. 1–36 (at p. 10).
5   Lord Byron, *The Complete Poetical Works*, ed. Jerome J. McGann, 7 vols (Oxford: Clarendon Press, 1980–93), 3. 256. In this section, Byron is quoted from this edition. *Lara* and 'When We Two Parted' are in the third volume, and *Manfred* and 'Stanzas to Augusta' are in the fourth.
6   Jonathon Shears, '"A tale untold": The Search for a Story in Byron's *Lara*', *The Byron Journal* 34.1 (2006): 1–8 (at 1).
7   Nigel Leask, 'Resolving *The Corsair*: *Lara* and *The Island*', in *Byron*, ed. and intro. Jane Stabler (London: Longman, 1998), pp. 67–78 (at p. 67).
8   Jerome McGann, 'Byron and "The Truth in Masquerade"', in *Romantic Revisions*, ed. Robert Brinkley and Keith Hanley (Cambridge: Cambridge University Press, 1992), pp. 191–209 (at p. 205).
9   Jane Stabler, *Byron, Poetics and History*, Cambridge Studies in Romanticism 52 (Cambridge: Cambridge University Press, 2002), p. 4.
10 Nigel Leask, *British Romantic Writers and the East: Anxieties of Empire* (Cambridge: Cambridge University Press, 1992), p. 56.
11 McGann, 'Byron and "The Truth in Masquerade"', p. 191.
12 McGann, 'Byron and "The Truth in Masquerade"', p. 191.
13 *BLJ* 5.96.
14 *BLJ* 8.187.
15 See Peter L. Thorslev, *The Byronic Hero: Types and Prototypes* (Minneapolis: University of Minnesota Press, 1962).
16 Jerome McGann, *Don Juan in Context* (Chicago: University of Chicago Press, 1976), p. 36.
17 *BLJ* 9.54.
18 Frederick Garber, *Self, Text, and Romantic Irony: The Example of Byron* (Princeton: Princeton University Press, 1988), p. 134.
19 Peter J. Manning, *Byron and His Fictions* (Detroit: Wayne State University Press, 1978), p. 72.

Lord Byron, *Childe Harold's Pilgrimage*

Byron's *Childe Harold's Pilgrimage, A Romaunt* was written and published in stages across the poet's career. The first two cantos, with their imitation or mockery of Spenserian 'romance' and their use of a travelogue format, were published in 1812. Canto 3, written in the aftermath of Byron's departure from England that year, and dealing, among other things, with his visit to the battlefield of Waterloo, and response to the Swiss Alps, was published in 1816. Much of it was composed after meeting Shelley in Geneva in May the same year. Canto 4, set in Italy, appeared from the press in 1818. Inevitably the work's focus and tones shift, but it still seems appropriate to refer to it as a single poem while bearing in mind the fact of its complicated publishing history; there are purposeful continuities and developments throughout, nowhere more so than in the room each canto gives itself to wander and digress, often dramatizing and enacting an interplay of feelings or attitudes.

Mainly written in 1809 and 1810, the original manuscript of the first two cantos underwent pre-publication revisions. Byron responded to criticism on political and religious grounds from his friend, R. C. Dallas, and his publisher, John Murray, and included additional stanzas prompted by events in his life, such as the stanzas (96–7) at the end of canto 2 about the deaths of various figures in his life, including his mother and John Edleston, a fellow Cambridge student with whom Byron was in love. The poem was an immediate sensation. His upper-middle-class readership delighted in accounts of travel to Spain, Greece, and Turkey, all areas of topical interest: Spain was a theatre of war, the Peninsular War being fought there against Napoleon's invading forces. Moreover, readers were intrigued by the way in which

The Romantic Poetry Handbook, First Edition. Michael O'Neill and Madeleine Callaghan.
© 2018 John Wiley & Sons Ltd. Published 2018 by John Wiley & Sons Ltd.

Byron depicted a version of his experiences through the figure of Childe Harold. The Byronic hero was launched, a brooding, self-divided figure, shifting between gloom and ardour, cloaked in impenetrable mystery, apart from the society which prompted his every antithetical move. This projected self is not quite identifiable with nor is it entirely separable from Byron the poet; at the same time, Harold and Byron share in one another's life, progressively so, until by the fourth canto Byron, in his Preface, concedes that 'there will be found less of the pilgrim than in any of the preceding [cantos], and that slightly, if at all, separated from the author speaking in his own person. The fact is,' Byron continues, 'that I had become weary of drawing a line which every one seemed determined not to perceive.'[1] But the provocative blurring of that line is among Byron's most arresting indeterminacies in the poem.

The poem handles with shrewd artistry the interplay between Harold and the poet-narrator; running on parallel lines, each figure embodies a process of what in canto 1 Byron calls 'Consciousness awaking to her woes' (1.92.941); each does so in the context of historical and geopolitical realities that are rendered with gusto. Harold may seem world-weary. Byron's narrative presence and extensive prose notes, at the foot of the page in the original edition, show a mind absorbed, even as he is often appalled, by what is happening in the world. An example is his assault on the Scottish Earl of Elgin's theft and selling of sculptures from Athens in canto 2. Here Byron is every inch the admiring disciple of Pope, depicting Elgin with swift contempt: 'Cold as the crags upon his native coast, / His mind as barren and his heart as hard' (2.12.102–3). A long Appendix reinforces the attack.

The poem is, thus, generically and tonally inclusive. It does not provide a smoothly comfortable reading experience, often dispatching a topic as vehemently as it addressed it; the Elgin Marbles stanzas, for instance, pass into the abrupt transition, 'But where is Harold? shall I then forget / To urge the gloomy wanderer o'er the wave?' (2.16.136–7). Yet these abruptnesses are inseparable from qualities that make the poem compelling: above all, a restless intensity of engagement with experience, a controlled narratorial impatience, and, as Jerome McGann notes, an implicit conviction that what seems disparate connects vitally. Thus, the longing for individual freedom (embodied in Harold) mirrors the desire for political liberation (the narrator's wish for Greece).[2] The first canto, setting up a rhythm that is pervasive, moves between discovery and disillusion, voyaging and finding that there is nothing new under the sun, responsiveness to contemporary history and an air of near-sardonic detachment. The 'Pilgrimage' of the title, as Alice Levine observes, is 'ironic, secular, Romantic', and yet the questing is real, finding its best image in the third canto's self-reflexive discovery of 'wanderers o'er

Eternity / Whose bark drives on and on, and anchor'd ne'er shall be' (3.70.669–70), an image Shelley replies to in the final stanza of *Adonais*, hearing an anticipatory echo of his own aspiring impulses in the enjambment and driving on that makes even 'Eternity' a realm of process.[3]

Sometimes the narrator's mood is that of Hamlet in the Gravedigger's scene, as when, at the Parthenon in Athens, he comments on a skull:

> Look on its broken arch, its ruin'd wall,
> Its chambers desolate, and portals foul:
> Yes, this was once Ambition's airy hall,
> The dome of Thought, the palace of the Soul … (2.6.46–9)

If life seems futile here, the thought only adds a spur to the narrator's subsequent re-embracing of experiential possibilities. Within a few stanzas he writes, with seemingly extempore immediacy, of a calm night at sea, 'when Meditation bids us feel / We once have lov'd, though love is at an end', when 'The heart, lone mourner of its baffled zeal, / Though friendless now, will dream it had a friend' (2.23.199–202). This writing unexpectedly and powerfully connects the reader to Byron. If it involves our acceptance of an achieved rhetoric, with its theatrical self-presentation, the rhetoric seems to well up from depths of feeling. Byron's syntax, bending back on itself, with its 'Though' clauses, is in touch with the way feelings move to and fro in time, and the pronoun 'We', rather seductively, includes the reader in Byron's depiction of what it is to have a 'heart' that is the 'lone mourner of its baffled zeal'.

Byron's public voice is among his most spectacular if not always comfortable successes. One of the novel guises he adopts in canto 1, as in later cantos, is that of the all-noticing, disenchanted eye-witness, or near-eye-witness. So, Albuera, which staged one of the bloodiest battles of the Peninsular War, earns the sardonic tag 'glorious field of grief' (1.43.459), before the idea of military glory is exploded as a meaningless 'game of lives' and the dead elicit a lip-curling lack of compassion, 'hirelings' (1.44.473) who fight 'for their country's good, / And die, that living might have prov'd her shame' (1.44.473–4). Yet within a few stanzas the poet commends the Maid of Saragossa as a fearsome warrior against the French invaders; she 'Stalks with Minerva's step where Mars might quake to tread' (1.54.566), wise in her forcefulness, or so the allusion to 'Minerva's step' suggests, yet ultimately a monstrous wonder rather than an admirable heroine.

Or, perhaps, she is both at the same time. The mobility of the poetry makes the Spenserian stanza a means of change and redirection, within and between stanzaic units. When Byron describes a bullfight at Cadiz, he finishes with a stanza in which the slain bull is, at first, brute animal and distant relation to tragic hero:

> Where his vast neck just mingles with the spine,
> Sheath'd in his form the deadly weapon lies.
> He stops – he starts – disdaining to decline:
> Slowly he falls, amidst triumphant cries,
> Without a groan, without a struggle dies.   (1.79.783–7)

The poet puts himself and the reader in the bloody arena, fascinated, sickened spectators who move beyond mere spectatorship as Byron ratchets up his intensity of perception. The ordering of the first two lines makes us see the fatal anatomical area first, the vulnerable place 'Where his vast neck just mingles with the spine', then the 'deadly weapon' securely located within it, 'Sheath'd', as Byron puts it with characteristically bitter wit. The third line captures, in little, a drama of defiance through its strong verbs and caesurae. Resistance to the inevitable is futile, and therefore in its own way, affecting. It is not that Byron says this; more that he implies it through the rendering of the animal's dignified descent, before the *b* rhymes find their focus in the pivotal verb, 'dies'. Capturing the crowd's satisfied sense of vicarious triumph, the mood of the stanza's last four lines changes; the bull becomes a corpse, a 'dark bulk' (1.79.790) both honoured – it is 'pil'd' (1.79.789) within 'The decorated car' (1.79.788) – and hurried off-stage. Few poets can match Byron's capacity to give us what feels like 'the thing itself', as he does in this celebrated passage and elsewhere.

Canto 2 addresses the plight of modern Greece, apostrophized as 'Fair Greece! sad relic of departed worth!' (2.73.693), a phrase that shows Byron's capacity for suggestive, epigrammatic speech. The 'worth' may have 'departed', but it lingers in the reader's mind, having as well as being the last word, and Byron looks into the future as he imagines the role he himself, in his own way, will undertake when he asks, invoking the memory of the Spartan hero Lysander, 'who that gallant spirit shall resume, / Leap from Eurotas' banks, and call thee from the tomb?' (2.73.700–1). The stanzas on Greece bookend an account of Albania and its ruler Ali Pacha, again demonstrating Byron's political savvy; Ali's 'dread command' in this outpost of the crumbling Ottoman Empire 'Is lawless law; for with a bloody hand / He sways a nation, turbulent and bold' (2.47.418–20). Byron senses that brutal autocracy is necessary if some kind of feudal stability is to hold, even as he admires the spirit of those who 'Disdain his power' (2.48.422).

Byron is looking into the crucible out of which our modern Europe, with its continued national conflicts, was being born. What is born coexists with what is dying, and, as noted above, he addresses the fact of mortality in two of the entire poem's finest stanzas (96 and 97); as always in Byron's best work, there is a strong sense of rising rhetorically yet passionately to the occasion, as in these lines:

> Oh! ever loving, lovely, and belov'd!
> How selfish Sorrow ponders on the past,
> And clings to thoughts now better far remov'd!
> But Time shall tear thy shadow from me last.   (2.96.900–3)

The quatrain deploys its rhymes to capture the movements of feeling, a glimmer of self-rebuke ('selfish Sorrow') eddying in the verse until the magnificent flourish of the final line makes 'Sorrow' the medium of unforgettable statement.

Canto 3 of the poem deploys this growing ability to move fluidly within the Spenserian stanza. The canto alludes to the previous cantos, as though Byron were at once in control of the possibilities offered by, and the sorrowful reader of, his past self:

> Again I seize the theme then but begun,
> And bear it with me, as the rushing wind
> Bears the cloud onwards: in that Tale I find
> The furrows of long thought, and dried-up tears ...   (3.3.21–4)

He is ready to 'seize the theme', but he looks back at his poem as though it bequeathed unalterable traces. The question of why he is writing the poem, and what he is doing in the process, finds expression in the remarkable stanzas, 6 and 7, in which he asserts that "Tis to create, and in creating live / A being more intense, that we endow / With form our fancy, gaining as we give / The life we image, even as I do now' (3.6.46–9). Byron approaches 'creating' from the perspective of the poet as his own first reader, able to 'live / A being more intense', an intensifying caught in the wording, with its air of catching new fire with each phrase and rhyme, and coming to an electrifying close in 'even as I do now'. The short supplementary clause brings with it a revitalized sense of the poem in process as means of living by other means for poet and reader. And yet the next stanza reminds us of the slumps as well as soarings of which this poem is capable. If stanza 6 prizes the 'Soul of my thought! with whom I traverse earth' (51), stanza 7 recoils from thought, now depicted not as benignly self-delighting, but as self-ravening, self-destructive: 'Yet must I think less wildly: —', Byron writes; 'I *have* thought / Too long and darkly' (3.7.55–6).[4]

Creativity is gift and curse, it transpires, and that double condition pervades the poem. Harold's own flights of idealistic star-gazing grant temporary relief from 'earth, and earth-born jars, / And human frailties' (3.14.120–1), but the 'jars' get the better of the 'stars' with which they collide in an expressively dissonant rhyme; 'this clay will sink / Its spark immortal', says Byron of the force that opposes the spirit's yearning, 'envying it the light / To which it mounts as if to break the link / That keeps us from yon heaven which woos us to its brink' (3.14.123–6). Remembered by Shelley in *Adonais*, that passage exemplifies Byron's control of overlapping tones: the sardonically disenchanted ('as if to break the link') dwells together or alongside the renewal of hope in '*yon* heaven' (emphasis added) and the suggestion of the almost agonizingly distant nearness of hope's realization in 'woos us to its brink'.

Harold, Byron's surrogate, still serves a purpose in this canto, less puppet than visitor who prompts a secondary commentary that quickly turns primary. He stands upon 'this place of skull, / The grave of France, the deadly Waterloo!' (3.18.154–5), which leads, after a powerful evocation of the ball before the battle and the subsequent destruction, to an inward poetry marked by external horror. 'And thus the heart will break, yet brokenly live on' (3.32.288), Byron concludes one stanza about those grieving for the dead, before he passes, in an enjambed stanza that was the last addition to the canto, into an extended comparison between the broken heart and a 'broken mirror' (3.33.289).[5] The comparison turns out to be an image for the poem itself, which 'makes / A thousand images of one that was' (3.33.290–1). Everywhere, as Byron reads modern history and the Swiss scenery, he sees a train of distorting mirrors of his own drives and energies: Napoleon and Rousseau are two such figures (both of whom are picked up by Shelley in *The Triumph of Life*, with *Adonais* his most impassioned and thoughtful responses to the canto). Napoleon induces in the verse an attempt to arrive at antithetically balanced judgement that reminds one, momentarily, of Dryden and Pope, but Byron's response to the figure he styles 'Conqueror and captive of the earth' (3.37.325) is never content with satirical detachment. One seems to watch a trembling beam that is now kicked one way, now another – but at the end of the tortuous labyrinth run through by diction and syntax Byron's identification with the fallen emperor is evident: 'But quiet to quick bosoms is a hell, / And *there* hath been thy bane' (3.42.370–1). And yet distance quickly reclaims the ascendancy: 'This makes the madmen who have made men mad / By their contagion' (3.43.379–80).

For Shelley, in *Prometheus Unbound*, 'The voice which is contagion to the world' (2.3.10) is transgressively inspiring. And, for Byron, the 'contagion' spread by 'Sophists, Bards, Statesmen, all unquiet things / Which stir too strongly the soul's secret springs' (3.43.382–3) is not wholly bad, even if it prompts him, 'dosed' by Shelley 'with Wordsworth physic even to nausea',[6] as he was that fateful Genevan summer, to turn to the apparent offer of quiet made by nature: 'to me', he asserts, 'High mountains are a feeling, but the hum / Of human cities torture' (3.72.682–3). But the feeling of 'torture' seems more plausible than the claimed-for 'feeling' in the presence of nature, and there is a strong sense in the verse of trying out a Wordsworthian recourse to nature, but not finding it completely convincing. Like Shelley, he finally sides with 'the human mind's imaginings' ('Mont Blanc', 143) rather than with the intuition of 'something far more deeply interfused' (Wordsworth, 'Tintern Abbey', 97). Yet whereas Shelley pursues a poetic-philosophical quest, when he uses the phrase 'secret springs' (4) in 'Mont Blanc', Byron is always and primarily, if not only, 'blood, bone, marrow, passion, feeling' (*Don Juan*, cancelled stanza, 2), his 'secrets springs' are always likely to give to tidal overflow, oceanic engulfments.

And yet, emotion in Byron is never so controlled as when at its most seemingly unbridled. A stanza resonant with apparently rhetorical questions – 'Are not the mountains, waves, and skies, a part / Of me and of my soul, as I of them?' (3.75.707–8) – is at once compelling in its urgency and knowingly aware of itself as Wordsworthian ventriloquism. The mood passes, 'But this is not my theme' (3.76.716); Byron is alone again, his poetic consciousness beginning its search for images of itself in a related but different direction, this time through reflections on 'the self-torturing sophist, wild Rousseau, / The apostle of affliction' (3.77.725–6). In his revolutionary ardour, eroticized yearning, Rousseau seems a double of Shelley, Byron's travelling companion round Lake Geneva, but he is also a version of an aspect of Byron himself, who, in canto 3 at any rate, is tempted by, even as he resists, a Shelleyan-Rousseauistic yearning after 'ideal beauty' (740). The stanza moves through various transitions, including further description of nature, back to where it started, thoughts of the poet's daughter, the last in a series of figures pulling at the poet's desire for relationship, confirming him in his isolation, or in the virtual companionship made possible by poetry. Movingly, chillingly, Ada becomes a chosen heir, responsive to her father's 'voice': 'My voice shall with thy future visions blend, / And reach into thy heart, — when mine is cold, — / A token and a tone, even from thy father's mould' (3.115.1073–5). There, the vision of futurity is comparable to Keats's warm and capable hand icily extended towards us; much has to do, in Byron's case, by the way in which 'reach' turns, across the line-ending, into a transitive verb, 'reaching' into the daughter's heart, 'A token and a tone'.

The final canto looks at art as a trophy, sometimes a hollow trophy, wrested from the ravages of history. History's '*one* page' (4.108.969) always involves 'the same rehearsal of the past' (4.108.965), Byron asserts on the Palatine Hill, surrounded by Roman ruins. This is a grimly pessimistic vision, one familiar from Edward Gibbon's monumental *Decline and Fall of the Roman Empire* (1776–88); the annals of Rome depict a cycle that runs its course from 'Freedom' through 'Glory' (4.108.966) to end up in 'barbarism at last' (4.108.967). Modern Venice tells a comparable story, even as Byron does not idealize the nature of her former power: 'Though making many slaves,' he says of the city when an independent republic, 'herself still free' (4.14.122). Venice lives on, for all its 'infamous repose' (4.13.117) under Austrian rule, as an idea, immortalized in literature, prompting Byron's reformulation of creativity as a form of compensation: 'The beings of the mind are not of clay; / Essentially immortal, they create / And multiply in us a brighter ray / And more beloved existence' (4.5.37–40); these beings are capable of 'replenishing the void' (4.5.45) which ordinary living creates.

Exemplifying the precarious status of its own ideal through its shifting, nervy caesurae and subliminally ironic diction ('more beloved' speaks volumes of the poet's disenchantment with love), such writing offers an exalted yet disquieting view of art. Later in the canto, art is not exempt from Byron's astonishingly eloquent assault on human values; a form of false projection like love, artistic creativity is, on this account, a form of illness: 'Of its own beauty is the mind diseased, / And fevers into false creation' (4.122.1090–1). That such 'false creation' has its own feverish beauty as it evokes the impossible origin and goal of art, 'The unreach'd Paradise of our despair' (4.122.1096), typifies the intensity, drive, and drama of canto 4, simultaneously bleak and unmelodramatically exhilarating, an instance of Romantic poetry driving to extremes, and finding in the end consolation in the sublimities of St Peter's and the ocean, and in the knowledge that, in the act of poetry, there is always the possibility of escape from mere hopelessness, of impressing on history and the world an answering imprint of poetic self. In Byron's words, which might be an epigraph for the canto and the whole poem, and, as suggested at the end of the previous section, his poetry more generally, 'There woos no home, nor hope, nor life, save what is here' (4.945).

Notes

1 Lord Byron, *The Complete Poetical Works*, ed. Jerome J. McGann, 7 vols (Oxford: Clarendon Press, 1980–93), 2.323. In this section, Byron is quoted from this edition. *Childe Harold's Pilgrimage* is in the second volume.

2 Of *Childe Harold* (1812) McGann writes: 'More than anything else this book says that the most personal and intimate aspects of an individual's life are closely involved with, and affected by, the social and political context in which the individual is placed.' 'The Book of Byron and the Book of a World' (1985), in *Byron's Poetry and Prose*, ed. Alice Levine (New York: Norton, 2010), p. 832.

3 *Byron's Poetry and Prose*, ed. Levine, p. 21.
4 For relevant commentary, see, among others, Harold Bloom, *The Visionary Company: A Reading of English Romantic Poetry*, rev. and enlarged edn (Ithaca, NY: Cornell University Press, 1971), pp. 240–1.
5 For relevant MS evidence, see *Childe Harold's Pilgrimage: A Critical, Composite Edition*, ed. David V. Erdman, with the assistance of David Worrall (New York: Garland, 1991), p. 203; vol. 6 of *Manuscripts of the Younger Romantics: Lord Byron*.
6 Thomas Medwin, *Conversations of Lord Byron* (London, 1824), p. 237.

Lord Byron, *Don Juan*, Cantos 1–4

Don Juan is a long, unfinished poem, written in *ottava rima*, a stanza written in iambic pentameter, consisting of three alternating couplets, rhyming *ab*, following by a rhyming couplet (*cc*). John Murray, who published the first two cantos in 1819, published the next three in 1821, before Byron changed publishers, moving to the more politically radical John Hunt, brother of Leigh Hunt. In 1823 John Hunt brought out, in three separate publications, cantos 6–8, 9–11, and 12–14; he published cantos 15–16 in 1824. In 1828, four years after Byron's death, the first sixteen cantos were published. The remaining unfinished canto was published by E. H. Coleridge as part of his monumental edition, 1899–1904.[1] The focus of this section is on the first four cantos, though passages from elsewhere in the work are also discussed.

The poem is a serio-comic masterpiece, satirical yet in many ways generously understanding of human nature, mock-epic in its subversions of seriousness, yet epic, too, in its range and sweep. The following stanza, cancelled from the opening canto, shows many of Byron's favoured procedures:

> I would to Heaven that I were so much Clay –
> > As I am blood – bone – marrow, passion – feeling –
> Because at least the past were past away –
> > And for the future – (but I write this reeling
> Having got drunk exceedingly to day
> > So that I seem to stand upon the ceiling)
> I say – the future is a serious matter –
> And so – for Godsake – Hock and Soda water.[2]

The Romantic Poetry Handbook, First Edition. Michael O'Neill and Madeleine Callaghan.
© 2018 John Wiley & Sons Ltd. Published 2018 by John Wiley & Sons Ltd.

The stanza illustrates the ease and brilliance of the poem's comic style. This style hinges on the use of *ottava rima*, a form whose confidently iambic rhythms, capacity for amusingly inventive rhyme, and clinching couplet suited Byron admirably. Each stanza, indeed, as here, seems to delight in a triadic structure; one thing is set against another before a resolution, of sorts, is attained.[3] In the above stanza, Byron is able to knock one line of thought off its perch by another, as he leaves 'the future' hanging in the air. Cleverly, feminine rhymes undermine pretentiousness: the serious Romantic word 'feeling' is made to look silly when rhymed with 'but I write this reeling' and ridiculous when paired with 'So that I seem to stand upon the ceiling'.

The wit serves as an exhilarating means of coping with despair. The effect of the final couplet, in which Byron calls out for his hangover remedy ('Hock and Soda water'), is stylish and amusing but there is pain in the debunking humour, too. Awareness of contradiction informs the stanza, which oscillates between wanting to escape from painful feeling and realizing that to be human is to be condemned to feel. William Hazlitt, no uncomplicated admirer of Byron, a feeling reciprocated by the poet who wrote that Hazlitt 'talks pimples',[4] was sensitive to Byron's underlying sense of unrest. Singling out '*Intensity*' as the 'great and prominent distinction of Lord Byron's writings', Hazlitt helps define a quality which continually if urbanely surfaces in *Don Juan* as well as his more evidently serious works.[5]

Byron himself seems to vacillate in his view of the poem. At one level, its only end is 'to giggle and make giggle';[6] at another, it is imbued with deadly satiric purpose. W. H. Auden writes in his 'Letter to Lord Byron', 'You are the master of the airy manner', praising him for 'A style whose meaning does not need a spanner',[7] and it is Byron's 'airy manner' that allows him to express different sides of a complicated poetic personality. An example occurs when Byron introduces Julia whose affair with Juan, the son of Donna Inez, the woman referred to in the first line, supplies the main plot-line of the first canto:

> Amongst her numerous acquaintance, all
>   Selected for discretion and devotion.
> There was the Donna Julia, whom to call
>   Pretty were but to give a feeble notion
> Of many charms in her as natural
>   As sweetness in the flower, or salt to ocean,
> Her zone to Venus, or his bow to Cupid,
> (But this last simile is trite and stupid.)   (1.55.433–40)

Donna Inez serves as a means by which Byron can aim some leisurely digs at his estranged wife, but she also has independent life as a character in Byron's often novel-like poem. Yet we are aware of the narrator's presence to a remarkable degree in the poem, delighting in the way in which, for all his show of respect, he is ironical about Inez's hypocrisy. There is a flicker of mockery in the second line which suggests that 'discretion and devotion' are commensurate and comparable virtues. In the last line Byron lets his stanza trip over the booby-trap of bathos he has laid; what is effective about the line is that, though we have sensed something comic in the offing (especially after the use of 'Cupid' as the rhyme prompt), Byron has beguiled us into thinking that he is going through the motions, dutifully idealizing his heroine. The last line, pulling the rug from under our feet, makes us conscious that this is a poet whose dealings with the hackneyed are continually critical.

In *Don Juan*, as his attacks on Wordsworth, Coleridge, and Southey bear witness, Byron puts into comedic practice his belief, expressed in a letter of September 1817, that 'we are upon a wrong revolutionary poetical system'.[8] A month later, Byron began work on *Beppo*, his first major poem in *ottava rima*. The poem is no mere dry run for *Don Juan*, but in its use of a magnetically captivating narrator, delighting in digression and leading his readership by the nose, and in its quicksilver switches of mood, *Beppo* anticipates aspects of *Don Juan*, as in these lines:

> I fear I have a little turn for satire,
>   And yet methinks the older that one grows
> Inclines us more to laugh than scold, though laughter
> Leaves us so doubly serious shortly after.　(*Beppo* 79.629–32)

The writing twists and turns. Byron admired Pope, but his syntax here overturns the shapeliness of the Augustan couplet, and the 'doubly serious' close manages to be coolly stage-managed yet almost confessionally affecting. *Don Juan* is a satire on manners and morals. Charles Mahoney, noting that the poem's first stanza involves rhymes on 'cant', persuasively discovers 'a pronounced commitment to poetic and political liberty, behind the veil of giggling and acting mad',[9] and the various inflections adopted by Byron in the poem can be related to this 'commitment'. At the same time, the poem's sweep is not constricted by the limits usually associated with the genre of satire: it is capable, in a way consonant with epic as well as mock-epic ambitions, of accommodating elegy, lyricism, narrative, pastoral, and other generic impulse.

Byron's poem unsheathes its satirical claws in its savage 'Dedication', unpublished until 1832. Cantos 1 and 2 were originally published anonymously, and Byron felt it inappropriate to 'attack the dog in the dark',[10] the 'dog' in question being the poet laureate Robert Southey. Byron saw in

Southey a perfect symbol of political self-interest. Having turned away from the radical politics of his youth, Southey was now for the younger poet an apostate: hence the Dedication signs off with a coolly questioning sneer of a couplet: 'To keep *one* creed's a task grown quite Herculean, / Is it not so, my Tory ultra-Julian?' (135–6). Southey had irked Byron for personal reasons; he suspected him of spreading rumours about having set up a 'League of Incest' with Shelley in 1816.[11] But he is also as a Lake poet a type, for Byron, of staid conservatism, and the satire moves on to criticize Southey, Wordsworth, and Coleridge as a trio of self-satisfied and insular writers, convinced of their special status.

Byron takes the fight to the three poets with gusto: 'There is a narrowness in such a notion / Which makes me wish you'd change your lakes for ocean' (39–40). The casual subjectivity of 'makes me wish' is at a studied distance from Popean appeals to abstractions, and yet a confidence about his scorn for 'narrowness' which is significantly a question of the writer's demeanour, how it carries itself. This scorn links with downright contempt for Castlereagh, dismissed as an 'intellectual eunuch' (88), an insult that rhymes with a previous gibe at Southey for soaring 'too high, Bob' (23) and falling 'for lack of moisture, quite adry, Bob!' (24). The allusion to Southey's supposed inability to ejaculate semen suggests a compulsion in both men to compensate for their sense of sexual failure by behaving with pert vanity in the poet's case and obstinate cruelty in the politician's.

If the Dedication is cool yet savage, Juvenalian, Byron can also entertain other modes, often doing so with a sense that every perspective, every style, every way of putting things involves performative self-awareness. A stanza from canto 15 talks about and illustrates Byron's manner and self-conscious mental agility in *Don Juan*:

> I perch upon an humbler promontory,
>   Amidst life's infinite variety:
> With no great care for what is nicknamed glory,
>   But speculating as I cast mine eye
> On what may suit or may not suit my story,
>   And never straining hard to versify,
> I rattle on exactly as I'd talk
> With any body in a ride or walk.   (15.19.145–52)

The art here lies in the writing's witty disdain for art. Byron adopts a nonchalant, take-it-or-leave-it tone. He is not going to be caught in the act of 'straining hard to versify', his seemingly chanced-on rhymes and regular iambic rhythms simulating an effortless, improvisatory air, as though he were guided by whims, casual inspirations. There is an urbane insolence about, say, 'what may not suit'. If we want a poem that sticks to a story-line, Byron seems to say, that's just too bad; we'll have to go elsewhere. Underpinning the insolence is great assurance; Byron knows that he can adopt this tone because his readers find it immensely winning. There is a hint, too, in the stanza's second line of self-justification: Byron implies that his style is suited to the real nature of existence, its contradictions and 'infinite variety'.

'I want a hero: an uncommon want' (1.1.1), begins the poem. Juan is at once charmingly unlike the predatory Don Juan of legend, and seemingly more acted-upon than acting. Byron uses him with great skill to take the story to its different location, and intended, on one account at least, to have led him finally to the Revolution in France where he would die on a guillotine. Yet the poem's 'hero' is less Juan than the wittily omnipresent narrator, commenting, qualifying, ironizing. Byron delights in blurring the boundaries between himself speaking 'in propria persona' and the narrator, and in teasing the reader, especially the reader who objected to the supposed immorality of the first two cantos: canto 3, stanza 12 is an instance:

> Haidée and Juan were not married, but
>   The fault was theirs, not mine: it is not fair,
> Chaste reader, then, in any way to put
>   The blame on me, unless you wish they were;
> Then if you'd have them wedded, please to shut
>   The book which treats of this unlawful pair,
> Before the consequences grow too awful;
> 'Tis dangerous to read of loves unlawful.   (3.12.89–96)

The control of tone in this stanza is expert: deference to the 'Chaste reader' barely holds laughter and contempt at arm's length. The suggestion that the reader 'shut / The book', with its reference to the fifth canto of the *Inferno*, in which Paolo and Francesca are hastened into adultery by reading a book, makes the reader wish to keep it open. Byron has his moral reader over a barrel; he has given us due warning – if we continue to read the poem, as we will, we risk being convicted of a hypocritical, not to say voyeuristic, fascination with 'loves unlawful'.

Elsewhere, Byron pretends that the joke is at his own expense, that the subject-matter with which he is dealing is growing too hot to handle. The developing physical intimacy between Juan and Julia in canto 1 gets the narrator into quite a tizzy, mimicking embarrassed confusion: 'I can't go on; / I'm almost sorry that I e'er begun' (1.115.919–20). Byron is never more in control than when he affects to be losing control. In the later cantos, where the poem grows more sombre as it deals with war, ageing, and various recurrent philosophical conundrums about, for example, truth and inconsistency or soul and matter,[12] Byron's contempt for the easily shockable is more snarlingly brusque. In canto 12, stanza 40, he writes: 'But now I'm going to be immoral; now / I mean to show things really as they are' (12.40.313–14). There, Byron surrounds 'immoral' with imaginary quotation marks, suggesting that what others call immorality is, in fact, a form of authentic truth-telling.

In other places, Byron fends off more lightly the charge of immorality. In canto 4, he notes that 'Some have accused me of a strange design / Against the creed and morals of the land, / And trace it in this poem every line' (4.5.33–5), archly brushing off the charge as ridiculous, even a misplaced compliment: 'I don't pretend that I quite understand / My own meaning when I would be *very* fine' (4.5.36–7). The italics are Byron's and capture a drolly dandified tone. The stanza is amusing with its new, post-*Childe Harold* commitment to being 'merry, / A novel word in my vocabulary' (4.5.39–40), an ingenious rhyme that stages Byron's comic self-fashioning in full sight of the reader. But the stanza's drollery needs to be seen in the perspective offered by its predecessor's opening:

> And if I laugh at any mortal thing,
> 'Tis that I may not weep; and if I weep,
> 'Tis that our nature cannot always bring
> Itself to apathy   (4.4.25–8)

This stanza comes close to explaining Byron's procedures in *Don Juan*, allowing us to understand his emotional 'mobility', to use his own term, to see a connection between the 'Romantic' and 'satirical' Byrons, between the idealist and the cynic. Laughter emerges as a defence against tears; tears, the many moments of pathos and sorrow in the poem, prove that the poet is still alive; 'apathy', the incapacity to feel, is a condition Byron at once fears and in some ways desires: the forgetfulness of 'Lethe' (4.4.32) has its attractions as the stanza goes on to observe.

As in *Childe Harold's Pilgrimage*, the poet-narrator's confessions and comments quicken our interest. Although such passages come thick and fast in the more reflective later cantos, one of the most impressive occurs towards the end of the first canto (stanzas 213–15), a passage that participates in the lamentation for change and disillusion often expressed in Romantic poetry (Coleridge's 'Dejection: An Ode' is a famous example). Byron is amusing and touchingly down to earth about ageing, flirting with wearing a wig, for instance: 'But now at thirty years my hair is gray— / (I wonder what it will be like at forty? / I thought of a peruke the other day) / My heart is not much greener' (1.213.1697–1700). He strikes a fine balance between lamenting the loss of youth and accepting the scanty consolations of maturity, managing not to be pompous about the 'judgement' (1.215.1719) he has gained, 'Though heaven knows it ever found a lodgement' (1.215.1720). The style mirrors the theme, Byron seems genuinely to experience a sense of sorrow, yet to send it up as well.

A judgement of the poem's worth depends on what is made of the poem's veering between comedy and seriousness, gravity and flippancy. Hazlitt puts the case against Byron's seesawing tones and attitudes with some force: 'He hallows in order to desecrate; takes a pleasure in defacing the images his hands have wrought ... It is not that Lord Byron is sometimes serious and sometimes trifling, sometimes profligate and sometimes moral—' (Hazlitt's own reversal of expectations in those couplings reflecting what he finds in Byron) 'but when he is most serious and most moral, he is only preparing to mortify the unsuspecting reader by putting a pitiful *hoax* upon him.'[13] Certainly there are many moments when Byron, true to his poem's Sternean genealogy ('a TRISTRAM SHANDY in rhyme' is Hazlitt's description of the way the poem has been seen by some),[14] does 'mortify the unsuspecting reader'. After the affecting stanzas in canto 4 depicting the tragic conclusion of the relationship between Juan and Haidee, Byron shifts into another gear:

> But let me change this theme, which grows too sad,
>   And lay this sheet of sorrows on the shelf;
> I don't much like describing people mad,
>   For fear of seeming rather touch'd myself –
> Besides I've no more on this head to add;
>   And as my Muse is a capricious elf,
> We'll put about, and try another tack
> With Juan, left half-kill'd some stanzas back.   (4.74.585–92)

Byron's flip tone comes close to taking 'a pleasure in defacing the images his hands have wrought', in Hazlitt's phrase. But it does not take anything from the sadness of what precedes it (the account of Haidee's final illness and death). It marks off that sadness, admits that pathos cannot be sustained indefinitely without turning into rhetorical indulgence. Byron is being tactless but honest when he says, 'Besides I've no more on this head to add' and frankly, jokily, admits that we are reading a work of fiction whose hero was 'left half-killed some stanzas back'. *Don Juan* is always reminding its reader that no one view of life exhausts its meaning. It strains away from closure. There is, too, the more personal note struck in the fourth line: 'For fear of seeming rather touch'd myself', where the slangy 'touch'd' behaves as though it conceals real anxiety.

Some passages from the first four cantos that develop preceding observations include a stanza from canto 1, which is part of Julia's love letter and 'the account of its being written', as Shelley put it. 'Where did you learn all these secrets?', Shelley goes on to ask: 'I should like to go to school there.'[15] Julia and Juan's relationship has come to light and Julia has been packed off to a convent. Byron goes to some pains to show her carrying out her romantic role with some care: 'This note was written upon gilt-edged paper / With a neat crow-quill, rather hard, but new … And yet she did not let one tear escape her; / The seal a sunflower; "*Elle vous suit partout*"' (1.198.1577–8, 1581–2). Byron does not merely poke fun at her. He may be wryly observant about the complexity of human behaviour, noting how this heart-broken woman is still composed enough to attend to the rituals of experience. But his humour does not merely debunk; often in the poem irony or humour is less reductive than inclusive, aware of different ways of viewing experience.

The poem is often sympathetic to the predicaments of its female characters. One of the jokes of the poem is that the hero is so unlike the traditional Don Juan, usually a licentious Lothario. Byron may annoy some readers by having Julia write to Juan: 'Man's love is of his life a thing apart, / 'Tis woman's whole existence' (1.194.1545–6). Yet his point is not that this is how things are immutably, but rather that it holds for the society he is delineating. Two stanzas from the close of canto 2 (199–200) are relevant in this context. The first stanza seems to trot out a stereotype, but to do so knowingly: 'Alas! the love of women! it is known / To be a lovely and a fearful thing' (2.199.1585–6). Yet the pity turns out to be neither patronizing nor undercut by mockery: 'yet, as real / Torture is theirs, what they inflict they feel' (2.199.1591–2). The last phrase is suddenly quite serious. The following stanza may exaggerate, but its dismal generalizations show an awareness of the unromantic realities in wait for women in Byron's society, after marriage: 'what rests beyond? / A thankless husband, next a faithless lover, / Then dressing, nursing, praying, and all's over' (2.200.1598–1600).

These stanzas occur straight after the description of Juan and Haidee together. Byron presents their idyllic but star-crossed love as a contrast to the usual relations between men and women. He presents their love as pure, more moral, for its spontaneity and naturalness, its freedom from hypocrisy. Haidee is 'Nature's bride' (2.202.1609): 'never having dreamt of falsehood, she / Had not one word to say of constancy' (2.190.1519–20). Yet, though idealized, the love is depicted credibly by Byron, partly because he implies, quite touchingly, his own distance from the raptures of first love: 'Alas! for Juan and Haidee! they were / So loving and so lovely—till then never, / Excepting our first parents, such a pair / Had run the risk of being damn'd for ever' (2.193.1537–40). Byron mocks and grimly concedes the idea that their love could lead to damnation. Throughout *Don Juan*, first love is a paradisal experience which inevitably brings about a fall into disillusion. Only Haidee's death prevents such disillusion in this case. The love is also credible because of the ease and tenderness of the writing: 'She sits upon his knee, and drinks his sighs, / He hers, until they end in broken gasps' (2.194.1549–50).[16]

This passage shows Byron at his most archetypally Romantic, yet it is a Romanticism that has its feet on the ground and its eye on familiar experience, as when he describes Haidee watching over the sleeping Juan (see stanza 197). Byron is detached enough to raise questions of constancy in relation to Juan and wittily confront or evade them (stanza 209). And, true to the poem's many-angled perspective, the romantic idyll follows the earlier account of the shipwreck in the same canto, one of the most powerful and controversial sections of the poem. Byron extracts grim humour from the fact that the immediate survivors are obsessed by food: 'They grieved for those who perish'd with the cutter, / And also for the biscuit casks and butter' (2.61.487–8). The reviewer for the *British Critic* was severe on this kind of thing: 'The poverty of a man's wit is never so conspicuous, as when he is driven to a joke upon human misery.'[17] But Byron's tone is that of a writer determined to make us see that from which we might wish to avert our eyes. The effect is less cynicism than savage realism, coloured by irony at the expense of our squeamishness as when the descent into cannibalism claims a Dantean precedent (via the story of Ugolino): 'if foes be food in hell, at sea / 'Tis surely fair to dine upon our friends, / When shipwreck's short allowance grows too scanty, / Without being much more horrible than Dante' (2.83.661–4). If, later, Byron praises nature as offering an ideal, here he sees it as force which makes a mockery of human taboos, as when he writes, of the drawing of lots to decide who should be eaten, 'None in particular had sought or plann'd it, / 'Twas nature gnaw'd them to this resolution' (597–8). Again, Byron does not deny that human beings are incapable of dignity *in extremis*.

The section demonstrates the poem's range of tones and inclusiveness of vision.[18] Throughout, though Byron comments, he rarely preaches. In the English cantos he is offering 'a satire on abuses of the present state of society', but he achieves much more, a recreation of aristocratic Regency England.[19] *Don Juan* is a poem which respects, even delights in, the muddle of experience. It is also a work given coherence by the attempt of its central narratorial consciousness to understand how social and individual histories mesh. Among the multitude of self-definitions and would-be explanatory images pervading the poem, the following from canto 7 comes as close as any to describing its overall impact: 'A non-descript and ever varying rhyme, / A versified Aurora Borealis, / Which flashes o'er a waste and icy clime' (7.2.10–12).

Notes

1   This account is indebted to *Byron's Poetry and Prose*, ed. Levine, p. 375.
2   Qtd as is all of *Don Juan* from vol. 5 (1986; 1992 corr.) of *Lord Byron: The Complete Poetical Works*, 7 vols (Oxford: Clarendon Press, 1980–93). The stanza was used as what McGann calls the 'Headpiece Stanza' in the 1832 edition of Byron's works.
3   Professor Jane Stabler made a comparable point in discussion following a lecture given by Michael O'Neill in Vechta in June 2014 at a conference on 'Byron and the Margins of Romanticism'.
4   *BLJ* 8.38.
5   William Hazlitt, *Complete Works*, ed. P. P. Howe (London: Dent, 1930–4), 11.72.
6   *BLJ* 6.208.
7   Qtd from *The English Auden*, ed. Edward Mendelson (London: Faber, 1977).
8   *Byron's Poetry and Prose*, ed. Levine, p. 729.
9   *Romantic Poetry: An Annotated Anthology*, ed. Michael O'Neill and Charles Mahoney (Malden, MA: Blackwell, 2008), p. 255.
10   See *Romantic Poetry*, ed. O'Neill and Mahoney.
11   See *Romantic Poetry*, ed. O'Neill and Mahoney.
12   See, for a discussion of this last doubling, essays in *Byron's Ghosts: The Spectral, the Spiritual, and the Supernatural*, ed. Gavin Hopps (Liverpool: Liverpool University Press, 2013).
13   Hazlitt, *Complete Works*, 11.225.
14   Hazlitt, *Complete Works*, 11.225n. Hazlitt says that 'it is rather a poem written about itself'.
15   *The Letters of Percy Bysshe Shelley*, ed. F. L. Jones, 2 vols (Oxford: Clarendon Press, 1964), 2.198.
16   See Christopher Ricks, *Keats and Embarrassment* (Oxford: Clarendon Press, 1974), p. 97: Ricks points out that the turn in 'He hers' implies the mutuality of the lovers.
17   Qtd from Theodore Redpath, *The Young Romantics and Critical Opinion 1807–1824* (London: Harrap, 1973), p. 252.
18   For more on the poem's irony, see Anne K. Mellor, *English Romantic Irony* (Cambridge, MA: Harvard University Press, 1980).
19   For the English cantos, see Peter W. Graham, *'Don Juan' and Regency England* (Charlottesville: University of Virginia Press, 1990), and Michael O'Neill, '"A Wilderness of the Most Rare Conceits": Imagining Politics in the English Cantos of *Don Juan*', in *Byron: The Poetry of Politics and the Politics of Poetry*, ed. Roderick Beaton and Christine Kenyon Jones (Abingdon: Routledge, 2006), pp. 144–56.

Percy Bysshe Shelley, *Queen Mab*; *Alastor, Laon and Cythna* [*The Revolt of Islam*]

This section looks at Shelley's earlier attempts at writing epic, romance, and quest-poetry. In *Queen Mab*, printed in a limited edition in 1813, the young Shelley's formidable intellect and ardour for reform are manifest. Among Shelley's most influential poems for later readers, fear of prosecution led to the poem being printed in a small print-run (250 copies) rather than published. Shelley seems to have distributed up to seventy copies himself, usually cutting out the evidence by which he could be identified as the author: the title-page, colophon, and dedicatory poem to his first wife, Harriet Shelley.[1] A pirated edition in 1821 led Shelley to write to Leigh Hunt, in the latter's capacity as editor of *The Examiner*, to dismiss the poem as written in 'a sufficiently intemperate spirit' and as 'perfectly worthless in point of literary composition', and to half-disclaim responsibility for 'having divulged opinions hostile to existing sanctions, under the form, whatever it may be, which they assume in this poem'. But the very way in which the letter concludes, with a sudden, calculated flare of contempt for the 'legal proceedings ... instituted against the publisher',[2] suggests that there is a strong continuity between the young man blazing with anti-establishment ideas who wrote the poem and the sadder, wiser, but still intransigent radical who looks back with a mixture of feelings, including covert pride, at his poem. George Bernard Shaw describes the poem as 'the Chartists' Bible' in the light of the poem's great influence over that movement in the 1830s and 1840s.[3]

The poem, written in nine cantos, recalls in its format eighteenth-century long poems such as Edward Young's *Night Thoughts*, also in nine sections. But *Queen Mab* overthrows rather than follows in the footsteps of its predecessors. The poem uses romance as the vehicle of a calculatedly 'intemperate' onslaught on current political and social ills, and imagines a

The Romantic Poetry Handbook, First Edition. Michael O'Neill and Madeleine Callaghan.
© 2018 John Wiley & Sons Ltd. Published 2018 by John Wiley & Sons Ltd.

millennial transformation.[4] The influence of French Enlightenment thinkers and of Godwin is clear in the poem, yet, as Reiman and Fraistat point out, Shelley 'resists as well as deploys his sources' and he constructs what they rightly describe as 'an original synthesis that constitutes the cosmopolitical and anti-Christian revolutionary discourse' of the poem.[5] This discourse is highlighted in the poem's accompanying 'Notes', long essays that imitate, in form, the extensive prose material provided in Southey's *Thalaba the Destroyer* and *The Curse of Kehama*, both poems that leave an impact on the rhythmic shape and irresistible driving force of Shelley's work.[6] The poem's epigraphs promise polemic: Voltaire's 'ECRASEZ L'INFAME!' (Crush the infamy!), Lucretius' determination to free human beings from superstition, and Archimedes' desire for a place to stand from where he could move the world. Yet Shelley first beguiles us with an account of the sleeping Ianthe visited by Queen Mab, the Fairy Queen, in her chariot. Queen Mab who sets about imparting visions of the present, past, and future to Ianthe, imagined as caught up in spirit by Queen Mab and taken on a journey; indeed, in its commitment to dream, vision, and a 'magic car' (or chariot), *Queen Mab* looks ahead to the voyage motif central to later poems, as in *Prometheus Unbound* 2.5. Moreover, its blend of feelings – ready to travel in imagination along 'The gradual paths of an aspiring change' (9.148), but setting that readiness against the awareness that a 'pathless wilderness remains' (9.144) – anticipates the double consciousness evident, say, at the end of the third act of *Prometheus Unbound*.

The first canto ends with an apostrophe to the 'Spirit of Nature' (1.264), present throughout creation, and a constant ideal in the poem in that it reproves the idea of a God made in any human likeness. Later, the 'Spirit of Nature' (3.214) is 'the judge beneath whose nod / Man's brief and frail authority / Is powerless as the wind / That passeth idly by' (3.219–22): lines whose varied lengths coexist with an 'authority' partly purchased by the echo of Shakespeare's *Measure for Measure* 2.2.117–18 and partly by the calmly inexorable movement of the rhythm. Nature's authority derives from the fact that it is an arena in which Necessity operates. In section 6, Shelley identifies the two in an appositional glissade: 'Spirit of Nature! all-sufficing Power, / Necessity! thou mother of the world!' (6.197–8).

By Necessity, Shelley means, as he puts it in an accompanying Note, 'that in no case could any event have happened otherwise than it did happen' (262), a bleak doctrine in many ways, yet a source of hope for the young Shelley, because, as Kenneth Neill Cameron glosses the matter, it allowed him to suppose that change 'took place in accordance with certain laws arising from the structural patterns of society',[7] much as change occurred in the physical world because of certain predetermining causes. Underpinning the doctrine, as Shelley would later see with near-tragic clarity, is a hopeful fiction that change is driven by a dynamic of betterment. Here Shelley's thought owes a debt to Godwin's idea of perfectibility: 'By perfectible', writes Godwin in *Political Justice*, 'it is not meant that [human beings are] capable of being brought to perfection. But the word seems sufficiently adapted to express the faculty of being continually made better and receiving perpetual improvement.'[8]

Such improvement finds an emblem in the poem's sense of cosmic symmetry. The beauty of the heavens mirrors the possibility of an ameliorated earth. With its Coleridgean 'fertile golden islands / Floating on a silver sea' (2.34–5), it suggests, too, an ever-present, ceaseless harmony that dwarfs human pride and serves as a model for the human condition.[9] The Fairy teaches a lesson about the transience of human power: 'Nile shall pursue his changeless way: / Those pyramids shall fall' (2.128–9). However, the poem is often topical in its political denunciations: section 3 focuses on the iniquity of kingship, since 'kings / And subjects, mutual foes, forever play / A losing game into each other's hands, / Whose stakes are vice and misery' (3.171–4). These lines illustrate the sharpness of the poem's radical critique. Shelley objects to the unequal power relations embedded in monarchy by suggesting it amounts to a game where all lose, succumbing either to 'vice' or 'misery'. This is a poetry with roots in Augustan practice, keenly tipping the foils of its abstractions with near-satirical venom, yet it jettisons the heroic couplet in favour of a measure more suited to an epic, necessitarian sweep and viewpoint. Canto 4 is an onslaught on war; canto 5 on unjust economic distribution; canto 6 on the concept of an omnipotent God, 'prototype of human misrule' (6.105); canto 7 introduces the figure of Ahasuerus, the Wandering Jew, who tells a narrative that allows Shelley to mock the vengefulness of the Christian God (as he sees it); cantos 8 and 9 imagine a redeemed earth in which human beings, no longer eaters of meat, live in a 'paradise of peace' (8.238).

Queen Mab is the matrix from which Shelley's more complex later poems will emerge. It is already a considerable achievement, balancing hopes for 'the omnipotence of mind' (8.236) and pressing material concerns, and justifying its subtitle 'A Philosophical Poem' through the series of long essays mentioned above. They address topics of vital concern for any hope of social amelioration: subjects covered, often with long quotations from different thinkers such as Holbach, Godwin, Condorcet, and Joseph Ritson, include cosmology with anti-Christian inflections, as when Shelley asserts that 'The works of his fingers have borne witness against him' (240); the horror of war; the injustice of wealth arrangements – 'There is no real wealth', writes

Shelley, 'but the labour of man' (248); the hypocrisy of the marriage institution; the nature of Necessity and the folly of believing in 'a creative Deity', though 'The hypothesis of a pervading Spirit coeternal with the universe' (263) escapes Shelley's censure as he, in effect, reprints *The Necessity of Atheism* with minor alterations; and the horrors of meat-eating (where Shelley – again with minor alterations – reprints his 1813 pamphlet *A Vindication of Natural Diet*). It is a work that has been dismissed as juvenilia, but to our own age, confronted by crises of various hues, it will often seem prescient and ponderable.

Alastor (1816), in part, represents a turn inwards, a movement away from the French *philosophes*. Its presiding spirit is the poetry of Wordsworth; its epigraph, a far cry from Voltaire crushing infamy, quotes Augustine on the desire for love. That desire leads Shelley to the delineation of 'the figure of the poet', to borrow Judith Chernaik's phrase.[10] And here Shelley can be seen less as retreating from the public sphere than exploring the poet's troubled relationship with that sphere; how do political ideals relate to the impulse to idealize which serves as an erotic energy in the poetry, too? And how do these energies relate to the impulse to explore the world? As Neil Fraistat notes, we should not 'forget that this apparently "inward" and "private" poem encompasses three continents geographically, as well as the history of Western civilization'.[11]

The focus, however, is on individual consciousness. In fact, the poem contains two poet-figures: in Earl Wasserman's terms, a Narrator and a Visionary.[12] The Narrator tells the story of the Visionary's longing for and vivid dream of an ideal soulmate, his inability to find her in this world, and his subsequent death in the lap of a natural world he loves but which will not requite his needs. The Narrator is so intimate with the Visionary's feelings that he seems, on occasions, to blur into him, and yet the poem's hypnotic, dream-like power to induce suspension of disbelief has much to do with the Visionary's inaccessibility to complete understanding.

Shelley's Preface seems torn about his poem's meaning. His stance seems coolly detached, as he professes to offer a poem that is 'allegorical of one of the most interesting situations of the human mind' (5), yet the Preface is at once sympathetic towards the Visionary and critical of him for a 'self-centred seclusion' that 'was avenged by the furies of an irresistible passion pursuing him to speedy ruin' (5). The poem itself seems for the most part to abandon such ambivalence towards the Visionary; only in equivocal lines about the Visionary spurning the 'choicest gifts' (205) sent by 'The spirit of sweet human love' (203) does a flicker of explicit criticism enter the poem. At the same time, many of the finest passages – the Narrator's invocation of nature, the Visionary's dream of a 'veiled maid' (151), the aftermath of his dream, his apostrophe to a swan, and final extinction in accord with the waning light of the moon – induce the reader to ask questions. Is the Narrator fearful of or violent towards the 'Mother of this unfathomable world' (18)? Is the Visionary's dream wholly delusory, or are we right to feel that such idealizing is not merely rejected by the poem? The eliciting of such questions is central to Shelley's poems which irresistibly supply a poetic experience and demand that the reader grapple with its meaning while refusing to offer a clear gloss that would mean the experience can be easily categorized. The dream of the 'veiled maid' is fascinating in this context:

> He dreamed a veiled maid
> Sate near him, talking in low solemn tones.
> Her voice was like the voice of his own soul
> Heard in the calm of thought; its music long,
> Like woven sounds of streams and breezes, held
> His inmost sense suspended in its web
> Of many-coloured woof and shifting hues.   (151–7)

The lines display Shelley's unusually nuanced poetic art. The poem's dream takes on a seemingly non-illusory reality; a dream of likeness, it refuses to be interpreted merely as a projection of sameness. What the poet hears as 'the voice of his own soul / Heard in the calm of thought' appears to be spoken from beyond as well as from within him. The voice possesses a 'music'; it holds 'his inmost sense suspended in its web', where 'inmost sense' means both his inmost capacity for apprehension and something close to his ultimate meaning. For the poet's subsequent awakening, disenchantment, and relentlessly driven pursuit to exercise the power over the reader that they do, it is vital for Shelley's hypnotic rhythms and diction to encourage a suspension of disbelief in the veiled maiden's otherness.

Alastor has an ambivalent attitude towards Wordsworth, as does the volume of which it is the title poem. 'To Wordsworth' is a sonnet that turns Wordsworth's tropes of loss against him as it laments the poet's alleged turning away from 'Songs consecrate to truth and liberty' (12). Wordsworth's long poem *The Excursion* (1814) left Shelley and Mary Godwin 'disappointed'; as the latter has it in a journal entry: 'He is a slave.'[13] The poem can be read as recommending the dousing of revolutionary ardour in the cooling streams of rural retreat. And yet the Solitary is a major influence on Shelley's portrait of the Visionary, as are the rhythms, imagery, and phrasing of Wordsworth's poetry more generally: the Preface ends with a quotation from Book 1 of *The Excursion* – 'The good die first, / And those whose hearts are dry as summer dust, / Burn to the socket' (6; Shelley replaces

Wordsworth's 'they' with 'those') – which may be aimed at Wordsworth's supposed falling away from the radical sympathies of his youth. But, as it concludes with an elegiac refusal of elegy, *Alastor* calls for support on the 'Ode: Intimations of Immortality' ('It is a woe "too deep for tears"', 713). If the poem's attitude to Wordsworth is finally and finely mixed, so, too, is its view of solitude. Solitude may have its dangers, but the poetry's fascination with the condition makes it difficult to see Shelley as simply writing a moral tale warning about the dangers of isolation. Rather, Shelley suggests that in isolation begins an ardent quest for ideals which can leave the spirit tragically unsatisfied.

Laon and Cythna, a long poem in twelve cantos of Spenserian stanzas, was first published in December 1817. Because of its hostility towards Christian ideas of God (for Shelley, too often conceived of as an anthropomorphized tyranny, invoked in support of repressive political systems) and because of its accommodating attitude towards a sexual relationship between the hero and heroine who are brother and sister, the poem roused fears in its publishers, the Olliers, that it would face prosecution, and it was released in an expurgated version in January 1818 as *The Revolt of Islam*. The poem is above all a reimagining of the French Revolution, as Shelley's energetic sketch of his poem's contents in his Preface makes clear; he lists, among the poem's elements, for example, after the depiction of 'the growth and progress of individual mind aspiring after excellence, and devoted to the love of mankind', a consequent 'awakening of an immense nation from their slavery and degradation to a true sense of moral dignity and freedom' (113). In turn, following the intervention of foreign powers, there is what Shelley calls 'the temporary triumph of oppression, that secure earnest of its final and inevitable fall' (114).

One can hear in that last clause a tone of the hopeful necessitarianism present in *Queen Mab*. But this poem's concern is as much with 'the growth and progress of individual mind aspiring after excellence' as it is with millennial triumph. The poem's emphasis is on the minds and hearts of the kindred revolutionary spirits, Laon and Cythna. Their relationship is a model for the love which, in his Preface's penultimate paragraph, Shelley says 'is celebrated every where as the sole law which should govern the moral world' (120). Their capacity to shape ideals of communal love bears witness to Shelley's conviction that the tide of reaction against revolutionary hope has now turned, and that 'those who now live have survived an age of despair' (114). His analysis of how defeated hopes led to such 'an age of despair' is masterly in its insights into the psychology of political disappointment, 'a disappointment that unconsciously finds relief only in the wilful exaggeration of its own despair' (115).

But the poem continually displays the defeat of collective action as well as its often inspiring successes. The opening canto rehearses, in the allegorical form of a witnessed flight between a snake and eagle, a struggle between forces of liberty and power, one that takes place 'When the last hope of tramped France had failed / Like a brief dream of unremaining glory' (1–2). That the eagle stands for power and the snake for liberty typifies the poem's affronts to conventional expectations. Shelley retells the Book of Genesis as a power struggle won by Evil: 'The darkness lingering o'er the dawn of things, / Was Evil's breath and life: this made him strong / To soar aloft with overshadowing wings; / And the great Spirit of Good did creep among / The nations of mankind' (1.28.244–8). Shelley continually stages such ideological reversal through clashing and dynamic remodellings.

Yet *Laon and Cythna* refuses to turn merely into a narrative of realized fantasy, in which revolutionary virtue earns easy triumphs, even as it is deeply preoccupied with fantasy – with the ways in which inner mental life links with collective political action. Laon's narrative of his development leads into his account of how he unsuccessfully fought against the tyrant's military forces; his delirious nightmares when imprisoned are among the most vivid passages in the poem, as are the sections in Cythna's inset narrative of her dreams (which turns out to be true) of having given birth and losing her child after she has been captured and taken to be the tyrant Othman's concubine, one of 'the thralls / Of the cold tyrant's cruel lust' (7.4.28–9). Dreams, fantasies, visions: all are the stuff, for Shelley, out of which historical reimaginings can be made.

There is much in the poem that reflects Shelley's revolutionary hopes, with great emphasis being laid on the inspiring effect of a radical oratory that appeals to people's best instincts and desire, as in Laon's speeches in canto 2 or Cythna's in canto 8. Often the writing has the fluent intensity of this stanza from canto 9, a stanza which begins mid-sentence, following on from an 'As' (9.3.26) clause at the end of the previous stanza:

> So from that cry over the boundless hills,
> Sudden was caught one universal sound,
> Like a volcano's voice, whose thunder fills
> Remotest skies,—such glorious madness found
> A path thro' human hearts with stream which drowned
> Its struggling fears and cares, dark Custom's brood,
> They know not whence it came, but felt around
> A wide contagion poured—they called aloud
> On Liberty—that name lived on the sunny flood.   (9.4.28–36)

The abstractions – Custom and Liberty – are caught up in the 'glorious madness' described and enacted in the language with its enjambments 'boundlessly' moving across line-endings, volcanic imagery, and rapturous imagery of agency and receptivity. Keats will rework in 'Ode to a Nightingale' in his lines about Ruth Shelley's image of finding 'A path thro' human hearts', suggesting his responsiveness to the power of Shelley's evocation of the communicative process, always a central concern in the work of this radical poet.

But 'struggling cares and fears', overcome momentarily in this stanza, and a sense of ultimate ignorance about the mind and the universe (joyously transfigured though it is) in 'know not whence they came', are also productive poetic presences in *Laon and Cythna*. There is a good deal in the poem that expresses Shelley's political fears and philosophical uncertainties. If he hopes that the relationship between Laon and Cythna will inspire a more general conversion to love, the poem reads in part like the account of an erotic love affair, one founded on shared political ideals, that is affectingly private. After being burned at the stake, the hero and heroine retreat to the Temple of the Spirit which has been first introduced in the opening canto. This conception speaks volumes about Shelley's need to locate abiding value in some realm immune from the shocks of historical circumstance, which can as easily restore the tyrant as topple him from his throne. For all its optimism and millennial imaginings, then, *Laon and Cythna* is a narrative poem whose convolutions and intricacies mirror the difficulty of translating hope-filled ideals into political practice.

Notes

1 See *The Complete Poetry of Percy Bysshe Shelley*, vol. 2, ed. Donald H. Reiman and Neil Fraistat (Baltimore: Johns Hopkins University Press, 2004), p. 496. The edition is cited hereafter as *CPPBS* (with volume number). *Queen Mab* is quoted from this edition; page numbers for prose quotations are supplied in parentheses. *Alastor* and *Laon and Cythna* are quoted from the third volume of this edition, gen. ed. Reiman, Fraistat, and Nora Crook (2012). Again page numbers for prose are supplied in the main text.

2 *Letters of Percy Bysshe Shelley*, ed. F. L. Jones, 2 vols (Oxford: Clarendon Press, 1964), 2.304, 305, 304.

3 George Bernard Shaw, 'Shaming the Devil about Shelley' (1892), qtd in *The Poems of Shelley*, vol. 1, *1804–1817*, ed. Geoffrey Matthews and Kelvin Everest (London: Longman, 1989), p. 25.

4 For the poem's millennial quality, see Morton D. Paley, *Apocalypse and Millennium in English Romantic Poetry* (Oxford: Oxford University Press, 1999). Paley writes (p. 225) that the poem 'is a rarity in English poetry – a long millennial (not millenarian) poem, projecting the slow growth of human society to a state of perfection'. For 'romance', see David Duff, *Romance and Revolution: Shelley and the Politics of a Genre* (Cambridge: Cambridge University Press, 1994), ch. 2.

5 See *CPPBS* 2.503. See also David Duff's comment that 'Shelley expressly disagrees with Godwin … in the importance that he attaches to "passion"'. *Romance and Revolution*, p. 106.

6 See Michael O'Neill, 'Southey and Shelley Reconsidered', *Romanticism* 17 (2011): 10–24.

7 K. N. Cameron, *The Young Shelley: Genesis of a Radical* (London: Gollancz, 1951), p. 273.

8 William Godwin, *Enquiry Concerning Political Justice*, ed. Isaac Kramnick (Harmondsworth: Penguin, 1976), pp. 144–5.

9 For the possible echo of *Kubla Khan*, which Shelley may have seen in manuscript, see *CPPBS* 2.532.

10 See Judith Chernaik, *The Lyrics of Shelley* (Cleveland, OH: Case Western Reserve University Press, 1972), ch. 1.

11 *CPPBS* 3.355.

12 See Earl R. Wasserman, *Shelley: A Critical Reading* (Baltimore: Johns Hopkins University Press, 1971).

13 Qtd in *CPPBS* 3.438.

Percy Bysshe Shelley, 'Hymn to Intellectual Beauty'; 'Mont Blanc'; 'Ozymandias'; 'Ode to the West Wind'; the late poems to Jane Williams

This section turns its attention to Shelley's lyric poetry, considering poems across his short, prolific career. 'Hymn to Intellectual Beauty' was composed during Shelley's productive summer in Geneva in 1816 and published by Leigh Hunt in *The Examiner* on 19 January 1817. Tilottama Rajan argues that 'Mont Blanc' and the 'Hymn' 'converge on the same problem: the mind's need to transcend life by positing some transcendent, form-giving fiction',[1] and this insight suggests the seriousness of the poetic philosophy explored in the poem. Shelley's poetry may be characterized by William Hazlitt as 'a passionate dream, a straining after impossibilities, a record of fond conjectures, a confused embodying of vague abstractions',[2] but the 'Hymn to Intellectual Beauty' offers an intricate challenge to and a rehabilitation of the hymn genre. That genre involves religious hymns, but also eighteenth-century hymns to abstractions, as well as French Revolutionary hymns.[3] There is, indeed, much cogency in Richard Cronin's observation that the poem 'is not a hymn, but an ode'.[4]

Rational analysis and emotional inspiration blur, as does the line between self and speaker. Where Judith Chernaik can discern a definite autobiographical voice,[5] Timothy Webb's erudite argument for Shelley as adopting the features of the genre seems convincing: 'Thus Shelley's exclamation is a highly-stylised cry of despair which must be seen as the culmination of a long tradition of prophetic poetry.'[6] These critical differences point to the ways in which Shelley makes the 'Hymn to Intellectual Beauty' an interpretative problem, as any certainties seem as evanescent for the reader as Intellectual Beauty is for Shelley himself.

The Romantic Poetry Handbook, First Edition. Michael O'Neill and Madeleine Callaghan.
© 2018 John Wiley & Sons Ltd. Published 2018 by John Wiley & Sons Ltd.

Stanza 1, moving from simile to simile, dramatically enacts a drive to persist in producing more descriptions, more images, to bring his poem as close to his thought as possible. The perplexing yet enriching difficulty of creating a poetic form capable of containing vision, re-visions, and adjusting perspectives plays throughout the 'Hymn'. Shelley captures the ever-shifting, ever-changing nature of Intellectual Beauty as the language mirrors the condition of its elusive presence. Rather than mounting a complaint against language's inadequacy, the poetry delights in capturing the fragility and evanescence of this visitant spirit. The strength of the speaker's desire to achieve a union with this figure animates the poem, sending the poet to meditate on varying states named in the poem as 'love and hate, despondency and hope' ('Hymn to Intellectual Beauty', 24). The rhetorical questions of stanza 2 show Shelley, after deliberately failing to define the named Power, in search of reasons why speaker and Intellectual Beauty cannot be completely unified. The mingled supplication, acceptance, and defiance in stanzas 2 to 4 keep the dramatic tension coursing through the lines, as Shelley moves between petition and plea, rebuke and demand. Stanza 3 begins in negatives as the poet gropes through uncertainty to get somewhere towards an understanding of the experience. Shelley skirts dangerously close to unveiling Intellectual Beauty as the divine but religion becomes a failed attempt to conceptualize its indefinable quality. 'God, and ghosts, and Heaven' (27) are revealed as labels attached to Intellectual Beauty by sages and poets, labels which stand as 'the records of their vain endeavour' (28) to define the ineffable. 'Doubt, chance, and mutability' (31) become the only certainties available. The figure of the poet comes under intense scrutiny as Shelley presents a gothic and autobiographical portrait where the visitant spirit touches him: 'Sudden, thy shadow fell on me; / I shrieked, and clasped my hands in ecstasy!' ('Hymn', 59–60). This self-portrait has, like many of Shelley's supposed self-revelations, attracted adverse criticism. Yet Shelley is creating a type of the self, a fictionalized 'I', rather than actually describing himself in a solely biographical way. Shelley the man paradoxically becomes both central to and unimportant for the creation of the poetic voice: 'Here the poet is only a poet in so far as he speaks to and for that community. As an individual he has ceased to exist.'[7] Shelley creates a distinctive poetic self within carefully wrought formal boundaries as the 'Hymn' represents his multi-layered poetry in its complex fullness.

Written in July 1816 while touring the Chamonix Valley, 'Mont Blanc' was published in 1817 in the Shelleys' *History of a Six Weeks' Tour*, a travel narrative concerning two trips taken by the Shelleys and Claire Clairmont (Mary Shelley's stepsister). 'Mont Blanc' reveals Shelley's technical accomplishments and imaginative power. This complex and fluctuating poem is suggestive of the kinds of ambiguity and sublimity developed and then questioned throughout Shelley's work through the power of language. Shelley makes poetic language a testing ground for his ideas as he places any theistic impulses in tension with his more questioning perspective.[8] One evident formal sign of this drive to test any overall coherence shows in the use of rhyme in the poem. Shelley rhymes his lines, but he does so irregularly and glancingly, and often in swiftly enjambed syntactical units; the effect is to make the poem's rhyming, in William Keach's words, 'both a stay against and a means of marking the chaos and blankness which are *Mont Blanc*'s special concerns'.[9] To include a sense of 'chaos and blankness' and 'stays' against them suggests the scale of the ambition in 'Mont Blanc'. Shelley's structural subtlety belies any reading of the poetry as an emotionally raw and technically poor creation.[10] Section 1 immediately situates Mont Blanc as an entity that is defined by its perception by the onlooker. It does not stress the static form of the mountain, concentrating instead on the fluid nature of perception:

> The everlasting universe of things
> Flows through the mind, and rolls its rapid waves,
> Now dark—now glittering—now reflecting gloom—   ('Mont Blanc', 1–3)

Passivity of the mind is suggested by the flow of things through it, and the process seems alogical as sense impressions are recorded. Shelley develops in the first half of the section an illusion of unfiltered vision, but this is partially shattered by Shelley's philosophic addition into the description of the scene: 'The source of human thought its tribute brings / Of waters, — *with a sound but half its own*' ('Mont Blanc', 5–6; emphasis added). The poem is created out of external impressions on his individual mind, which overflows with different connections and ways of conceptualizing the mountain. Shelley refuses to impose one kind of controlling mould on to the natural world. Instead he relishes the plurality of interpretations possible by exposure to external stimuli. In section 2, Shelley shows a heightened awareness of the subjectivity of his imaginings in the second part of the second stanza: 'Dizzy Ravine! and when I gaze on thee / I seem as in a trance sublime and strange / To muse on my own separate fantasy' ('Mont Blanc', 34–6). Geoffrey Hartman points out with reference to 'Mont Blanc' that 'the trance induced by the sublime landscape does not point to a loss or sacrifice of intellect',[11] and this possibility allows the poet to be entranced even as he remains in control of his mental landscape. Section 3 of 'Mont Blanc' opens up a questioning vein, aware of the temptation to mythologize even as he cannot resist creating a myth of origin: 'Is this the scene / Where the old

Earthquake-daemon taught her young / Ruin? Were these their toys?' ('Mont Blanc', 71–3) and the speaker longs for the mountain to 'repeal / Large codes of fraud and woe; not understood / By all, but which the wise, and great, and good / Interpret, or make felt, or deeply feel' ('Mont Blanc', 80–3). The reader is left to question if the speaker can be included in this illustrious roll call, and if so, if he can manage this act of interpretation or sensibility. The exploration of the mountain's great power continues into section 4, and an elegiac sense creeps into the lines which lament that 'So much of life and joy is lost. The race / Of man flies far in dread; his work and dwelling / Vanish, like smoke before the tempest's stream, / And their place is not known' ('Mont Blanc', 117–20).

By section 5, a sense of higher knowledge and inevitability creeps into the tone, as Shelley seems to comprehend some of the mountain's knowledge:

> Mont Blanc yet gleams on high:—the power is there,
> The still and solemn power of many sights,
> And many sounds, and much of life and death.   ('Mont Blanc', 127–9)

Yet this unnamed power seems to contradict the thrust of the poem; 'Mont Blanc' offers a statement of belief in profusion. These lines would reduce the poem to a single belief, but the poem continues as Shelley insists on holding all possibilities open to the reader. The final three lines represent Shelley at his most skilful, demonstrating his ability to pivot from one point to another without dismissing the previous idea or prioritizing the present concept. They are an affirmation of the power of the human mind to vivify and conceptualize the landscape with the imagination's perceptive power:

> And what were thou, and earth, and stars, and sea,
> If to the human mind's imaginings
> Silence and solitude were vacancy?   ('Mont Blanc', 142–4)

While affirming the power of the imagination, the lines contain an underlying ambivalence that Shelley communicates by formulating a question. The question seems a real enquiry rather than a rhetorical trope. While the densely packed perceptions of the poem attest to the primacy of the imagination, there is an underlying fear of vacancy as the inverse of the teeming mind of the poet. Shelley in 'Mont Blanc' creates and dismisses each attempt at coming up with a theory,[12] indicating nothing more keenly than the fluidity and plurality of the human imagination. But glimmering beneath the narrator's confident imaginative exercise is a fear that the human mind's imaginings might finally point to humanity's alienation from nature. The imagination's need to fill a vacuum could prevent a possible interchange between man and nature, rendering it impossible for people to see nature in its own physical majesty. On the other hand, the fear that nature may indeed be dumb is equally horrifying. Either way it is apparent that the interchange between man and nature, if ever there was one, is broken. Careful observation and perception of the mountain entwine with Shelley's demonstration of the colouring that 'the human mind's imaginings' project on to nature, but ultimately, for Shelley, the human mind takes centre stage, becoming the final point of contemplation.

Written in late 1817, 'Ozymandias' was Shelley's contribution to a competition with Horace Smith, and was published under a pseudonym in Hunt's *Examiner* on 11 January 1818. As François Jost writes, 'In English literature the prize for prosodic variety in sonnet composition undoubtedly goes to Shelley, if we restrict the competition to major poets up to his time … He never used the same [rhyme scheme] twice.'[13] Shelley put pressure on the sonnet form and on his subject matter. Preoccupied by the relationship between art and history, Shelley's sonnet refuses to settle for a single interpretation:

> I met a traveller from an antique land
> Who said—'Two vast and trunkless legs of stone
> Stand in the desert. Near them, on the sand,
> Half sunk, a shattered visage lies, whose frown,
> And wrinkled lip, and sneer of cold command,
> Tell that its sculptor well those passions read
> Which yet survive, stamped on these lifeless things,
> The hand that mocked them and the heart that fed;
> And on the pedestal these words appear:
> "My name is Ozymandias, King of Kings:
> Look on my Works, ye Mighty, and despair!"
> Nothing beside remains. Round the decay
> Of that colossal Wreck, boundless and bare
> The lone and level sands stretch far away.'

The face, only half sunk, is shattered. But apparently, despite the weathered-looking nature of the stone, the traveller can see clearly a 'wrinkled lip, and sneer of cold command'. Ozymandias is depicted as a tyrant, making the inscription on the statue seem like a mockery. Ozymandias' boast could seem almost laughably hollow. Yet Ozymandias' great works guaranteed immortality, of a sort. Shelley and all the poets and artists that judge him have to contend with the enduring legacy of this powerful leader, the self-proclaimed King of Kings. Yet what the traveller describes is the triumph of art over history. It is the sculptor who defines the way in which Ozymandias is remembered. It is the artist, not Ozymandias in his own right, who has survived history. Nothing else remains; the statue is merely a 'colossal Wreck' in a sea of bare sands. The reader can expect history to yield us no certainties, no truths, nothing but a sculptor's interpretation or a traveller's story. We are returned to Shelley's imaginative power, the poet who imagined the sculptor's achievement and legacy, and presumably, the testimony of the traveller. Art and history come together, ensuring that 'every act of reading the sonnet must pay attention to the precariousness of what we have just identified as the message of that writing'.[14] The message of the sonnet is unstable, the opposite of the enduring universal monument. But the power of 'Ozymandias' is to open out the possibilities of art and history, viewing them less as competing forces than as irrevocably bound together.

'Ode to the West Wind', begun in Florence in October 1819 and published in Shelley's 1820 volume, *Prometheus Unbound, with Other Poems*, encompasses 'rebirth and regeneration in the personal and political spheres'.[15] This *terza rima* poem turns on movement as Shelley makes it seem ceaselessly fluid even as he transforms each section into sonnets of a kind in his five-part poem. Preoccupied by myth-making and poetic power, Harold Bloom views the poem as deeply metapoetic: 'The "Ode to the West Wind" is actually a poem about this process of making myths, a poem whose subject is the nature and function of the nabi and his relation to his own prophecies.'[16] Shelley shows the development from priest, to prophet, to poet in 'Ode', as its sparkling *terza rima* swiftness moves the poem forward irresistibly. Opening with an invocation that views the 'wild West Wind' (1) as a godlike force, Shelley's opening section positions the speaker as supplicant to the 'unseen presence' (2) of the wind. The 'Pestilence-stricken multitudes' (5), a phrase that turns leaves into people, seem passively driven by the wind's force, as 'from an enchanter fleeing' (3). Hymning the wind's power in the second section, Shelley's powerful lines almost delight in 'thy congregated might' (26) where the destructive power of the West Wind brings 'Black rain, and fire, and hail' to 'burst' (28) upon the earth. The poem then moves into a dreamily beautiful passage in section 3, where the wind wakes the Mediterranean, and then darkens the calm of the section's earlier lines through fear of the West Wind's violence in the closing couplet. Only by the fourth section does Shelley bring in the personal pronoun, changing from impersonal supplication to personal identification with the 'wild West Wind' (1). The lines show Shelley initially asking to be borne by the wind as a dead leaf, then requesting to become a cloud 'to fly with thee' (44), and finally to share in 'The impulse of thy strength' (46). Yet this yearning admits it cannot be fulfilled; the speaker is unable to be a natural phenomenon, even as he longs to be 'only less free / Than thou, O, Uncontrollable!' (47).

The climactic lines, 'Oh! lift me as a wave, a leaf, a cloud! / I fall upon the thorns of life! I bleed!' (53–4), have been imbued with biographical readings, but Harold Bloom's terse summary – 'By now it ought to be evident that the thorns of life have nothing to do with Lord Chancellors, quarterly reviews, despotic fathers, etc'[17] – has been instrumental in returning the focus to the poetry itself. Here, Shelley demonstrates the struggle and the agony involved in the process of myth-creation. The final section is a confident invocation of the wind, as Shelley turns from supplicant into commander of this wind, insisting on controlling the change he imagines. The poetry ripples with potency as the poet demands that his words be scattered by the wind among mankind. This poetry, though it looks forward to 'direct political action' as William Keach argues,[18] is at least as fascinated with poetic legacy and the dissemination of words as well as ideas by the 'incantation of this verse' (65). Such prophetic certainty is not sustained; the final two lines reveal less confidence than the rest of the section: 'O, wind, / If Winter comes, can Spring be far behind?' (69–70). The magisterial voice has given way to something more circumspect.

In 1822, Shelley began writing poems for Jane Williams, including 'With a Guitar. To Jane', 'To Jane ("The keen stars were twinkling")', 'To Jane. The Invitation', 'To Jane—The Recollection', 'To — ("The serpent is shut out from Paradise")', 'The Magnetic Lady to her Patient', and 'Lines Written in the Bay of Lerici'. These poems 'illustrate the intimate entanglement of Shelley's personal life and poetic ambition',[19] and display Shelley's mastery of tonal complexities. The Shelleys met Jane and her second husband, Edward Ellerker Williams, early in 1821 while living in Pisa, and Shelley himself had a strong regard for both Jane and her husband. As Emilia Viviani was for *Epipsychidion*, so Jane Williams became for his lyrics; she is the idealized subject onto which Shelley could project his imagination.

'To — ("The serpent is shut out from Paradise")', composed in January 1822 and sent to Edward Williams, shows Shelley testing the limits of artifice and biography in his modified *ottava rima*. The reference to the serpent, Byron's nickname for his fellow poet, suggests that Shelley is the subject of the lines, and his adoption of Byron's *ottava rima* suggests the older, rival poet is a presence in the poetry, perhaps ghosting the lines as his worldly success contrasts with the speaker's disappointment with his reception at the hands of 'the world's carnival' (31). The poem displays creativity even in the midst of its despair. The opening stanza offers three possible incarnations of the poet-figure, 'serpent,' 'wounded deer', recalling *Adonais* and its 'frail Form' who 'Actaeon-like' flees 'With feeble steps o'er the world's wilderness' (*Adonais* 31.271, 276, 277), and 'widowed dove'. Creative potential is undimmed despite the speaker's exiled and wounded state and the rhyme of 'again' with 'pain' offers a poetic mastery that cannot quite redeem the speaker's misery. Quasi-Byronic in its initial proud scorn and 'Indifference' (10), this emotion gives way to grief and loneliness. Wearied sadness slows the lines as death seems to provide the only possible way out: 'Doubtless there is a place of peace / Where *my* weak heart and all its throbs will cease' (47–8), where the couplet rhymes insistently point to the grave as the only solution to the poet's 'forced part in life's dull scene' (4.28). Closing with an affirmation of his friends' empathy, his hope comes to 'look[ed] more like Despair' (*The Mask of Anarchy* 88). 'To Jane. The Invitation' and 'To Jane—The Recollection' draw on an excursion taken by Jane Williams and the Shelleys and show Shelley's command of the pastoral mode, where the poet almost transcends time with his polished summoning of 'the universal Sun' ('To Jane. The Invitation', 69). Mary's disappearance from the poems seems less a troubling aporia than Shelley transmuting the dross of experience into the gold of poetic artifice. 'To Jane. The Invitation' almost resembles a *carpe diem* poem, but rather than allowing dark and melancholy undertones to lurk in the poem, Shelley openly banishes them, picking off Sorrow, Despair, Care, Death, and Expectation to affirm that 'Today is for itself enough—' (40). The invitation's ephemerality lends the lines a poignancy as their beauty seems sustained by an act of the poet's will. By the time of 'To Jane—The Recollection', Shelley recollects 'The giants of the waste, / Tortured by storms to shapes as rude / As serpents interlaced' (2.22–4), yet this threatening scene does not disrupt the serenity he discovered. Section 3 is the still centre of the turning world of the poem, where 'How calm it was!' (3.33) seems both delighted memory and painful contrast to his present circumstances. The speaker's disturbed mind closes the poem, offering no sign of a future without torment on the horizon. 'The Magnetic Lady to her Patient' sees the speaker mired in tortured thought, where he is told to 'forget me, for I can never / Be thine.—' (26–7). As in 'To — ("The serpent is shut out from Paradise")', Shelley is tormented by what momentarily mitigates his agony; the presence of the Magnetic lady. Moving strikingly close to biographical disclosure, the final lines instruct her to 'tempt me not to break / My chain' (44–5), with his marriage seeming as much like physical bondage as spiritual (dis)union. 'Hymn to Intellectual Beauty', 'Mont Blanc', 'Ozymandias', 'Ode to the West Wind', and the late poems to Jane Williams are united by their experimentation with the lyric genre; each questions even as it fashions a poet-self.

Notes

1 Tilottama Rajan, *The Dark Interpreter: The Discourse of Romanticism* (Ithaca, NY: Cornell University Press, 1980), p. 84.

2 William Hazlitt, qtd in Theodore Redpath, *The Young Romantics and Critical Opinion 1807–1824* (London: Harrap, 1973), p. 388.

3 See *The Complete Poetry of Percy Bysshe Shelley*, vol. 3, gen. ed. Donald H. Reiman, Neil Fraistat, and Nora Crook (Baltimore: Johns Hopkins University Press, 2012), p. 483.

4 *Shelley's Poetic Thoughts* (London: Macmillan, 1981), p. 224.

5 'The personal experience dramatized in lines 49–72 is almost painfully authentic.' Judith Chernaik, *The Lyrics of Shelley* (Cleveland, OH: Case Western Reserve University Press, 1972), p. 36.

6 Timothy Webb, *Shelley: A Voice Not Understood* (Manchester: Manchester University Press, 1977), p. 38.

7 Webb, *Shelley: A Voice Not Understood*, p. 38.

8 Stuart Curran, *Poetic Form and British Romanticism* (Oxford: Oxford University Press, 1986), p. 61.

9 In *Shelley's Style* (New York: Methuen, 1984), qtd from *Shelley's Poetry and Prose*, ed. Donald H. Reiman and Neil Fraistat (New York: Norton, 2002), p. 671.

10 'The "poetical faculty," we are left no room for doubting, can, of its very nature, have nothing to do with any discipline, and can be associated with conscious effort only mechanically and externally.' F. R. Leavis, *Revaluation: Tradition and Development in English Poetry* (Harmondsworth: Penguin, 1964), p. 175.

11 Geoffrey Hartman, 'Gods, Ghosts, and Shelley's "*Atheos*"', *Literature & Theology* 24.1 (2010): 4–18 (at 10).

12 For a discussion of Shelley's use of mythographs, see Jerrold E. Hogle, *Shelley's Process: Radical Transference and the Development of His Major Works* (New York and Oxford: Oxford University Press, 1988).

13 François Jost, 'The Anatomy of an Ode: Shelley and the Sonnet Tradition', *Comparative Literature* 34 (1982): 223–46 (at 232).

14 Christoph Bode, 'Discursive Constructions of the Self in British Romanticism', *Romanticism and Victorianism on the Net* 51 (2008): http://www.erudit.org/revue/ravon/2008/v/n51/019264ar.html#s1n3.

15 *Shelley: Major Works*, p. 762.

16 Harold Bloom, *Shelley's Mythmaking*, Yale Studies in English, 141 (New Haven, CT: Yale University Press, 1959), p. 67.

17 Bloom, *Shelley's Mythmaking*, p. 85.

18 William Keach, *Arbitrary Power: Romanticism, Language, Politics* (Princeton: Princeton University Press, 2004), p. 129.

19 Shahidha Bari, 'Lyrics and Love Poems: Poems to Sophia Stacey, Jane Williams, and Mary Shelley', in *The Oxford Handbook of Percy Bysshe Shelley*, ed. Michael O'Neill and Tony Howe, with the assistance of Madeleine Callaghan (Oxford: Oxford University Press, 2012), pp. 275–390 (at p. 375).

Percy Bysshe Shelley, *Prometheus Unbound; Adonais; The Triumph of Life*

Prometheus Unbound, Adonais, and *The Triumph of Life* stand as three of the finest writings of Shelley's middle to late period, showcasing the breadth of his poetic range and the pinnacle of his achievement.[1] *Prometheus Unbound,* written at intervals between August or September 1818 and mid-1820, is a lyrical drama that espouses 'beautiful idealisms' ('Preface to *Prometheus Unbound*', 232) while remaining alert to the pain-fraught challenges to the liberty finally celebrated in the work. *Adonais,* Shelley's 1821 elegy for John Keats, stands as a monument to both his esteem for Keats and his continual scrutiny of the role of the poet and poetry, as he performs, questions, and challenges the generic rules of elegy. *The Triumph of Life,* begun in 1822, became, by reason of Shelley's premature death, his final and incomplete poem. Its fragmentary status has not damaged its appeal to generations of critics, with many, including T. S. Eliot,[2] judging it to be his masterpiece. The three works are united by their powerful engagement with the possibilities inherent in poetry, the intensity with which Shelley imbues language, and their swift-winged imaginative movement.

Prometheus Unbound moves between poetry and drama; the subtitle, 'A Lyrical Drama', offers the reader an insight into Shelley's imaginative scheme, a scheme which seeks to explore and exploit the possibilities of both genres. The emphasis on language over action after the first act shows Shelley deliberately shifting the plot from physical to mental action, yet the importance of Prometheus' self-overcoming in the first act reveals Shelley's intellectual debt to Aeschylus, the Greek playwright whose *Prometheus Bound* offered the impetus for the lyrical drama. Drawing on a number of influences, from Aeschylus to Milton, *Prometheus Unbound* shows Shelley working out a distinctively Shelleyan brand of poetry. Prometheus begins the

The Romantic Poetry Handbook, First Edition. Michael O'Neill and Madeleine Callaghan.
© 2018 John Wiley & Sons Ltd. Published 2018 by John Wiley & Sons Ltd.

play mired in loathing for Jupiter, his nemesis. Renouncing his hatred, Prometheus is tormented by the Furies, but overcomes them through affirming his autonomy. In Act 2, Panthea, witness to Prometheus' self-liberation, tells Asia of events, and then Asia and Panthea visit Demogorgon, who, during their interview, pronounces that the hour of Prometheus' freedom is upon them. In Act 3 Demogorgon, revealed as Jupiter's son, overthrows Jupiter, dragging him into the abyss, and Prometheus affirms humanity's new-found freedom after being reunited with Asia. Act 4 is where Shelley creates 'an ocean of splendour and harmony' (4.134) as the poetry ascends into an exultation and analysis of love and the possibilities of the human mind.

As critics have frequently pointed out, Act 1 is the site of the main action and drive of the entire play, leaving the remaining three acts to develop as a result of the earlier psychodrama. The first act also includes some of the most impressive poetry of the entire lyrical drama, as Prometheus is forced to confront the Furies, Mercury, and the spectre of his former self. Despite the 'emergence of creative possibility' that closes the act,[3] the mental suffering endured by Prometheus, and witnessed by Panthea and Ione, underscores Shelley's clear-eyed assessment of the challenges to self-rule. Shelley's psychological acuity comes to the fore as Prometheus fears for his autonomy in the face of the torments he faces:

> He whom some dreadful voice invokes is here,
> Prometheus, the chained Titan. Horrible forms,
> What and who are ye? Never yet there came
> Phantasms so foul through monster-teeming Hell
> From the all-miscreative brain of Jove;
> Whilst I behold such execrable shapes,
> Methinks I grow like what I contemplate,
> And laugh and stare in loathsome sympathy. (*Prometheus Unbound* 1.444–51)

Prometheus' potential to mirror Jupiter appears as Prometheus is forced to see the terrible spectres that emanate from the mind of his oppressor, and this moment of weakness reminds the reader of his earlier resemblance to Jupiter at the opening of the lyrical drama. The fearful questioning, horrified description of the foul phantasms, and the terror of becoming inured and then complicit in such ugliness shows Shelley emphasize the level of torment and struggle attendant on achieving psychological freedom. Prometheus is forced to face the abject horror conjured by the Furies. Yet, despite the rhetorical strength of the Furies' arguments, and the terrifying visions imposed on Prometheus, Prometheus cuts through their attempts to make words into unchangeable physical reality. Without physically battling the Furies, Prometheus banishes what Blake described as 'mind-forged manacles' from his discourse.[4] The poetry enacts the mental dexterity required of Prometheus as he extricates himself from Jupiter's psychological prison.

Shelley never allows plot to overshadow language. *Prometheus Unbound* attains its dazzling quality through its many facets, the formal experiments attempted throughout the 'composite order' of his lyrical drama.[5] Shelley does not simply subvert or resist formal fixity; rather, the poem ranges through a variety of forms, each form deliberately developing its own internal direction. The rhythmic and phonetic form of the poetry goes beyond mirroring the content of the lines. It is almost impossible to divide the semantic meaning from the formal construction of the poem. Asia's ecstasy following Prometheus' victory over himself showcases some of the finest poetry of *Prometheus Unbound* as Shelley explores the beauty of language and its ability to embody heightened emotional states:

> It seems to float ever, forever,
> Upon that many-winding river,
> Between mountains, woods, abysses,
> A paradise of wildernesses!
> Till, like one in slumber bound,
> Borne to the ocean, I float down, around,
> Into a sea profound, of ever-spreading sound: (2.5.78–84)

Asia's words embody the trance-like tranquillity of her feeling, as she floats upon the 'silver waves' of her metaphor. The almost echoing quality of 'float ever, for ever' demonstrates without insisting upon the waves on which she is borne, while the feminine half-rhyme of 'ever' and 'river' brings out the 'seeming' nature of Asia's experience of eternity. Reaching the ecstatic affirmation of 'a paradise of wildernesses', Asia glories in the natural beauty of the 'mountains, woods, abysses', as the poetry luxuriates in the paradise it enacts. The reader is bound around in sound, as the music of the poem embodies its description of the 'sea profound, of ever-spreading sound'.

Prometheus Unbound closes with a far from uncritical affirmation of human potential, one that pivots on the importance of remaining vigilant against the forces that would again imprison the human spirit, even as it cautiously celebrates the achievement of Prometheus and mankind. Despite the judgement of William Butler Yeats, whose harshest criticism often reveals engagement with rather than censure of his predecessors, *Prometheus Unbound* does not witness Shelley setting out a simplistic formula for wish-fulfilment.[6] But Yeats's emphasis on the 'nightmare-ridden' quality of *Prometheus Unbound* suggests its complexity. Harold Bloom's claim, 'The uncritical millenarianism that critics have found in "Prometheus" is what they have brought to the poem themselves',[7] seems supported by the text's insistence on the struggle that must be faced in order to create and then sustain the climactic change that it advocates. Prometheus must become 'king over myself' (1.492), just as humanity must be willing 'Neither to change, nor falter, nor repent' (4.575).

Adonais brings into sparkling poetic life Shelley's concerns and confidence about poetry, his ideas on the afterlife, and shows him experiment with the boundaries of genre. Michael O'Neill writes, 'What Shelley does assert, with desperate conviction, is that great poetry endures',[8] and, rather than assume such endurance, Shelley forces poetry to earn its claims of transcendence. Written in the Spenserian stanza, the elegy displays Shelley's formal mastery as he, like Byron, wrests the challenging form to match his distinctive poetic voice. Moving from slowed stanzas, where the poet seems acted upon, 'And others came … Desires and Adorations, / Wingèd Persuasions and veiled Destinies, / Splendours, and Glooms, and glimmering Incarnations / Of hopes and fears, and twilight Fantasies' (*Adonais* 13.109–12), to the toweringly dramatic: 'Alas! that all we loved of him should be, / But for our grief, as if it had not been, / And grief itself be mortal! Woe is me! / Whence are we, and why are we? of what scene / The actors or spectators?' (*Adonais* 21.181–5), Shelley's poem runs the gamut of emotional intensity while retaining tight formal control.

Drawing attention to the constructedness of *Adonais*, Shelley describes it as a 'highly wrought *piece of art*.'[9] His admiration for the younger poet, which he referred to in terms of Keats's potential to outstrip his own poetic power, added a tense dimension to his representation of Adonais / Keats.[10] Arthur Bradley emphasizes the scale of Shelley's artistic challenges in the work: 'Shelley's *Adonais* is both an attempt to monumentalise Keats's loss and an attempt to resist or evade all monumentalising gestures',[11] and this is one of many vacillations between extremes housed in the poetry. Shadowing the death of the elegized poet is the continuing existence of the elegizing poet, whose creation of self-portrait becomes fraught task equal to the struggle to commemorate Keats. The parade of 'inadequate mourners' offers scant consolation to the elegist,[12] who is forced to face the limitations of poetic consolation, and strive to find effective strategies to memorialize the dead poet. The first seventeen of fifty-five stanzas stand as desperate attempts to find comfort for the assembled mourners, 'sobbing in their dismay' (*Adonais* 14.126). After returning to the stark fact, '*He* will awake no more, oh, never more!' (*Adonais* 22.190), Shelley turns to portraiture, painting Keats / Adonais as a weak, though beautiful child who courted his own destruction: 'Defenceless as thou wert, oh where was then / Wisdom the mirrored shield, or scorn the spear?' (*Adonais* 27.239–40). Despite some censure for this presentation of Keats / Adonais,[13] Shelley's artistic ends were far greater than to denigrate a dead rival as *Adonais* gains imaginative strength from the fluctuation between admiration for Adonais's power and sadness for his vulnerability. Though Kelvin Everest views *Adonais* as showing Shelley as figuring himself as inferior to Keats,[14] it is the close identification between the two poets that lends the poem its sublimity. The self-portrait created by the elegist comes close to twinning the elegist and the elegized through their weakness,[15] though the former is distinguished by his status as 'neglected and apart' (*Adonais* 33.296) from his fellow mourners, who include Byron, Moore, and Hunt.

The final stanzas show Shelley taking artistic flight, wresting transcendence from the previously intractable agony of Keats's / Adonais's loss. Shifting gear in stanza 38, *Adonais* begins a swift ascent, the force of the elegist's poetry seems to propel him forward, drawing him, almost against his will, into 'the white radiance of Eternity' (*Adonais* 52.463). This sense of Shelley as being compelled rather than choosing ecstatic surrender is encapsulated by the beginning of stanza 53, which suggests the urge to draw away from the intensity of his vision: 'Why linger, why turn back, why shrink, my Heart? / Thy hopes are gone before: from all things here / They have departed; thou shouldst now depart!' (*Adonais* 53.469–71). What had been the struggle to achieve transcendence darkens into terror of realizing just what that transcendence means for the still mortal poet. Shivering on the edge of transfiguration, the final stanza shows Shelley in the process of being drawn into the eternity which he had previously courted:

> The breath whose might I have invoked in song
> Descends on me; my spirit's bark is driven
> Far from the shore, far from the trembling throng
> Whose sails were never to the tempest given;
> The massy earth and spherèd skies are riven!
> I am borne darkly, fearfully, afar;
> Whilst burning through the inmost veil of Heaven,
> The soul of Adonais, like a star,
> Beacons from the abode where the Eternal are.   (*Adonais* 55.487–95)

The elegy has transformed from an act of commemoration into a menacingly hypnotic spell which now threatens the very life of the elegist. The passive verbs proliferate as Shelley is propelled away from the markers of mortal life, and his fearful passage seems neither positive nor negative, but inevitable. Adonais, the dead and commemorated poet, now figures as a beacon, compelling Shelley forward into his final state. Leaving the reader with this chilling ending, Shelley's elegy reveals how far he has explored and pushed the limits of the genre. What had offered consolation has, under Shelley's masterful poetic manipulation, become dangerously ambiguous.

The Triumph of Life, with its fleet of foot *terza rima* stanzas and darkly ambiguous music, is Shelley's final and unfinished fragment poem. Indebted to Petrarch, Dante, Milton, and Goethe, amongst others,[16] the poem shows Shelley weaving together his influences alongside his individual preoccupations to form a poem that speaks with his own distinctive voice. Unfolding with dazzling intensity, the poem recounts 'the tenour of my waking dream' (*Triumph of Life*, 42) where the poet watches the 'sad pageantry' (176) of humanity, the 'captive multitude' (119) driven along by Life. Interviewing Rousseau, who is disfigured into 'an old root which grew / To strange distortion out of the hillside' (182–3), the poet attempts to discover the meaning of 'this harsh world in which I wake to weep' (334). The poem scrutinizes history, philosophy, and poetry itself to create a sombre and haunting vision that asks but never answers its final question, '"Then, what is Life?"' (544). The critical approbation received by the poem has occasionally led to the sense that his final poem shows Shelley finally surrendering to a belief in the futility of life. Paul de Man's sense that '"The Triumph of Life" can be said to reduce all of Shelley's previous work to nought' represents this strain of critical thought, but it understates the relationship between the poem and its predecessors.[17] Like *Prometheus Unbound* and *Adonais*, *The Triumph of Life* admits a complex emotional range into its parameters. Bursting with aesthetic flare even as it grieves for the plight of 'that deluded crew' (184), *The Triumph of Life* is distinguished by its ability to embody 'many sounds woven into one / Oblivious melody, confusing sense / Amid the gliding waves and shadows dun' (340–2).

The image of these 'gliding waves and shadows dun' suggests the content as well as the behaviour of the poetry. Shelley capitalizes on the quick moving *terza rima*, using its evasive structure to court as well as defy the mind's desire for meaning. Walking an uneasy line between unfettered pessimism and incautious optimism, the poetry deliberately refuses the solace of certainty. From the beginning of the poem, the speaker withholds from the reader 'thoughts which must remain untold' (21), and offers a vision which stubbornly refuses to define itself as 'slumber' (30) or truth. The central action of the poem, where Rousseau relates his encounter with the Shape all Light, is equally equivocal. Asking the Shape all Light, 'Show whence I came, and where I am, and why— / Pass not away upon the passing stream' (398–9), Rousseau pleads, with an affecting poignancy masquerading as assertiveness, for answers. Yet no answers come. Instead, Rousseau drinks the 'bright Nepenthe' (359) offered: '"I rose; and, bending at her sweet command, / Touched with faint lips the cup she raised, / And suddenly my brain became as sand"' (403–5). Despite the temptation to form a moral judgement of Rousseau, as Hugh Roberts amongst others has,[18] Shelley carefully alerts the reader to the dangers of subscribing to a single view of events through the relentlessly shifting parameters of his poem. No single emotional state takes control of the poem as Shelley proliferates possibility throughout *The Triumph of Life*.

This artistic principle of mutability comes, paradoxically, to be the closest thing to constancy in the poem. Even as it seems that Shelley creates a single tone, the poetry undermines any overwhelming despair:

> — ... 'Let them pass',
>   I cried, '—the world and its mysterious doom
>
> 'Is not so much more glorious than it was
>   That I desire to worship those who drew
> New figures on its false and fragile glass   (243–7)

Apparently chilling in their denunciation of 'the world and its mysterious doom', the lines swell with imperious self-will, revealing assertiveness that glories in the strength of its own rhetorical power. The soaring lines emphasize the will of the speaker and the right of the individual to refuse worship to 'those who drew / New figures on its false and fragile glass'. Immediately following this declaration of independence, Rousseau reminds the speaker of the connection between 'those' and himself, '"Figures ever new / Rise on the bubble, paint them how you may; / We have but thrown, as those before us threw, / "Our shadows on it as it passed away"' (248–51), refusing the speaker's nihilistic avowal.[19] *The Triumph of Life* swithers away from any final statement of a single vision, carefully performing doubts, shifts, and uncertainties even as its poetic power shines through the lines. The three poems are united by their determined questioning of the power of the poet and their challenge to and affirmation of the potential of poetry.

Notes

1 Percy Bysshe Shelley, *A Defence of Poetry*, in *Percy Bysshe Shelley: The Major Works*, ed. Zachary Leader and Michael O'Neill, Oxford World's Classics (Oxford: Oxford University Press, 2003), p. 701. All quotations from the poetry and prose of Shelley in this section (unless specified otherwise) will be taken from this edition.

2 T. S. Eliot, *The Use of Poetry and the Use of Criticism* (London: Faber, 1964), p. 90.

3 Daniel Hughes, 'Prometheus Made Capable Poet in Act One of *Prometheus Unbound*', *Studies in Romanticism* 17.1 (1978): 3–11 (at 4).

4 William Blake, 'London', 8, in *Blake's Poetry and Designs: Illuminated Works, Other Writings, Criticism*, sel. and ed. Mary Lynn Johnson and John E. Grant, 2nd edn (New York: Norton, 2008), p. 53.

5 As suggested by Stuart Curran's chapter 'Composite Orders' in Stuart Curran, *Poetic Form and British Romanticism* (New York and Oxford: Oxford University Press, 1986), p. 181.

6 W. B. Yeats, 'Prometheus Unbound', in *Essays and Introductions* (London: Macmillan, 1961), pp. 419–25.

7 Bloom, *Shelley's Mythmaking*, p. 95.

8 Michael O'Neill, '*Adonais* and Poetic Power', *The Wordsworth Circle* 35.2 (2004): 50–7 (at 52).

9 *Letters of Percy Bysshe Shelley*, ed. F. L. Jones, 2 vols (Oxford: Clarendon Press, 1964), 2.294. All quotations from Shelley's letters will be taken from this volume.

10 'I am aware indeed in part [tha]t I am nourishing a rival who will far surpass [me] and this is an additional motive & will be an added pleasure.' *Letters* 2.240.

11 Arthur Bradley, '"Until Death Tramples It to Fragments": Percy Bysshe Shelley after Postmodern Theology', in *Romanticism and Religion from William Cowper to Wallace Stevens*, ed. Gavin Hopps and Jane Stabler, The Nineteenth Century Series (Aldershot: Ashgate, 2006), pp. 191–206 (at p. 201).

12 Peter M. Sacks, *The English Elegy: Studies in the Genre from Spenser to Yeats* (Baltimore: Johns Hopkins University Press, 1987), p. 148.

13 'Enough has been said, I think, to show that this strange story of Keats's death was deliberately fabricated by Shelley. But it is not only a fabrication; it is also an insult.' James A. W. Heffernan, '*Adonais*: Shelley's Consumption of Keats', in *Romanticism: A Critical Reader*, ed. Duncan Wu (Oxford: Blackwell, 1995), pp. 173–91 (at p. 177).

14 '*Adonais* differs from other English elegies in celebrating its subject throughout as a more important poet than the author, which is what Shelley really judged Keats to be.' Kelvin Everest, 'Shelley's *Adonais* and John Keats', *Essays in Criticism* 57.3 (2007): 237–64 (at 237).

15 '[T]he elegist is lamenting his own fate.' Judith Chernaik, *The Lyrics of Shelley* (Cleveland, OH: Case Western Reserve University Press, 1972), p. 20.

16 *Shelley: Major Works*, pp. 815–16.

17 Paul de Man, 'Shelley Disfigured', in *The Rhetoric of Romanticism* (New York and London: Columbia University Press, 1984), pp. 93–123 (at p. 120).

18 'If we return to *The Triumph of Life* and, turning actor not spectator, avoid Rousseau's mistake of demanding a value that is not at risk in the flux of process, then we find the apparent nightmare of life's dance is a product of incorrect seeing, or choosing an inappropriate scale.' Hugh Roberts, 'Spectators Turned Actors: *The Triumph of Life*', in *Shelley's Poetry and Prose*, sel. and ed. Donald H. Reiman and Neil Fraistat, Norton Critical Edition, 2nd edn (New York: Norton, 2002), p. 766.

19 Donald H. Reiman, *Shelley's 'The Triumph of Life': A Critical Study*, Illinois Studies in Language and Literature 55 (Urbana: University of Illinois Press, 1965), p. 57.

John Keats, *Endymion*; 'Sleep and Poetry'; The Sonnets

This section seeks to display Keats's generic variety in the first half of his brief career. In an 1818 review originally signed 'Z', John Gibson Lockhart dismisses Keats's literary aspirations in the same vein that John Wilson Croker would in his essay in the *Quarterly Review*: 'so back to the shop Mr John, back to "plasters, pills, and ointment boxes", &c. But, for Heaven's sake, young Sangrado, be a little more sparing of extenuatives and soporifics in your practice than you have been in your poetry.'[1] With his reviewers linking politics and poetry, class and rhyme,[2] Keats suffered for his 'Cockney' rhymes in 'Sleep and Poetry'. *Endymion: A Poetic Romance* received mixed reviews, but the power of Keats's early 'poetic romance' is increasingly recognized by critics. Experimenting with the possibilities of poetry in lush couplets, *Endymion* blends genres, myths, and ideas in an 'indistinct profusion' that highlights the beauty of the poetry and the power of the poet.[3] The sonnets extend this experimentation as Keats, like his fellow romantics, adapted the sonnet form, which, like other genres, became '[a] time-bound entit[y], not transcendent form[s]'.[4] Keats adopted and then adapted the sonnet, revivifying it to bear witness to the range and depth of his poetic voice.

'Sleep and Poetry', written while residing at Leigh Hunt's Hampstead cottage, was started in the autumn of 1816 and completed in December of the same year. A manifesto for Keats's poetic preoccupations, 'Sleep and Poetry' seemed, to many of its readers, to embody Hunt's reformist political beliefs. Keats was denigrated as one of Hunt's coterie rather than as a poet in his own right; for John Wilson Croker, Keats was 'unhappily a disciple of the new school of what has been somewhere called Cockney poetry; which may be defined to consist of the most incongruous ideas in the most uncouth

The Romantic Poetry Handbook, First Edition. Michael O'Neill and Madeleine Callaghan.
© 2018 John Wiley & Sons Ltd. Published 2018 by John Wiley & Sons Ltd.

language'.⁵ Though Keats did, following Hunt, adopt 'a freer spirit of versification',⁶ 'Sleep and Poetry' moves between doubt and assertion of his poetic beliefs: Susan J. Wolfson notes that 'what makes "Sleep and Poetry" a drama of rather than a dramatization of aspiration is its rhythm of hesitation: this poet keeps retracing the plan, the tracing becoming the tale'.⁷ The drama that she suggests forms the greater part of the poem's importance, with Keats's recurring questions in the poem opening up challenges to his assertions rather than implying faith via rhetorical questions. Teetering on the brink of admitting his fear that he may be unsuccessful, Keats's pleas gain poignancy from their longing:

> O Poesy! for thee I hold my pen
> That am not yet a glorious denizen
> Of thy wide heaven—Should I rather kneel
> Upon some mountain-top until I feel
> A glowing splendour round about me hung,
> And echo back the voice of thine own tongue?
> O Poesy! for thee I grasp my pen
> That am not yet a glorious denizen
> Of thy wide heaven; yet, to my ardent prayer,
> Yield from thy sanctuary some clear air,
> Smoothed for intoxication by the breath
> Of flowering bays, that I may die a death
> Of luxury, and my young spirit follow
> The morning sunbeams to the great Apollo
> Like a fresh sacrifice;   ('Sleep and Poetry', 47–61)⁸

Repeating the rhyme of 'pen' and 'denizen', Keats does not labour under the assumption that 'it might work better on a second attempt than the first'.⁹ Rather, Keats theatrically restages the scene, moving from the image of kneeling on the mountain-top, to praying, to yearning to 'die a death / Of luxury'. Asking direction from Poesy, the questions seem both anxious and amused as Keats suggests a wry irony in his stagey apprenticeship.¹⁰ The echo intimates self-consciousness as the line repeats to allow the rhymes to fall into place with ease, but it also underscores a potential immaturity as the rhyme embodies the poem's fears with an ironic edge. Rather than being Apollo's inheritor or double, Keats characterizes himself as '[l]ike a fresh sacrifice', feminizing himself into an Andromeda-like pose in an almost eroticized passage focused on luxury and intoxication. But Keats is not content to remain intoxicated. Conflict enters the poem as he joins the attack on neoclassical poetry.

After delighting in the realms of 'Flora, and old Pan' ('Sleep and Poetry', 102), Keats feels pressure to return to 'the agonies, the strife / Of human hearts' (124–5) but remains preoccupied with his vision of a charioteer and its passage through the enchanted landscape. When the vision breaks down, Keats bleakly records:

> The visions all are fled—the car is fled
> Into the light of heaven, and in their stead
> A sense of real things comes doubly strong,
> And, like a muddy stream, would bear along
> My soul to nothingness: but I will strive
> Against all doubtings, and will keep alive
> The thought of that same chariot, and the strange
> Journey it went.   ('Sleep and Poetry', 155–62)

Despite vision slipping away, Keats fights against the almost overpowering nature of 'real things' which would destroy poetry. Forced to 'strive' to 'keep alive', Keats struggles to prolong his imaginative vision in explicit opposition to the forces of mundane life even as the poem does not ignore the age itself.[11] Such immersion in the world could only extinguish the vital self, numbing 'My soul to nothingness', but determination to refuse such a fate adds spice to Keats's fear. The dulled repetition of 'fled' in the first line suggests that which Keats must struggle against. Poetry cannot descend into a repeated elegy for what has been lost, and this sparks Keats's outburst against the neoclassical 'foppery and barbarism' (182) which had its subjects deluded by its 'musty laws' (195) as 'with a puling infant's force / They swayed about a rocking horse, / And thought it Pegasus' (185–7). Far more than a simple rebuke to the eighteenth century's Pope, Dryden, and so on, Keats explicitly aligns himself with Leigh Hunt and his radical peers in what was the 'canonical canon controversy' of the century.[12] Provoking the ire of fellow poets, such as Byron, and that of Tory critics, Keats seemed to set out his stall against the past. Yet the energy with which Keats defends his poetic beliefs rivals Byron's only half-mocking parody of the Ten Commandments in *Don Juan*, 'Thou shalt believe in Milton, Dryden, Pope; / Thou shalt not set up Wordsworth, Coleridge, Southey',[13] suggesting that both poets had gained from Pope's example. Pope's *Essay on Criticism*, curiously enough, informs Keats's 'Sleep and Poetry'. Though Keats loosens his rhyme, mostly enjambing rather than endstopping his couplets, couplets are still those he chooses in which to announce his poetic beliefs rather than Wordsworth's blank verse.[14] 'Sleep and Poetry' seems an exercise in testing and performing his fitness as a poet: 'Be sure yourself and your own reach to know, / How far your genius, taste, and learning go' (*Essay on Criticism* 1.48–9).[15]

Endymion: A Poetic Romance, composed in 1817 and published in 1818, shows Keats, like his contemporaries Byron and Shelley, using Edmund

Spenser's example to create his central questing theme.[16] Viewing the poem's composition as 'a trial of my Powers of Imagination, and chiefly of my invention',[17] *Endymion* is the testing ground for Keats to explore and experiment with poetry. John Bayley and Christopher Ricks have rejected Keats's own and some of his contemporaries' judgement that the poem reflects his immaturity, with Bayley claiming that 'this vulnerable and virginal self' is the defining strength of his poetry.[18] Although Keats avowed the weaknesses of *Endymion* in his Preface, there remains an underlying sense of the poem's worth in his preface to the poem: 'It is just that this youngster should die away; a sad thought for me, if I had not some hope that while it is dwindling I may be plotting, and fitting myself for verses fit to live.'[19]

Divided into four books, *Endymion: A Poetic Romance* centres on Endymion and Cynthia's love affair. Book 1, after the priest's address to Pan, focuses on the mortal Endymion's story of his visionary experience of love, a story addressed to his sister Peona after she calms him with a soothing song. By Book 2, Endymion, in his misery, goes wandering and first encounters a naiad who pities his pain before he meets Venus and Adonis, immortal and mortal lovers, and Venus blesses Endymion's love affair with immortal Cynthia. Then, reunited with Cynthia, his immortal lover relates her passion and love, but warns him that their love must remain secret as she lacks the power to make him immortal nor can she inform her fellow gods: 'Yet, can I not to starry eminence / Uplift thee; nor for very shame can own / Myself to thee' (2.777–9). Leaving him after their brief encounter, Endymion's misery closes Book 2. Book 3 continues with Endymion's torment. Journeying under water, he pleads with Cynthia to release her hold on him before he encounters Glaucus, Circe's imprisoned lover. Relating his tale and how he came under Circe's enchantment, Endymion recognizes Glaucus as his double, crying: 'We are twin brothers in this destiny!' (3.713), and Endymion then frees the lovers that Glaucus had arranged in rows under the sea, including Glaucus' beloved, Scylla. Book 4 shows Endymion encounter an Indian maid, with whom he falls in love despite the torment of his love for Cynthia. He decides to reject Cynthia for his mortal lover, and the Indian maid tells Endymion that she cannot be his lover. Miserably alone, Endymion is reunited with his sister Peona, and they encounter the Indian maiden who then reveals her true identity as Cynthia herself. *Endymion* ends with Peona's surprised joy and Endymion's passionate elation.

Despite *Endymion* suggesting itself as a narrative poem, the 'poetic romance' subtitle is more suggestive of Keats's design. Seeming almost like a corrective to *Alastor*, Shelley's earlier visionary poem, where the Poet falls in love with an unearthly 'veilèd maid',[20] *Endymion* reverses the tragic fate of *Alastor*'s protagonist to offer a more optimistic coupling between a mortal and an immortal. Yet both Keats and Shelley are fascinated by the metapoetic ramifications of visionary poetry. Viewing *Endymion* as an apprenticeship for Keats, Stuart Curran sees him as writing a failed but ultimately instrumental poem for his future poetic career: 'Tracing Endymion through convoluted paths and frequently losing him in a luxurious vegetation hastily transplanted from the conservatory, Keats nevertheless taught himself the craft of poetry.'[21] This assessment, though rightly emphasizing Keats's often self-conscious performance as neophyte, ends up doing an injustice to *Endymion*. Loaded with lush and luxuriant lines, visionary beauties, and a strong self-consciousness about the possibilities of myth for the poet, Keats creates a poem that is recognizably in his own style. Keats meditates on poetry as both craft and imaginative overflow. Byron's crude remark that *Endymion* engages in 'mental masturbation'[22] is suggestive of the poetry's self-delighting artistry, but it misses the mark as to the distinctive beauty of the poetry and Keats's clear-eyed awareness of his struggle to write a poem of the scope that he desires.

Book 3, where Endymion encounters Glaucus, is the metapoetic heart of the poem. John Barnard suggests that Book 3 shows Endymion 'progressively learning to sympathise with the sufferings of others'.[23] More than enlarging sympathy, Book 3 blends allegory with narrative, lyric with romance as Keats explores the possibilities of poetry. For Karen Swann, 'Glaucus is a patently poetic figure: a figure for the poet and the charm of poetry. As literary predecessor to the belated Endymion, his first act is to anoint the youth as his successor, "the man" who has come to complete and redeem his work'.[24] Yet Endymion had been anointed successor by Venus, whose well wishes for his immortal love affair had the effect of replacing her and Adonis' story with Endymion and Cynthia's newer legend. Rescuing Glaucus from the stultifying order of his own creation, where Glaucus patterned lover with lover in his prison beneath the ocean, Endymion revives the ageing and imprisoning structures in an analogous act to Keats's own desire to remould poetry in looser imaginative vision after neoclassical stricture. Ambitious yet deliberately vague in the identification between Keats and Endymion, Keats evades rendering the book open only to allegory's clarifying structure, keeping the poem dream-like and flowing. If poetry requires revivification by Keats's aspirant imagination, the young poet would not be didactic enough to insist on such a conclusive reading.

Despite such ambition, Keats does not bask in certainty at the power of his new poetic voice. Keats becomes a kind of Endymion to poetry's Cynthia as he longs to achieve the visionary heights of the poetry to which he aspires. The shadow of self-doubt creeps in throughout the poem as '[a] sense of real things comes doubly strong' ('Sleep and Poetry', 157) on the apprentice poet, who doubts his fitness as poet. Book 4 opens with an invocation to England's muse, where Milton's *Paradise Lost* shimmers in the background as the great English epic that Keats was reading as he wrote *Endymion.* Referring to Dante and Virgil, Keats's aspirations are laid out before the reader, and his swell of patriotism as he hymns the muse's constancy gives way to the anxious sense that he does not belong to the lineage of the great English poets who have won their muse her 'full accomplishment' (*Endymion* 4.18):

> Long have I said, how happy he who shrives
> To thee! But then I thought on poets gone,
> And could not pray—nor could I now—so on
> I move to the end in lowliness of heart.   (*Endymion* 4.26–9)

At the opening of Keats's final book, the haunting fear that *Endymion* has failed even as it is being composed comes to the fore. Keats paints himself as longing to give himself to his muse, but the crushing weight of his illustrious predecessors means that he 'could not pray—nor could I now' (*Endymion* 4.28). Despite his despair, Keats will finish his tale. Yet, rather than this moment defining the tone of the rest of the book, Keats draws an implicit parallel between himself and Endymion. At the close of Book 3, Endymion had been transported from under the sea by Neptune to land, as 'Imagination gave a dizzier pain' (*Endymion* 3.1009) to the mortal lover. The imaginative and visionary Book 3 gives way to Book 4, which opens with Endymion marooned far from his lover and far from his native land. Likewise, Keats must descend from his metapoetic exploration of Glaucus and Circe into closing his narrative, drawing the loose threads of his poem together. Once Endymion awakes, his despair is equal to Keats's, with his first words being to express his anguish, 'Ah, woe is me!' (*Endymion* 4.30). Yet such identification is seamless, subtle, and teasingly incomplete. Keatsian artistry transmutes narrative to luxuriant aesthetic couplets that reveal *Endymion* as poetic apprenticeship but also expression of his poetic power.

Keats's sonnets show the young poet entering a crowded arena of sonneteers with a confidence. With the second-generation Romantic poets arriving late to the sonnet mania that had been ongoing since the 1780s, the sonnet tradition was wide open for reconsideration and exploration.[25] Keats was a major figure in such tradition reshaping; poems such as 'On sitting down to read *King Lear* once again' and 'On first looking into Chapman's Homer' suggest the range and complexity of his ability. 'On sitting down to read *King Lear* once again' opens with a farewell to Romance, the chosen genre of Edmund Spenser's *Fairie Queene* which had been deeply influential for Keats in *Endymion* and elsewhere. Keats instead chooses to venture into the 'fierce dispute / Betwixt damnation and impassion'd clay' (5–6) embodied in *King Lear*. Rather than suggesting an absolute rejection of the Romance genre, Keats implies that his embrace of *King Lear* is predicated on the need for a kind of bracing difficulty. Romance's seductive escapism is no longer open to the poet. It is Shakespeare's tragic perfection that Keats requires. Addressing Shakespeare in the sestet, Keats praises the fire of *King Lear*, savouring 'The bitter-sweet of this Shakespearian fruit' (8), choosing the burning flame of Shakespeare's passion rather than the 'barren dream' (12) of Romance. The poem is loosely composed as a Petrarchan sonnet, and Keats carefully eschews writing in Shakespeare's anglicized sonnet form, making the most of the volta to turn from the apostrophe to Romance to an apostrophe for Shakespeare. In embracing the Italian form, Keats subtly emphasizes his status as no mere aspirant, despite his claim to 'humbly assay' (7) the fruits of *King Lear*.

'On first looking into Chapman's Homer' sees Keats proclaim the power of Homer's poetry, but he reserves more attention for Chapman, his translator: 'Yet did I never breathe its pure serene / Till I heard Chapman speak out loud and bold' (7–8). If Homer was a superb poet, it required Chapman to translate the blind poet with care and a poet's ear so as to deliver to Keats such 'pure serene' poetry. Where the octave opens with Keats's mental travels to 'the realms of gold' and the second quatrain is dedicated to the combined poetic power of Homer and Chapman, the sestet moves to a compelling reimagining of Keats's feeling as he entered into the new world of Homer's imagination recreated in Chapman's language:

> Then felt I like some watcher of the skies
>   When a new planet swims into his ken;
> Or like stout Cortez when with eagle eyes
>   He stared at the Pacific—and all his men
> Looked at each other with a wild surmise—
>   Silent, upon a peak in Darien.   (9–14)

The energy of the sestet looks forward to *Hyperion* when Apollo experiences a similar kind of awakening; here, there is a powerful potential unlocked by Keats's new-found land. Though critics and readers have been quick to note that it was, in fact, Vasco Nuñez de Balboa who sighted land, Keats's mistake when he chose to name 'stout Cortez' in place of Balboa offers an insight into the poem. It was Cortez who had led the expedition that ended the Aztec Empire as his warlike approach to colonization brought Mexico under

Spanish rule. Cortez's 'eagle eyes' are trained on controlling the land he discovers, bringing it mercilessly under Spanish dominion. The image of Cortez's powerful gaze and the wonder of his men is suggestive of Keats's own poetic power. Keats would glory in Homer's 'realms of gold' and then have dominion over that which he surveyed. The sonnet becomes a statement of Keats's poetic ability; the young poet is not in thrall to Homer's imagination, but given licence by Homer's poetry to pursue his own vision.

Notes

1   Review signed 'Z', *Blackwood's Edinburgh Magazine* (August 1818), iii, pp. 519–24, in *Keats: The Critical Heritage*, ed. G. M. Matthews (London: Routledge & Kegan Paul, 1971), pp. 97–110 (at p. 110).

2   Jerome McGann comments, 'if we return to the early reviewers who named and defined the Cockneyism of Hunt and Keats, we find most of [these qualities] deplored. [...] The reviewers who censure Keats's vulgarity consistently see him from a class-conscious perspective. Keats is low born and ought not to be writing poetry in the first place; he lacks the appropriate education for the office.' Jerome McGann, 'Keats and the Historical Method in Literary Criticism', *MLN* 94 (1979): 988–1032 (at 997–8).

3   *Letters* 2.221.

4   David Duff, *Romanticism and the Uses of Genre* (Oxford: Oxford University Press, 2009), p. 145.

5   Unsigned review, *Quarterly Review* (dated April 1818, published September 1818), xix, pp. 204–8, in *Keats: The Critical Heritage*, ed. Matthews, pp. 110–14 (at p. 111).

6   Leigh Hunt, 'Preface' to *The Story of Rimini*, in *Poetical Works, 1801–1821*, ed. John Strachan, vol. 5 of *The Selected Writings of Leigh Hunt*, gen. eds. Robert Morrison and Michael Eberle-Sinatra, 6 vols (London: Pickering & Chatto, 2003), p. 167.

7   Susan J. Wolfson, *Borderlines: The Shiftings of Gender in British Romanticism* (Stanford, CA: Stanford University Press, 2006), p. 220.

8   John Keats, 'Sleep and Poetry', in *John Keats: The Complete Poems*, ed. John Barnard, 3rd edn (Harmondsworth: Penguin, 1988). All poetry by John Keats will be quoted from this edition in this section unless otherwise specified.

9   Peter McDonald, *Sound Intentions: The Workings of Rhyme in Nineteenth-Century Poetry* (Oxford: Oxford University Press, 2012), p. 123.

10 As suggested by Wolfson, *Borderlines*, p. 219.

11 Daniel P. Watkins, *Keats's Poetry and the Politics of the Imagination* (London: Associated University Presses, 1989), p. 33.

12 James Chandler, 'The Pope Controversy: Romantic Poetics and the English Canon', *Critical Inquiry* 10.3 (1984): 481–509 (at 481).

13 Lord George Gordon Byron, *Don Juan* 1.205, 1633–4, in *Lord Byron: The Major Works*, ed., intro., and notes by Jerome McGann, Oxford World's Classics (Oxford: Oxford University Press, 2000).

14 '[B]y 1817–1818, blank verse had come to be inevitably associated with Wordsworth, whose political conservatism Hunt frequently criticized even as he made efforts to align himself with Wordsworth's power as a poet of nature.' William Keach, 'Cockney Rhymes: Keats and the Politics of Style', *Studies in Romanticism* 25.2 (1986): 182–96 (at 185).

15 Alexander Pope, *Major Works*, ed. with intro. and notes by Pat Rogers, Oxford World's Classics (Oxford: Oxford University Press, 2006).

16 'Among the leading epic poems of the younger Romantics, however, Spenserianism becomes essential. It provides the stanza for Byron in *Childe Harold's Pilgrimage* and Shelley in *The Revolt of Islam* (1817), the central questing motif for Keats in *Endymion* (1817), and the dynamic of mental doubling that underpins all three poems.' Greg Kucich, *Keats, Shelley, and Romantic Spenserianism* (University Park: Pennsylvania State University Press, 1991), p. 103.

17 *Letters* 2.169.

18 See Christopher Ricks, *Keats and Embarrassment* (Oxford: Clarendon Press, 1974), pp. 7–8 and John Bayley, 'Keats and Reality,' in *The Uses of Division: Unity and Disharmony in Literature* (London: Chatto & Windus, 1976), p. 150.

19 John Keats, 'Preface' to *Endymion*, in *John Keats: The Complete Poems*, ed. John Barnard, 3rd edn (1988; London: Penguin, 2006 corr.), p. 505.

20 Percy Bysshe Shelley, *Alastor*, l. 151, in *Shelley: The Major Works*, ed. Leader and O'Neill.

21 Stuart Curran, *Shelley's Annus Mirabilis: The Maturing of an Epic Vision* (San Marino, CA: Huntington Library, 1975), p. 5.

22 Lord Byron, Letter to John Murray, 9 November 1820, in *BLJ* 7.225.

23 *Keats: The Complete Poems*, ed. Barnard, p. 36.

24 Karen Swann, 'Endymion's Beautiful Dreamers', in *The Cambridge Companion to Keats*, ed. Susan J. Wolfson (Cambridge: Cambridge University Press, 2001), pp. 20–36 (at p. 26). Vincent Newey concurs that 'Glaucus himself is, whatever else, a type of the Poet, bearing the insignia of "book", "wand", and priestly "stole" (III. 196–230); Endymion, "the youth elect", is at once his counterpart – they are "twin brothers in this destiny" (III. 713) – and his successor'. Vincent Newey, 'Keats, History and the Poets', in *Keats and History*, ed. Nicholas Roe (Cambridge: Cambridge University Press, 1995), pp. 165–93 (at p. 174).

25 'Starting in the 1780s and continuing for some four decades of rediscovery, this most exacting form of the British tradition was bent, stretched, reshaped, rethought.' Stuart Curran, *Poetic Form and British Romanticism* (Oxford: Oxford University Press, 1986), p. 30.

John Keats, *Hyperion* and *The Fall of Hyperion*

Hyperion and *The Fall of Hyperion*, despite their status as fragments, represent Keats's successful forays into epic territory. Keats had long been preoccupied by the myth of Hyperion and his hope was to write an epic that would propel him into the lofty poetic realm where 'epic was of all the king, / Round, vast, and spanning all like Saturn's ring'.[1] *Hyperion* was largely composed between late September 1818 and the death of Tom Keats on 1 December 1818, and eventually abandoned in April 1819 before its publication in 1820. Keats had begun writing *The Fall* in mid-July 1819 but gave up around 21 September 1819, and it was never published in his lifetime. Yet these fragments reveal what Herbert Tucker calls 'tantalizingly consummate imperfection',[2] where the poet's burning desire to write the high language of epic propels the poetry forward, investing both *Hyperion* and *The Fall of Hyperion* with a yearning that moves the apparently impersonal genre of epic towards the condition of lyric intensity. 'The two *Hyperions* read each other';[3] both fragments manage to attain epic grandeur even as they collapse under the weight of their achievement.

For Jack Stillinger, *Hyperion* marks a dividing line: 'for all its astonishing epic resplendence, [the poem] just sits there apart from the rest, like Saturn himself, "quiet as stone" (*Hyperion*, I. 4), almost as if it had been written by someone other than Keats.'[4] The sense of strangeness comes through as the poem begins after an event rather than in its midst, divorced from personal avowal, allowing the fallen gods to take centre-stage. Unlike *Paradise Lost*, which begins after the defeat of the fallen angels only to

The Romantic Poetry Handbook, First Edition. Michael O'Neill and Madeleine Callaghan.
© 2018 John Wiley & Sons Ltd. Published 2018 by John Wiley & Sons Ltd.

shift to the larger action, the Fall of Adam and Eve, there is no sense that any action will follow. Book 1 moves from Saturn's mournful passivity and loss of identity, to Thea's pity, to Hyperion's fearful rage, where Book 2 recalls *Paradise Lost*'s council of fallen angels, only to replace their energy and hatred with a numbed despair, and Book 3 stages an encounter between Mnemosyne and Apollo which shows the latter affirm the dizzying power of his newfound divinity. Within the three books, *Hyperion* moves from elegizing the defeat of the Titans to celebrating the advent of a new order. Each emotional inflection is masterfully sculpted as Keats's poetry captures the subtleties of tone generated, in part, by his choice to engage in 'writing a poem which does not have a clear case to make'.[5] The sorrowful solitude of *Hyperion* begins immediately in Keats's description of Saturn's broken fallenness:

> Deep in the shady sadness of a vale
> Far sunken from the healthy breath of morn,
> Far from the fiery noon, and eve's one star,
> Sat grey-haired Saturn, quiet as a stone,
> Still as the silence round about his lair;
> Forest on forest hung above his head
> Like cloud on cloud. No stir of air was there,
> Not so much life as on a summer's day
> Robs not one light seed from the feathered grass,
> But where the dead leaf fell, there did it rest.
> A stream went voiceless by, still deadened more
> By reason of his fallen divinity   (*Hyperion* 1.1–12)

Saturn's deadened posture oppresses the description. Keats has nature stifled 'By reason of his fallen divinity'. Numbed in its exile from 'the healthy breath of morn', the oppressive situation mirrors his dethroned state. Repeated clauses fill the lines, as 'Forest on forest' and 'cloud on cloud' weigh down the blank verse, stilling it into the sullen atmosphere appropriate for mourning the loss of worldly dominion.[6] The dominating 's' sounds slow down the lines until Thea's pity enters the poem as she arrives to share 'our weary griefs' (*Hyperion* 1.66) in a sorrowful frieze of joy departed from the world. Saturn's confusion over his shattered identity offers an affecting pathos: 'I am gone / Away from my own bosom; I have left / My strong identity, my real self, / Somewhere between the throne and where I sit' (*Hyperion* 1.112–15). Here, Saturn's defeat seems actively chosen; it is he who has left behind who he was, and this confusion between being defeated and choosing exile suggests the bewilderment suffered by the dispossessed Titan. Defeat and loss of status breed loss of self, and Keats does not flinch from presenting Saturn's misery at losing his creativity in lines that seem both personal in a metapoetic sense and epically striking:

> But cannot I create?
> Cannot I form? Cannot I fashion forth
> Another world, another universe,
> To overbear and crumble this to naught?   (*Hyperion* 1.141–4)

Keats keeps the lines relevant to his own poetic ambition without becoming openly personal. Saturn's questioning witnesses a desire to create something entirely new, completely without reference to any pre-existing order, and the spectre of Milton rises in the lines as the fashioner of an epic world which Keats cannot escape. Keats wrote, 'I have but lately stood on my guard against Milton. Life to him would be death to me. Miltonic verse cannot be written but in the vein of art—I wish to devote myself to another sensation.'[7] But *Hyperion* thrives on this tension, as Keats senses a place for his own epic achievement in the wake of Milton just as Apollo feels that 'the liegeless air / Yields to my step aspirant' (*Hyperion* 3.92–3).

Book 2 collects together the broken Titans, where the strongest are 'Dungeoned in opaque element, to keep / Their clenchèd teeth still clenched, and all their limbs / Locked up like veins of metal, cramped and screwed' (*Hyperion* 2.23–5). Shifting from physical agonies to the despairing suffering of the unimprisoned Titans, this version of *Paradise Lost*'s council of Hell is marked by passivity. Saturn cannot rouse them into an energetic response to their loss nor can he ask them to remain fallen: 'O Titans, shall I say, "Arise!"?—Ye groan: / Shall I say "Crouch!"?—Ye groan. What can I then?' (*Hyperion* 2.157–8). Oceanus, described as 'Sophist and sage from no Athenian grove' (*Hyperion* 2.168), gives a speech that for Herbert Tucker offers 'somewhat deliberate cheer'.[8] But this is not 'cheer' so much as an attempt to find a reason for suffering, poignant in both its effort to dispel pain and its inevitable failure:

> So on our heels a fresh perfection treads,
> A power more strong in beauty, born of us
> And fated to excel us, as we pass
> In glory that old Darkness: nor are we
> Thereby more conquered, than by us the rule
> Of shapeless Chaos.   (2.212–17)

This prophecy, borne from meeting his younger Olympian counterpart, cannot assuage the suffering experienced by the Titans, despite Clymene's testimony of a similar experience. 'Fresh perfection' and the abstract sense of perfectibility cannot assuage pain. Oceanus' sophistry can offer intelligent argument but not emotional succour, and Keats's poetry captures the eloquent force of Oceanus' ideas even as it reveals that reason does not unseat feeling. The poet raises no more than two cheers for the relentless process of history. Enceladus' rage and Hyperion's return see the Titans attempt to rekindle their supremacy, shouting Saturn's name from their 'hollow throats' (*Hyperion* 2.391). Yet, by Book 3, their woes remain, despite their momentary rallying against desolation.

Book 3 turns its attention away from the Titans to the birth of the new god, Apollo, 'once more the golden theme!' (*Hyperion* 3.28). Yet the poem witnesses no relief from pressure in its turn from the defeated to the victor. To borrow T. S. Eliot's phrase, in the case of Apollo, 'this Birth was / Hard and bitter agony'.[9] Of the Titans, Mnemosyne, goddess of memory, demands an explanation for Apollo's weeping, and Apollo describes the 'dark, dark, / And painful vile oblivion' (*Hyperion* 3.86–7) that torments what ought to be sublime achievement.

> Knowledge enormous makes a God of me.
> Names, deeds, grey legends, dire events, rebellions,
> Majesties, sovran voices, agonies,
> Creations and destroyings, all at once
> Pour into the wide hollows of my brain,
> And deify me, as if some blithe wine
> Or bright elixir peerless I had drunk,
> And so become immortal.   (*Hyperion* 3.113–20)

Knowledge transfigures Apollo, as 'wild commotions shook him' (*Hyperion* 3.124) as the poet experiences the electric force of history, listed as 'Names, deeds, grey legends, dire events, rebellions, / Majesties, sovran voices, agonies', showing Apollo speeding through the annals of history. His brain becomes the site for history to be reconceived through the poet's eyes. 'Creatings and destroyings', though listed as part of the ideas to which he has access, signals the poetic power available to Apollo, a power which looks forward to *The Fall of Hyperion* and the speaker's drinking of 'That full draught [which] is parent of my theme' (*The Fall of Hyperion* 1.46). Yet Apollo's triumph is less than complete. Apollo 'seems', as Vincent Newey notes, 'less a god being born than a man dying'.[10] Edward Bostetter's sense that the poem's abandonment 'was a sign of doubt and imaginative failure' downplays Keats's achievement in *Hyperion*,[11] which reveals a perplexed power.

The Fall of Hyperion puts poetry centre-stage, revealing Keats's 'vale of Soul-making' as dependent on vision wrested into poetry by disciplined struggle.[12] Drawing an immediate distinction between fanatic and dreamer,

Keats weaves, like the fanatics he describes, an intricate relationship between poetry and vision. Though fanatics dream, Keats emphasizes the significance of poetry, which offers the only medium to facilitate vision: 'For Poesy alone can tell her dreams' (*The Fall of Hyperion* 1.8). The task of the reader comes to the fore, where we are called upon to participate in the poetic vision in the role of auditor, but unlike Shelley's *Defence*, where the musician is 'unseen',[13] Keats places himself in our line of vision:

> Whether the dream now purposed to rehearse
> Be Poet's or Fanatic's will be known
> When this warm scribe my hand is in the grave. (*The Fall of Hyperion* 1.16–18)

Where Milton addressed his muse at the opening of *Paradise Lost*, Keats's self-reflexive epic addresses the reader. Almost formulated as a challenge to the recipient of these lines, the stakes are overtly acknowledged; Keats must be judged. The reader's role anticipates Moneta's later role, which, as Stuart Sperry claims, shows Keats assigning her the 'role of interrogator and judge on the one hand and intercessor and redeemer on the other'.[14] Though Helen Vendler sees Moneta as a figure who stands for a denial of audience,[15] Moneta seems more aptly described as a figure of the 'eternal Being, the principle of Beauty, – and the Memory of great Men' that Keats places in opposition to the public,[16] but it is a figure that still 'reads' Keats, just as posterity will judge 'this warm scribe my hand'. Despite Keats's frequent and near irritable claims to avoid courting his reader,[17] here, the compact between reader and poet is in the foreground. The lines, concentrated and distinctly preoccupied with what John Barnard calls his desire to 'question the limits and sufficiency of the imagination's claim to truth',[18] show Keats loading every rift with ore. The limits and possibilities of the imagination and its effect on the reader become central to the poem's achievement, an achievement which Keats forces the reader to consider before moving into his poetic vision. Vision in *The Fall of Hyperion* is attended by struggle:

> I heard, I looked: two senses both at once,
> So fine, so subtle, felt the tyranny
> Of that fierce threat, and the hard task proposed.
> Prodigious seemed the toil; the leaves were yet
> Burning—when suddenly a palsied chill
> Struck from the pavèd level up my limbs,
> And was ascending quick to put cold grasp
> Upon those streams that pulse beside the throat.
> I shrieked; and the sharp anguish of my shriek
> Stung my own ears—I strove hard to escape

The numbness, strove to gain the lowest step.
Slow, heavy, deadly was my pace: the cold
Grew stifling, suffocating, at the heart;
And when I clasped my hands I felt them not.   (*The Fall of Hyperion* 1.118–31)

Metapoetic in the extreme, the tyrannous demands of the epic place enormous pressure on the apprentice poet. The shriek, which recalls Shelley's
'Hymn to Intellectual Beauty', underscores the demands of visionary process.
Forced to hear and to look at once, as the toil becomes climactic, Keats uses
the blank verse to make it mimetic of his struggle. 'Slow, heavy, deadly' like
a bell are adjectives that toll Keats back to his sole self, a self he places under
visionary stress. Though temping to read the lines as Jonathon Shears does
when he notes 'a curious masochism in the fact that Keats chooses Moneta
or memory when he desires to escape the influence of Milton',[19] the struggle
against Milton's influence also seems reminiscent of the Spenserian quest to
earn the rewards of Romance. Keats deliberately stages the struggle to
become an epic protagonist in his epic poem. The difficulty of such a task is
not understated. Keats fails repeatedly in his own eyes, buckled by the intensity of his vision:

Without stay or prop,
But my own weak mortality, I bore
The load of this eternal quietude,
The unchanging gloom, and the three fixèd shapes   (*The Fall of Hyperion*
    1.388–91)

'The unchanging gloom' oppresses the poet, forcing him to sit, as he writes
to Shelley, 'with [his] wings furl'd'.[20] The load to bear becomes almost too
heavy, as Moneta seems to displace Keats from his poem. The close of canto
1 shows Keats turn over his epic task to her, shifting from telling the tale
to recording her talk. Memory becomes the site of epic daring, and it is
memory of her speech that must be delivered: 'I must delay, and glean my
memory / Of her high phrase—perhaps no further dare' (*The Fall of
Hyperion* 1.467–8). Canto 2 opens in her voice, as she assures the poet that
this vision is 'Too huge for mortal tongue' (*The Fall of Hyperion* 2.9), diminishing the poet's capacity to 'tell [his] dreams' (*The Fall of Hyperion* 1.8)
with 'the fine spell of words' (*The Fall of Hyperion* 1.9) required. Yet this
marks no failure of the visionary poet, who recovers himself to take possession of his vision. Unlike *Hyperion*, the close of the poem remains in the first
person; the words '[m]y quick eyes ran on' (*The Fall of Hyperion* 2.53)
reveal Keats as embedded in his epic. He underscores his status as visionary
arbiter who has proven capable of 'sav[ing] / Imagination from the sable
charm / And dumb enchantment' (*The Fall of Hyperion* 1.10–11).

Notes

1 John Keats, 'To Charles Cowden Clarke', ll. 66–7, in *Keats: The Complete Poems*, ed. Barnard.

2 Herbert F. Tucker, *Epic: Britain's Heroic Muse 1790–1910* (Oxford: Oxford University Press, 2008), p. 199.

3 Michael O'Neill, *Romanticism and the Self-Conscious Poem* (Oxford: Clarendon Press, 1997), p. 223.

4 Jack Stillinger, *The Hoodwinking of Madeline, and Other Essays on Keats's Poems* (Chicago: University of Illinois Press, 1971), pp. 47–8.

5 O'Neill, *Romanticism and the Self-Conscious Poem*, p. 224.

6 Andrew Bennett, *Keats, Narrative and Audience* (Oxford: Clarendon Press, 1994), p. 146.

7 *Letters* 2.212.

8 Tucker, *Epic*, p. 211.

9 T. S. Eliot, 'Journey of the Magi', in *The Complete Poems and Plays* (London: Faber, 1969).

10 Vincent Newey, '*Hyperion, The Fall of Hyperion*, and Keats's Epic Ambitions', in *The Cambridge Companion to Keats*, ed. Susan J. Wolfson (Cambridge: Cambridge University Press, 2001), pp. 69–85 (at p. 76).

11 Edward E. Bostetter, *The Romantic Ventriloquists: Wordsworth, Coleridge, Keats, Shelley, Byron* (Seattle: University of Washington Press, 1963), p. 8.

12 *Letters* 2.102.

13 Percy Bysshe Shelley, *A Defence of Poetry*, in *Shelley: Major Works*, ed. Leader and O'Neill, p. 681.

14 Stuart M. Sperry, *Keats the Poet* (Princeton: Princeton University Press, 1973), p. 326.

15 Helen Vendler, *The Odes of John Keats* (Cambridge, MA: Harvard University Press, 1983), pp. 216, 222, 224.

16 *Letters* 1.266.

17 For example, Keats writes: 'I have not the slightest feel of humility towards the Public – or to any thing in existence – but the eternal Being, the principle of Beauty, – and the Memory of great Men' (*Letters* 1.266).

18 John Barnard, *John Keats* (Cambridge: Cambridge University Press, 1987), p. 129.

19 Jonathon Shears, *The Romantic Legacy of Paradise Lost* (Farnham and Burlington, VT: Ashgate, 2009), p. 176.

   The poem's belatedness is often considered specifically in terms of Keats's indebtedness to Milton, e.g. Stuart Sperry, 'Keats, Milton and *The Fall of Hyperion*', *PMLA*, 77.1 (1962), 77–84.

20 *Letters* 2.222.

John Keats, The 1820 Volume

Keats's 1820 volume *Lamia, Isabella, The Eve of St. Agnes, and Other Poems*, among the major achievements of Romantic poetry, includes three narrative poems – *Lamia, Isabella*, and *The Eve of St. Agnes* – that focus on questions of imagination and reality, and their many related dualisms.[1] In *Lamia* Keats sought to address an issue he deals with humorously in his review of 21 December 1817 on the acting of Edmund Kean. Kean, for Keats, 'is a relict of romance; – a Posthumous ray of chivalry'. He is implored at the essay's end to 'Cheer us a little in the failure of our days! for romance lives but in books. The goblin is driven from the heath, and the rainbow is robbed of its mystery!'[2] The twentieth-century American poet Amy Clampitt sees *Lamia* as 'a weird trophy / hung among the totems of his own ambivalence', and about nothing is it more ambivalent than its view of romance.[3]

The heroine is more than the metamorphic monster of Keats's source, added at the end of the 1820 printing, as though to point up what the poet had done with his originating material. In that note, from Robert Burton's *Anatomy of Melancholy*, potential poignancy flickers, but passes into exposure of illusion; after her unmasking as 'a serpent, a lamia' by Apollonius, the heroine 'wept, and desired Apollonius to be silent, but he would not be moved'.[4] In the poem, Keats deepens and complicates 'Burton's straightforward account of witchcraft uncovered by the wisdom of philosophy'.[5] Questions of judgement are in play throughout.

At the beginning Lamia gains or regains a female form as a result of a questionable bargain with the lascivious Hermes in pursuit of a nymph made invisible by Lamia's powers. The first prolonged description of her is a fireworks display of 'dazzling' contraries and oppositions: 'She was a gordian shape of dazzling hue, / Vermilion-spotted, golden, green, and blue'

The Romantic Poetry Handbook, First Edition. Michael O'Neill and Madeleine Callaghan.
© 2018 John Wiley & Sons Ltd. Published 2018 by John Wiley & Sons Ltd.

(47–8). This description blinds the reader's sight with colour and possibility, suggesting as one sombre possibility that Lamia is a 'Gordian' knot that only a sword-cut can untie, as proves to be the case when she is pitilessly unmasked by Apollonius, the rationalist mentor of Lycius, who is beguiled by Lamia into falling in love with her. But this opening passage also includes hints that Lamia may be worthy of sympathy as well as mistrust:

> ... rainbow-sided, touched with miseries,
> She seemed, at once, some penanc'd lady elf,
> The demon's mistress, or the demon's self.   (54–6)

Keats's Drydenesque couplets allow for doubleness in a phrase such as 'touched with miseries'. The rhyme of 'elf' and 'self' suggests the flitting elusiveness of selfhood.[6] The phrase 'rainbow-sided' anticipates a narratorial intrusion towards the end of the poem where Keats appears to align himself with his heroine, who is identified with the rainbow, deprived of its capacity to induce 'awe' by the malign effect of Newtonian optics: 'Do not all charms fly', asks the poet-narrator,

> At the mere touch of cold philosophy?
> There was an awful rainbow once in heaven:
> We know her woof, her texture; she is given
> In the dull catalogue of common things.
> Philosophy will clip an Angel's wings,
> Conquer all mysteries by rule and line,
> Empty the haunted air, and gnomed mine –
> Unweave a rainbow, as it erewhile made
> The tender-personed Lamia melt into a shade.   (2.229–38)

Though Keats, like other Romantics, had deep interest in science, a typically Romantic hostility to reason's murderous, hubristic dissections shows itself here. One detects such hostility in the grimace which the down-at-the-mouth phrasing of 'We know her woof, her texture' invites us to imagine. This 'knowledge' is a reductive instrument, a foe to 'mysteries', an emptying-out of 'haunted air'. And yet in 'We know' is a hint of complicity in disenchantment. Keats draws his moral from Hazlitt, who suggested in his lecture 'On Poetry in General' that one cannot have enlightenment without a diminishment of enchantment, asserting 'that the progress of knowledge and refinement has a tendency to circumscribe the limits of the imagination, and to clip the wings of poetry'.[7] *Lamia* is a poem which has sympathy with 'The tender-personed Lamia', who will 'melt into a shade' when confronted by Apollonius' gaze. That this gaze is itself by no means as coolly detached as it would like to be offers little comfort. Apollonius may only behold what he wishes to see – Lamia as merely 'A serpent' – but his discourse holds sway in his culture as the imaginings of Lycius do not.

Lamia is a poem in which head and heart conflict; it seems aware that it is unable to do justice to the full reality of either. Something is forcing Keats to see 'illusion' as 'mere illusion' rather than as possessing its own kind of reality. Arguably, his greatest poems grant 'dream', imagination, illusion a fuller sense of worth, even as that granting is rarely unembattled. However, *Lamia* is still, in its control of tone, its evenhandedness, and its seeing through to the predestined end of its bitter fable, a virtuosic poem that manages to evade imaginative circumscription while confronting forces that would 'clip the wings of poetry'. Keats's slightly wry claim for the poem is justified: 'I am certain there is that sort of fire in it which must take hold of people in some way – give them either pleasurable or unpleasurable sensation. What they want is a sensation of some sort.'[8]

The Eve of St. Agnes, written at the start of 1819, half a year before *Lamia*, also treats themes of enchantment, once again focusing on the possibilities of erotic fulfilment. Madeline believes she will dream of (and possibly encounter) her future husband if she obeys the rites and superstitions of St. Agnes's Eve; Porphyro is determined to win her affections. Both wishes are fulfilled, though whether Madeline is a 'hoodwinked dreamer' and Porphyro a 'ruffian' seducer has been much debated.[9] In his final letter, Keats writes to Charles Brown of 'the knowledge of contrast, feeling for light and shade' required by a poem.[10] *The Eve* is among his greatest poems because of the sensuous power with which it makes us feel on our pulses that 'knowledge of contrast,' a knowledge which is also connectedness.

If warmth and erotic ardour are at the poem's centre, haunting its periphery are cold, old age, and death. 'The hare limped trembling through the frozen grass' (3), a detail from the poem's first stanza, helps to introduce this motif, and illustrates Keats's ability, evident throughout the poem, to be, in his own words, 'in for – and filling some other Body'.[11] Here the rhythm limps in sympathy (the result of a strong stress on 'limped') with the trembling animal; the reader experiences a kinetic, quasi-muscular identification. At the poem's unsparing close, cold has the last word: 'The Beadsman, after thousand aves told, / For aye unsought for slept among his ashes cold' (377–8), a conclusion that suggests this world is all there is. The poem's religious imagery is secularized, subordinated to its dreams of erotic fulfilment. Whether these dreams can be realized or represent fantasy is a question that never quite takes centre-stage, for all its hovering urgency.

What does occupy the mind and imagination are scenes, conveyed through gorgeously descriptive, slow-paced Spenserian stanzas, in which romance comes alive through the opulent beauty of the writing. Porphyro following Angela, 'Brushing the cobwebs with his lofty plume' (110); his planning a stratagem to gain access to Madeline's bedchamber in such a way that 'a thought came like a full-blown rose, / Flushing his brow' (136–7); the description of 'A casement high and triple-arched' (208), of Madeline disrobing as she gets ready for bed and 'Loosens her fragrant boddice' (229), and of the feast prepared for her by Porphyro – all these richly figurative moments have an air of entranced but sensuously apprehensible inevitability. True, the reader wonders about Madeline's good sense and Porphyro's motivation, but the poetry's drive is towards a momentary realization of erotic dream, climaxing in the stanza depicting the two figures making love, a stanza that seems, momentarily, hazardously, to bring the poetry to a 'Solution sweet' (322). 'Into her dream he melted' (320), writes Keats in language that concentrates sexual suggestiveness and thematic coherence. The stanza concludes with a return of the quickened, because temporarily forgotten, threat of the passing moment: 'Meantime the frost-wind blows / Like Love's alarum pattering the sharp sleet / Against the window-panes; St Agnes' moon hath set' (322–4). Romance, poetry itself, compete with and take notice of a world indifferent to dream and desire.

Keats's poetry is at once expressive of the imagination's yearning for beauty and responsive to the awareness that, as he puts it in his 'Chamber of Maiden-Thought' letter, 'the World is full of Misery and Heartbreak, Pain, Sickness and oppression'.[12] In his epic fragment *Hyperion*, more fully discussed in the previous section, Keats brings beauty and sorrow memorably together. The poem recounts the aftermath of the Titans overthrown by the Olympians, an overthrow seen as tragedy and beautiful necessity. After the initial account of the fallen Saturn, a figure utterly motionless and downcast, who in an open-vowelled music of sumptuous delicacy is rendered 'Still as the silence round about his lair' (5), Keats describes the face of Thea, the wife of the still-unfallen Hyperion, in this way: 'How beautiful, if sorrow had not made / Sorrow more beautiful than Beauty's self' (35–6).

In his revision Keats omitted these lines, as though reacting against them as illustrating 'the false beauty proceeding from art',[13] as aestheticizing the ugly facts of 'sorrow'. But they illustrate his attempt in *Hyperion* to balance the claims of poetic beauty and experiential sorrow, doing so in a post-Miltonic blank verse that possesses pathos and majesty. F. R. Leavis found in the verse a 'decorative preoccupation'.[14] But in passage after passage the poetry gets beyond decorativeness to imply unfathomable and mysterious depths to the suffering brought about by historical change. Oceanus tries to persuade the other Titans that their fall is part of a progressivist, near-evolutionary tendency, and that ''tis the eternal law / That first in beauty should be first in might' (2.228–9), but possibly the deepest note he strikes is one of contemplative acquiescence when, in lines of stoical nobility, he recommends that 'the top of sovereignty' (2.205) is 'to bear all naked truths, / And to envisage circumstance, all calm' (2.203–4).

Ideas floated in the journal letter of February to May 1819 about the possibility or difficulty of a 'complete disinterestedness of Mind' find expression here,[15] but Oceanus cannot talk the poem out of its sympathy for Saturn's loss and pain. Hyperion himself, at the close of Book 1, also alerts us to the poem's 'transcendental cosmopolitics', in Leigh Hunt's fine phrase;[16] he is urged by Coelus to 'Be ... in the van / Of circumstance' (1.343–4). But action, in this poem that contemplates revolution without fully endorsing it, yet again gives way to contemplation as Hyperion, before his plunge towards the earth, and hearing his father's 'region-whisper' (1.349), 'on the stars / Lifted his curved lids, and kept them wide / Until it ceased; and still he kept them wide; / And still they were the same bright, patient stars' (1.350–3). Prefiguring the dynamics of the sonnet 'Bright star', the passage reaches out to a domain beyond suffering, that of 'the bright, patient stars', whose 'patience' commends itself as an ethical virtue and poetic ideal. The poem breaks off as it tries to imagine the deification of Apollo, Hyperion's destined successor: 'Knowledge enormous make a God of me' (3.113); he asserts to the muse-figure Mnemosyne, but the claim seems premature, even presumptuous, as is registered by the indecent haste with which the fragment rushes to bestow godhead upon him. Apollo sketches what Keats feels a poet of epic tragedy requires, and *The Fall of Hyperion* (not published until 1856) begins by reverting directly to the question of poetic authenticity: 'Whether the dream now purposed to rehearse / Be Poet's or Fanatic's will be known / When this warm scribe my hand is in the grave' (1.16–18). *The Fall*, subtitled 'A Dream', contains the view that 'The poet and the dreamer are distinct' (1.199), spoken by Moneta, but the poet's investment in 'dream', understood as poetic imagining, is still strong. As ever in Keats, though with deepened force, poetic dream in *The Fall* is in vigorous dialogue with the nervous reality suggested by that startlingly held-towards-us 'warm scribe my hand'.

The first major Ode, 'Ode to Psyche', also dwells on the limits and possibilities associated with being a modern poet, who, like the goddess he hymns (herself a part of the poet, his 'psyche'), is 'Too, too late for the fond believing lyre, / When holy were the haunted forest boughs' (37–8). Initially in the poem, Keats longs for unmediated mythical vision, of a kind briefly rehearsed in the opening stanza, when he imagines coming upon Cupid and Psyche. But he redefines vision as a matter of subjective inspiration: 'I see, and sing, by my own eyes inspired' (43). This line serves as a springboard for the final stanza's embracing of the modern poet's role as an imaginative 'priest' (50), a role involving internalization of worship, with its double-edged emphasis on the breakthroughs made possible by 'all the gardener Fancy e'er could feign' (62), where 'feign' chimes to ambivalent effect with the 'fane' (50) being built by the poet for Psyche; comparable equivocations surround the 'soft delight / That shadowy thought can win' (64–5), where 'shadowy' quivers with oscillating suggestions. As Miriam Allott puts it, shadowy might mean 'either musing thought that evolves obscurely or, perhaps, thought that is shadowy as the mere ghost of sensation'.[17] Keats is not prepared simply to yield up the external world in favour of the internal, as is shown by the ambiguity here, the thrown-open casement at the poem's end in order 'To let the warm Love in' (67), and the way in which mindscape and landscape merge in details such as the metaphorical 'dark-clustered trees' (55) and 'wild-ridgèd mountains' (56).

In 'Ode to a Nightingale', placed first in the section marked 'Poems' in the 1820 volume, the 'sole self' (72) of the poet is also to the fore. As in all the great odes, the poem's stanzaic form, normally ten lines consisting of a Shakespearean quatrain followed by a Petrarchan sestet (with in 'Ode to a Nightingale' one shorter line), reaps the harvest of his experimentation with the sonnet. Keats expressed witty dismay at the constraints imposed by the sonnet in his meta-sonnet 'If by dull rhymes our English must be chain'd', expressing his hope in that poem that he might find 'Sandals more interwoven and complete / To fit the naked foot of Poetry' (5–6). In the odes he develops a form that sustains the impressions of change of direction and transition associated with the sonnet, but condenses that effect in stanzaic units that, for all their fluctuations, come across as 'interwoven and complete'. This technical discovery goes hand in hand with Keats's ability, especially in evidence in this ode and 'Ode on a Grecian Urn', to create lyric poetry out of the ebb and flow of conflicting feelings. Leavis speaks of the 'Ode to a Nightingale' as 'an extremely subtle and varied interplay of motions, directed now positively, now negatively'.[18] This movement outwards in the odes results in moments of intense empathy with something beyond the self, whether bird, goddess, season, or urn. The poetry's moving outwards can result in recoils back to the 'sole self', even as it speaks of the desires of the self to move beyond itself.

An example is provided by the crucial stanzas 7 and 8 of 'Ode to a Nightingale'. Stanza 7 begins with an assertion of the bird's immortality as Keats seeks to discover a permanence which he can set against the transience of human life. In effect, this immortality is the birdsong's transhistorical continuance, which leads Keats to think of those who have listened to it, a movement that turns the poem away from the trope of immortal song to the thought of suffering human auditors, as when Keats comments that the song is 'Perhaps the self-same song that found a path / Through the sad heart of Ruth, when, sick for home, / She stood in tears amid the alien corn' (65–7). Ruth reminds the poet, 'stationed' amongst 'the alien corn', of the human condition of being 'sick for home'.[19] She detains us as an image of abiding human sorrow, open to the consolations of a song that 'found a path / Through [her] sad heart', lines that suggest the connection yet distance between longing human being and mysteriously potent song. In a final effort to reimagine the relationship between song and listener, Keats wins too 'perilous' a victory as he thinks of the song as having 'Charmed magic casements, opening on the foam / Of perilous seas, in faery lands forlorn' (69–70). The 'faery lands forlorn' expose the poet to a world where the air, though beautiful, is too rarefied to breathe, and the journey homeward to habitual self begins. That it is catalysed by the poet's own hearing in the poem of a word he has just spoken – 'Forlorn!', he writes, 'the very word is like a bell / To toll me back from thee to my sole self!' (71–2) – brings out the metapoetic immediacy of Keatsian transitions. Throughout, there are shiftings of ground as the imagination outruns some initial impulse, complicating it, evolving an experience whose value and meaning remain richly in doubt, even at the very end, with its wondering questions: 'Was it a vision, or a waking dream? / Fled is that music – Do I wake or sleep?' (79–80).

The poem's fifth stanza begins, 'I cannot see what flowers are at my feet' (41), seeming to announce sensory deprivation. In fact, it encourages an outward-going sensuousness. In his attempt to 'guess each sweet' (43), Keats uses his imagination to come to terms with process, picturing not only 'Fast fading violets' (47), but also 'The coming musk-rose' (49), things fading and growing held in the same act of imaginative apprehension. In 'Ode to a Nightingale', the moment will pass into the poet's own state of being 'half in love with easeful Death' (52), from which he will subsequently recoil. But stanza 5 might be seen as heralding the later ode 'To Autumn', a poem from which the self is markedly absent.

In 'To Autumn', Keats, having emerged as one of the major subjective lyricists in the language, writes a poem which will exercise great influence over later poets as it seeks a language that comes to terms with existence in itself. Imagination here is less the vehicle for imagined transcendence than the means by which – finely and implicitly – poetry can address the fact and mystery of being. It is a world in which beauty and sorrow coalesce in an act of restrained acceptance, caught in the line, 'While barrèd clouds bloom the soft-dying day' (25), where 'bloom' and 'soft-dying' enter into a contrapuntal relationship. Throughout, the poem reaches for hyphenated formulations as though to build bridges between different states. The season, from the start, is associated with the near-antithetical 'mists and mellow fruitfulness' (1); it is at once addressed as 'Close bosom-friend of the maturing sun' (2), allegorized as a figure with 'hair soft-lifted by the winnowing wind' (15), and noted as a time when 'full-grown lambs loud bleat from hilly bourn' (30). The phrases encourage intensified awareness of dualities and mergings: that the 'lambs' are 'full-grown', for example, hints at the equivocal nature of the maturing processes typical of the season.

The poem's stanza form has an extra line (eleven rather than the ten in the 'Nightingale', 'Grecian Urn', and 'Melancholy' odes) which creates effects of lingering arrest, contemplation, and acceptance. At the poem's close, there is, implicit in the choice of verbs, a refusal to project meaning on to the landscape, a chastening of earlier elegiac hints in words such as 'mourn', applied to 'small gnats' (27), and 'lives or dies', applied to the 'light wind' (29).[20] As 'Hedge-crickets sing' (31), a 'red-breast whistles' (32), and 'gathering swallows twitter' (33), there is a Keatsian steadfastness of recognition; what this poem presents us with is the cyclical life of nature, our apprehension of which undergoes revivifying aid within and through the elegantly constructed stanzas.

'To Autumn' proves in its own way the provisional validity of the Grecian Urn's identification of 'truth' and 'beauty'. 'Ode on a Grecian Urn', written some months earlier, is a poem of eternal Spring whereas the later ode is a poem of an autumn doomed to pass yet prolonged for our contemplation through a wealth of devices: the extra line in each stanza, the contemplative attitude struck, in particular, at the close of stanza 2 where the personified season watches 'the last oozings hours by hours' (22). In 'Grecian Urn', the poet, addressing the carved lovers and even vegetation, cheats himself into believing they enjoy a happiness that is 'All breathing human passion far above' (28). The very 'boughs' are 'happy' (21) in that they 'cannot' (21) 'ever bid the Spring adieu' (22). But, in this poem, that 'cannot' begins to sound like limitation rather than transcendence, and resistance to change sounds like frozen arrest. For all its asserted inferiority, 'breathing human passion' recommends itself, the two adjectives fighting against the airlessness of art's triumph over time.

Subtly, almost in an unnoticed way, the poem forgets the hypothesis that 'Heard melodies are sweet, but those unheard / Are sweeter' (11–12). Even when it is first stated, the use of the word 'soft' in 'therefore, ye soft pipes, play on' (12) threatens to undo the speaker's certainty since it implies a residual attachment to the sound which is supposedly being foresworn.

In stanza 4, the poet turns to a procession of figures 'coming to the sacrifice' (31), until, as if blurring the worlds of urn and historical reality that gave rise to the urn's representations, the speaker wishes to locate a 'little town' (35) not to be found on the urn's surface. The pathos of his subsequent realization that the town is unpopulated, gone for ever, 'desolate' (40), is intense.

It leads, in the final stanza, to an initial disenchantment with the urn, now merely an artwork, an 'Attic shape' (41), the object of veiled scorn as it withstands a series of barbed puns aimed at its removal from generation and sexuality; it may be 'overwrought' (42) 'with brede / Of marble men and maidens' (41–2), but it cannot 'breed' and is incapable of housing 'overwrought' passion. Yet, said to 'tease us out of thought / As doth eternity' (44–5), the urn continues to vex, unsettle, fascinate. 'Cold Pastoral!' (45) is the nearest Keats comes to fixing the urn in a near-oxymoronic phrase, at once a vessel of idealized beauty and 'Cold'. That outcry gives way to a six-line sentence, concluding with the famous equation of 'beauty' and 'truth', and full of supple weighings and reservations.

Keats, above all, finds his way to a balance – between the fact that 'old age shall this generation waste' (46) and the real if not wholly adequate consolation offered by the fact of the urn's longevity, and the witness it bears to the human need to believe that art offers a knowledge, truth, and beauty superior to the life from which they spring and to which they seek to bring comfort. Art may be 'a friend to man' (48), for Keats, but it cannot offset the fact that, in the world as we know it, change and transience have the final word. 'She dwells with Beauty—Beauty that must die' (21), Keats writes of the mistress in 'Ode on Melancholy', holding in tension the longing for abiding presence in 'dwells' and the awareness of the perishable nature of beauty in 'must die'. His great odes found themselves on the 'lyric debate', in Walter Jackson Bate's phrase, to which this tension gives rise.[21]

Notes

1   For good commentary on the volume and its organization, see the relevant chapter in Neil Fraistat, *The Poem and the Book* (Chapel Hill: University of North Carolina Press, 1985).

2   Qtd, as are all Keats's poems, from *John Keats: The Complete Poems*, ed. John Barnard, 3rd edn (1988; London: Penguin, 2006 corr.).

3   Amy Clampitt, 'The Isle of Wight' from 'Voyages: A Homage to John Keats', in *What the Light Was Like* (London: Faber, 1985).

4   *Keats: Complete Poems*, ed. Barnard, p. 690.

5   *Keats: Complete Poems*, ed. Barnard, p. 690.

6   Kingsley Amis associates it with another example in Keats in which the same rhyme evinces 'mythological incongruity even if the simile is just in other ways', in 'The Curious Elf: A Note on Rhyme in Keats', *Essays in Criticism* (1951) I (2): 189–92 (at 191).

7   Qtd in *Keats: Complete Poems*, ed. Barnard, p. 697.

8   *Letters* 2.189.

9   See, especially, Jack Stillinger, 'The Hoodwinking of Madeline: Scepticism in "The Eve of St. Agnes"', *Studies in Philology* 58 (1961): 533–55.

10 *Letters* 2.360.

11 *Letters* 1.387.

12 *Letters* 1.281.

13 *Letters* 2.167.

14 F. R. Leavis, *Revaluation: Tradition and Development in English Poetry* (Harmondsworth: Penguin, 1964), p. 267.

15 *Letters* 2.79.

16 Leigh Hunt, *Autobiography* (London: Smith, Elder and Co., 1850), 2.202.

17 Qtd in *Keats: Complete Poems*, ed. Barnard, p. 671.

18 Leavis, *Revaluation*, p. 246.

19 See Keats's praise for Milton's *'stationing or statu[a]ry'* in his note on *Paradise Lost* 7.420–3; in *Keats: Complete Poems*, ed. Barnard, p. 525.

20 See Vendler, *The Odes of John Keats*, p. 261.

21 Walter Jackson Bate, *John Keats* (Cambridge, MA: Harvard University Press, 1963), p. 500. Bate's discussion is characteristically nuanced and resistant to easy paraphrase.

Third-Generation Romantic Poets

John Clare: Lyrics

John Clare is a poet of 'strange doubleness', as Hugh Haughton puts it.[1] He is alert to the natural world, intently, raptly so, yet he is also self-conscious about his role as a poet, as Haughton's memorable discussion of 'The Nightingales Nest' displays. He often has us in his spell because we think we are reading a poetry that has laid artifice aside, and yet there is much skill in his apparent casualness. Indeed, a critical difficulty posed by Clare is how the reader should respond to his seeming preference for accident over purpose, artlessness over formal control. This section explores such issues in a consideration of a group of poems from across Clare's career.

Poems state his love for the natural world and catalogue the sights and sounds that he loved with what may look like indifference to overall coherence. Yet, in Stephanie Kuduk Weiner's words, his 'anti-closural endings align his poetry in unexpected ways with the meditative lyric and the fragment'.[2] Intuitively or by design (words that often lose an absolute sureness in the work of many poets and especially Clare), his poetry continually surprises, less by virtue of a carefully exhibited complexity than by changes of tone, nuances of expression. He can be 'wittily artless in a way that performed and undermined his image as an unlettered rustic poet', as Mina Gorji has it, but he can also be uncannily affecting.[3]

Clare's poems about birds' nests show his capacity for intent observation and sympathy. In 'The Yellowhammers Nest', he uses a mixture of rhymes: mainly alternate quatrain rhymes, but also couplets and more irregular chimes to convey the flow of consciousness induced by the sight and thought of the nest. As though in the just-gone past, 'a bird flew up / Frit by the cowboy as he scrambled down / To reach the misty dewberry' (1–3). The scene is alive, Clare's dialect word 'Frit' for 'frightened' bringing the vitality of

The Romantic Poetry Handbook, First Edition. Michael O'Neill and Madeleine Callaghan.
© 2018 John Wiley & Sons Ltd. Published 2018 by John Wiley & Sons Ltd.

non-standard English into the poem. We are invited to accompany the poet on his solicitous search: 'let us stoop / And seek its nest' (3–4) before the in-the-moment, quiet excitement of the nest's discovery: 'Aye here it is stuck close beside the bank' (7), authenticated by the country-dweller's eye for detail: the nest is made up of 'bleached stubbles and the withered fare / That last years harvest left upon the land / Lined thinly with the horses sable hair' (10–12). The syntax of these lines suits their powers of quick observation; it has a spun-out connectedness, marked off by the sharply precise, spondaic 'Lined thinly'.

The poet then knowingly admits the play of 'fancy' (14) into the poem, as he compares 'Five eggs pen-scribbled over lilac shells' (13) to the 'writing scrawls' (14) which 'pen-scribbled' has already metaphorically brought to mind. But Clare's metaphors do not imply a retreat into any falsifying idyll; they serve as the basis for a robust rural poetic, namely, that the yellowhammer is like the poet and 'that old molehill like as parnass hill' (19). Not untypically, this movement into something like assertive reverie is not allowed the final word. The poet goes on to sense, as though by an instinctive reaction, that a serpent might, literally, enter what has turned unostentatiously into an Eden, as well as being a real habitat. He thinks of how 'snakes' (25) might 'seize the helpless young' (26). The thought rounds itself out in the uncoiling syntax, as the depressing, dawning possibility of 'ill' (23) threatens the poet's wish that the spot he has taken us to should be left 'A happy home of sunshine flowers and streams' (22). Instead, the snakes 'are known' (25) to come and go, each an unwanted 'guest' (27),

Leaving a housless-home a ruined nest
And mournful hath the little warblers sung
When such like woes hath rent its little breast.   (28–30)

The 'little warblers' become self-elegists in this glimpse of paradise lost, the ruination of the nest. In thirty lines, Clare has moved from keen-eyed naturalist, to playful presider over poetic 'fancy', to sombre recognizer and mourner of 'such like woes'.

Loss is unignorable for Clare, precisely because he values that which is caught up in transience, perishability. At the same time, a later sonnet, 'The Yellowhammer', seems to speak back to the earlier poem, as it reaffirms the creative, nest-building instinct of the bird. The poem finishes thus:

In early Spring when winds blow chilly cold
The yellow hammer trailing grass will come
To fix a place and choose an early home
With yellow breast and head of solid gold   (11–14)

With an almost proto-Yeatsian emphasis, the poet places his trust in ringingly firm rhymes, concluding with the bird's 'head of solid gold' that clinches the poem (the fine phrase unimpeded by any closing punctuation) and outbraves the Spring's 'chilly cold'. Verbs are firm and active: 'fix' and 'choose'. There's an evident if latent admiration for the bird's instinctual pluck and concern to make a home, and the poem itself becomes an improvised, shapely haven, a verbal bird's nest, composed from what lies to hand, overrunning artificial boundaries between octave and sestet: 'Dead grass, horse hair and downy headed bents / Tied to dead thistles ... / Close to a hill o' ants' (7–9).

In 'The Flitting', describing his movement from Helpston to Northborough in 1832, Clare authenticates feelings of loss through details that have an odd, almost inconsequential but ignorable force: 'I sit me in my corner chair / That seems to feel itself from home' (17–18) is an example, where Clare knows the chair does not, but only 'seems to feel itself from home', but also knows he cannot escape the feeling that it does, because his sense of estrangement is pervasive. The poem's eight-line stanzas employ two sets of alternating rhymes (*ababcdcd*), as though to point up the speaker's movement between then and now, even as he criticizes himself for doing so, as in the lines: 'I dwell on trifles like a child / I feel as ill becomes a man / And still my thoughts like weedlings wild / Grow up to blossom where they can' (57–60). In those lines one hears a note of resilience in the midst of unhappiness often found in Clare.

Elsewhere, as in '[O could I be as I have been]', Clare brings complex feelings into connection with limpid balladic lyricism. In this poem, Clare leaves unexplained the reason for his inability to be as he has been, contrasting in this respect with Wordsworth whose sentiments in the 'Ode: Intimations of Immortality' he echoes.[4] Clare deflects attention from his current sadness by focusing on his former delights, and yet he heightens interest in it, too. The result is a blend of ardent pleasure in the past and a strain of pathos. The repeated exclamations of the opening two stanzas – 'O could I be' (1, 5) – sound a chord of lament that sustains itself through the poem's return to the past, when Clare was 'A harmless thing in meadows green / Or on the wild sea shore' (3–4), 'A dweller in the summer grass' (7), and 'A tennant of the happy fields' (9). Here the nouns bring out Clare's major theme of dwelling, of being part of a known and treasured landscape. They also, by implication, suggest his great counter-theme, that of displacement and loss. Clare famously deplored the impact on his home village Helpston of enclosure (lands being taken out of common use) as a result of which 'he saw venerable trees cut down, whole coppices destroyed, and the streams diverted from their natural courses'.[5]

There is, in '[O could I be as I have been]', a shift of mood in stanza 4, where Clare recalls his status as a dweller, discussing what he did, first through an infinitive, 'To sit on a deserted plough' (13), that tangles doing with contemplation. The poem mingles an ease of phrasing with an economical particularity, as in the stanza:

> The harrows resting by the hedge
> The roll within the Dyke
> Hid in the Ariff and the sedge
> Are things I used to like.   (17–20)

Place-names and words for instruments of labour ('roll' is a 'large, heavy wooden roller for breaking clods', p. 513) are 'things I used to like' – and still do, the poem suggests, through the touching naturalness with which 'like' responds to the rhyming prompt of 'the Dyke / Hid in the Ariff' (or 'goosegrass', p. 506). The poem shows Clare's love of dialect – the 'headaches' that 'left a stain' (24) are 'common poppies' (p. 510) – but even those much-loved words seem to belong to 'what I have been', 'when I roved in shadows green / And loved my willow tree' (26, 27–8). Clare contrives a shift here from the earlier 'meadows green', 'valleys green' (6), and 'places green' (8) that speaks of a movement towards darkness and dissolution as well as the contending impulse to celebrate his own recollected experience: one notes the possessive adjective 'my'.

Tilting away from sadness, however, the final stanza picks up on the earlier infinitive construction ('To sit') and suggests that the origin of Clare's poetic career lay, perhaps paradoxically, in his past:

> To gaze upon the starry sky
> And higher fancies build
> And make in solitary joy
> Loves temple in the field   (29–32)

The lines complicate a clear division between past and present as Clare aligns the building of 'higher fancies' with a time of hope from which he is now excluded, and yet he re-enters that time through memory. The lines resonate less with loss than with recovery: past and present converge as Clare both recalls and imagines the ability to 'make in solitary joy / Loves temple in the field'.

'I am — yet what I am, none cares or knows' explores the poet's sense of madness at a time of existential crisis. Self is experienced as a desolation and desertion.

> I am—yet what I am, none cares or knows;
> My friends forsake me like a memory lost:—

I am the self-consumer of my woes;—
    They rise and vanish in oblivion's host,
Like shadows in love's frenzied stifled throes:—   (1–5)

The opening 'I am' echoes wryly and ironically God's self-definition to Moses, 'I AM THAT I AM' (Exodus 3:14), summoned up by Coleridge in his definition of the 'primary IMAGINATION' in chapter 13 of *Biographia Literaria* as 'a repetition in the finite mind of the eternal act of creation in the infinite I AM'.[6] Yet there's an obstinate energy pulsing below and through the nihilism and despair of 'I am the self-consumer of my woes'. The speaker's 'woes' are forces that seem inextricably internal and external. 'They rise and vanish in oblivion's host' as though they compose an endless self-easing 'host'. And, strangely, they also challenge comparison with erotic intensity and frustration since 'They rise and vanish' 'Like shadows in love's frenzied stifled throes'. The stanza's enjambed last line, passing over the stanza break, opens with a steeled, sad repetition, 'And yet I am, and live', where 'and live' is alert to the fact that being involves becoming; he not only is but he has to live with the fact of who he is now, a state at once irrefutable and inexplicable.

Comparison, 'like vapours tost // Into the nothingness of scorn and noise, —/ Into the living sea of waking dreams' (6–8), drives the poem on into further exploration of the poet's predicament. The drum-beat struck up by the relentless pattern of interlacing *ab* rhymes takes on a different form in the second stanza in which, as in the third and final stanza, Clare inserts a third concluding couplet rhyme after the *ab* rhymes of the stanza's first four lines. It's a technical feature that accompanies his way of altering his tones and angles, helping to make his self-representation at once powerfully affective and open to development. So, the 'nothingness of scorn and noise' passes 'Into the living sea of waking dreams'. The second line, there, moves from a feeling of external oppression, 'scorn and noise', into a sense of internalized confusion, 'the living sea of waking dreams' (8), that amplifies the earlier statement that 'I am, and live'. These 'waking dreams' involve and evolve a metaphor of 'the vast shipwreck of my lifes esteems' (10) which Mark Sandy aptly describes as a 'turbulent, surreal, seascape' and where 'lifes esteems' means both what he has esteemed and those who have esteemed him.[7] This second meaning comes clear in the stanza's final couplet: 'Even the dearest, that I love the best, / Are strange—nay, rather stranger than the rest' (11–12). The modulation in 'nay, rather stranger' typifies the way in which emotion in the poem is able to comment on itself and change, even as it remains intense throughout.

The final stanza moves from regret to longing, longing for an ungendered space never peopled yet at one with his 'childhood':

> I long for scenes, where man hath never trod
>   A place where woman never smiled or wept
> There to abide with my Creator, God;
>   And sleep as I in childhood, sweetly slept,
> Untroubling, and untroubled where I lie,
> The grass below—above the vaulted sky.   (13–18)

Harold Bloom may overstate the case when he writes, in accord with his idea that Clare is negotiating between extremes of attachment to nature and desperate trust in imagination, that 'The yearning is apocalyptic – not for childhood but for scenes "where man hath never trod"'.[8] Clare's final position is more mixed than Bloom would have us believe, both a pure imaginative space, created by longing, and a product of memory, nostalgia, and residual piety. Yet the final line abolishes any sentimentality, as it intimates that the only peace the poet knows is, if not in, then in anticipation of the tomb. Here, as in other late poems, as Bloom notes,[9] the self that won't or can't wholly lose itself in Clare's beloved nature stalks the poetry, an unexorcisable presence.

Even when haunting the poetry, however, the Clarean self looks for company. Clare's 'An Invite to Eternity' extends an initially tender yet increasingly sardonic invitation to the poem's addressee: 'Wilt thou go with me sweet maid / Say maiden wilt thou go with me' (1–2). The tetrameters overthrow acceptance of what is; they become the medium through which Clare can imagine a 'Where' that is the shadowy mirror world of this-worldly nature, a place 'Where life will fade like visioned dreams / And mountains darken into caves' (11–12). It is a place, one might hazard, familiar to Romantic poetry, found in such works as Coleridge's *Kubla Khan*, a place that is antithetical to the real as it bears witness to the misshaping as well as shaping possibilities of imagination. It is a place of and speaking to a state of 'sad non-identity / Where parents live and are forgot / And sisters live and know us not' (15–16). Familial roles still exist but 'we' – perhaps gladly, perhaps sadly – have been airbrushed out of knowledge. It is a post-Coleridgean 'strange death of life' (18), a world in which the usual markers of belonging or identity have been erased and yet in which we are still able 'to see / Things pass like shadows' (23–4). The final stanza offers its queasily triumphalist QED; the invitation to accompany the poet into this place is, it's implied, perilous, impossible, and the only way to access a vision to which the speaker has unique access:

The land of shadows wilt thou trace
And look—nor know each others face
The present mixed with reasons gone
And past, and present all as one
Say maiden can thy life be led
To join the living with the dead
Then trace thy footsteps on with me
We're wed to one eternity   (25–32)

Clare becomes an impossible Jesus-like figure, admonishing his would-be companion to abandon all she knows and follow him. At the same time, even as he gives her space to accept or decline an offer that grows increasingly bewildering (they won't 'know each others face'), he implies, half grimly, that they're already married, 'wed to one eternity' (the line can be read as a statement of how things are or as an anticipation of how they would be). Viewed as a poem about Clare's isolation and need for an audience, it attaches itself to a group of Romantic poems, from 'Tintern Abbey' onwards, that thematizes the difficult, necessary role of the reader and implies the impossible, preciously ambivalent gift proffered by the poet.

Notes

1 'Progress and Rhyme: "The Nightingales Nest" and Romantic Poetry', in *John Clare in Context*, ed. Hugh Haughton, Adam Phillips, and Geoffrey Summerfield (Cambridge: Cambridge University Press, 1994), p. 53.

2 Stephanie Kuduk Weiner, *Clare's Lyric: John Clare and Three Modern Poets* (Oxford: Oxford University Press, 2014), p. 72.

3 Mina Gorji, *John Clare and the Place of Poetry* (Liverpool: Liverpool University Press, 2008), p. 17.

4 Clare is qtd from *John Clare*, ed. Eric Robinson and David Powell, Oxford Authors (Oxford: Oxford University Press, 1984).

5 *John Clare*, ed. Robinson and Powell, pp. xvii–xviii.

6 Samuel Taylor Coleridge, *Biographia Literaria*, ed. James Engell and W. Jackson Bate, 2 vols (Princeton: Princeton University Press, 1983), 1.304.

7 Mark Sandy, *Romanticism, Memory, and Mourning* (Farnham: Ashgate, 2013), p. 143.

8 Harold Bloom, *The Visionary Company: A Reading of English Romantic Poetry*, rev. and enlarged edn (Ithaca, NY: Cornell University Press, 1971), p. 454.

9 See Bloom, *The Visionary Company*, esp. pp. 454–5.

Felicia Hemans, *Records of Woman: With Other Poems*

Felicia Hemans was one of the highest paid and most critically feted poets of her day,[1] but her star has waned since her death, with critics only recently beginning to rediscover her work in the wake of the efforts of Stuart Curran, Susan J. Wolfson, and Norma Clarke, amongst others.[2] Hemans published her first poems in 1808 at fourteen years old, poetry that made Shelley long to make her acquaintance, though she and her mother, perhaps wisely, chose not to respond to his somewhat disingenuous invitation. She continued to write throughout her life, despite the breakdown of her marriage and the difficulty of coping with a large family, and her work is highly attuned to its audience, finely wrought, and deeply engaged with self-fashioning. *Records of Woman: With Other Poems* stands as her most important achievement.[3] In the collection, Hemans imagines, recovers, and rewrites stories of women, from 'The American Forest Girl' to 'Joan of Arc'. The poems featured in the collection are united by suffering, particularly suffering caused by men, who feature as either malicious or inadvertent sources of female misery. Michael Williamson thoughtfully argues that *Records of Woman* sees Hemans refiguring the elegiac tradition: 'Instead of responding to death as an occasional intrusion into life, Hemans writes elegiac poems that lament the waste of women's psychic and imaginative energy on a world tainted by male death, deplore the absence of any commemorative interest in the histories of dead women, and represent dramatically disfiguring subject positions for women mourners.'[4] Eschewing self-pity or anger, *Records of Woman* creates its dramatic records by adopting various female voices.

Records of Woman was Hemans's most popular volume, going into four editions from May 1828 to October 1830. The volume was dedicated to Joanna Baillie, the gifted Scottish poet and playwright, and Susan J. Wolfson

The Romantic Poetry Handbook, First Edition. Michael O'Neill and Madeleine Callaghan.
© 2018 John Wiley & Sons Ltd. Published 2018 by John Wiley & Sons Ltd.

quotes Hemans's letter to Mary Russell Mitford where she writes: 'I have put my heart and individual feelings into it more than in any thing else I have written.'[5] Containing nineteen poems and seven scholarly endnotes, *Records of Woman* joins, as Wolfson notes, the developing genre of 'women's lives',[6] but it also enters into dialogues with male peers, from Byron and Shelley to Wordsworth, as Hemans refigures 'male' themes through female voices. 'The Bride of the Greek Isle' shows Hemans returning to the Greek themes explored in her earlier and overlooked *Modern Greece*, but she also weaves in allusions to Shelley and Byron. *Hellas* and *Don Juan*'s 'The Isles of Greece' linger in the poem, but it is Byron's Tales which are most drastically reconceived. The poem is written largely in heroic couplets like Byron's Tales, but Hemans changes the form with each spoken section, cross-rhyming 'The Bride's Farewell' and shortening the lines to tetrameter to create dramatic interest. The poem opens with Eudora's initially unwilling departure from her mother: 'She turns to her lover, she leaves her sire' (84). After the wedding ceremony, the party are attacked by Ottoman pirates. When her husband, Ianthis, passively dies, Eudora builds a funeral pyre and casts herself on top where the admiring narrator asks, 'could this work be of woman wrought?' (210). While Hemans's narrator invokes suttee as the point of reference for Eudora's suicide, here it seems an act of resistance in the manner of Sardanapalus' self-sacrifice (her epigraph is from the play) but purged of the egotism of Byron's hero. Alert to the political and literary contexts at work in her choice of her heroine and locale, Hemans's Eudora is the perfected heroine of a Byronic tale.

'Properzia Rossi', the most accomplished poem in the collection,[7] shows Hemans engaging in a self-conscious act of doubling where the poet creates Properzia Rossi and Properzia creates her sculpture of Ariadne. Properzia openly avows her intention to channel herself into her artistic creation, Ariadne, and the haunting question becomes how far Hemans uses her artistic creation with the same intention. Properzia Rossi was a highly gifted and regarded artist; Ariadne, despite assisting her beloved Theseus and saving his life, was abandoned by him as he sailed away from Crete. Both of these figures reveal Hemans's care in her selection of her protagonists. In Hemans's poem, Properzia too has been abandoned, suggesting an oblique identification between Properzia and Ariadne, and a subtle biographical link between Properzia and Hemans. Hemans had been deserted by her husband for a new life in Italy, a trauma which was, as Norma Clarke argues, 'the central event in her life as a woman artist'.[8] The poem reveals the intoxication of and the ultimate disappointment of art, as the 'bright work' cannot make up for the pain of such romantic loss even as creative potency ripples through the poem.

Written in couplets that in places recall Shelley's *Epipsychidion*, 'Properzia Rossi' disrupts the smoothness of the iambic beat to make it more jaggedly reflective of human speech. Like Shelley, however, Hemans uses the 'I' to lyrical, even vertiginous effect. This 'keenly performative' ekphrastic verse shows Hemans entering into Properzia's creative process.[9] Hemans lays bare the artistic triumph and personal defeat of the artist. Her work aims to be 'this farewell triumph' (1.8) to be held against her vain love. Seeking to place her soul into her art, Properzia aims to affect her lover deeply, providing him with proof of her devotion. Angela Leighton's description of the speaker, 'a courtesan in her art, displaying her emotional wares to the imagined eye of her lover', suggests a deliberate tension in the poem.[10] Disturbing any sense of art as 'Cold Pastoral' (Keats, 'Ode on a Grecian Urn,' 45), as Grant F. Scott shows, 'Hemans creates a profoundly mortal image, sensuous and impermanent, imbued with the fragility of its human creator. The poem returns *ekphrasis* to its classical origins, showing its artwork in the process of creation and privileging the voice over the perpetuity of the visual image; Hemans ensures that the object "speak out" in the warm words of its creator.'[11] Art as a self-delighting and self-sufficing power comes into conflict with the artist's intention, where the failure of the latter does not affect the success of the former, but shows art slip out of the controlling artist's hands to shine with aesthetic rather than personal glory. Though the voice is privileged, it is the monument that will remain to communicate Properzia's soul 'When its full chords are hush'd' (4.123).

The power of art is unambiguously celebrated by Hemans in 'Properzia Rossi'; though art is unable to heal personal wounds, its magnificence remains:

> …Yet once again
> I greet it proudly, with its rushing train
> Of glorious images:—they throng—they press—
> A sudden joy lights up my loneliness,—
> I shall not perish all!   (2.28–32)

As Properzia celebrates the 'glorious images' that rise before her, Hemans becomes a spectral double of her creation. It is Hemans's 'rushing train' of images that is captured in poetry that demands the immortality of the artist through her art. Hemans catches the creative joy experienced by Properzia in her artistic process, her imaginative prowess. Yet this is coupled with anxiety, as where she laments the limits of her chosen art form: 'Oh! could I throw / Into thy frame a voice, a sweet, and low, / And thrilling voice of song!' (2.49–51). Sculpture lacks voice, but the 'thrilling voice of song' suggests Hemans's own concerns. Left 'Too much alone' (3.66), Properzia lacks the audience for which she longs and the support needed by the artist. By the final section, the fame and glory of the artwork mock the artist who sought to be a lover:

> Worthless fame!
> That in *his* bosom wins not for my name
> Th' abiding place it ask'd! Yet how my heart,
> In its own fairy world of song and art,
> Once beat for praise!—Are those high longings o'er?
> That which I have been can I be no more?   (4.81–6)

Painfully admitting that her art cannot win the affections of her lover, the rhyme of 'heart' and 'art' seems bitterly ironic. Yet more troubling is the lack of interest in the audience for whom the 'fairy world of song and art' had once been created. Seeming to recall Wordsworth's line, 'The things which I have seen I now can see no more' (9) from 'Ode. Intimations of Immortality', Properzia's loss shows how Hemans aligns her with the poet's own contemporaries. Properzia rallies to discover an 'abundant recompence' ('Tintern Abbey', 89) of the kind that characterizes Wordsworth's most affecting poetry. The images of the love she desperately recollects are united by memories of silence. In her longing to watch the sky without speaking, to listen silently to music, to gaze on art, Properzia dreams of being an appreciator of art rather than an artist herself. For her, 'This had been joy enough' (5.117), but she continues to imagine that such silence would feed her art, and then she would sculpt perfectly, and make her fame 'A glory for thy brow' (5.120). Avowing that such hopes are 'dreams', a quiet acceptance closes the poem, where Properzia's ambition is reduced to hoping that her lover will remember her because of her art. This solving acceptance is suggested by the final lines' firm masculine rhyme. Susan Wolfson refers to the poem as revealing a 'calculus of heart and art',[12] and Properzia's self-fashioning melds the glory of her art with a profound understanding of her own necessary failure. 'Properzia Rossi' is a celebration and a lament for the lot of the female artist. The 'deep thrill' (5.122) of the lines lies in Hemans's doubling between Ariadne and Properzia, and between Properzia and Hemans herself.

'Imelda' and 'Gertrude, or Fidelity till Death' shows Hemans using historical figures that she reanimates, using their stories to draw out the female fidelity and bravery displayed by her characters. Yet such agony does not go rewarded in the poems, with Imelda's death and Gertrude's pain availing them nothing. The 'Indian Woman's Death Song' is marked by clear allusions to Byron's *Childe Harold's Pilgrimage* 4 and Shelley's *Alastor*, but Hemans carefully feminizes their poetry, turning an historical account of infanticide into a protest against and a considered response to 'woman's weary lot' (36). The poem opens with an irregular and unrhymed fifteen-line stanza that carefully refuses the sonnet form. It then transforms into seven quatrains of heptameter couplets, borrowing its form from Chapman's translation of Homer's *Iliad*.[13] Hemans's confident long lines stretch out the Indian woman's lamentation, where her misery gains part of its pathos from its triumphant embrace of coming destruction. 'Pauline' also draws on historical fact, but Hemans intensifies the story from a tale of maternal sacrifice where Pauline saves her daughter from a fire to having both mother and daughter die in the blaze. Maternal courage comes to the fore, but in the final lines, Hemans insists on the necessity of belief: 'Oh! we have need of patient faith below, / To clear away the mysteries of such wo!' (89–90). Rather than seeming a trite response to tragedy, this couplet makes faith seem like the only possible response to pain, with the unspoken alternative being only an endless agony of grief. In 'Juana' and 'Costanza' Hemans underscores the injustice to which both women were subject. Juana, who had been carelessly treated by her husband because 'I am not fair like thee' (25), attempts to win affection from the already dead man: 'I have but a woman's heart, wherewith *thy* heart to seek' (28). As Susan Wolfson notes, the heptameter couplets are arranged into quatrains, as in 'The Indian Woman's Death Song' and the 'Sicilian Captive', suggesting that Hemans creates a formal link between such songs of feminine despair.[14] The poem creates a dichotomy between Costanza as a physical figure and as an ideal abstraction, as Michael T. Williamson shows: 'Costanza's bodily presence as a woman thus hovers beneath her saintly aura and her role as an abstraction; Cesario's breath both exalts and effaces the ideal of saintly feminine forgiveness.'[15] The 'solemn fervour' (11) announced early on in the poem reveals the paradox Hemans creates, where Costanza is both a woman and an archetype of female mercy. Hemans also deliberately mingles the physical with the metaphysical in her presentation of her protagonist in 'Joan of Arc, in Rheims'. While retaining Joan of Arc's power, Hemans domesticates her subject as she imagines Joan's infancy, rural background, and longing to return to a time of such innocence. Though Hemans allows 'The crown of glory unto woman's brow' (94), she insistently combines the real woman with the political myth; power and femininity vie for importance in her poem.

Childhood as the locus amoenus of joy reverberates through many other poems in the volume. 'The American Forest-Girl' links youth to virtue in a manner suggestive of Wordsworth's 'My Heart Leaps Up', as the young female child's pity convinces the group of 'red warriors' (4) to free their European captive. But it is in 'Madeline, A Domestic Tale', 'arguably the most autobiographical poem in this self-revealing collection',[16] that infancy and the mother–daughter bond become vitally important. After Madeline's husband dies before Madeline reaches him in America, she longs to return home to her mother: 'This voice echoes many such regressive Romantic longings – ones heard in Shelley, Wordsworth, and Keats, whose texts often involve images of maternal nurture. But Hemans's conception is a more specific fantasy of the actual maternal home, and Madeline's yearning for the "true and perfect love" (149) of its care evokes a gender-specific paradise lost.'[17] Romantic love comes a poor second to the domestic bliss of the maternal home, and Madeline's instinct is not to find a new husband, but to remain with her mother. Hemans's heroic couplets wistfully record loss as the pentameter elegiacally captures pain with stoic forbearance:

> ... Alas! we trace
> The map of our own paths, and long ere years
> With their dull steps the brilliant lines efface,
> On sweeps the storm, and blots them out with tears.   (47–50)

The felt loss in the lines hints at a speaker alive to and empathetic of the suffering of Madeline. Longing for home is neither ironized nor lamented by Hemans's speaker. Madeline's mother heroically rescues her child, sailing to the new world to bring her child safely back to the domestic sphere where 'Peace will be ours beneath our vines once more' (102). The bond between women becomes the unbreakable tie far beyond that of marriage, and 'The Memorial Pillar' reinforces this when mother and daughter rejoin one another after death, and Hemans's 'gender-specific paradise lost' comes in the afterlife, if not in this one.

Records of Woman seeks to represent female experience, attempting to give a voice to her chosen women throughout culture and history. Experimenting with genre, form, and voice, using famous and anonymous speakers, the collection reveals Hemans's subtle ability to imagine experience and channel her own experience into the voices of others. 'The Lost Pleiad' shows Hemans making poetic capital of Byron's and Shelley's poetry to make even her most allusive moments absolutely her own, as Michael O'Neill argues: 'Hemans's poem is sumptuously musical, yet self-aware, attentive, sorrowful and courageous, equal to the challenge presented by "glory from the heavens departed"'.[18] Complex and self-conscious, Hemans's *Records of Woman* is a major Romantic achievement.

Notes

1 According to Paula R. Feldman, 'ledger books reveal that Hemans was the single highest paid contributor to Blackwood's Edinburgh Magazine'. Paula R. Feldman, 'The Poet and the Profits: Felicia Hemans and the Literary Marketplace', *Keats-Shelley Journal* 46 (1997): 148–76 (at 149).

2 See works such as Start Curran, 'The "I" Altered', in *Romanticism and Feminism*, ed. Anne K. Mellor (Bloomington: Indiana University Press, 1988), pp. 185–207; Marlon B. Ross, *The Contours of Masculine Desire: Romanticism and the Rise of Women's Poetry* (New York: Oxford University Press, 1989), pp. 232–310; Norma Clarke, *Ambitious Heights: Writing, Friendship, Love – The Jewsbury Sisters, Felicia Hemans, and Jane Welsh Carlyle* (London: Routledge, 1990); *Felicia Hemans: Selected Poems, Letters, Reception Materials*, ed. Susan J. Wolfson (Princeton: Princeton University Press, 2000).

3 Angela Leighton, *Victorian Women Poets: Writing Against the Heart* (Hemel Hempstead: Harvester Wheatsheaf, 1992), p. 36.

4 Michael T. Williamson, 'Impure Affections: Felicia Hemans's Elegiac Poetry and Contaminated Grief', in *Felicia Hemans: Reimagining Poetry in the Nineteenth Century*, ed. Nanora Sweet and Julie Melnyk, foreword by Marlon B. Ross (Basingstoke: Palgrave, 2001), pp. 19–35 (at p. 19).

5 *Felicia Hemans*, ed. Wolfson, p. 329.

6 See *Felicia Hemans*, ed. Wolfson, p. 330.

7 Leighton agrees, referring to it as follows: 'The best monologue in the collection represents Hemans' most ambitious version of the Sappho-Corinne myth.' Leighton, *Victorian Women Poets*, p. 38.

8 Clarke, *Ambitious Heights*, p. 80.

9 Grant F. Scott, 'The Fragile Image: Felicia Hemans and Romantic Ekphrasis', in *Felicia Hemans: Reimagining Poetry in the Nineteenth Century*, ed. Sweet and Melnyk, pp. 36–54 (at p. 41).

10 Leighton, *Victorian Women Poets*, p. 39.

11 Scott, 'The Fragile Image', p. 49.

12 Susan J. Wolfson, '"Domestic Affections" and "the spear of Minerva": Felicia Hemans and the Dilemma of Gender', in *Re-Visioning Romanticism: British Women Writers, 1776–1837*, ed. Carol Shiner Wilson and Joel Haefner (Philadelphia: University of Pennsylvania Press, 2004), pp. 128–66 (at p. 157).

13 *Felicia Hemans*, ed. Wolfson, p. 379n.

14 *Felicia Hemans*, ed. Wolfson, p. 388.

15 Williamson, 'Impure Affections', p. 28.

16 Anne K. Mellor, *Romanticism and Gender* (New York and London: Routledge, 1993), p. 132.

17 Wolfson, '"Domestic Affections" and "the spear of Minerva"', p. 140.

18 Michael O'Neill, '"Materials for Imagination": Shelleyan Traces in Felicia Hemans's Poetry After 1822', *Women's Writing* 21.1 (2014): 74–90 (at 78).

Letitia Elizabeth Landon, 'Love's Last Lesson'; 'Lines of Life'; 'Lines Written under a Picture of a Girl Burning a Love-Letter'; 'Sappho's Song'; 'A Child Screening a Dove from a Hawk. By Stewardson'

Letitia Elizabeth Landon, or L. E. L. as she was known to the public, occupies the hinterland between Romantic and Victorian poetry, and this section offers comments on a few of her lyrics. Publishing her first poem in 1820 at the age of eighteen, the year before Keats's death, Landon, like Hemans who also published her mature work post-1820, seems to belong to a third generation of Romantic poets.[1] Publishing her first poem, 'Rome', in the *Literary Gazette*, and more poems in the same journal in 1821, Landon also enjoyed the prestige of being the chief reviewer of the journal. Though her first collection of poetry, *The Fate of Adelaide: a Swiss Tale of Romance; and other Poems*, published under her own name, went largely without comment, her subsequent 1824 collection, *The Improvisatrice, and other Poems*, published under the mysterious and tantalizing nom de plume of *L. E. L.*, was very popular, running to six editions in its first year. Along with Felicia Hemans, Landon's earnings propelled her to the top of the financial list in the 1820s and 1830s, with Paula Feldman noting the parity between Hemans and Landon in terms of their monetary success.[2] Publishing more poetry collections, including *The Troubadour: Poetical Sketches of Modern Pictures, and Historical Sketches* in 1825, followed by *The Golden Violet* (1827) and *The Venetian Bracelet* (1829), Landon also edited several annuals. She also began to write novels, including her *Romance and Reality* (1831), which garnered some approving critical notices. Despite her impressive earnings, money remained a source of difficulty throughout her life, and, like Felicia Hemans, the pressure to be a financially as well as creatively successful poet shaped her poetic practice.

Despite an obvious resemblance to Felicia Hemans, Landon most closely recalls Byron, owing to the scandal that surrounded her, and to her interest in the role of the self in her poetry. Jerome McGann draws out this similarity, referring to her (along with Edgar Allan Poe) as 'a second-order Byron'.[3] But this diminishes her considerable achievement. Landon's poetry drips with references to secret romances, romantic misery, and abandonment, choosing to focus on erotic love unlike Hemans's poetry of 'domestic and maternal love'.[4] Like Byron, Landon tried to disavow biographical readings, but she was equally unsuccessful at repelling prurient interest, which was compounded by her status as an independent female poet. Though Landon continually experimented with the self in her poetry, such experimentation is not in the simply autobiographical sense that her early critics believed. Rather, Landon deliberately works with the parameters of the self, blending a wry detachment with effusions of feeling so as to create poetry that both participates in and challenges the self's emotional responses to pain. Self-consciousness, rather than crippling her work, offers her a means with which to figure the self.

Glennis Stephenson argues for Landon as a highly self-conscious poet fascinated by the role of the poet to the extent that she seems a 'relentlessly Romantic' poet, even more so than her male predecessors.[5] Where Stephenson sees the role of the female poet as limiting, for Daniel Riess, 'Her poetry did not simply acquiesce in the increasing commodification of literature and art; rather, it was an active, willing participant'.[6] Femininity is, in the poetry, a means for self-fashioning, much as Byron made use of a version of masculinity and heroism to create his poetry. Landon's poetry explores femininity as a gilded cage as she exposes both its imprisoning quality and its aesthetic potential. In 'Love's Last Lesson', she meditates through the speaker who acts as another 'I' for her to inhabit. Opening with a love letter, the poem begins with an insight into the agony of a woman whose lover has abandoned her and her letter to him. But Landon reframes this rejection as a means for considering the act of writing:

> She flung aside the scroll, as it had part
> In her great misery. Why should she write?
> What could she write? Her woman's pride forbade
> To let him look upon her heart, and see
> It was an utter ruin;—and cold words,

And scorn and slight, that may repay his own,
Were as a foreign language, to whose sound
She might not frame her utterance. Down she bent
Her head upon an arm so white that tears
Seem'd but the natural melting of its snow,
Touch'd by the flush'd cheek's crimson; yet life-blood
Less wrings in shedding than such tears as those. (61–72)

If, as a biographical reading would have it, she writes to bare her heart, these lines compellingly dismiss the idea. Pride prevents self-exposure of a simplistic kind, even between former lovers. Self-preservation demands withdrawal, but the problem of language continues as Landon's speaker will not return the tenor of her lover's 'cold words', unable and unwilling to speak in the 'foreign language' and 'scorn and slight' that colour his speech. McGann views such lack of emotional revelation as showing Landon's careful mode of self-exposure, claiming: 'Landon had to negotiate her way with great care and deliberation. The consequence is a (socially) self-conscious style of writing that often – especially in the later work – comes inflected with a disturbing mood or tone of bad faith. Again and again the poetry seems oblique, or held in reserve, or self-censored.'[7] Yet, within the poetry, such reserve accords with Byron's deliberate silencing of his heroes. Lara, the Giaour, and countless Byronic hero-figures increase their mystery in direct proportion to their speechlessness, and Landon creates intensity out of what her speaker refuses to say. Landon knowingly creates an aestheticized image of feminine anguish to appeal to her reader.

At the same time, seemingly insisting on her purpose as higher than aesthetic beauty, Landon aligns herself with ethical poets, such as Pope, Byron's poetic father.

What is the tale that I would tell? Not one
Of strange adventure, but a common tale
Of woman's wretchedness; one to be read
Daily in many a young and blighted heart.
The lady whom I spake of rose again
From the red fever's couch, to careless eyes
Perchance the same as she had ever been.
But oh, how alter'd to herself! ('Love's Last Lesson', 99–106)

Underscoring the frequency of such pain, and the commonness of misadventures, Landon points up the dissimulation demanded of the wounded female. Forced to hide her pain, the goal is to appear unaltered 'to careless eyes'. Like Jane Austen's *Sense and Sensibility* and the pressure for Marianne to hide her misery when Willoughby cruelly jilts her, Landon shows young women as forced to perform as if untouched by misery until they are alienated from themselves. Asking 'Are words, then, only false?' ('Love's Last Lesson', 117), this question forms the heart of the poem. Despite the love letter taking up the first sixty lines, its inability to console or help the young woman's situation demands the question as to the point of writing. Her lover's ambition turned him from the young woman, and the world-weary speaker offers no salve for either lover: 'For man's most golden dreams of pride and power / Are vain as any woman dreams of love;' (129–30). 'Love's Last Lesson' appears to be the inevitability of loss, a loss that poetry cannot or will not transform into aesthetic gain.

'Lines of Life' also shows Landon working in a metapoetic mode. Landon's speaker witnesses the corrupting influence of society and her separation from the sneering masses, but rather than only lamenting her solitude, poetry becomes a means of creating a connection between the present and the future:

> Why write I this? because my heart
>   Towards the future springs,
> That future where it loves to soar
>   On more than eagle wings.
>
> The present, it is but a speck
>   In that eternal time,
> In which my lost hopes find a home,
>   My spirit knows its clime.
>
> Oh! not myself,—for what am I?—
>   The worthless and the weak,
> Whose every thought of self should raise
>   A blush to burn my cheek.
>
> But song has touch'd my lips with fire,
>   And made my heart a shrine;
> For what, although alloy'd, debased,
>   Is in itself divine.
>
> I am myself but a vile link
>   Amid life's weary chain;
> But I have spoken hallow'd words,
>   Oh do not say in vain!   ('Lines of Life', 73–92)

Written in ballad metre, the determined regularity of the form suggests unadorned honesty, but it is an honesty coloured by close attention to her poetic peers, Byron, Shelley, and Keats. The poet, Landon's speaker claims, looks to the future, placing her in the tradition of Shelley's sense of the importance of writing for posterity. Landon's poetic instinct seems to spring less from a sense of self-preservation than a yearning to communicate with future readers, distinguished by her song, not her self. Divorcing self from song, the speaker claims to be a weak creature who never considers herself, but it is song, those 'hallowed words', which elevates her. Reminiscent of Byron's *Childe Harold's Pilgrimage* 3, where the poet insists: 'What am I? Nothing; but not so art thou / Soul of my thought!' (3.6.50–1), Landon, like Byron, sees vitality as a condition of art, not of the self. Yet where Byron's meditation displays a confident power, Landon endangers the security of her 'hallow'd words' when her final quoted exclamation, 'Oh do not say in vain!', shakes the certainty that divine song will guarantee an immortality for her poetry. Going on to imagine her work read by men and women, it seems that her poetry is justified by the response of her readers, as in Keats's *The Fall of Hyperion* where Keats defers decision about his status as a poet until a time 'When this warm scribe my hand is in the grave' (*The Fall of Hyperion* 1.18). Landon's poetry is inflected by Romanticism only to reframe its concerns in a new context.

'Lines Written under a Picture of a Girl Burning a Love-Letter' showcases Landon's poetic gift by means of its brilliant economy. The poem is suggestive of the sonnet as it opens with a two-line epigram that contextualizes the following twelve lines: 'The lines were filled with many a tender thing, / All the impassioned heart's fond communing'. Landon's cross-rhymed lines increase rather than solve the ambiguity that builds in the poem.

> I took the scroll: I could not brook,
>   An eye to gaze on it save mine;
> I could not bear another's look
>   Should dwell upon one thought of thine.
> My lamp was burning by my side,
>   I held thy letter to the flame,
> I marked the blaze swift o'er it glide,
>   It did not even spare thy name.
> Soon the light from the embers past,
>   I felt so sad to see it die,
> So bright at first, so dark at last,
>   I feared it was love's history. ('Lines Written under a Picture of a Girl Burning a Love-Letter', 1–12)

Curiously clipped, this self-contained poem offers a record of an anonymous woman burning a letter sent by her former lover. The detachment of the poem distances the reader even as it seems to recount an intimate event.

Refusing to allow the reader access to even 'one thought of thine', the speaker's interest in destroying the letter is bound up less with an attempt to destroy a record of him than to prevent any onlooker from looking upon their shared history. Affecting in its careful denial of disclosure or emotion, the heart of the poem, 'It did not even spare thy name', shows the absent lover to whom she speaks being effaced completely. The reader turns voyeur, reading lines written as a response to destroying other lines for fear of being read. Christopher Nagle rightly shows that the poem does not even attempt to behave as a consolation for or replacement of the original lines.[8] That it is 'Love's history', not merely their personal history that burns, 'So bright at first, so dark at last', shows the speaker including the fate of all love affairs in the same conflagration.

Angela Leighton shows that 'Poetry is the single motive and motif for all her [Landon's] verse',[9] and Landon's repeated invocation of Sappho bears witness to Landon's intense self-consciousness as a poet. Yet the source of fascination is Sappho's divided status, where her femininity and her poetic power seem not incongruent but that the latter cannot rescue the former from pain and disappointment. 'And Sappho knew that genius, riches, fame, / May not soothe slighted love' ('Sappho', 71–2). While Landon celebrates Sappho's genius without equivocation or any apology for her vocation, her status as a poet becomes almost painful for its inability to soothe or salve love's pain. 'Sappho's Song', a poem within a poem in Landon's bestselling *The Improvisatrice*, shows Landon reaching for lyrical intensity by embodying Sappho, her chosen ancient Greek double. Sappho comes to 'personify lyric',[10] as Landon mingles poetic pride with personal loss. While the opening of the poem sought to blame her romantic loss on her lyrical brilliance, by the second stanza, Sappho is forced to admit that art did not exact any heavy cost to her life:

> Yet wherefore, wherefore should I blame
>   Thy power, thy spell, my gentlest lute?
> I should have been the wretch I am,
>   Had every chord of thine been mute.   ('Sappho's Song',
>   *The Improvisatrice*, 145–8)

Refusing to create a binary between the personal and poetic, Landon does not compromise her poetic art by blaming it for romantic suffering. Despite the first stanza blaming the 'poison' and 'fever' of song, here, Sappho seems almost carried away by 'Thy power, thy spell, my gentlest lute', rising to a celebration of the beauty of the lute even in the midst of a lament for her wretched state. 'A Child Screening a Dove from a Hawk. By Stewardson' also avoids empty moralizing. Setting itself up as an exemplar of balanced simplicity, the surface blandness of the apparent moral, 'Ever amid the sweets of life / Some evil thing must be' (7–8), becomes a kind of disguise. The following line, 'Ah moralize!', suggests that such moral certainty does not prevent pain, and this sardonic fatalism allows Landon to ironize didactic poetry.

Here as elsewhere, the reader senses the force of Nagle's argument that 'Only by struggling to see the value in the "artificial" – in its commercial, aesthetic, epistemological, and affective senses – its splendid, multi-layered and poly-vocal *artifice* – will the substantive richness of Landon's poetry emerge for readers of the present century'.[11]

Notes

1 'The 1820s and 1830s have long posed a problem to English literary periodization.' Daniel Riess, 'Laetitia Landon and the Dawn of English Post-Romanticism', *Studies in English Literature, 1500–1900* 36.4 (1996): 807–27 (at 808).

2 Paula R. Feldman, 'The Poet and the Profits: Felicia Hemans and the Literary Marketplace', *Keats-Shelley Journal* 46 (1997): 148–76 (at 175–6n).

3 Jerome McGann, *The Poetics of Sensibility: A Revolution in Literary Style* (Oxford: Clarendon Press, 1996), p. 146.

4 McGann, *The Poetics of Sensibility*, p. 146.

5 Glennis Stephenson, 'Letitia Landon and the Victorian Improvisatrice: The Construction of L.E.L.', *Victorian Poetry* 30.1 (1992): 1–17 (at 1).

6 Riess, 'Laetitia Landon and the Dawn of English Post-Romanticism', p. 810.

7 McGann, *The Poetics of Sensibility*, p. 146.

8 Christopher C. Nagle, 'Landon, Letitia Elizabeth', in *The Encyclopedia of Romantic Literature*, ed. Frederick Burwick, 3 vols (Oxford: Blackwell, 2012), 1.763–72 (at 1.769).

9 Angela Leighton, *Victorian Women Poets: Writing Against the Heart* (Hemel Hempstead: Harvester Wheatsheaf, 1992), p. 60.

10 Yopie Prins, *Victorian Sappho* (Princeton: Princeton University Press, 1999), p. 14.

11 Nagle, 'Landon, Letitia Elizabeth', p. 771.

Thomas Lovell Beddoes, *Death's Jest-Book* and Lyrics

Thomas Lovell Beddoes is a poet who exists between worlds, a belated Romantic, a proto-Modern. Continual efforts to raise his poetic profile have been made, and yet he seems obstinately to fail to enter the mainstream of poetry in English, as he uncannily predicts in his death-note: 'I am food for *what I am good* for – worms ... I ought to have been among other things a good poet.'[1] He was more than 'a good poet', but often one whose poetic virtues demonstrate themselves as a questioning of ambition, wish, and desire, and through what Michael Bradshaw calls 'a deeply ambivalent attitude to a reader's wish for imaginative completion and fusion'.[2]

His great lyric 'Dream-Pedlary' evokes and mocks the activity of peddling dreams, a veiled reference to writing poems for an indifferent audience. Its prosody and haunting rhyming, often monorhyming, create a miniature drama in five stanzas. A voice asks the speaker in the first stanza which dreams he would buy, 'If there were dreams to sell', spelling out the differences between kinds of dreams, some grave, some light, some 'Merry and sad', finally all blurring into the one composite form. The opening 'If' transmits a chord of plangent conditionality – half-lament, half-sardonic grimace – through the stanza, a note that amplifies its music in the triple rhyme that appears only in the first stanza (in which there are ten lines, the other four each having nine lines): 'If there were dreams to sell', says Beddoes, reprising his lyric's first line, 'Merry and sad to tell, / And the crier rung the bell, / What would you buy?' The penultimate line does much to deepen the poem's emotional impact. This, one feels, is the reason for the extra line, the thought of a crier ringing a bell to communicate news – as though he were calling out that there were dreams to sell, but also as though he were

The Romantic Poetry Handbook, First Edition. Michael O'Neill and Madeleine Callaghan.
© 2018 John Wiley & Sons Ltd. Published 2018 by John Wiley & Sons Ltd.

announcing a death, perhaps of the dream-pedlar (Beddoes's mocking equivalent to the pedlar who stands for robust good living and high thinking in Wordsworth's *The Excursion*). The thought of a 'passing bell' tolls through the stanza and the poem.

In the second stanza the speaker voices a wish for a subjective retreat into nature, living in 'A cottage lone and still'. In the third the voices entangle: the speaker addresses himself as 'thou' and rebukes himself as falling into the trap of prizing mere dreams, before he switches to 'I' and takes seriously what he'd seemed to pour scorn on, namely the idea of 'wishing ghosts to rise'. The movingly Orphic fourth stanza imagines the poet raising the ghost of 'my loved longlost boy' (among the clearest textual evidence that Beddoes nursed a deep homosexual passion, possibly for Bernhard Reich with whom he lived for a year in Göttingen), until it comes back to earth with a mono-syllable bump:

> There are no ghosts to raise;
> Out of death lead no ways;
> > Vain is the call.

The bareness and terseness of these lines, along with the poem's bewitching melody, typify Beddoes's lyric power, evident too in the graceful acquiescence of the fifth and final stanza, in which the speaker recommends that a quiet death is the best medicine for hopeless hope, but does so in the context of seeing and accepting that the pursuit of ghosts is the price paid by love. The art, pathos, and tragic insight of this fine poem are equally impressive.

Although Beddoes looks back to the devices and concerns of Elizabethan lyricism and Jacobean tragedy, he is no mere pasticheur. Rather, he is able to use echoes and illusions with a creative, ironic intelligence. His poetry attracted the approval of Ezra Pound, for whom he was 'the prince of morticians' (Canto LXXX);[3] it sings with a reckless poetic life of its own, a life that derives in part from the poetry's preoccupation with death and the liminally spectral states surrounding it. Spirit is at war with mortal flesh throughout his work, even as he speculates darkly about a physical organ of resurrection:

> > a seed-shaped bone,
> Aldabaron, called by the Hebrews Luz,
> Which, being laid into the ground, will bear
> After three thousand years the grass of flesh,
> The bloody, soul-possessed weed called man. (*Death's Jest-Book* 3.3.456–60)

Spoken by the ambivalent figure of Ziba, half sage, half necromantic villain, the lines exemplify the monodramatic nature of Beddoes's maverick Romantic play; 'a sort of spectral dramatic fantasia' is Arthur Symons's description of the work.[4] Yet if a spectral aura surrounds its language, hand in hand with a sense that the dramatis personae are all ventriloquizing variations on a single poetic voice, there is a pungent physicality too in the writing.

In the lines above, Beddoes wields a sonorous pentameter made to hold clashing registers and inflections. Here, the reference to 'Luz' lifts the tone on to a plane that's Hebraic and solemn, even as the word and the idea of grotesque resurrection it betokens seem on the edge of being what Beddoes in a letter calls 'an excellent joke' (p. xxxviii).

The sardonic, weightily stressed last line of the quoted passage suggests how he thrives on the jar of contraries. Man is 'bloody' in that he's physically and metaphorically 'bloody'; he's 'soul-possessed' in that he possesses, and is possessed by the idea of, a soul; and if traditionally all flesh is grass Beddoes sardonically finds in that truism grounds for the notion of human beings as a 'weed', the chime with 'seed-shaped' reminding us yet again of this poet's constant way of bringing together yearning and mockery.

Such a compounding, leavened with macabre irony, emerges in the lyric, 'Squats on a toad-stool under a tree / A bodiless childfull of life, in the gloom, / Crying with frog voice, "What shall I be?"' (3.3.328–30). Isbrand offers this as his genre-subverting version of a Romantic kind ('I hate your ballads that are made to come / Round like a squirrel's cage, and round again', 3.3.324–5), and certainly it avoids anything like mechanical circularity as its imagined speaker occupies a strange zone between foetal anomaly and Romantic ur- or counter-poem questing for a new mode of being, crying '"What shall I be?"'. In a fascinating reading, Ute Berns explores the width and depth of Beddoes's lyrical intellectualism in the poem, bringing out ways in which it 'highlights', from the perspective of an informed interest in new biological sciences, 'the grotesque creativity of "life"', and questions 'idealist assumptions about the course of the history of mankind'.[5] Beddoes the poet of soul and spirit is also the poet of body and matter, of embryological fantasy and haphazard evolutionary tendencies. Indeed the poem crackles with zestful, slightly revolted physicality. Yet it is, for all its interest in science, imagined as the product of 'A bodiless childfull of life in the gloom', where 'gloom' edges towards metaphor, rather as it does in Hardy's later poem about loss of religious belief, 'The Oxen', which finishes, 'I should go with him in the gloom, / Hoping it might be so' (11–12).[6] The fact that the poem is so metapoetic, followed as it is by Siegfried's and Isbrand's glosses ('tis perhaps a little / Too sweet and tender', says the latter out of a twisted, good-humoured corner of his mouth, 'but that is the fashion' (376–7)), allows us to see it as a self-proclaimed 'new Dodo' (373), delightedly cancelling its own exhilarating if strained life.

Poetic strains in Beddoes are often, quite consciously, strained, as though he were conceding his inability to write in any available idiom; questing for something new, he, self-mockingly, declares his own originality to be instantly obsolete. Frequently it is when imagining the dead, though, that Beddoes's verse comes most alive, as in Siegfried's explanation of why haunting is out of fashion, now that so many have gone over to death:

> But now great cities are transplanted thither,
> Memphis, and Babylon, and either Thebes,
> And Priam's towery town with its one beech.　(3.3.399–401)

Again taking a leaf out of Shelley's *Prometheus Unbound*, Beddoes offers his own version of the shadow-world conjured into being by Earth in Act 1 of Shelley's lyrical drama, finding a feisty, memorable embodiment for what Shelley calls 'Dreams and the light imaginings of men' (1.200). In that last detail, he releases the Romantic obsession with singularity, apparent in Wordsworth's line, 'But there's a Tree, of many one' ('Ode. Intimations of Immortality', 51), into his poetry's highly singular form of ghost-ridden life.

At one point in *Death's Jest-Book*, Isbrand, the cynical yet beguilingly intrepid and candid anti-hero, addresses himself as a 'tragic fool', telling himself, with a nonchalant command of ordinary idiom, to 'Cheer up'. If he is 'alone', 'Why, so should be / Creators and destroyers' (1.1.207–9). That casual coupling suggests the work's closeness to Romantic irony, the idea that creativity exhibits itself most compellingly in the act of destroying its own productions. Throughout the work, characters destroy what they love and destroy because they love, as when, in the central action of the play as revenge tragedy, the Duke murders Wolfram, less because the latter loves Sibylla than because he inflicts the humiliation of forgiveness on the Duke. The work is alert to the dynamics of sibling hatreds and loves, and has more insight psychologically than is sometimes allowed.

At his most Romantically transcendent, as in his poem in praise of Shelley, 'Lines Written in a Blank Leaf of the *Prometheus Unbound*', Beddoes imagines a poetic triumph over the material world. In these lines Beddoes utters a chant of affirmation in praise of his immediate forebear's creative achievement: Shelley was like a 'providence', whose 'Angelic sounds / Alive with panting thoughts sunned the dim world', where intertextual references handsomely acknowledge the vision of a poet who sought to bring libertarian light to what Shelley calls 'this dim world' ('Ode to Liberty', 227).

Normally, however, such longing for transcendence betrays itself as death-dealing, macabre or parodic. In the 1829 version of *Death's Jest-Book*, discussed here, the version Beddoes sent to friends in England who deflatingly advised against publication, there is, running through the mechanism of the revenge tragedy plot, a suggestion that the poem itself is subtly dangerous. When Wolfram's ghost speaks with Sibylla, she conjures him to

> Speak as at first you did: there was in the words
> A mystery and music, which did thaw
> The hard old rocky world into a flood,
> Whereon a swan-drawn boat seemed at my feet
> Rocking on its blue billows ...   (4.2.47–51)

Her exhortation deploys images drawn from Shelley's *Prometheus Unbound* 2.5, in lyrics such as 'My soul is an enchanted boat'. Beddoes's effects are knowingly self-referential and allusive. He evokes the primal rapture of Romantic poetry here, its ability to turn 'The hard old rocky world into a flood' available for song and harmony. But such an evocation contends with a different, harsher recognition, a sense that human imaginings may be illusory and tempt their creators and auditors towards states of death and oblivion. Again there are sources in Shelley, whose darkest work *The Cenci*, admired greatly by Beddoes, finds its way into Wolfram's warning reply:

> Listen not to me, look not on me more,
> I have a fascination in my words,
> A magnet in my look, which drags you downwards,
> From hope and life.   (64–7)

That 'fascination' is serpent-like, treacherous; it intimates the power of 'words' to drag the listener 'downwards', destroying 'hope and life'. Count Cenci, imagining the corruption of his daughter, says parenthetically that 'what she most abhors / Shall have a fascination to entrap / Her loathing will' (4.1.85–7), and Beddoes adapts that sadistic inflection to his own more insinuating hints of 'fascination' with death. Wolfram's warning only increases Sibylla's fascination with 'death', depicted by her lyrically as a means of achieving a pleasing loss of self: 'let me pass praying away into thee, / As twilight still does into starry night' (4.2.128–9). The extended vowel music of 'praying away' is characteristic of Beddoes's impulse and ability to create rhythms that embody feeling.

Moving between states, then, Beddoes's poetry encompasses a host of possible meanings: literary, personal, psychological, political, national. His poetry's despair is the reflex of a barely acknowledged radical hope; his cultural aloneness speaks of a wish to set going a dialectic between two cultures, England and Germany. He belongs to a period when revolutionary ardour seemed largely to have been repressed, but in his non-conforming, often unruly conduct and in his sympathy for the cause of freedom and liberty, he maintains at an unpropitious time and in however ironized a form ideals championed by Byron and Shelley.

The motif of resurrection is potent in Beddoes. 'The buried, dead, and slain / Rise again' in a late lyric ('Song from the Waters') inserted into the much-revised and incrementally enlarging *Death's Jest-Book*. That claim and ambiguous hope make his work far other than the morbidly lugubrious curiosity it is sometimes represented as being. There is an evidently buoyant sense of hitting the target in Auden's witty clerihew, 'Thomas Lovell Beddoes / Could never walk through meadows / Without getting the glooms / And thinking of tombs'.[7] But 'Song from the Waters' bears witness to a dynamic energy that pushes its force through dimeters that are simultaneously post-mortal, almost brutally impersonal, and vibrant with life. The final stanza reveals the poem's pressure to make words the seeds of a form of future life:

> As wake the morning
>   Trumpets bright;
> As snowdrop, scorning
>   Winter's might,
> Rises warning
>   Like a sprite:
> The buried, dead, and slain
>   Rise again.

Those 'morning / Trumpets' seem more metaphorical than literal; possibly they refer to the trumpet-shapes of flowers. Certainly they recall Shelley's 'trumpet of a prophecy' (69) in 'Ode to the West Wind'. Because of the extreme compression of such effects, the 'sense of the piece', as Bradshaw notes, 'is at first confusing, hard to grasp'.[8] And not merely 'at first' since the syntactical pressure is great, setting emblematic 'snowdrop' (minus any article, as in some proto-Modernist impatience with such a thing) against 'Winter's might' and making 'The buried, dead, and slain' both different categories and, in Bradshaw's phrase, 'a pregnant synonymity' as 'the list works backwards'.[9] The final 'Rise again' rhymes ruefully with 'slain'; men are 'slain', die, and are buried, before, as in some natural cycle, they inevitably 'Rise again'. But if that cyclical process involves death, often of a violent kind, it also promises recurrence, even if that new vitality is often admonitory, spectral, a near-grotesque simulacrum of Romantic renewal.

Notes

1   Qtd from *Poems and Plays of Thomas Lovell Beddoes*, ed. with intro. H. W. Donner (London: Routledge, 1950), p. lxviii. This edition, which prints the 1829 version of *Death's Jest-Book*, is used for all quotations from Beddoes's poetry and letters.
2   Michael Bradshaw, *Resurrection Songs: The Poetry of Thomas Lovell Beddoes* (Aldershot: Ashgate, 2001), p. 117.
3   Ezra Pound, *The Cantos* (London: Faber, 1975).
4   Quoted in *Poems and Plays*, ed. Donner, p. lxxx.
5   Ute Berns, *Science, Politics, and Friendship in the Works of Thomas Lovell Beddoes* (Newark, DE: University of Delaware Press, 2011), p. 256.
6   Thomas, *Selected Poems*, ed. Tim Armstrong (London: Longman, 1993).
7   Qtd from *The Ashgate Research Companion to Thomas Lovell Beddoes*, ed. Ute Berns and Michael Bradshaw (Aldershot: Ashgate, 2007), p. xvi.
8   Bradshaw, *Resurrection Songs*, p. 123.
9   Bradshaw, *Resurrection Songs*, p. 123.

Part 5 **Further Reading**

General Critical Reading

M. H. Abrams, *The Mirror and the Lamp: Romantic Theory and the Critical Tradition* (Oxford: Oxford University Press, 1953).

M. H. Abrams, *Natural Supernaturalism: Tradition and Revolution in Romantic Literature* (New York: Norton, 1971).

M. H. Abrams, *The Correspondent Breeze: Essays on English Romanticism* (New York: Norton, 1984).

Andrew Bennett, *Romantic Poets and the Culture of Posterity*, Cambridge Studies in Romanticism 35 (Cambridge: Cambridge University Press, 1999).

Harold Bloom, *The Visionary Company*, enlarged edn (Ithaca, NY: Cornell University Press, 1971).

Marshall Brown, *Preromanticism* (Stanford, CA: Stanford University Press, 1991).

Marilyn Butler, *Romantics, Rebels, and Reactionaries: English Literature and its Background, 1760–1830* (Oxford: Oxford University Press, 1981).

Carmen Casaliggi and Porscha Fermanis, *Romanticism: A Literary and Cultural History* (London: Routledge, 2016).

James Chandler (ed.), *The Cambridge History of English Romantic Literature* (Cambridge: Cambridge University Press, 2009).

James Chandler and Maureen N. McLane (eds), *The Cambridge Companion to British Romantic Poetry* (Cambridge: Cambridge University Press, 2008).

Stuart Curran, *Poetic Form and British Romanticism* (Oxford: Oxford University Press, 1986).

Stuart Curran (ed.), *The Cambridge Companion to British Romanticism*, 2nd edn (Cambridge: Cambridge University Press, 2010).

David Duff, *Romanticism and the Uses of Genre* (Oxford: Oxford University Press, 2009).

Beth Lau (ed.), *Fellow Romantics: Male and Female British Writers, 1790–1835* (Aldershot: Ashgate, 2009).

The Romantic Poetry Handbook, First Edition. Michael O'Neill and Madeleine Callaghan.
© 2018 John Wiley & Sons Ltd. Published 2018 by John Wiley & Sons Ltd.

Jerome J. McGann, *The Romantic Ideology* (Chicago: University of Chicago Press, 1983).

Maureen N. McLane, *Balladeering, Minstrelsy, and the Making of British Romantic Poetry* (Cambridge: Cambridge University Press, 2008).

Charles Mahoney (ed.), *A Companion to Romantic Poetry* (Malden, MA: Wiley Blackwell, 2011).

Anne K. Mellor, *English Romantic Irony* (Cambridge, MA: Harvard University Press, 1980).

Lucy Newlyn, *'Paradise Lost' and the Romantic Reader* (Oxford: Clarendon Press, 1992).

Lucy Newlyn, *Reading, Writing, and Romanticism: The Anxiety of Reception* (Oxford: Oxford University Press, 2003).

Michael O'Neill, *Romanticism and the Self-Conscious Poem* (Oxford: Clarendon Press, 1997).

Michael O'Neill (ed.), *The Cambridge History of English Poetry* (Cambridge: Cambridge University Press, 2010).

Alan Rawes (ed.), *Romanticism and Form* (Basingstoke: Palgrave Macmillan, 2007).

Mark Sandy, *Romanticism, Memory and Mourning* (Farnham: Ashgate, 2013).

Jane Stabler, *Burke to Byron, Barbauld to Baillie, 1790–1830* (Basingstoke: Palgrave Macmillan, 2001).

J. R. Watson (ed.), *Pre-Romanticism in English Poetry of the Eighteenth Century: The Poetic Art and Significance of Thomson, Gray, Collins, Goldsmith, Cowper* (London: Macmillan, 1989).

Susan J. Wolfson, *Formal Charges: The Shaping of Poetry in British Romanticism* (Stanford, CA: Stanford University Press, 1997).

Jonathan and Jessica Wordsworth (eds.), *The Penguin Book of Romantic Poetry* (London: Penguin, 2001).

Duncan Wu (ed.), *Romanticism: An Anthology*, 4th edn (Malden, MA: Wiley Blackwell, 2012).

Duncan Wu, *30 Great Myths about the Romantics* (Malden, MA: Wiley Blackwell, 2015).

Anna Laetitia Barbauld (1743–1825)

Evan Gottlieb, 'Fighting Words: Representing the Napoleonic Wars in the Poetry of Hemans and Barbauld', *European Romantic Review* 20.3 (2009): 327–43.

Harriet Guest, *Small Change: Women, Learning, Patriotism, 1750–1810* (Chicago: University of Chicago Press, 2000).

William Keach, 'A Regency Prophecy and the End of Anna Barbauld's Career', *Studies in Romanticism* 33.4 (1994): 569–77.

Emma Major, 'Nature, Nation, and Denomination: Barbauld's Taste for the Public', *ELH* 74.4 (2007): 909–30.

Orianne Smith, *Romantic Women Writers, Revolution and Prophecy: Rebellious Daughters, 1786–1826* (Cambridge: Cambridge University Press, 2013).

Thomas Lovell Beddoes (1803–1849)

Ute Berns, *Science, Politics, and Friendship in the Work of Thomas Lovell Beddoes* (Newark, DE: University of Delaware Press, 2012).

Ute Berns and Michael Bradshaw (eds), *The Ashgate Research Companion to Thomas Lovell Beddoes* (Aldershot: Ashgate, 2007).

Michael Bradshaw, *Resurrection Songs: The Poetry of Thomas Lovell Beddoes* (Aldershot: Ashgate, 2001).

H. W. Donner, *Thomas Lovell Beddoes: The Making of a Poet* (Oxford: Blackwell, 1935).

Alan Halsey, *Homage to Homunculus Mandrake: A New Reading of Death's Jest-Book* (Belper: Thomas Lovell Beddoes Society, 1996).

Michael O'Neill, '"A storm of ghosts": Beddoes, Shelley, Death and Reputation', *Cambridge Quarterly* 28.2 (1999): 102–15.

Alan Richardson, 'Death's Jest-Book: "shadows of words"', in *A Mental Theater: Poetic Drama and Consciousness in the Romantic Age* (University Park, PA: Pennsylvania State University Press, 1988), pp. 154–73.

William Blake (1757–1827)

Hazard Adams, *William Blake: A Reading of the Shorter Poems* (Seattle: University of Washington Press, 1963).

G. E. Bentley, Jr, *The Stranger from Paradise: A Biography of William Blake* (New Haven, CT: Yale University Press, 2001).

V. A. De Luca, *Words of Eternity: Blake and the Poetics of the Sublime* (Princeton: Princeton University Press, 1991).

David Erdman, *Blake: Prophet against Empire*, 3rd edn (Princeton: Princeton University Press, 1977 [1954]).

David Fuller, *Blake's Heroic Argument* (London: Croom Helm, 1988).

Joseph Viscomi, *Blake and the Idea of the Book* (Princeton: Princeton University Press, 1993).

Robert Burns (1759–1796)

Alex Broadhead, *The Language of Robert Burns: Style, Ideology, and Identity* (Lewisburg, PA: Bucknell University Press, 2013).

Robert Crawford (ed.), *Robert Burns and Cultural Authority* (Edinburgh: Edinburgh University Press, 1997).

Robert Crawford, *The Bard: Robert Burns, A Biography* (Princeton: Princeton University Press, 2009).

Nigel Leask, *Robert Burns and Pastoral: Poetry and Improvement in Late Eighteenth-Century Scotland* (Oxford: Oxford University Press, 2010).

Carol McGuirk, *Robert Burns and the Sentimental Era* (Athens, GA: University of Georgia Press, 1985).

Murray Pittock, *Scottish and Irish Romanticism* (Oxford: Oxford University Press, 2008).

Lord George Gordon Byron (1788–1824)

Bernard Beatty and Vincent Newey (eds), *Byron and the Limits of Fiction* (Liverpool: Liverpool University Press, 1988).

Jerome Christensen, *Lord Byron's Strength: Romantic Writing and Commercial Society* (Baltimore: Johns Hopkins University Press, 1993).

Frederick Garber, *Self, Text, and Romantic Irony: The Example of Byron* (Princeton: Princeton University Press, 1988).

Robert Gleckner, *Byron and the Ruins of Paradise* (Baltimore: Johns Hopkins University Press, 1967).

Anthony Howe, *Byron and the Forms of Thought* (Liverpool: Liverpool University Press, 2013).

Jerome J. McGann, *Don Juan in Context* (London: John Murray, 1976).

Alan Rawes, *Byron's Poetic Experimentation: Childe Harold, the Tales, and the Quest for Comedy* (Aldershot: Ashgate, 2000).

Jane Stabler, *Byron, Poetics and History* (Cambridge: Cambridge University Press, 2003).

Sarah Wootton, *Byronic Heroes in Nineteenth-Century Women's Writing and Screen Adaptation* (Basingstoke: Palgrave Macmillan, 2016).

John Clare (1793–1864)

Timothy Brownlow, *John Clare and Picturesque Landscape* (Oxford: Clarendon Press, 1983).

Paul Chirico, *John Clare and the Imagination of the Reader* (New York: Palgrave Macmillan, 2007).

Johanne Clare, *John Clare and the Bounds of Circumstance* (Kingston: McGill-Queen's University Press, 1987).

Mina Gorji, *John Clare and the Place of Poetry* (Liverpool: Liverpool University Press, 2008).

Hugh Haughton, Adam Phillips, and Geoffrey Summerfield (eds), *John Clare in Context* (Cambridge: Cambridge University Press, 1994).

Stephanie Kuduk Weiner, *Clare's Lyric: John Clare and Three Modern Poets* (Oxford: Oxford University Press, 2014).

Samuel Taylor Coleridge (1772–1834)

John Beer, *Coleridge's Poetical Intelligence* (London: Macmillan, 1977).

Frederick Burwick (ed.), *The Oxford Handbook of Samuel Taylor Coleridge* (Oxford: Oxford University Press, 2009).

Paul Hamilton, *Coleridge's Poetics* (Oxford: Basil Blackwell, 1983).

Humphry House, *Coleridge* (London: Hart-Davis, 1953).

Nigel Leask, *The Politics of Imagination in Coleridge's Critical Thought* (New York: St Martin's Press, 1988).

Morton Paley, *Coleridge's Later Poetry* (Oxford: Clarendon Press, 1996).

Seamus Perry, *Coleridge and the Uses of Division* (Oxford: Clarendon Press, 1999).

Max F Schulz., *The Poetic Voices of Coleridge* (Detroit: University of Illinois Press, 1963).

Felicia Hemans (1793–1835)

Norma Clarke, *Ambitious Heights: Writing, Friendship, Love – The Jewsbury Sisters, Felicia Hemans, and Jane Welsh Carlyle* (London: Routledge, 1990).

Paula R. Feldman, 'The Poet and the Profits: Felicia Hemans and the Literary Marketplace', *Keats-Shelley Journal* 46 (1997): 148–76.

Angela Leighton, *Victorian Women Poets: Writing Against the Heart* (Hemel Hempstead: Harvester Wheatsheaf, 1992).

Nanora Sweet and Julie Melnyk (eds), *Felicia Hemans: Reimagining Poetry in the Nineteenth Century*, foreword by Marlon B. Ross (Houndmills: Palgrave, 2001).

Susan J. Wolfson (ed.), *Felicia Hemans: Selected Poems, Letters, Reception Materials* (Princeton: Princeton University Press, 2000).

(James Henry) Leigh Hunt (1784–1859)

Michael Eberle-Sinatra, *Leigh Hunt and the London Literary Scene: A Reception History of his Major Works, 1805–1828* (New York: Routledge, 2005).

Rodney Stenning Edgecombe, *Leigh Hunt and the Poetry of Fancy* (London: Associated University Presses, 1994).

Theodore Fenner, *Leigh Hunt and Opera Criticism: The 'Examiner' Years, 1808–1821* (Lawrence: University Press of Kansas, 1972).

Nicholas Roe (ed.), *Leigh Hunt: Life, Poetics, Politics* (London: Routledge, 2003).

Nicholas Roe, *Fiery Heart: The First Life of Leigh Hunt* (London: Pimlico, 2005).

John Keats (1795–1821)

W. J. Bate, *John Keats* (Cambridge, MA: Harvard University Press, 1963).

Thomas McFarland, *The Masks of Keats: The Endeavour of a Poet* (Oxford: Oxford University Press, 2000).

Michael O'Neill (ed.), *John Keats in Context* (Cambridge: Cambridge University Press, 2017).

Christopher Ricks, *Keats and Embarrassment* (Oxford: Clarendon Press, 1974).

Nicholas Roe, *John Keats and the Culture of Dissent* (Oxford: Clarendon Press, 1997).

Stuart Sperry, *Keats the Poet* (Princeton: Princeton University Press, 1973).

Helen Vendler, *The Odes of John Keats* (Cambridge, MA: Belknap Press of Harvard University Press, 1983).

Susan J. Wolfson, *Reading John Keats* (Cambridge: Cambridge University Press, 2015).

Letitia Elizabeth Landon (1802–1838)

Angela Leighton, *Victorian Women Poets: Writing Against the Heart* (Hemel Hempstead: Harvester Wheatsheaf, 1992).

Jerome McGann, *The Poetics of Sensibility: A Revolution in Literary Style* (Oxford: Clarendon Press, 1996).

Anne K. Mellor, 'The Female Poet and the Poetess: Two Traditions of British Women's Poetry, 1780–1830', *Studies in Romanticism* 36.2 (1997): 261–76.

Daniel Riess, 'Laetitia Landon and the Dawn of English Post-Romanticism', *Studies in English Literature, 1500–1900* 36.4 (1996): 807–27.

Glennis Stephenson, 'Letitia Landon and the Victorian Improvisatrice: The Construction of L.E.L.', *Victorian Poetry* 30.1 (1992): 1–17.

Thomas Moore (1779–1852)

Ronan Kelly, *Bard of Erin: The Life of Thomas Moore* (London: Penguin, 2009).

Alison Morgan, '"Let no man write my epitaph": The Contributions of Percy Shelley, Thomas Moore and Robert Southey to the Memorialisation of Robert Emmet', *Irish Studies Review* 22.3 (2014): 285–303.

Jeffery W. Vail, *The Literary Relationship of Lord Byron and Thomas Moore* (Baltimore: Johns Hopkins University Press, 2001).

Robert Welch, *Irish Poetry from Moore to Yeats* (Gerrards Cross: Smythe, 1980).

Harry White, *Music and the Irish Literary Imagination* (Oxford: Oxford University Press, 2008).

Mary Robinson (1758–1800)

Paula Byrne, *Perdita: The Life of Mary Robinson* (London: HarperCollins, 2004).

Elizabeth Eger, 'Spectacle, Intellect and Authority: The Actress in the Eighteenth Century', in *The Cambridge Companion to the Actress*, ed. Maggie B. Gale and John Stokes (Cambridge: Cambridge University Press, 2007), pp. 33–51.

Amy Garnai, *Revolutionary Imaginings in the 1790s: Charlotte Smith, Mary Robinson, Elizabeth Inchbald* (New York: Palgrave Macmillan, 2009).

Judith Pascoe, *Romantic Theatricality: Gender, Poetry, and Spectatorship* (Ithaca, NY: Cornell University Press, 1997).

Judith Pascoe, '"Unsex'd Females": Barbauld, Robinson, and Smith', in *The Cambridge Companion to English Literature 1740–1830*, ed. Thomas Keymer and Jon Mee (Cambridge: Cambridge University Press, 2007), pp. 210–26.

Percy Bysshe Shelley (1792–1822)

Harold Bloom, *Shelley's Mythmaking* (New Haven, CT: Yale University Press, 1959).

Madeleine Callaghan, *Shelley's Living Artistry: Letters, Poems, Plays* (Liverpool: Liverpool University Press, 2017).

Jerrold E. Hogle, *Shelley's Process: Radical Transference and the Development of His Major Works* (Oxford: Oxford University Press, 1988).

William Keach, *Shelley's Style* (London: Methuen, 1984).

Michael O'Neill, *The Human Mind's Imaginings: Conflict and Achievement in Shelley's Poetry* (Oxford: Clarendon Press, 1989).

Michael O'Neill and Anthony Howe (eds), with the assistance of Madeleine Callaghan, *The Oxford Handbook of Percy Bysshe Shelley* (Oxford: Oxford University Press, 2013).

Hugh Roberts, *Shelley and the Chaos of History: A New Politics of Poetry* (University Park, PA: Pennsylvania State University Press, 1997).

Ross Wilson, *Shelley and the Apprehension of Life* (Cambridge: Cambridge University Press, 2013).

Charlotte Smith (1749–1806)

Stuart Curran, 'The "I" Altered', in *Romanticism and Feminism*, ed. Anne K. Mellor (Bloomington: Indiana University Press, 1988), pp. 185–207.

Loraine Fletcher, *Charlotte Smith: A Critical Biography* (Basingstoke: Macmillan, 1998).

Amy Garnai, *Revolutionary Imaginings in the 1790s: Charlotte Smith, Mary Robinson, Elizabeth Inchbald* (New York: Palgrave Macmillan, 2009).

Diane Long Hoeveler, *Gothic Feminism: The Professionalization of Gender from Charlotte Smith to the Brontës* (Liverpool: Liverpool University Press, 1998).

Jacqueline M. Labbe, *Charlotte Smith: Romanticism, Poetry and the Culture of Gender* (Manchester: Manchester University Press, 2003).

Robert Southey (1774–1843)

Carol Bolton, *Writing the Empire: Robert Southey and Romantic Colonialism* (London: Pickering & Chatto, 2007).

Geoffrey Carnall, *Robert Southey and his Age: The Development of a Conservative Mind* (Oxford: Clarendon Press, 1960).

David M. Craig, *Robert Southey and Romantic Apostasy: Political Argument in Britain, 1780–1840* (Woodbridge: Boydell, 2007).

Lynda Pratt (ed.), *Robert Southey and the Contexts of English Romanticism* (Aldershot: Ashgate, 2006).

Christopher J. P. Smith, *A Quest for Home: Reading Robert Southey* (Liverpool: Liverpool University Press, 1997).

William Wordsworth (1770–1850)

James Averill, *Wordsworth and the Poetry of Human Suffering* (Ithaca, NY: Cornell University Press, 1980).

Jonathan Bate, *Romantic Ecology: Wordsworth and the Environmental Tradition* (London: Routledge, 1991).

James K. Chandler, *Wordsworth's Second Nature: A Study of the Poetry and the Politics* (Chicago: University of Chicago Press, 1984).

Stephen Gill, *Wordsworth's Revisitings* (Oxford: Oxford University Press, 2011).

Richard Gravil and Daniel Robinson (eds), *The Oxford Handbook of William Wordsworth* (Oxford: Oxford University Press, 2015).

Geoffrey H. Hartman, *Wordsworth's Poetry 1787–1814* (New Haven, CT: Yale University Press, 1971).

Mary Jacobus, *Tradition and Experiment in Wordsworth's 'Lyrical Ballads'* (Oxford: Clarendon Press, 1976).

Nicholas Roe, *Wordsworth and Coleridge: The Radical Years* (Oxford: Clarendon Press, 1988).

Jonathan Wordsworth, *The Music of Humanity* (London: Nelson, 1969).

Jonathan Wordsworth, *The Borders of Vision* (Oxford: Clarendon Press, 1982).

Ann Yearsley (1753–1806)

Kerri Andrews, *Ann Yearsley and Hannah More: Poetry and Patronage* (London: Pickering & Chatto, 2013).

Moira Ferguson, 'Resistance and Power in the Life and Writings of Ann Yearsley', *The Eighteenth Century* 27.3 (1986): 247–68.

Moira Ferguson, *Subject to Others: British Women Writers and Colonial Slavery, 1670–1834* (London: Routledge, 1992).

Dustin Griffin, *Patriotism and Poetry in Eighteenth-Century Britain* (Cambridge: Cambridge University Press, 2002).

Claire Knowles, 'Ann Yearsley, Biography and the "Pow'rs Of Sensibility Untaught!"', *Women's Writing* 17.1 (2010): 166–84.

Index

Abrams, M.H., 7, 179, 180
Ackroyd, Peter, 56
Addison, Joseph, 50
Aeschylus, 11, 260
   Prometheus Bound, 11, 260
Aikin, Charles Rochemont, 49
Aikin, John, 49
Aikin, Lucy, 50
Akenside, Mark, 50
Alighieri, Dante, 11, 127, 139, 212, 214,
   240, 265, 273
   Inferno, 212, 236
Allott, Miriam, 289
Andrews, Kerri, 94, 110
Ariosto, Ludovico, 87, 141
Armour, Jean, 57, 58
Artis, E.T., 62
Auden, W.H., 16
   'Letter to Lord Byron,' 167, 233
Austen, Jane
   Sense and Sensibility, 313

Bainbridge, Simon, 8
Barbauld, Anna Laetitia, 8, 9, 14, 15, 49, 50,
   97–100
   Eighteen Hundred and Eleven, A Poem,
     50, 97, 98, 99
   'Epistle to William Wilberforce, Esq.,
     on the Rejection of the Bill for
     Abolishing the Slave Trade,' 49,
     97, 98
   Hymns in Prose for Children, 49
   Lessons for Children, 49

'The Rights of Woman,' 97, 98
   Washing-Day, 98
Barbauld, Rochemont, Reverend, 49
Barnard, John, 272, 281
Basire, James, 54
Bate, Jonathan, 62
Bate, Walter Jackson, 65, 292
Bayley, John, 271
Beaton, Roderick, 60
Beatty, Bernard, 215
Beddoes, Thomas Lovell, 8, 15, 16, 51–53,
   318–324
   Death's Jest-Book, or, The Fool's Tragedy,
     52, 318, 319, 321–323
   'Dream-Pedlary,' 318
   'Lines Written in a Blank Leaf of the
     Prometheus Unbound,' 321
   Love's Arrow Poisoned, 51
   'Song from the Waters,' 323
   The Brides' Tragedy, 51
   'The Comet,' 51
   *The Improvisatore, in Three Fyttes, with
     other Poems*, 51
   The Last Man, 51
   The Second Brother, 51
   Torrismond, 51
Beer, John, 65
Behn, Aphra
   Oroonoko, 111
Behrendt, Stephen C., 116
Berns, Ute, 320
Berlin, Isaiah, 8
Berlioz, Hector, 209

The Romantic Poetry Handbook, First Edition. Michael O'Neill and Madeleine Callaghan.
© 2018 John Wiley & Sons Ltd. Published 2018 by John Wiley & Sons Ltd.

Bieri, James, 83, 84
Blackwood, 52, 72
  Edinburgh Magazine, 70
Blake, Robert, 54
Blake, William, 5, 6, 8, 11, 12, 14, 16, 49,
    54–56, 115–123, 124–131, 137,
    174, 261
  'A Poison Tree,' 118
  'A Song of Liberty,' 124, 128
  America a Prophecy, 55
  An Island in the Moon, 115, 119
  'Auguries of Innocence,' 55
  'Christian forbearance,' 96
  Early Illuminated Books, 127
  'Earth's Answer,' 117
  Europe, 55
  'Holy Thursday,' 115, 119
  'Introduction' to *Songs of Experience*,
    116, 117, 118
  'Introduction' to *Songs of Innocence*, 121
  'London,' 12, 121, 129
  Jerusalem, 55, 129, 130
  Milton, 55, 126, 129
  'My Pretty Rose Tree,' 118
  Poetical Sketches, 54
  'Shewing the Two Contrary States of the
    Human Soul,' 118
  Songs of Experience, 115, 116, 119,
    120, 121
  Songs of Innocence, 5, 49, 55, 115, 116,
    119, 120, 121
  Songs of Innocence and of Experience, 11,
    55, 115, 118
  The Book of Thel, 55
  The Book of Urizen, 124, 126, 128,
    129, 130
  'The Chimney Sweeper,' 12, 120
  'The Clod & the Pebble,' 118
  'The Echoing Green,' 121
  'The Little Girl Lost,' 116
  'The Little Girl Found,' 116
  The Marriage of Heaven and Hell, 11, 55,
    124–128, 130
  'The Mental Traveller,' 55, 124,
    129, 130
  'The School Boy,' 116
  'The Tyger,' 116
  'The Voice of the Ancient Bard,' 116
  Vala, or, The Four Zoas, 55, 129, 174
  Visions of the Daughters of Albion, 55
Bloom, Harold, 6, 16, 116, 121, 126, 256,
    257, 262, 302
Bostetter, Edward E., 188, 280

Boucher, Catherine, 54
Bourne, J.G.H., 52
Bowles, Caroline Anne, 88
Boydell, John, 54
Boydell, Josiah, 54
Bradley, Arthur, 263
Bradshaw, Michael, 52, 318, 323
Bradshaw, Penny, 98
Brawne, Fanny, 73
Brisman, Leslie, 215
Bristol Gazette, The, 111
British Critic, The, 204
Brock, Claire, 81
Brontë, Emily, 209
Brougham, Henry, 69
Brown, Charles, 286
Browne, George, 66
Browne, Henry, 66
Browning, Robert, 6, 7
  'Childe Roland to the Dark Tower
    Came,' 7
Bulwer-Lytton, Edward, 75
Burke, Edmund, 7, 132, 163
Burnes, William, 57
Burns, Robert, 6, 8, 12, 14, 15, 57–58,
    137–143, 153
  'Address to the Deil,' 140
  Letters Addressed to Clarinda, 58
  'Man Was Made to Mourn. A Dirge,' 137
  Poems, Chiefly in the Scottish Dialect, 5,
    57, 137
  'Tam o' Shanter,' 139
  The Jolly Beggars, 58
  *The merry muses of Caledonia: a
    collection of favourite Scots songs,
    ancient and modern, selected for use
    of the Crochallan Fencibles*, 58
  'The Vision, Duan Second,' 140
  'To a Mountain Daisy, On Turning One
    Down, with the Plough, in April—
    1786,' 141
  'To a Mouse, on Turning Her Up in Her
    Nest with the Plough, November,
    1783,' 142
Burton, Robert, 284
  Anatomy of Melancholy, 284
Byrne, Paula, 81
Byron, Ada, 60
Byron, Allegra, 60
Byron, Catherine, 59
Byron, George Gordon, Lord, 4, 7, 8, 9, 14,
    15, 16, 51, 57–60, 62, 65–67, 70, 74,
    77, 78, 83, 85, 88, 101, 139, 148,

174, 191, 198, 205, 206, 208, 211,
    215–222, 223–231, 232–241, 257,
    258, 263, 264, 270, 272, 305, 308,
    309, 312, 313, 315, 323
Beppo, 60, 234
Childe Harold's Pilgrimage, A Romaunt,
    8, 14, 59, 148, 222, 223–231, 237,
    308, 315
'Darkness,' 51
Don Juan, 7, 14, 60, 83, 88, 139, 229,
    (Cantos, 1-4), 232–241, 270, 305
English Bards and Scotch Reviewers, 59,
    77, 101
Fugitive Pieces, 59
Hours of Idleness, 59
Lara, 7, 9, 16, 215–218, 313
Letters and Journals (BLJ), 17n, 222n,
    241n, 276n
Manfred, 16, 215, 219–222
Marino Faliero, 60
'Stanzas to Augusta' ('Epistle to Augusta'),
    215, 219
The Corsair, 215
The Giaour, 217, 313
The Liberal, 70, 83
The Two Foscari, 60
The Vision of Judgement, 88
'Turkish Tales,' 59, 215
'When We Two Parted,' 215, 218–219
Byron, Glennis, 75
Byron, John, 59

Cameron, Kenneth Neill, 243
Carbonari, Neapolitan, 60
Carnall, Geoffrey, 79, 89
Casaliggi, Carmen, 209n
Cavendish, Georgiana, 80
Chapman, Alison, 76, 273, 274, 308
Chatterton, Thomas, 138, 153
'An Excelente Balade of Charitie,' 153
Chaucer, Geoffrey
    Troilus and Criseyde, 153
Chernaik, Judith, 245, 251
Chorley, H.F., 68
Clairmont, Claire, 60, 82, 83, 252
Clampitt, Amy, 284
Clare, Ann, 61
Clare, John, 6, 8, 15, 16, 61–62,
    297–303
'An Invite to Eternity,' 302
'[O could I be as I have been],' 299
*Poems Descriptive of Rural Life and
    Scenery*, 61

'The Flitting,' 299
'The Nightingales Nest,' 297
The Rural Muse, 62
The Shepherd's Calendar, 62
The Village Minstrel, 61
'The Yellowhammer,' 298
'The Yellowhammers Nest,' 297
Clare, Parker, 61
Clarke, Charles Cowden, 72
Clarke, Norma, 304, 305
Clarkson, Oliver, 156
Coleridge, Berkeley, 64
Coleridge, E.H., 232
Coleridge, George, 63
Coleridge, Hartley, 183
Coleridge, John, Reverend, 63
Coleridge, Samuel Taylor, 3, 5, 6, 8–10,
    12–16, 61, 63–65, 69, 81, 87, 88, 91,
    92, 97, 134, 137, 139, 144–151, 152,
    154, 158, 163, 164, 168, 179–186,
    187–195, 196, 197, 234, 235, 237,
    244, 270, 301, 302
Aids to Reflection, 65
Biographia Literaria, 3, 65, 187, 301
Christabel, 64, 134, 187, 189, 191–194
'Dejection: An Ode,' 13, 152, 179,
    183–185, 237
'Effusion XXXV,' 180
'Frost at Midnight,' 13, 147, 179,
    182–183
Kubla Khan, 5, 12, 64, 134, 168, 187,
    188–191, 194
Lyrical Ballads, 5, 10, 16, 64, 91,
    144–151, 187, 191, 196
'Preface to *Christabel*,' 191
Religious Musings, 15
Remorse, 65
Sibylline Leaves, 180
'The Eolian Harp' (see 'Effusion XXXV'
    above), 179, 180–181, 185
The Friend, 64, 181
'The Nightingale, a Conversational Poem'
    ('The Nightingale, written in April,
    1798'), 147
'The Pains of Sleep,' 187, 189–191
The Rime of the Ancient Mariner, 64, 145,
    187–188, 191
The Watchman, 64
'This Lime-Tree Bower My Prison,' 168,
    179, 181–182
'To William Wordsworth,' 184
Coleridge, Sara, 144
Collins, William, 13, 50

Comberbache, Silas Tomkyn, 63
Condorcet, Marquis de, 244
Cottle, Joseph, 88
Cowper, William, 13, 104, 179, 182
    The Task, 13, 182
Crabbe, George, 9, 10
    Peter Grimes, 9
Crawford, Robert, 58
Critical Review, The, 135, 144
Crocco, Francesco, 99
Croker, John Wilson, 99, 268
Cronin, Richard, 251
Curran, Stuart, 4, 85, 86, 101, 272, 304

Dacre, Tom, 12, 120
Dallas, R.C., 223
Darby, John, 80
Darley, George, 51, 52
Davie, Donald
    'Remembering the 'Thirties,' 13
Darwin, Erasmus
    The Botanic Garden, 55
Deane, Seamus, 205, 206
De Balboa, Vasco Nuñez, 274
De Beaupuy, Michel, Captain, 91
De Man, Paul, 265
De Quincey, Thomas, 167
Degen, Konrad, 52
Drury, Edward, 61
Dryden, John, 9, 11, 228, 270, 285

Edgeworth, Anna, 51
Edgeworth, Maria, 51
Edinburgh Review, the, 59
Edleston, John, 223
Eliot, T.S., 6, 115, 260, 280
Emmet, Robert, 77, 206
Empson, William, 169, 188
Enfield, William, 49
Erdman, David V., 115, 116, 119, 120
Essick, Robert N., 56
European Magazine, 90
Evans, Mary, 63
Everest, Kelvin, 73, 264

Fraistat, Neil, 243, 245
Feldman, Paula, 311
Ferguson, Adam, 58
Ferguson, Moira, 94, 113
Fletcher, Loraine, 86
Forster, John, 75
Fox, Charles James, 81, 150
Franklin, Caroline, 50

Frend, William, 63
Fricker, Edith, 63, 87
Fricker, Sara, 63, 87, 180
Frye, Northrop, 119
Fulford, Tim, 198

Garber, Frederick, 221
Garrick, David, 80
Gibbon, Edward
    *Decline and Fall of the Roman
        Empire*, 230
Gill, Stephen, 92
Gillman, James, 65
Gleckner, Robert, 117
Godwin, Fanny, 83
Godwin, Mary (Shelley, Mary), 82, 83, 246
Godwin, William, 82, 91, 163, 243, 244
    Political Justice, 244
Goldsmith, Oliver
    The Deserted Village, 148
Goethe, Johann Wolfgang von, 265
Gorji, Mina, 297
Gray, Thomas, 13
    'Elegy Written in a Country
        Churchyard,' 142
Griffin, Andrew, 146
Griffin, Dustin, 110
Guiccioli, Teresa, 60

Hallam, Arthur, 15
Halsey, Alan, 52
Hardy, Thomas
    'Tenebris II,' 130
    'The Oxen,' 320
Hartman, Geoffrey, 253
Hastings, Francis Rawdon, 77
Haughton, Hugh, 297
Haydon, Benjamin Robert, 70, 72
Hayley, William, 55, 103, 104
Hazlitt, William, 7, 10, 57, 61, 64, 70,
        115, 174, 187, 205, 233, 238,
        251, 285
    'On Poetry in General,' 285
Hegel, Georg Wilhelm Friedrich, 125
Hemans, Alfred, Captain, 66
Hemans, Felicia, 7, 8, 12, 15, 16, 66–68, 74,
        304–310, 311, 312
    'Corinne at the Capitol,' 67
    'Costanza,' 308
    *England and Spain; or, Valour and
        Patriotism*, 66
    'Gertrude, or Fidelity till Death,' 307
    'Joan of Arc, In Rheims,' 304, 308

'Juana,' 308
'Imelda,' 307
'Indian Woman's Death Song,' 307
'Madeline, A Domestic Tale,' 309
Modern Greece, 66, 305
Poems, 66
'Properzia Rossi,' 305–307
Records of Woman: With Other Poems, 7,
    12, 16, 67, 304–310
'Sicilian Captive,' 308
Songs of the Affections, with Other
    Poems, 67
'The American Forest Girl,' 304, 308
The Domestic Affections &c, 66
The Forest Sanctuary &c, 67
'The Lost Pleiad,' 67, 309
The Restoration of the Works of Art to
    Italy, 66
The Siege of Valencia, 67
Henderson, J., 62
Hervey, Frederick Augustus, 94
Hessey, James, 61, 72
Hogarth, William, 54
Hogg, Thomas Jefferson, 82
Holbach, Baron, 244
Holmes, Richard, 65, 179
Home, John, 58
Homer, 11, 273, 274, 275, 308
House, Humphry, 181
Hume, David, 5
Hunt, Isaac, 69
Hunt, John, 69, 232
Hunt, Leigh (James Henry), 8, 9, 15, 69–71,
    72, 83, 211–214, 232, 242, 251, 255,
    264, 268, 269, 270
    Critical Essays on the Performers of the
        London Theatres, 69
    Foliage, 70
    Imagination and Fancy, 70
    Juvenilia, 69
    Literary Pocket-Book, or, Companion
        for the Lover of Nature and
        Art, 70
    Lord Byron and some of his
        Contemporaries, 70
    Poetical Works, 70
    Preface to *The Story of Rimini*, 212
    'Round Table,' 70
    The Descent of Liberty, 70
    The Examiner, 69, 70, 242, 251
    The Liberal, 70, 83
    The Story of Rimini, 9, 70, 211–214
Hunt, Marianne, 69

Hutchinson, Mary, 64, 91
Hutchinson, Sara, 64, 183

Jefferson, Thomas, 7
Jeffrey, Francis, 77, 92
Jerdan, William, 74, 75
Johns-Putra, Adeline, 98
Johnson, James, 58
Jones, Robert, 90
Jost, François, 255
Joyce, James
    A Portrait of the Artist as a Young Man, 77
Joyce, Mary, 61

Keach, William, 253, 257
Kean, Edmund, 284
Keats, Georgiana (Augusta Wylie), 73
Keats, George, 73
Keats, John, 5, 8, 9, 12–16, 70, 72–73, 83,
    99, 133, 139, 174, 176, 192, 197,
    214, 229, 249, 260, 263, 264,
    268–276, 277–283, 284–293, 306,
    309, 311, 315
    Endymion, 5, 9, 72, 99, 268–276
    Hyperion, 8, 73, 197, 274, 277–283,
        287, 288
    Isabella, 73
    'La Belle Dame Sans Merci,' 192
    Lamia, 9, 13, 73, 284–286
    'Ode on a Grecian Urn,' 176, 289, 291
    'Ode on Melancholy,' 291, 292
    'Ode to a Nightingale,' 12, 14, 16, 249,
        289, 290
    'Ode to Psyche,' 288
    'On Visiting the Tomb of Burns,' 139
    Poems (1817), 72
    'Sleep and Poetry,' 268–272
    The, 1820 Volume (*Lamia, Isabella, The*
        Eve of St. Agnes, and Other Poems),
        16, 284–293
    The Eve of St. Agnes, 73, 284, 286
    The Eve of St. Mark, 73
    The Fall of Hyperion, 277–283, 288, 315
    'To Autumn,' 290, 291
Keats, Tom, 277
Kelly, Ronan, 79, 207
Kelsall, T.F., 51, 52
Knowles, Claire, 112

La Cassagnère, Christian, 13
Labbe, Jacqueline, 101, 108
Lamb, Caroline, Lady, 218
Lamb, Charles, 61, 63, 69, 181, 182

Lamb, Mary, 181
Landon, Catherine Jane, 74
Landon, John, 74
Landon, Letitia Elizabeth, 8, 12, 14–16,
    74–76, 311–317
  'A Child Screening a Dove from a Hawk.
    By Stewardson,' 316
  Ethel Churchill, 75
  Francesca Carrera, 75
  'Lines of Life,' 12, 14, 311, 314–315
  'Lines Written under a Picture of a Girl
    Burning a Love-Letter,' 311, 315–316
  'Love's Last Lesson,' 311–314
  Romance and Reality, 75, 311
  'Sappho's Song,' 311, 316–317
  The Easter Gift, 75
  *The Fate of Adelaide: a Swiss Tale
    of Romance; and other Poems*,
    74, 311
  The Golden Violet, 75, 311
  The Improvisatrice, and other Poems, 74,
    311, 316
  The Troubadour, 75, 311
  The Venetian Bracelet, 75, 311
  The Vow of the Peacock, 75
Landor, Walter Savage, 88
Leader, Zachary, 84
Leask, Nigel, 216, 218
Leavis, F.R., 169, 287, 289
Leigh, Augusta (Byron's half-sister), 60
Leighton, Angela, 306, 316
Levine, Alice, 224
Levy, Martin J., 81
Linnell, John, 55
Literary Gazette, The, 74, 311
Lockhart, John Gibson, 70, 268
Lorington, Merinah, 80
Louis XVI, 91
Lucretius, 243

MacCarthy, Fiona, 60
Mackay, James A., 58
Macpherson, Hugh, 208
Maginn, William, 75
Mahoney, Charles, 191, 234
Major, Emma, 97
Manini, Luca, 102
Manning, Peter, 222
Marchand, Leslie A., 60
McCarthy, William, 50
McGann, Jerome J., 3, 13, 60, 132, 149, 217,
    218, 220, 224, 312, 313

McLean, George, Captain, 75
Mellor, Anne K., 112
Merry, Robert, 81
Metastasio, Pietro, 101, 104
Milbanke, Annabella, 59
Milton, John, 11, 13, 54, 97, 99, 101,
    102, 104, 105, 117, 124, 126–129,
    132, 140, 141, 147, 162, 164,
    166, 172, 174, 184, 191, 218,
    221, 222, 260, 265, 270, 273,
    279, 281, 282, 287
  'Methought I saw my late espoused
    saint,' 162
  Paradise Lost, 128, 140, 141, 164, 166,
    190, 191, 273, 277–279, 281, 298
  Samson Agonistes, 184
Mitford, Mary Russell, 305
Montagu, Elizabeth, 64, 110
Moore, Barbara, 78
Moore, Jane, 205, 206
Moore, Thomas, 8, 15, 16, 77–79,
    205–210, 264
  Epistles, Odes, and other Poems, 77
  'Erin! The Tear and the Smile in Thine
    Eyes,' 208
  Fables for the Holy Alliance, 78
  History of Ireland, 78
  *Intercepted Letters, or, The Twopenny
    Post-Bag*, 78
  Irish Melodies, 16, 77, 205–210
  Lalla Rookh, 78
  Memoirs of Captain Rock, 78
  *Memoirs of the Life of the Right
    Honourable Richard Brinsley
    Sheridan*, 78
  M.P., or The Blue-Stocking, 78
  Fables for the Holy Alliance, 78
  Odes of Anacreon, 205
  *Poetical Works of the Late Thomas
    Little*, 77
  The Fudge Family in Paris, 78
  *The Life and Death of Lord Edward
    Fitzgerald*, 78
  The Spirit of the Age, 205
  *Travels of an Irish Gentleman in Search
    of Religion*, 78
More, Hannah, 93, 94, 110, 111
Morning Chronicle, The, 69
Morning Post, The, 51, 64
Motion, Andrew, 73
Murray, John, 60, 66, 78, 137, 191,
    223, 232

Nagle, Christopher, 316, 317
Napoleon (Bonaparte), 8, 61, 69, 99, 107, 200, 223, 228
Newey, Vincent, 280
Newton, Isaac, 285
Nurmi, Martin K., 125

Oldfield, J.R., 111
Ollier, C. and J., 72, 247
O'Neill, Michael, 191, 263, 309

Paine, Thomas, 7
Paton, Elizabeth, 57
Paley, Morton D., 130
Palmer, Samuel, 118
Perry, Seamus, 6, 194
Petrarch, Francesco, 101–104, 132, 161, 265, 274, 289
Pindar, 158
Pinney, Azariah, 91
Pinney, John, 91
Pittock, Murray, 137
Plato, 5, 157
Poe, Edgar Allan, 312
Pope, Alexander, 9, 11, 98, 102, 135, 200, 211, 213, 224, 228, 234, 235, 270, 313
    'Eloisa to Abelard,' 102
    Essay on Criticism, 270
    Sappho to Phaon, 135
Pound, Ezra, 319
Priestley, Joseph, 49, 63
Procter, Bryan Waller, 51, 52
Punter, David, 56

Quarterly Review, The, 72, 88, 268

Raine, Kathleen, 56
Rajan, Tilottama, 251
Rawlings, Frances, 72
Rees, Shelley S., 53
Reich, Bernhard, 319
Reiman, Donald, 243
Reynolds, J.H., 72
Ricks, Christopher, 271
Riess, Daniel, 312
Ritson, Joseph, 244
Roberts, Hale, 148
Roberts, Hugh, 265
Robinson, Daniel, 132
Robinson, Eric H., 62

Robinson, Mary, 8, 14, 15, 80–81, 132–136
    Captivity: A Poem, 80
    History of the Campaigns of, 1780 and, 1781 in the Southern Provinces of North America, 81
    Lyrical Tales, 81
    Poems (1775), 80
    Sappho and Phaon: In a Series of Legitimate Sonnets, 132–136
        Sonnet VI, 134
        Sonnet XI, 134
        Sonnet XXIV, 132
        Sonnet XXVII, 133
        Sonnet XXXV, 135
        Sonnets XLI to XLIII, 133
    The World, 81
    'To the Poet Coleridge,' 134
Robinson, Mary Elizabeth, 80
Robinson, Thomas, 80
Rodgers, Betsy, 50
Roe, Nicholas, 69, 71, 73
Rose, Sarah, 85
Rousseau, Jean-Jacques, 7, 228, 229, 265, 266
    Julie, 212
Rowe, Elizabeth Singer, 97
Ryan, Alan, 7

Sandy, Mark, 301
Sayers, Frank, 198
    Poems, Containing Sketches of Northern Mythology, 198
Schulz, Max F., 181, 183
Scolfield, John, 55
Scott, Grant F., 306
Scott, Walter, 8, 58, 137
    Marmion, 8
    The Lady of the Lake, 8
Severn, Joseph, 73
Shakespeare, William, 80, 103, 104, 193, 243, 274, 289
    King Lear, 273, 274
    Romeo and Juliet, 80
    Measure for Measure, 243
Shaw, George Bernard, 242
Shears, Jonathon, 282
Shelley, Charles, 83
Shelley, Clara, 83
Shelley, Harriet, 83, 242
Shelley, Ianthe, 82, 83
Shelley (Godwin), Mary, 60, 70, 83, 252
    Frankenstein, 83

Shelley, Percy Bysshe, 4, 5, 7, 8, 10–12,
	14–16, 51, 60, 67, 70, 72, 73, 82–84,
	87, 88, 108, 127, 134, 138, 139, 148,
	157, 165, 174, 175, 189, 192,
	196–198, 200, 206, 208, 209, 212,
	223, 225, 228, 229, 235, 239,
	242–250, 251–259, 260–267,
	270–272, 281, 282, 304–306, 308,
	309, 315, 321–323
	A Defence of Poetry, 4, 14, 127
	Adonais, 5, 70, 72, 83, 148, 208, 225, 228,
		257, 260, 263–264, 265
	Alastor, 7, 175, 196, 197, 242, 245–247,
		271, 308
	A Vindication of Natural Diet, 245
	History of a Six Weeks' Tour, 252
	Epipsychidion, 257, 306
	Hellas, 305
	'Hymn to Intellectual Beauty' 11, 15, 165,
		189, 196, 251–252, 258, 282
	Laon and Cythna (The Revolt of Islam),
		242, 247–249
	'Lines Written in the Bay of Lerici,' 257
	'Mont Blanc,' 108, 229, 251,
		252–255, 258
	'Ode to Liberty,' 321
	'Ode to the West Wind,' 12, 14, 209, 251,
		256–257, 258, 323
	Original Poetry by Victor and Cazire, 82
	'Ozymandias,' 251, 255–257, 258
	Preface to *Alastor*, 175
	*Posthumous Fragments of Margaret
		Nicholson*, 82
	Prometheus Unbound, 8, 10, 11, 83, 122,
		196, 206, 228, 243, 256, 260–263,
		265, 321, 322
	Queen Mab, 82, 174, 242–245, 247
	St. Irvine, 82
	The Cenci, 51, 83, 322
	'The Magnetic Lady to her Patient,'
		257, 258
	The Mask of Anarchy, 83, 258
	The Necessity of Atheism, 82, 245
	The Triumph of Life, 138, 157, 200, 228,
		260, 265–266
	'The Two Spirits: An Allegory,' 192
	'To Jane. The Invitation,' 257, 258
	'To Jane—The Recollection,' 257, 258
	'To —— ("The serpent is shut out from
		Paradise"),' 257, 258
	'To Wordsworth,' 246
	'With a Guitar. To Jane,' 257
	Zastrozzi, 82
Shelley, Ruth, 249
Shelley, Timothy, 65
Shelley, William, 83
Sheridan, Richard Brinsley, 80
Smith, Anna Augusta, 86, 104
Smith, Benjamin, 85
Smith, Charlotte, 5, 6, 8, 14, 15, 74, 85–86,
	101–106, 107–109, 132, 135
	Beachy Head, Fables, and Other Poems,
		86, 107–109
	*Elegiac Sonnets, and Other Essays
		by Charlotte Smith of Bignor Park,
		Sussex*, 5, 85, 86, 101–106, 108, 135
	'Preface to the Sixth Edition,' 102
	Sonnets III, VII, and LV, 102
	Sonnets XXI to XXV, 104
	Sonnet XXXII, 104
	Sonnet LXXXVIII, 'To Nepenthe,' 104
	Sonnet XCII, 'Written at Bignor Park in
		Sussex, in August, 1799,' 105
	'To a nightingale,' 102
	'to Mr. Hayley, on receiving some
		elegant lines from him,' 103
	'Written on the sea shore.—October,
		1784,' 103
	The Emigrants, 86, 104
	The Young Philosopher, 86
Smith, Horace, 72, 255
Smith, Richard, 85
Speck, W.A., 89
Spenser, Edmund, 9, 67, 87, 125, 148, 193,
	197, 199, 207, 223, 227, 247, 263,
	271, 273, 282, 287
	The Faerie Queene, 197, 273
	The Shepheardes Calender, 145
Sperry, Stuart, 281
Southey, Robert, 8, 15, 16, 63, 64, 87–89,
	91, 144, 196–201, 234, 235, 243, 270
	Annual Review, The, 88
	A Tale of Paraguay, 88
	A Vision of Judgement, 88
	Colloquies of Society, 88
	History of Brazil, 88
	History of the Peninsular War, 88
	Joan of Arc, 87, 88
	Letters from England, 88
	*Letters Written during a Short Residence
		in Spain and Portugal*, 88
	Lives of the British Admirals, 88
	Madoc, 88
	Oliver Newman: a New-England Tale, 88
	Thalaba the Destroyer, 16, 87, 88,
		196–199, 243

The Curse of Kehama, 16, 87, 88, 196, 197, 199–200, 243
Wat Tyler, 88
Stabler, Jane, 211
Stafford, Fiona, 144
Steele, Richard, 50
Stephenson, Glennis, 76, 312
Stillinger, Jack, 277
Strachan, John, 211
Stuart, Arabella, 12
Sullivan, Brad, 97
Swann, Karen, 272
Swedenborg, Emanuel, 54, 55, 124
  'Memorable Relations,' 124
Sweet, Nanora, 67
Symons, Arthur, 320

Tarleton, Banastre, Colonel, 81
  History of the Campaigns of, 1780 and, 1781 in the Southern Provinces of North America, 81
Tasso, Torquato, 87
Taylor, John, 61, 62, 72
Tennyson, Alfred, 15, 16, 213
  'Mariana,' 16
  'Tears, Idle Tears,' 213
The London Magazine, 52
Thelwall, John, 15
Thompson, James R., 53
Thomson, James, 13, 97, 112, 143, 179
  The Seasons, 179
Tucker, Herbert F., 277, 279
Turner, Martha, 61
Tyler, Elizabeth, 87

Vallon, Annette, 90, 171
Van-Hagen, Stephen, 94
Vanacott, Hester, 80
Vaughan, Henry, 138
  'They Are All Gone into the World of Light,' 138
Vendler, Helen, 281
Vico, Giambattista, 8
Virgil, 11, 155, 273
Viscomi, Joseph, 116
Vivian, Charles, 83
Voltaire, Francois Marie Arouet
  'ECRASEZ L'INFAME!,' 243

Waldron, Mary, 94
Waller, Nicholas, 51
Ware, Tracy, 150
Wasserman, Earl, 245

Waters, Mary, 50
Watkins, Daniel P., 9
Webb, Timothy, 251
Webster, Frances Wedderburn, Lady, 218
Wedgwood, Josiah, 64
Wedgwood, Thomas, 64
Weiner, Stephanie Kuduk, 297
Wellek, René, 5
Westbrook, Harriet, 82
Wheeler, Kathleen, 189
Williams, Edward Elleker, 83, 257
Williams, Helen Maria, 15, 50, 90
  'The Bastille, A Vision,' 15
Williams, Jane, 257, 258
Williamson, Michael T., 304, 308
Wilner, Joshua, 164
Wolfson, Susan J., 66, 67, 269, 304, 305, 307, 308
Wollstonecraft, Mary, 55, 82, 97, 98
  Original Stories from Real Life, 55
  Vindication of the Rights of Woman, 97, 98
Wordsworth, Caroline, 91, 92
Wordsworth, Catharine, 91, 161
Wordsworth, Dorothy (Dora), 15, 64, 90, 91, 148, 163
Wordsworth, John, 91, 92, 160
Wordsworth, Jonathan, 164, 166
Wordsworth, Thomas, 91
Wordsworth, William, 4–16, 57, 64, 65, 81, 85, 87, 88, 90–92, 97, 101, 103, 108, 137–139, 143, 144–151, 152–162, 163–173, 174–178, 182–185, 187, 196, 211, 229, 234, 245–247, 270, 299, 305, 307–309, 319, 321
  A Letter to the Bishop of Llandaff, 91
  Adventures on Salisbury Plain, 91
  'Anecdote for Fathers,' 147
  An Evening Walk, 91
  Descriptive Sketches, 91
  'Elegiac Stanzas, Suggested by a Picture of Peele Castle in a Storm, Painted by Sir George Beaumont,' 152, 160–161
  'Goody Blake and Harry Gill: A True Story,' 145
  'Lines Composed [originally 'Written'] a Few Miles above Tintern Abbey,' 5, 108, 148, 149, 166, 182, 229, 303, 307
  Lyrical Ballads, 5, 10, 16, 64, 91, 144–151, 152, 191, 196
  Michael: A Pastoral Poem, 10, 11, 149
  'My Heart Leaps Up,' 308

Wordsworth, William (*cont'd*)
  Note to 'The Thorn,' 4
  'Nutting,' 149
  'Ode: Intimations of Immortality,' 7, 13, 152, 155–160, 183, 247, 299
  'On Seeing Miss Helen Maria Williams Weep at a Tale of Distress,' 90
  Poems, Chiefly of Early and Late Years, 92
  Poems, in Two Volumes 92
  Preface to *Lyrical Ballads*, 6, 10
  'Preface to *Poems* (1815)' 153
  'Resolution and Independence' ('The Leech Gatherer'), 138, 152–153, 155
  'Simon Lee: The Old Huntsman,' 12, 145, 146
  'Surprized by Joy,' 152, 160–162
  The Borderers, 91
  The Brothers, 150
  'The Complaint of a Forsaken Indian Woman,' 147
  The Excursion, 14, 16, 92, 174–178, 246, 319
  'The Female Vagrant,' 148, 150
  'The Idiot Boy,' 147
  'The Last of the Flock,' 148
  'The Mad Mother,' 147, 148
  'The Old Cumberland Beggar: A Description,' 146
  The Prelude, 7, 8, 13, 14, 91, 92, 159, 163–173, 174, 177
  The Recluse, 14, 174
  The Ruined Cottage, 91, 175
  'The Thorn,' 4, 146, 192
  'We are Seven,' 146
  Yarrow Revisited, 92
Worthen, John, 92
Wroe, Ann, 84
Wu, Duncan, 56, 64, 65, 92

Yearsley, Ann, 8, 14, 15, 93–94, 110–114
  'A Poem on the Inhumanity of the Slave-trade,' 111–112
  'Bristol Elegy,' 94, 110, 112–113
  Earl Goodwin: an Historical Play, 94, 110
  Poems on Several Occasions, 93, 110
  Poems, on Various Subjects, 94, 110
  'Slavery, A Poem,' 111
  The Royal Captives: a Fragment of Secret History, Copied from an Old Manuscript, 94, 110
  The Rural Lyre, 94, 110
Yearsley, John, 93
Yeats, William Butler, 262, 299
Young, Edward
  Night Thoughts, 55, 174, 242

Zimmerman, Sarah M., 86